The MICHELIN Guide

San Francisco

Bay Area & Wine Country

RESTAURANTS

2012

Manufacture française des pneumatiques Michelin

Société en commandite par actions au capital de 504 000 004 EUR
Place des Carmes-Déchaux — 63000 Clermont-Ferrand (France)
R.C.S. Clermont-Fd B 855 200 507

Dépot légal Octobre 2011
Made in Canada
Published in 2011

The MICHELIN Guide
One Parkway South
Greenville, SC 29615 USA
www.michelinguide.com
michelin.guides@us.michelin.com

Dear Reader

We are thrilled to present the sixth edition of our MICHELIN Guide to San Francisco.

Our dynamic team has spent this year updating our selection to wholly reflect the rich diversity of San Francisco's restaurants and hotels. As part of our meticulous and highly confidential evaluation process, our inspectors have anonymously and methodically eaten through all the city's neighborhoods including the bay area and wine country to compile the finest in each category for your enjoyment. While these inspectors are expertly trained food industry professionals, we remain consumer driven: our goal is to provide comprehensive choices to accommodate your comfort, tastes, and budget. Our inspectors dine, drink, and lodge as 'regular' customers in order to experience and evaluate the same level of service and cuisine you would as a guest.

Furthermore, we have delved deeper into the dining scenes south of San Francisco in order to provide a more thorough selection of notable and unique restaurants in both the Peninsula and South Bay. Don't miss the scrumptious "Small Plates" category, highlighting those establishments with a distinct style of service, setting, and menu; and the further expanded "Under $25" listings which also include a diverse and impressive choice at a very good value.

Additionally, you may follow our Michelin Inspectors on Twitter @MichelinGuideSF as they chow their way around town. Our anonymous inspectors tweet daily about their unique and entertaining food experiences.

Our company's two founders, Édouard and André Michelin, published the first MICHELIN Guide in 1900, to provide motorists with practical information about where they could service and repair their cars, find quality accommodations, and a good meal. Later in 1926, the star-rating system for outstanding restaurants was introduced, and over the decades we have developed many new improvements to our guides. The local team here in San Francisco enthusiastically carries on these traditions.

We sincerely hope that the MICHELIN Guide will remain your preferred reference to San Francisco restaurants and hotels.

Contents

SFCVB/Phillip H.Coblentz

SFCVB/Phillip H. Coblentz

Contents

The Michelin Guide

"*This volume was created at the turn of the century and will last at least as long".*

This foreword to the very first edition of the MICHELIN Guide, written in 1900, has become famous over the years and the Guide has lived up to the prediction. It is read across the world and the key to its popularity is the consistency in its commitment to its readers, which is based on the following promises.

→ Anonymous Inspections

Our inspectors make anonymous visits to hotels and restaurants to gauge the quality offered to the ordinary customer. They pay their own bill and make no indication of their presence. These visits are supplemented by comprehensive monitoring of information—our readers' comments are one valuable source, and are always taken into consideration.

→ Independence

Our choice of establishments is a completely independent one, made for the benefit of our readers alone. Decisions are discussed by the inspectors and the editor, with the most important decided at the global level. Inclusion in the guide is always free of charge.

→ The Selection

The Guide offers a selection of the best hotels and restaurants in each category of comfort and price. Inclusion in the guides is a commendable award in itself, and defines the establishment among the "best of the best."

How the MICHELIN Guide Works

→ Annual Updates

All practical information, the classifications, and awards, are revised and updated every year to ensure the most reliable information possible.

→ Consistency & Classifications

The criteria for the classifications are the same in all countries covered by the Michelin Guides. Our system is used worldwide and is easy to apply when choosing a restaurant or hotel.

→ The Classifications

We classify our establishments using XXXXX-X and ⌂⌂⌂⌂⌂-⌂ to indicate the level of comfort. The ✿✿✿-✿ specifically designates an award for cuisine, unique from the classification. For hotels and restaurants, a symbol in red suggests a particularly charming spot with unique décor or ambiance.

→ Our Aim

As part of Michelin's ongoing commitment to improving travel and mobility, we do everything possible to make vacations and eating out a pleasure.

How to Use This Guide

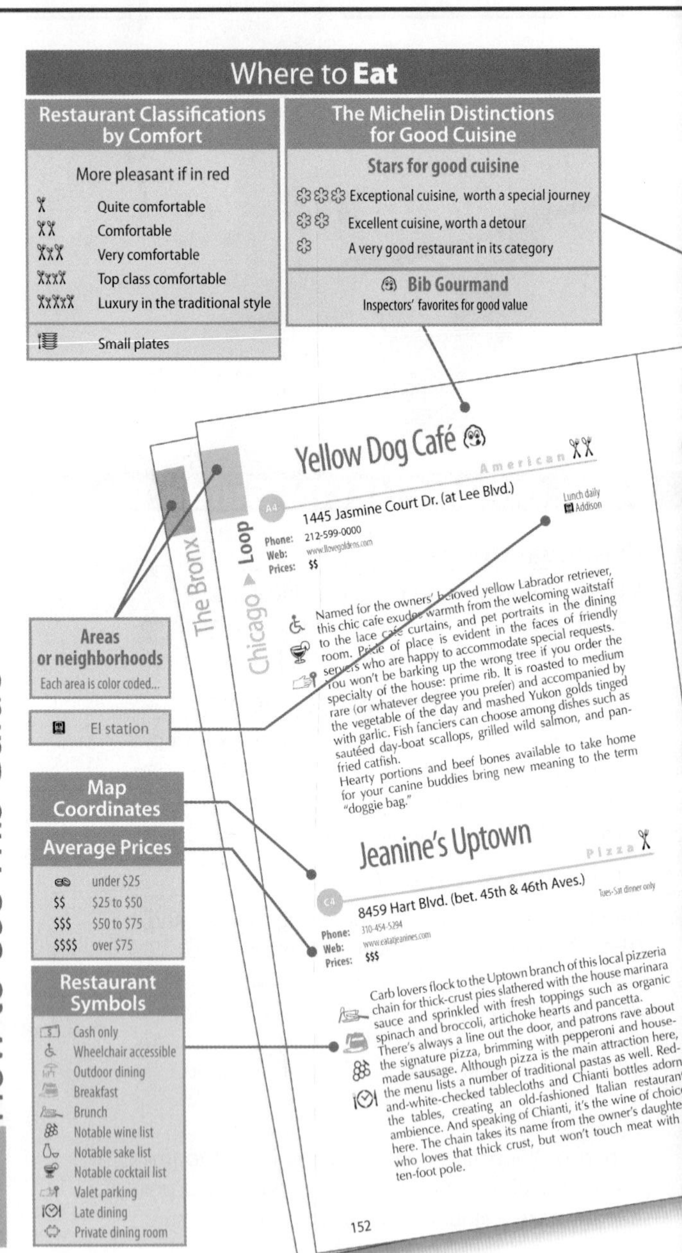

Where to **Stay**

Average Prices	Hotel Symbols	Hotel Classifications by Comfort
Prices do not include applicable taxes	149 rooms — Number of rooms & suites	More pleasant if in red
$ under $200	Wheelchair accessible	Quite comfortable
$$ $200 to $300	Exercise room	Comfortable
$$$ $300 to $400	Spa	Very comfortable
$$$$ over $400	Swimming pool	Top class comfortable
	Conference room	Luxury in the traditional style
	Pet friendly	
	Wireless	

Map Coordinates

Palace

italian

er Pl. (at 30th Street)

Dinner daily

oulouspalace.com

Manhattan ▸ Chelsea

David Buffington/Getty Images

ome cooked Italian never tasted so good than at this pretentious little place. The simple décor claims no big-me designers, and while the Murano glass light fixtures e chic and the velveteen-covered chairs are comfortable, is isn't a restaurant where millions of dollars were spent n the interior.

nstead, food is the focus here. The restaurant's name may not be Italian, but it nonetheless serves some of the best pasta in the city, made fresh in-house. Dishes follow the seasons, thus ravioli may be stuffed with fresh ricotta and herbs in summer, and pumpkin in fall. Most everything is liberally dusted with Parmigiano Reggiano, a favorite ingredient of the chef.

For dessert, you'll have to deliberate between the likes of creamy tiramisu, ricotta cheesecake, and homemade gelato. One thing's for sure: you'll never miss your nonna's cooking when you eat at Sonya's.

153

D1

The Fan Inn

135 Shanghai Street, Oakland

Phone: 650-345-1440 or 888-222-2424
Web: www.superfaninnoakland.com
Prices: $$

45 Rooms
5 Suites

John A. Rizzo/Getty Images

San Francisco ▸ Civic Center

oused in an Art Deco-era building, the venerable Fan Inn ently underwent a complete facelift. The hotel now fits with the new generation of sleekly understated hotels ring a Zen-inspired aesthetic, despite its 1930s origins. othing neutral palette runs throughout the property, uated with exotic woods, bamboo, and fine fabrics. e lobby, the sultry lounge makes a relaxing place for mixed cocktail or a glass of wine.

ens and down pillows cater to your comfort, while n TVs, DVD players with iPod docking stations, less Internet access satisfy the need for modern For business travelers, nightstands convert to les and credenzas morph into flip-out desks. nter, fax or scanner? It's just a phone call away. st, the hotel will even provide office supplies.

alf of the accommodations here are suites, xury factor ratchets up with marble baths, ng areas, and fully equipped kitchens. nn doesn't have a restaurant, the nearby arly everything you could want in terms of dumplings to haute cuisine.

315

Where to Eat

San Francisco Convention & Visitors Bureau photo by Phil Coblentz

San Francisco

Castro

Cole Valley · Haight-Ashbury · Noe Valley

It's raining men in the Castro, the world famous "gayborhood" that launched the career of civil rights icon, Harvey Milk, and remains devoted to celebrating the gay and lesbian community (yes, ladies are allowed here too). The hub for all things LGBT–including Gay Pride in June and the Castro Street Fair each October–the Castro is a constant party with a mélange of bars from shabby to chic and dance clubs that honor the ruling class of multi-platinum wonder women—Madonna, Beyoncé, Babs, Cher, and Lady Gaga.

The Castro teems with casual cafés to feed its buzzing population of gym bunnies, leather daddies, and drag queens, as well as a flood of vibrant out-of-towners on pilgrimage to mecca. **Café Flore**'s quaint patio is more evocative of its Parisian namesake than the plain-Jane continental fare. But, if you go to eat, you're missing the point: this is prime cruising territory with cheap drinks and DJs. There are white napkin restaurants dishing worthwhile cuisine–**La Méditerranée** for instance–but the best flavors of the Castro are served on the run.

Thai House and **Noe Valley Bakery & Bread Company** are mainstays for a quick and heavenly bite; and **Marcello's Pizza** is a satisfying post-cocktail joint. Speaking of booze, SF's first openly gay bar, **Twin Peaks Tavern**, and **Castro Village Wine Company** continues to lure. The younger hotties, however, sweat it out at **Badlands**' colorful (and sceney) dance floor. **Café du Nord** draws hipsters for live music in a former speakeasy built in 1907. This area is also chock-full of darling specialty shops. The **Castro Cheesery** pours fresh-roasted gourmet coffees and offers a small selection of cheeses; **Drewes Brothers** struts its meats; **Samovar Tea Lounge** brews artisan loose-leaf; and **Swirl**, a sleek space brimming with stemware and accessories, offers tastings of boutique wine varietals. Take home a nosh from Italian foods purveyor **A.G. Ferrari**, or indulge your sweet tooth at the kitschy kiosk, **Hot Cookie**.

Nearby Cole Valley is home to **Say Cheese**, full of quality international cheeses and a small stock of sandwiches; and **Val de Cole**, with value table wines galore. On Monday nights, dog-lovers treat the whole family to dinner on the garden patio at **Zazie**. Counterculturalists, of course, have long sought haven in the hippiefied Haight-Ashbury where, despite recent Gap-ification, head shops and record stores continue to dominate the landscape.

Eschew any notions of fine dining here and join the locals at more laid-back hot spots. **Cha! Cha! Cha!** is a groovy tapas bar flowing with fresh-fruit sangria; and for the morning after, **Pork Store Café** draws a cliquey following for greasy hash browns and hotcakes.

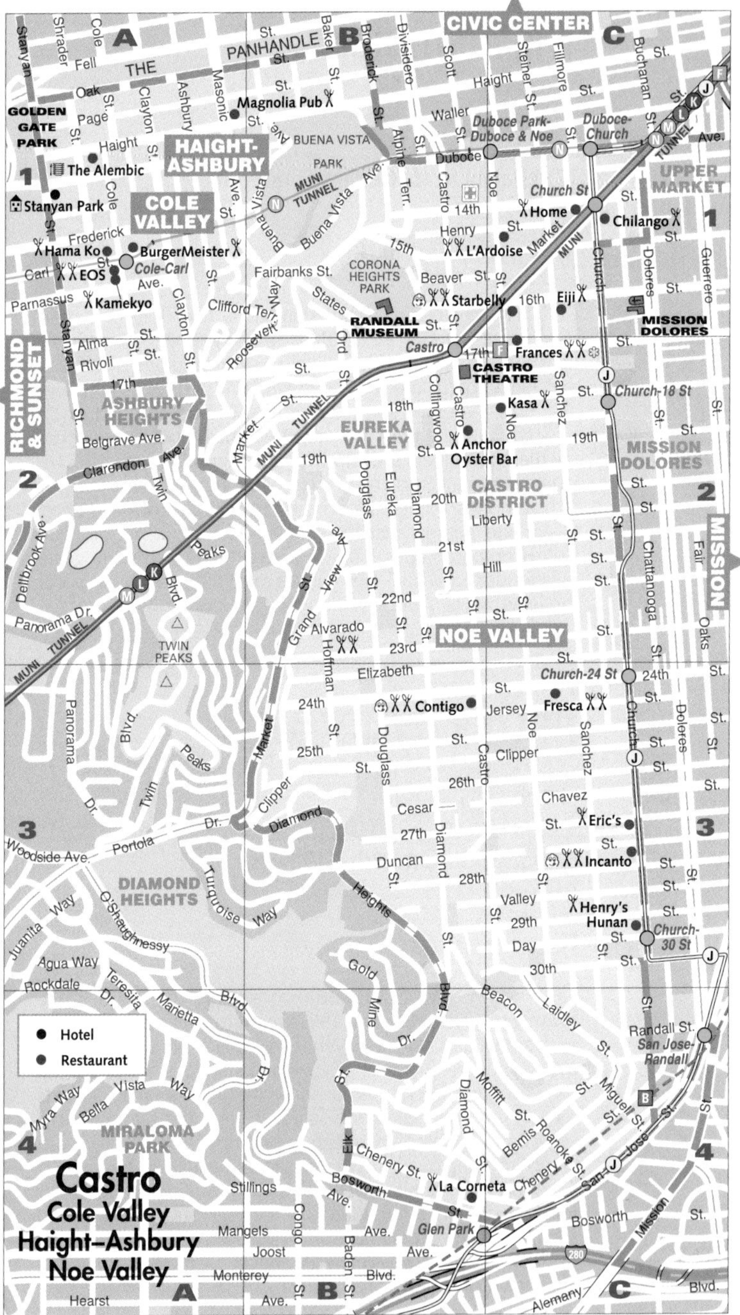

Castro
Cole Valley
Haight–Ashbury
Noe Valley
Hotel
Restaurant
CIVIC CENTER
RICHMOND & SUNSET
MISSION
GOLDEN GATE PARK
THE PANHANDLE
HAIGHT-ASHBURY
COLE VALLEY
BUENA VISTA PARK
CORONA HEIGHTS PARK
RANDALL MUSEUM
UPPER MARKET
MISSION DOLORES
CASTRO THEATRE
ASHBURY HEIGHTS
EUREKA VALLEY
CASTRO DISTRICT
NOE VALLEY
TWIN PEAKS
DIAMOND HEIGHTS
MIRALOMA PARK
Magnolia Pub
The Alembic
Stanyan Park
Hama Ko
BurgerMeister
EOS
Kamekyo
Home
Chilango
L'Ardoise
Starbelly
Eiji
Frances
Kasa
Anchor Oyster Bar
Contigo
Fresca
Eric's
Incanto
Henry's Hunan
La Corneta
Duboce Park-Duboce & Noe
Duboce-Church
Church St
Cole-Carl
Castro
Church-18 St
Church-24 St
Church-30 St
San Jose-Randall
Glen Park
MUNI TUNNEL
Stanyan
Shrader
Cole
Clayton
Ashbury
Masonic
Baker
Broderick
Divisidero
Scott
Steiner
Fillmore
Buchanan
Fell
Oak
Page
Haight
Waller
Duboce
Frederick
Carl
Parnassus
Alma
Rivoli
17th
Belgrave Ave.
Clarendon Ave.
Twin Peaks Blvd.
Dellbrook Ave.
Panorama Dr.
Buena Vista Ave.
Alpine Terr.
14th
Henry
15th
Beaver
16th
Fairbanks St.
States
Clifford Terr.
Roosevelt Way
Ord
Castro
Noe
Market
Church
Dolores
Guerrero
Sanchez
18th
Collingwood
19th
Douglass
Eureka
Diamond
20th
Liberty
21st
Hill
22nd
Grand View Ave.
Alvarado
Hoffman
23rd
Elizabeth
24th
Jersey
25th
Clipper
26th
Cesar Chavez
27th
Duncan
28th
Valley
29th
Day
30th
Chattanooga
Fair Oaks
Portola Dr.
Woodside Ave.
O'Shaughnessy Blvd.
Turquoise Way
Juanita Way
Agua Way
Rockdale
Teresita
Marietta
Diamond Heights Blvd.
Gold Mine Dr.
Beacon
Laidley
Randall St.
Moffitt
Bemis
Roanoke
Miguel St.
Chenery St.
Elk St.
Bosworth St.
San Jose Ave.
Mission
Myra Way
Bella Vista Way
Stillings
Congo
Mangels
Joost
Monterey Blvd.
Baden St.
Hearst
Alemany Blvd.
280

The Alembic

Gastropub

1725 Haight St. (bet. Cole & Shrader Sts.)

Phone: 415-666-0822 — Lunch & dinner daily
Web: www.alembicbar.com
Prices: $$

Culinary kudos aside, The Alembic is first, foremost, and proudly a watering hole. Bare filament bulbs do little to light the bar fashioned from old Kezar Stadium bleachers, and blackboards are hand-scrawled with artisanal whiskeys and ryes. Whether you crave a classic old-fashioned or an education on the finer points of small-batch bourbons, these talented bartenders are happy to accommodate.

With passionate cooking and a well-worn vibe, this purveyor of fine moods and local foods fits the term gastropub to a tee. Here, find patrons feasting on braised Wagyu beef tongue sliders prepared *sous vide* or a sweet-tangy whiskey glaze over tender baby back ribs. Unlike most pubs, dinner is worth the lengthy wait; weekend lunches are more low-key.

Anchor Oyster Bar

Seafood 

B2

579 Castro St. (bet. 18th & 19th Sts.)

Phone: 415-431-3990 — Lunch Mon – Sat
Web: www.anchoroysterbar.com — Dinner nightly
Prices: $$

For a warm bowl of chowder on a foggy day, head home to Anchor Oyster Bar, the 1977 mainstay that's always ready with a beer and a bivalve. While the homey bar may not have the soigné hip of its younger neighbors, it does have the solid seafood and cheeky humor (note the adult-themed T-shirts for sale) to keep everyone sated. In fact, the place itself is something of an oyster: clean, a bit briny, some claim it has an aphrodisiac quality, and occasional pearls can be found.

Cozy up at a stainless steel table or the marble-topped bar and check the whiteboard for classics such as steamed shellfish, seafood cocktails, and variations on chowder. Their fresh oysters are always expertly shucked—the only thing that changes here are the daily specials.

BurgerMeister

American

86 Carl St. (at Cole St.)

Phone: 415-566-1274 Lunch & dinner daily
Web: www.burgermeistersf.com
Prices:

This daddy of burger joints with up-market eats and a low-key vibe stacks up to Bay Area standards with all-natural Niman Ranch beef and eco-friendly packaging. Moreover, these juicy quarter- and half-pounders, cooked to order and tossed on a freshly baked bun, are greatly delicious and make a near mockery of the trendy little slider.

Though not cheap, the "Meister Favorites" (starting at nine dollars) offer quality and creativity, as in the "San Diego" topped with roasted jalapeños and melted pepper jack. Fries come in curly, sweet potato, chili, and roasted garlic varieties; beer-battered onion rings arrive without a trace of grease. Salads and wines by the glass are offered, though milk shakes are more popular here, and are best eaten with a spoon.

Chilango

235 Church St. (bet. 15th & Market Sts.)

Phone: 415-552-5700 Lunch & dinner daily
Web: www.chilangococina.com
Prices:

This unexpected taqueria brings wholesome and sophisticated tastes of Mexico City to the Castro. Black-and-white photos depicting life in Mexico DF decorate most of the interior and are a sure sign of the authenticity (and deliciousness) behind the kitchen's flavors. These same flavors suit the palate of natives (called *Chilangos*) and locals, so expect a complex fare of fresh produce and free-range meats. *Lo siento*, no burritos.

Here most *antojitos* begin with a house-made corn tortilla. Tacos may be stuffed with braised beef brisket or filet mignon, while sliced grilled short ribs and fixings top the *huraches chilango*, an open-faced torta resting on an oval tortilla sandal. *Sopes*, ceviche, and posole complement local wines from Latino vintners.

Contigo

Spanish XX

B3

1320 Castro St. (at 24th St.)

Phone: 415-285-0250 — Dinner Tue – Sun
Web: www.contigosf.com
Prices: $$

This Noe Valley darling's name (Spanish for "with you") is the first clue that Contigo is best when shared with friends. Single diners sit cozily at the wine bar or front counter, for truly, this contemporary neighborhood eatery was designed in the spirit of conviviality.

Reclaimed wood and ceramic tiles lend an earthy balance to a modish setting, where small groups nosh on authentic Catalonian fare–think bite-sized tapas such as salt cod *croquetas* with *piment d'Espelette allioli*–over glasses of sparkling cava. *Raciones* are slightly larger plates ideal for sharing: look for oxtail-stuffed piquillo peppers and fried caper-studded Brussels sprouts. Do not miss the prized *jamòn Iberico,* sliced tissue thin, or the heated garden patio out back.

Eiji

Japanese X

317 Sanchez St. (bet. 16th & 17th Sts.)

Phone: 415-558-8149 — Lunch & Dinner Tue – Sun
Web: N/A
Prices:

Differentiating one sushi house from another is a personal matter, but Eiji's wooden shingle siding layering a tree-flanked façade, marked by an oblong flag reading "sushi" and "tofu" on either side is sure to lure. Eiji Onoda's eponymous eatery brings to life a vegan's dream—think of inordinately luscious custard and fresh, homemade tofu and you will start to get the drift.

Go for a bowl of silky, made-to-order *oboro*—delicate curds of tofu just separated from the soymilk; or try the melt-in-your-mouth *ankake* tofu topped with a *konbu*-soy sauce. Aptly representing the "sushi" side is pristine seafood like *ankimo* or monkish liver. Also proffered are *sunomono,* seafood casseroles, *yosenabe,* and *misonabe*—bring your own bowl if you want either *nabe* to-go.

EOS

Asian XX

901 Cole St. (at Carl St.)

Phone: 415-566-3063 Dinner nightly
Web: www.eossf.com
Prices: $$

In the heart of tiny Cole Valley lies this bouncy, bohemian charmer. Happy hour during the week boasting several wine and food selections has EOS buzzing with families, young professionals, and gaggles of diners from all parts of the city. Intricate bamboo window treatments and soft green walls match both the contemporary dining room and cozy (adjoining) wine salon replete with stellar wine flights, sake cocktails, and a separate menu of fusion small plates.

No matter your locale, order teeny portions of tasty Thai salads, curries, or perhaps *poke* rolls (ahi tuna and salmon) and share them family-style. You can even take home a portion of their sweetness via ice cream flavors (Thai tea and pineapple mint sorbet maybe?) that are available to-go.

Eric's

1500 Church St. (at 27th St.)

Phone: 415-282-0919 Lunch & dinner daily
Web: N/A
Prices: ⊖

A neighborhood favorite and Noe Valley fixture with a line out the door since 1991, Eric's is just the sort of godsend that everyone comes to appreciate. This little house packs its bright yellow, mirrored interior with regulars who feast on Hunan and Mandarin lunches for under $10 (including soup and tea) and dinner for just a few bills more.

Prices belie the portions, so expect ample specialties such as rainbow fish with pine nuts in garlic sauce, or tender Shanghai chicken breast with crispy seaweed and al dente brown rice. While some discerning palates may claim the cuisine is somewhat Americanized, no one denies that it is nonetheless delicious.

Reservations are not accepted (hence the line), but service is as very fast as it is friendly.

Frances ✿

Californian 

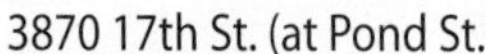

C2

3870 17th St. (at Pond St.)

Phone: 415-621-3870 Dinner Tue – Sun
Web: www.frances-sf.com
Prices: **$$$**

Jennifer Yin

Do not be misguided by the fact that everything about Frances is small and humble. The menu lists just a handful of bouchées (small bites), appetizers, main dishes, and sides. The dining room is furnished with a sprinkling of snug tables packed with locals amid smiling servers who seem like life-long friends. The hype, crowds, and one-month wait for reservations are all worth it, thanks to the petite and ponytailed Chef/owner Melissa Perello, who is a true force in the kitchen with a culinary prowess that shines through every dish.

Named for the chef's Texan grandmother, Frances prefers to keep it straightforward and simple, but by no means standard. It has that fresh-from-the-farm look, feel, and taste of superb produce that is sourced locally. The bouchées are particularly spirited, with the likes of bacon beignets and crispy chickpea fritters. You can't go wrong with any of the five entrée offerings like thickly slicked Liberty Farms duck breast on a bed of plump Italian butter beans, balanced with the flavors of braised chicory and Sicilian olives.

Without reservations, arrive early and expect to sit shoulder-to-shoulder at the bar, but lucky types snag a coveted parking spot.

Fresca

3945 24th St. (bet. Noe & Sanchez Sts.)

Phone: 415-695-0549 Lunch & dinner daily
Web: www.frescasf.com
Prices: **$$**

Inside this cheery room with a raw bar and open kitchen in back, Fresca offers patrons a unique rendition of Peruvian flavors and creative cocktails to be sampled and sipped amid catchy Latin beats. The front seating area with its bright yellow walls, arched ceilings, skylights, and outdoor views lends a fresh, open feel.

Likewise, the purity of their ingredients is patent in fresh seafood items like crisp and creamy *tequeños* (fried wontons packed with shrimp, crab, and cream cheese, with an *aji amarillo* aïoli), while the salmon BLT provides a very satisfying sandwich experience, if not authentically Peruvian. A morsel of the ahi mignon or *lomo saltado* further illustrates the concept of culinary invention. Two other locations are equally pleasing.

Hama Ko

108 Carl St. (bet. Cole & Stanyan Sts.)

Phone: 415-753-6808 Dinner Tue – Sun
Web: N/A
Prices: **$$**

It may be easy to miss this simple sushi shop (only a few sake bottles line its sidewalk window and there is no sign), but that would be blasphemous as you won't find a more authentic, mom-and-pop affair than Hama Ko. He mans the sushi bar, deftly assembling nigiri samplers; and she serves the serene space with a cheerful smile. This feels like the home of your (imaginary) Japanese grandparents.

The open kitchen is a touch worn, but the food is super fresh and lovingly prepared. Forget those trendier sushi spots, and be sure to inquire about the chef's hot and cold creations including deliciously succulent tuna, buttery scallops, and simple maki. While the chef is serious and focused, when you share your enjoyment, witness big beams around the room.

Henry's Hunan

Chinese

C3

1708 Church St. (bet. Day & 29th Sts.)

Phone: 415-826-9189 Lunch & dinner daily
Web: www.henryshunan.com
Prices: ⊜

Believe this: Henry's Hunan has some of the best hot and sour soup in San Francisco City, and they *give* it away at lunch. This fourth outpost in Noe Valley is perhaps the most stylish, featuring delicious and fantastically spicy classics for heat-addicts.

Begin, of course, with the aforementioned soup, floating thin slices of carrot and green onion, chopped tofu, scrambled egg, and red chilies in a silky, spicy-hot broth. Howard's special *kung pao* pork and Liling chicken wings provide a unique and tasty turn; while the hot and sour beef has a memorable kick, with tender strips of beef stir-fried with carrots and onions in a pungent vinegar-chili sauce. And with such low prices and large portions, this place is truly a *bijou.*

Home

American

C1

2100 Market St. (at Church St.)

Phone: 415-503-0333 Lunch & dinner daily
Web: www.home-sf.com
Prices: **$$**

All the comforts of home and some of the best people-watching around bring crowds to this spot on the edge of the Castro District. Homespun starters soothe senses with the likes of decadent macaroni and cheese with chives and breadcrumbs or Sloppy Joe dip with chips. Mom's cooking comes to mind in every wholesome bite of a tender pot roast with mashed potatoes or hearty chicken potpie.

On foggy nights, a roaring fire in the enclosed patio coaxes any chill from the air. Inside, red banquettes, white tile walls, and black lacquer chairs compose the diner-like space, as it caters to its highly supportive, local alternative community. Don't forget to try one (or several) of their bottomless organic mimosas during brunch on the weekends.

Incanto

Italian XX

1550 Church St. (at Duncan St.)

Phone: 415-641-4500 — Dinner Wed – Mon
Web: www.incanto.biz
Prices: $$

The quintessential neighborhood spot in the Noe Valley, Incanto is enchanting and inviting. Evoking nostalgic notions are classic street cars that rumble by; and an interior lined with agricultural prints and a trippy Animal Farm-meets-Timothy Leary painting (courtesy of a local artist) lends a bucolic vibe.

This is a great place for those that think tripe, tongue, and tendons are tasty. Chef Chris Cosentino is big on the pig, and his Italian-Californian menu dances with the season offering a variety of pork-based dishes. The more squeamish can rest easy—they will be warmed by soulful combinations of burnt flour rigatoni with chanterelles and watercress; while grilled lamb's heart with julienned beets and horseradish is sure to sate the less squeamish.

Kamekyo

943 Cole St. (bet. Carl St. & Parnassus Ave.)

Phone: 415-759-5693 — Lunch & dinner daily
Web: N/A
Prices: $$

Cole Valley's go-to for sushi lovers since 1996, Kamekyo is an intimate dining room anchored by a polished blonde wood bar and minimalist décor. A lavender ceiling and gold-hued walls warm the space, though the stoic chefs can be chilly. Still, a seat at the counter while the seafood is cleaned could yield a taste that should not be refused.

Deftly cut nigiri, sashimi, and maki make big waves here, but wholesome Japanese favorites including piping hot soba and udon noodles, light and crispy shrimp tempura, teriyaki, perfectly steamed white rice, and budget-friendly lunchtime bento boxes should not be overlooked. For visitors looking to keep with the theme, the Japanese Tea Garden in neighboring Golden Gate Park is just a Prius hop away.

Kasa

C2 — Indian

4001 18th St. (at Noe St.)

Phone: 415-621-6940 — Lunch & dinner daily
Web: www.kasaindian.com
Prices: $$

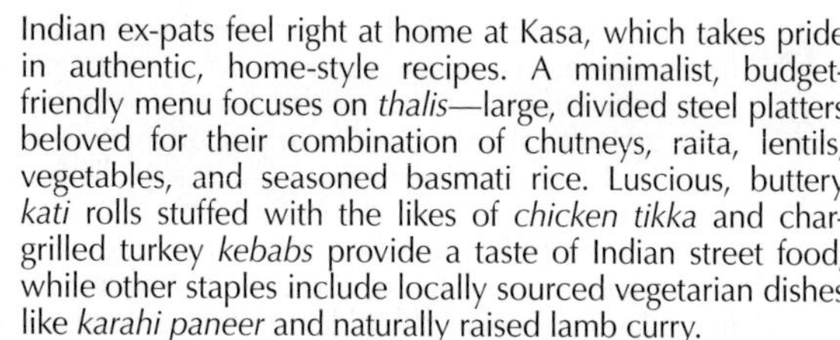

Indian ex-pats feel right at home at Kasa, which takes pride in authentic, home-style recipes. A minimalist, budget-friendly menu focuses on *thalis*—large, divided steel platters beloved for their combination of chutneys, raita, lentils, vegetables, and seasoned basmati rice. Luscious, buttery *kati* rolls stuffed with the likes of *chicken tikka* and char-grilled turkey *kebabs* provide a taste of Indian street food; while other staples include locally sourced vegetarian dishes like *karahi paneer* and naturally raised lamb curry.

In keeping with the low-key affair, the vibe is self-service casual with a high communal table that is ideal for on-the-go eats. A modern palette and brushed aluminum accents make this a sleek spot for a home cooked meal.

La Corneta

B4 — Mexican

2834 Diamond St. (bet. Bosworth & Chenery Sts.)

Phone: 415-469-8757 — Lunch & dinner daily
Web: www.lacorneta.com
Prices: $$

A smiley sunshine mural beams atop cheery yellow walls at this awesome taqueria. Upbeat, tidy, and vibrant, La Corneta serves up fresh, fast, and very filling fare from prawn burritos to sautéed salmon fish tacos—cooked to order from fresh fillets. Queue up and mosey down the food line where servers pile your favorite ingredients into a mouthwatering heap of Mexican deliciousness.

Try to tackle the carne asada super burrito—expertly wrapped to contain the gargantuan mix of grilled beef, beans, rice, cheese, guacamole, sour cream, lettuce, tomato, and *pico de gallo*. If the nachos, tacos, burritos, and quesadillas haven't defeated you, end with a warm, sugary *churro*. A word to the wise: any item with the word "super" means it, so grab a knife and fork.

L'Ardoise

C1

151 Noe St. (at Henry St.)

Phone: 415-437-2600 — Dinner Tue – Sat
Web: www.ardoisesf.com
Prices: $$

Laying low on a tree-lined residential street with tight-knit wood tables, a few seats at the kitchen-facing counter, and a house full of French-speaking ex-pats, L'Ardoise is the traditional Gallic bistro every neighborhood wishes it had. If this were our neighborhood, we would likely become regulars. Still, we might not be guaranteed a seat in their petite and charming interior.

Newcomers may trust the Francophile clientele and know that L'Ardoise is authentic. Here traditional recipes such as coq au vin, falling off the bone and into the *pommes purée* are exquisitely simple and tasty every time. Pair your wine-soaked chicken with a glass of smooth Châteauneuf-du-Pape and finish with an oh-so-buttery and flaky apple-laden tarte Tatin.

Magnolia Pub

A1

1398 Haight St. (at Masonic Ave.)

Phone: 415-864-7468 — Lunch & dinner daily
Web: www.magnoliapub.com
Prices: $$

Hippies and hipsters alike flock to this Haight-Ashbury mainstay where a hoppy aroma fills the wood-clad interior. Tufted leather booths are a cozy spot for noshing despite the steam clinging to the windows—thanks to the beloved work of the micro-brewery.

Obviously, beer is the nip of choice: locals (and characters who give this place its personality) crowd the bar, made of salvaged wood, for home-brewed draughts whose names are scribbled on the blackboard next to their BUs, or bitterness units, according to Brit tradition. In SF style, Slow Food rules at this gastropub, serving creative updates on classic pub grub like homemade sausages. Pair an artisanal pint with Scotch quail eggs or a seafood boudin; Anglophiles rejoice in the fish and chips.

Starbelly

C1  Californian XX

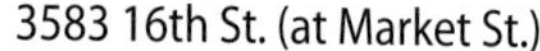

3583 16th St. (at Market St.)

Phone: 415-252-7500

Web: www.starbellysf.com

Prices: **$$**

Lunch & dinner daily

This local darling bears all the trigger words–*salumi*, pizza, pork, organic, reclaimed wood–that catch the local love. Starbelly struts a chic, green design with its bowling lane turned communal table and a cozy patio lined with potted herbs. The Castro clientele is expectedly stylish and come to devour a menu of Cali comfort food.

Here, pig manifests in many forms from house-made bacon in tangles of spaghetti, tomato, basil, and jalapeños, to *chilaquiles* with homemade chorizo, corn chips, scrambled eggs, and chili sauce. Fans of sister spot Beretta are familiar with the cerebral pizzas, perhaps topped with autumn squash, sage, and *pepitas*.

An instant hit since its inception, expect clever wine- and beer-based cocktails as well as a line at the door.

Good food without spending a fortune? Look for the Bib Gourmand.

Peter L. Wrenn/MICHELIN

Civic Center

Hayes Valley · Lower Haight · Tenderloin

The gilded Beaux-Arts dome of City Hall marks the main artery of the Civic Center, where graceful architecture houses the city's finest cultural institutions, including the War Memorial & Performing Arts Center and the Asian Art Museum. On Wednesdays and Sundays, the vast promenade outside City Hall hosts **Heart of the City**, San Francisco's oldest farmer's market. Priced to attract low-income neighborhood families, the market brims with such rare Asian produce as young ginger, Buddha's hand, and bergamot lemons.

Ground zero for California's marriage equality movement and protests of every stripe, City Hall is also prime territory for festivals, including Love Fest; the SF Symphony's biennial Black & White Ball; and the Lao New Year Festival in April. This same mall also witnessed the harvest of Alice Waters' Slow Food Nation Victory Garden in 2008.

With an enormous Asian, and particularly Vietnamese, population in the neighboring Tenderloin, there is an incredible array of authentic dining options, especially on Larkin Street. Mom-and-pop shop **Saigon Sandwiches** leads the way with spicy *báhn mì* made with fresh, crusty baguettes. These tasty subs are only three bucks a pop. Nearby, the *pho ga* at **Turtle Tower** is said to be a favorite of Slanted Door's chef, Charles Phan, while **Bodega Bistro** is a romantic purple nook with an infusion of French flavors and *pho*.

Best known for a seedy mess of strip clubs, liquor stores, and drug deals, the Tenderloin is a go-to for both a dingy and decadent nightlife. On the site of a former speakeasy, **Bourbon & Branch** is a sultry hideaway with a tome full of classic and creative cocktails. Other sleek lounges with interesting beats and delicious concoctions include the famed **Slide**. This is a rather unique and sophisticated

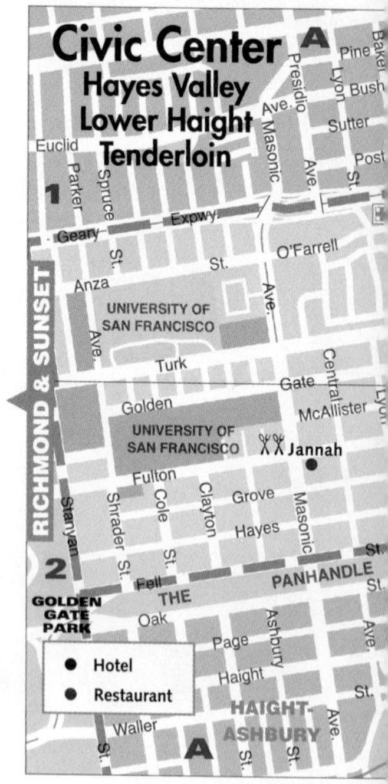

playground despite its unusual entrance—that's right, a snaking mahogany slide.

West of the Civic Center, Hayes Valley is positively polished, with a coterie of chic design shops and boutiques; as well as an interesting medley of stylish restaurants. The excellent menu at **Paulette Macarons** includes uniquely-flavored macarons (violet cassis and Madagascar vanilla?) in a French-style setting. **Destino** is a mainstay for *"nuevo Latino"* cuisine, and **Miette Confiserie** is an impossibly charming, old-fashioned style candy store jam-packed with hard-to-find European chocolates, salted licorice, taffy, and gelées. Apostles of **Blue Bottle Coffee** get their daily dose at the kiosk on Linden Alley. To the west, the Lower Haight draws hipsters for foosball and 21 tap beers at **The Page**; sake cocktails at **Noc Noc**; and live shows at the Independent. However, it's the Fillmore Jazz District that seduces true music lovers. Settled by African-American GIs at the end of World War II, the neighborhood hummed with jazz greats like Billie Holiday and Miles Davis.

Today, with the attempted resurgence of the jazz district, large restaurants present live music and contemporary stars grace the stage. The Fillmore still echoes with the voices of Pink Floyd, Hendrix, and the Dead, and the annual Fillmore Jazz Festival is also a must-see.

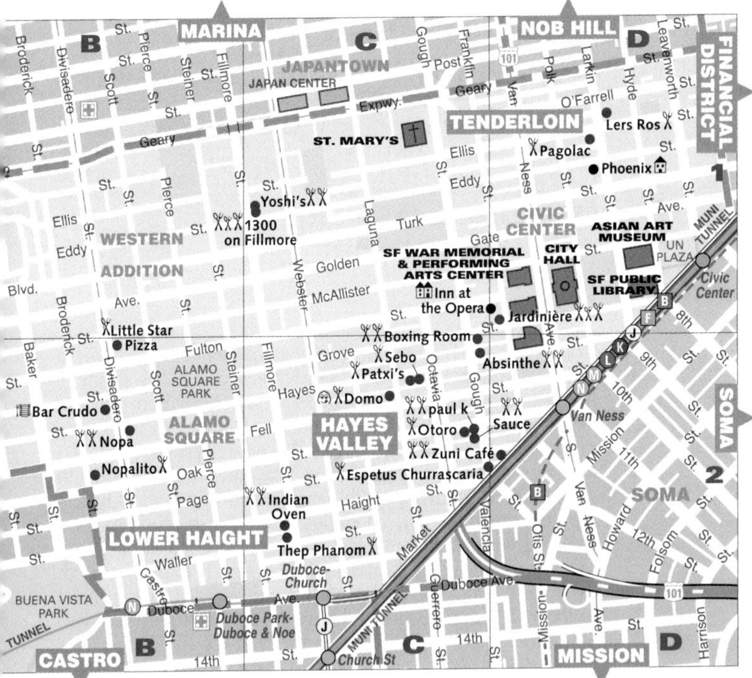

Absinthe

Mediterranean

C2

398 Hayes St. (at Gough St.)

Phone: 415-551-1590 Lunch & dinner Tue – Sun
Web: www.absinthe.com
Prices: **$$$**

A longtime favorite among cosmopolites looking for a bite near the performing arts district, Absinthe offers a performance of its own. The set: a bustling Parisian brasserie with pressed-tin ceilings and mischievous green fairies spying on red velvet banquettes from mural-coated walls. The actors: well-heeled ladies and business types at lunch; adoring couples and artisanal cocktail enthusiasts by night.

Choreography in the kitchen focuses on Mediterranean-French delicacies composed of Californian ingredients. Dishes may include country pâté with kumquat marmalade; potato-crusted Arctic char with Niçoise olive tapenade; and Valrhona chocolate *pot de crème*.

Take home a bit of Absinthe in the restaurant's beloved beverage tome, *The Art of the Bar*.

Bar Crudo

Seafood

B2

655 Divisadero St. (at Grove St.)

Phone: 415-409-0679 Dinner Mon – Sat
Web: www.barcrudo.com
Prices: **$$**

With super-fresh seafood artfully prepared, Bar Crudo is a bright idea. But be warned: San Francisco is a city of savvy foodies and, on any given night, you'll find them packed like sardines into this modern, narrow Divisadero space and ordering their fill of raw, cold, and hot small plates.

Regulars line the kitchen-facing bar and small balcony to slurp seafood chowder with caramelized applewood bacon and an enticing kick from chilies. A butterfish crudo may be flavored with asparagus-pistachio pesto and garnished with beet *brunoise*, while butterflied Idaho trout is roasted with toasty potatoes. Dessert is not served here, but chalk it up to the chef's expertise—he knows you'll be stuffed anyway. Schooled diners park in the nearby DMV lot.

Boxing Room

Southern

C2

399 Grove St. (at Gough St.)

Phone: 415-430-6590 Dinner nightly
Web: www.boxingroom.com
Prices: $$

Laissez les bon temps rouler at Boxing Room, the Civic Center newcomer serving a raucous taste of the Bayou. A far cry from the neighborhood's more posh post-theater environs, this corner space with floor-to-ceiling windows has a contemporary urban vibe with exposed steel beams, reclaimed wood tables, and a long zinc counter popular among cocktailing bartenders after work. In all, it's a party.

The kitchen too turns out jazzy cuisine with flavorful Cajun and Creole notes. Get your groove on with cornmeal-battered fried alligator (tastes like chicken); spicy andouille sausage and chicken gumbo; or a delicious fried shrimp Po'boy with creamy tartar sauce. For dessert, try fluffy beignets with espresso cream and pretend you're at Café du Monde.

Domo

Japanese

C2

511 Laguna St. (bet. Fell & Linden Sts.)

Phone: 415-861-8887 Lunch Mon – Fri
Web: www.domosf.com Dinner nightly
Prices: $$

Just two narrow counters and a prep kitchen dress the space at Domo, a *tobiko*-sized Japanese haunt that serves creative, ingredient-driven cuisine. The constant crowd is as much a sign of fine food as it is of cramped quarters, and the sunny vibe–imagine citrus-hued walls and blonde wood accents–makes up for the lack of elbow room.

Wherever you sit, you'll be treated to a view: one counter faces streetfront windows; the other overlooks the kitchen, where the aroma of torched Kobe beef will make you drool. Make it quick, however, because Domo turns the seats. You'll have no trouble wolfing down spicy tuna crudo with *sriracha*, cilantro, and avocado; fresh *unagi* sashimi; or the unbeatable $12 lunch special, served with soup and salad.

Espetus Churrascaria

Brazilian

1686 Market St. (at Gough St.)

Phone: 415-552-8792 Lunch & dinner daily
Web: www.espetus.com
Prices: $$

This is nirvana for carnivores with a penchant bordering on gluttony. "All you can eat" takes on new meaning at this Brazilian *rodizio*-style haven, where gallant *gauchos* deliver (via swords) an endless parade of roasted and grilled proteins. Turn the wheel to green if you want "more please," and show red (or scream "uncle") when you're "taking a meat break." So after several servings of Parmesan pork, homemade sausage, chicken thighs, and beef sirloin, it's code red!

During lunch, you may see a lot of repeat visits from the sirloin stud, but as accoutrements, a generous buffet overflows with salads, fresh veggies, and other side dishes. Dinner ups the meat ante as well as the prices, but one glass of the malbec and you'll be set for a lusty feast.

Indian Oven

233 Fillmore St. (bet. Haight & Waller Sts.)

Phone: 415-626-1628 Lunch & dinner daily
Web: www.indianovensf.com
Prices: $$

Fillmore residents who take out from Indian Oven on weeknights can now enjoy the restaurant's two walls of windows flooding the space with sunlight—this colorful little eatery with Indian folk art murals and a second dining room upstairs is great for private parties.

Surrounded by upscale boutiques, bustling bars, and restaurants along this popular stretch of Fillmore, Indian Oven is a great spot for an inexpensive bite after dropping your dough at the neighboring shops. The open kitchen turns out milder versions of authentic North Indian signatures such as tandoori chicken; fragrant *murgh masala* with turmeric and cumin; and tender lamb *vindaloo*. Also try homemade cheese dumplings, *gulab jamun*, and the specialty rice dish, *Kashmiri biryani*.

Jannah

1775 Fulton St. (bet. Central & Masonic Aves.)

Phone: 415-567-4400 Lunch & dinner daily
Web: www.yayacuisine.com
Prices: $$

From its walls and ceilings painted with bright blue skies and puffy clouds, to the Arabic music streaming through the dining room, Jannah is like a trip to the Medina without the jet lag. Bright, upbeat, and full of energy, Jannah's boundaries extend to a pleasing outdoor patio—just right for enjoying the hookah pipes that sit at the ready.

It is California-meets-Middle East on the menu, which features interesting, authentic, and unique dishes. A trained team of cooks punctuate their cooking with bold flavors and sweet/savory spices to create their own mark on everything from tabbouleh to *kuzi*—phyllo dough stuffed with lamb, fruit, vegetables, and an enticing blend of spices. Don't dismiss the chef's specials like smoked spice-crusted trout (*maskoof*).

Jardinière

300 Grove St. (at Franklin St.)

Phone: 415-861-5555 Dinner nightly
Web: www.jardiniere.com
Prices: $$$

Posh couples and culture vultures have long counted this arts district mainstay as home base for pre- and post-curtain revelry. Downstairs, indulgent regulars unwind on low-slung sofas and nosh on decadent bar bites in j lounge, while Jardinière's upstairs dining room sets the stage for Chef/owner Traci Des Jardins' French-Californian cuisine.

Nestle into a velvet booth beneath the golden dome or grab a two-top near the balustrade that hugs a view of Champagne on ice at the bar below. Wherever you sit, these meals are expertly choreographed. Order oysters or caviar à la carte, or settle in for the chef's seven-course menu with wine pairings. Savor such fare as herbaceous and crispy bacon-wrapped quail or pan-seared duck breast with chestnut spätzle.

Lers Ros

Thai

730 Larkin St. (bet. Ellis & O'Farrell Sts.)

Phone: 415-931-6917 — Lunch & dinner daily
Web: www.lersros.com
Prices: ⓈⓈ

A cheap and tasty meal isn't worth braving this shady stretch of Tenderloin by night. But come daylight, another story unfolds. Lers Ros is a cult favorite lunch spot you can count on. Union Square and Civic Center suits pour over heaping plates of flavorful Thai cuisine; visitors from across town are wise to park in a nearby garage.

At Lers Ros, you've barely set your menu down before the food arrives. Sample red curry, sweetened with coconut milk and loaded with beef, Thai eggplant, and Kaffir lime leaves; minced chicken stir-fried with basil, garlic, and chili (*pad kra pow kai*); or *pad kee mow*, a spicy pan-fried noodle ensemble topped with juicy pork and bean sprouts. Rumor is Lers Ros is moving or opening a second location this year.

Little Star Pizza

Pizza 

B2

846 Divisadero St. (bet. Fulton & McAllister Sts.)

Phone: 415-441-1118 — Dinner Tue – Sun
Web: www.littlestarpizza.com
Prices: ⓈⓈ

This is a hip, chic, and minimalist spot for local twenty-somethings to pop in, put some of-the-moment music on the jukebox, grab an ice cold P.B.R., and wait for their eponymous Little Star deep dish pies to arrive, topped in creamy spinach, feta, and mushrooms. The Classic deep-dish (sausage, mushrooms, green peppers, and onions) is likewise a favorite, but lovers of thin-crust find nirvana in roasted chicken and basil pesto atop a crispy, flaky cornmeal crust.

The dimly lit dining room is always packed, loud, and not a kid-friendly spot, so the Chuck E. Cheese set should stay home with a sitter. Expect waits during prime time, so consider calling for a pie to-go. If too packed, give their Valencia Street or Albany location in the East Bay a shot.

Nopa

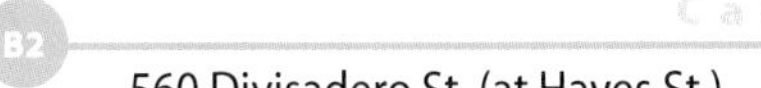

Californian

560 Divisadero St. (at Hayes St.)

Phone: 415-864-8643 — Dinner nightly
Web: www.nopasf.com
Prices: $$

Only an outsider would be fooled by the spacious interior of Nopa. Size may matter but, in this case, it won't guarantee you a table. Seats abound in the lofty, minimalistic dining room whether at the kitchen counter, on the mezzanine, or inside a cozy booth, but rest assured they are filled with savvy locals who made a reservation.

Here the Bay Area's signature organic fare gets the wood-fired treatment, where such dishes as Italian sausage flatbread with seasonal fava beans are soul-warming and delicious. Even a flaky halibut is hearty when wood-roasted, topped with sugar snap peas and earthy wild mushrooms. Nopa is at once urban and rustic—just taste the molten-rich and heavenly chocolate soufflé that flaunts a blooming garnish of lavender.

Nopalito

Mexican

306 Broderick St. (at Fell St.)

Phone: 415-437-0303 — Lunch & dinner daily
Web: www.nopalitosf.com
Prices:

Painted in zesty shades of green evocative of its namesake, Nopalito is both a piquant bit of edible cactus used in Mexican cooking and the cheeky little sibling of Nopa, the neighborhood's destination restaurant. Here, budget-conscious hipsters come for satisfying Mexican fare of the local, organic variety.

Housed in Falletti Plaza, Nopalito is minimally adorned with just a few canvas coffee bags and a crowded, heated patio. But flavors are big in dishes such as complimentary fried chickpeas tossed in *guajillo* salsa; quesadilla *roja* with braised pork shoulder and crispy *chicharron*; and a seasonal fish taco spiced with adobo and ancho chili.

Nopalito may be kid friendly, but the grownups will find plenty of tequila and mescal at the bar.

Otoro

Japanese  

C2

205 Oak St. (at Gough St.)

Phone: 415-553-3986 — Lunch Mon – Sat
Web: www.otorosushi.com — Dinner nightly
Prices: $$

As any sushi aficionado knows, *otoro* is the Japanese term for the prized yet scarce, melt-in-your-mouth cut of tuna belly that is rich in fat and healthful omega-3 fatty acids. At this tiny Hayes Valley sushi spot, *otoro* is featured among a wide range of raw, composed, and hot dishes.

Slurp through noodle bowls like miso ramen or tempura udon while checking out the dry erase board behind the sushi counter for seasonal offerings, such as seared hamachi belly and monkfish liver pâté. Or, feel free to get creative and suggest your own sushi roll ideas here.

A good selection of sake lines the shelves by the entrance, but if you are new to the field of rice wine, rest assured that the list here is well-illustrated and explained for novices.

Pagolac

Vietnamese

D1

655 Larkin St. (at Ellis St.)

Phone: 415-776-3234 — Dinner Tue – Sun
Web: N/A
Prices:

San Francisco's Tenderloin district demands quality restaurants like Pagolac to lure folks to this less savory area. The owners of this tiny and very popular family-run business clearly pour their hearts into both the service and the fresh, vibrant Vietnamese food.

The weathered pink awning may not seem enticing, but once inside you'll be embraced by the friendly staff and captivated by the good food at bargain-basement prices. Do-it-yourself cooking and tableside dining are taken to the next level with the "7 Flavors of Beef," a multicourse feast that you prepare using tabletop firepots and a grill—delicious, unforgettable, and just plain fun. The kitchen is equally happy to oblige those seeking less hands-on eating, with claypots and noodle bowls.

Patxi's

Pizza

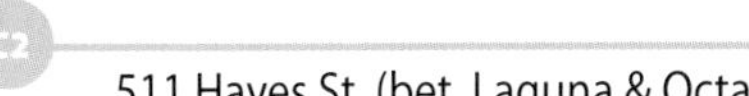

C2

511 Hayes St. (bet. Laguna & Octavia Sts.)

Phone: 415-558-9991 — Lunch & dinner daily
Web: www.patxispizza.com
Prices: $$

An exuberant din of neighborhood pizza lovers rocks the rafters at Patxi's, the Hayes Valley outpost of the Palo Alto original. Exposed brick walls, concrete floors, and bright paintings from a nearby gallery give this location a distinctly San Francisco feel, though many of the pies actually nod to Chicago.

While Patxi's does offer cracker-crisp cornmeal pies for thin-crust devotees, deep dish is the main draw here. Expect to wait half an hour or more for that flakey-buttery, two-inch-deep sensation stuffed with gooey cheese; the "Favorite" is heavily heaped with pepperoni, mushrooms, and black olives. Salads and pizzas by the slice play well to the loyal lunch crowd, while half-baked take-home pies are a smart reward at the end of a long day.

paul k

Mediterranean

C2

199 Gough St. (at Oak St.)

Phone: 415-552-7132 — Lunch Sat – Sun
Web: www.paulkrestaurant.com — Dinner Tue – Sun
Prices: $$

As its name suggests, paul k is a low-key Hayes Valley haunt favored by fun-loving thirty-somethings on a first-name basis with the staff. The delightful bistro is done in charcoal gray and red, with a zinc-topped bar and linen-clad tables serving tasty Mediterranean fare. By day, take in the view of passersby on Gough Street; at night, vibrant artworks and pretty florals are illuminated by candlelight.

On the menu, choose from a vegetarian meze platter laden with marinated artichokes, roasted beets, and hummus; or a deliciously fresh seafood stew spiked with harissa and chili. Meat lovers will find Syrian-spiced duck breast with forbidden rice and pomegranate-braised lamb riblets with garlic yogurt. Wash it all down with a crisp, dry gruner veltliner.

Sauce

C2 American XX

131 Gough St. (bet. Oak & Page Sts.)

Phone: 415-252-1369 Dinner nightly
Web: www.saucesf.com
Prices: $$

Laying off the Sauce isn't an option for Hayes Valley locals who can't help but kick back at their neighborhood mainstay, anticipating comfort food classics like baked mac and cheese with ham hock or fried chicken with whipped potatoes and gravy.

The Gough Street locale is as cozy as the food: upholstered booths are warmed by light from the semi-open kitchen; dark coffered ceilings and white tablecloths add just enough chichi to make this a hot night out. An international bent is evident in lettuce steak wraps with chili-garlic sauce or butterfish wrapped with *Prosciutto di Parma*. Desserts are a crowd pleaser as in the cinnamon-sugar donuts with vanilla-bourbon dipping sauce. Don't forget the other sauce, in a glass of crisp, local rosé.

Sebo

C2 Japanese X

517 Hayes St. (bet. Laguna & Octavia Sts.)

Phone: 415-864-2122 Dinner Tue – Sun
Web: www.sebosf.com
Prices: $$$

Local sushi lovers craving the quality easily found in New York and L.A. are happy to wait for a coveted spot (no reservations are taken) at the six-seat sushi bar of this Hayes Valley favorite. Trapezoidal tables are the lone design flourish in an otherwise minimalist space, but a glass of crisp, dry sake is all one needs to savor the experience.

Sebo is best known for its hard-to-find fish offerings such as seasonal firefly squid, gizzard shad, and blue fish gracing the nigiri selection. The sashimi omakase is silky, fresh, and pretty looking with its fan of carrots, shredded daikon, and shiso leaves. Cut rolls may appear less refined, but the *maguro* roll with avocado, radish, sesame oil, and sea salt bursts with memorable flavor.

Thep Phanom

Thai

C2

400 Waller St. (at Fillmore St.)

Phone: 415-431-2526 — Dinner nightly
Web: www.thepphanom.com
Prices: $$

Fillmore residents tired of the bar scene step up to a different type of bar—the to-go counter at 20-year mainstay Thep Phanom, where a creamy Thai iced tea is as good as any cocktail. Family types not in the mood to sully their kitchens with takeout, however, are content to eat in the friendly dining room, dressed in simple wood furnishings and exotic art with two windowed walls for a view of neighborhood bustle.

Authentic dishes such as grilled beef salad and crispy prawns are boldly flavored with the cuisine's ubiquitous fresh basil, cilantro, garlic, and chili; heat-seekers will relish the sinfully spiced "Thaitanic" chicken with string beans and yellow curry. Don't miss the Birds of Paradise, otherwise known as the chef's famous fried quails.

1300 on Fillmore

American

C1

1300 Fillmore St. (at Eddy St.)

Phone: 415-771-7100 — Lunch Sun
Web: www.1300Fillmore.com — Dinner nightly
Prices: $$$

1300 on Fillmore is pitch-perfect in bridging jazz-era nostalgia with a sultry, urbane vibe. A backlit wall of sepia-toned images and black-and-white photos of jazz greats add smooth notes to the posh leather-clad lounge, while gray and chocolate tones dress the soaring dining room. However, the menu of appetizing American soul food headlines the show and makes this a favorite in the Fillmore Jazz Preservation District.

Come hungry and prepared to devour an array of comfort food. A culinary performance might warm up with cornbread smothered in honey butter and pepper jelly; crescendo at supremely tender maple-braised beef short ribs with buttermilk mashed potatoes; and wind down with a hot apple cobbler. Classic cocktails sing spirited backup.

Yoshi's

C1 — Japanese XX

1330 Fillmore St. (at Eddy St.)

Phone: 415-655-5600 — Dinner nightly
Web: www.yoshis.com
Prices: **$$$**

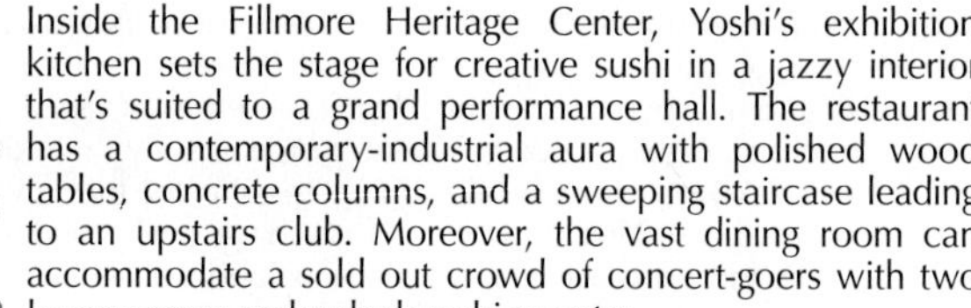

Inside the Fillmore Heritage Center, Yoshi's exhibition kitchen sets the stage for creative sushi in a jazzy interior that's suited to a grand performance hall. The restaurant has a contemporary-industrial aura with polished wood tables, concrete columns, and a sweeping staircase leading to an upstairs club. Moreover, the vast dining room can accommodate a sold out crowd of concert-goers with two lounge areas and a sleek sushi counter.

Service may be slow but the wait is worth it for such expertly prepared dishes as the "High Note," a sushi-sashimi combo including *maguro,* hamachi, and *unagi*; grilled *robata* plates; and rolls like the spicy dragon with shrimp tempura and creamy avocado. A glass from the well-curated sake list perfectly washes it all down.

Zuni Café

D2 — Mediterranean XX

1658 Market St. (bet. Franklin & Gough Sts.)

Phone: 415-552-2522 — Lunch & dinner Tue – Sun
Web: www.zunicafe.com
Prices: **$$**

If you haven't eaten at nationally famed Zuni Café, then you're a tourist. And if you're a tourist who hasn't been to this Europe-evoking eatery, then you're not a very good tourist. Having marked its triangular footprint on Market St. in 1979 and luring the height of local fashion, it was Zuni that made the wood-fired brick oven cool and functional, producing the most perfect pizzas or the much-heralded chicken for two that takes an hour to cook.

Denim-clad revelers sip aperitifs at the long copper bar or mezzanine (complete with a delicious view) as they await mesquite grill thrills like grouper with a carto-fennel slaw and potatoes; or starters including house-cured anchovies with celery, Parmesan, and Niçoise olives.

Peter L. Wrenn/MICHELIN

Financial District

Embarcadero · Union Square

Though San Francisco may be famed for its laid-back image, its bustling business district is ranked among the top financial centers in the nation. On weekdays, streetcars, pedestrians, and wildly tattooed bicycle messengers clog the streets of the triangle bounded by Kearny, Jackson, and Market streets. Lines snake out the doors of the better grab-and-go sandwich shops and salad bars at lunch; and both day and night, a host of fine-dining restaurants in this quarter cater to clients with expense accounts. Along Market Street, casual cafés and chain restaurants focus on floods of tourists and shoppers. Despite all that the area has to offer, its greatest culinary treasures may be within the Ferry Building. This 1898 steel-reinforced sandstone structure was among the few survivors of the 1906 earthquake and fire

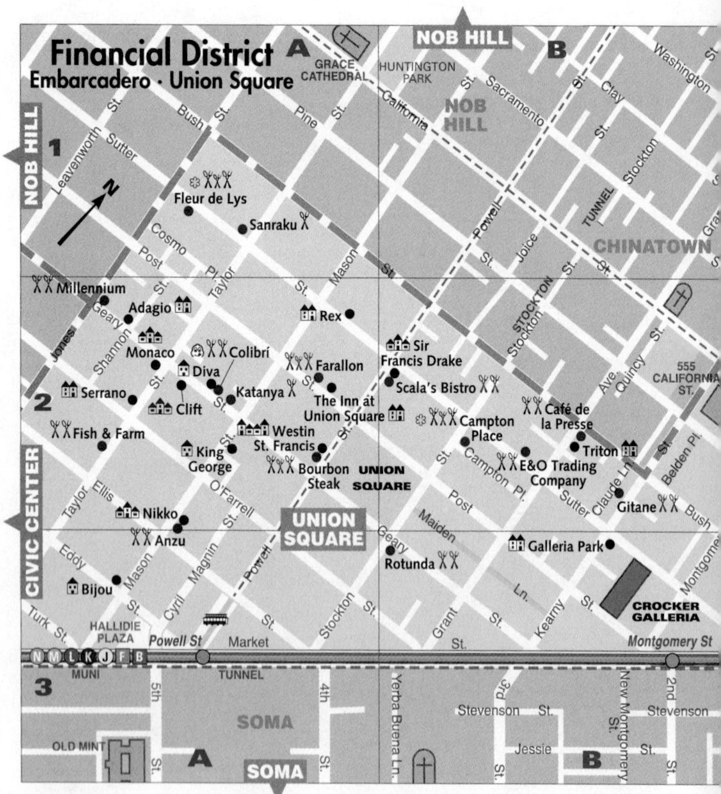

that destroyed most of the area. It remains a clear neighborhood standout, easily recognized by its 244-foot clock tower rising from Market Street above the waterfront promenade known as The Embarcadero ("boarding place" in Spanish). Renovated in 2004, its soaring interior arcade now makes an architecturally stunning culinary showcase for local and artisanal foods, fine Chinese teas, and everything in between. Known as the **Ferry Building Marketplace**, this is a true foodie pilgrimage and includes Lauren Kiino's **Il Cane Rosso**—a quick serve rotisserie and casual sandwich shop that pleases patrons with a weekday brunch (starring an olive oil fried egg sandwich); lunch menus replete with salads, soups, and sandwiches; and family-stlye, 3-course dinners prettily priced at $25. The marketplace strives to support the local and artisanal food community by highlighting small regional producers. Among these, two of the most popular are the acclaimed **Cowgirl Creamery** farmstead cheeses, and the organic breads of Berkeley's **Acme Bread Company**. Discover exotic, organic mushrooms, medicinals, and themed products at **Far West Fungi**. Patient enthusiasts can even purchase logs on which

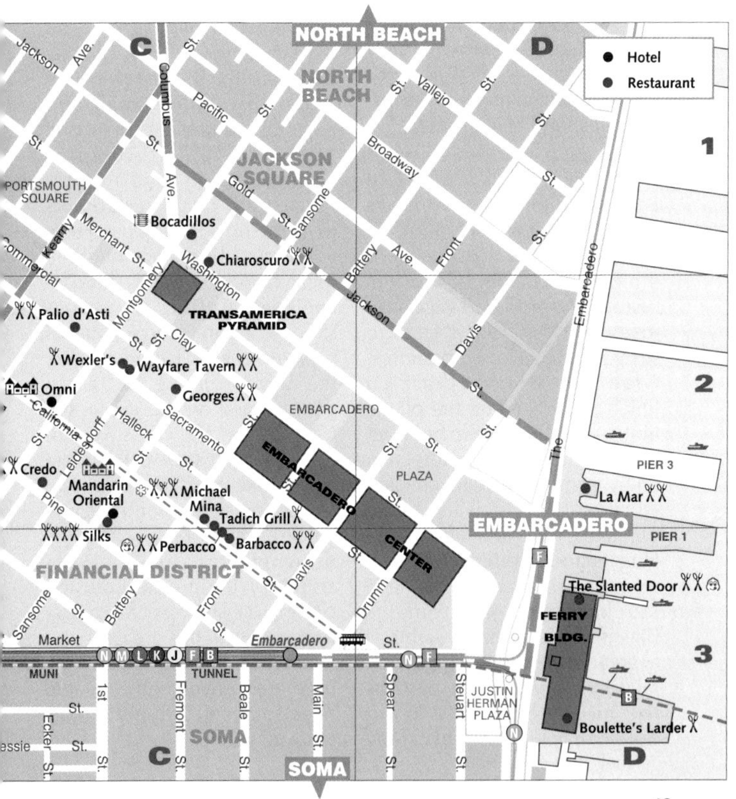

to grow their own harvest. The legendary **Frog Hollow Farms** also has an outpost here, offering luscious seasonal fruit as well as a myriad of organic chutneys and marmalades. **Recchiuti Confections** elevates the art of crafting Parisian-style chocolates and caramels to a level that can only be described as heavenly! The owners (Michael and Jacky Recchiuti) successfully take on the charge of introducing Americans to "real chocolate" via their best sellers.

Even the retail offerings are food-themed here, and include a number of cookware shops and home-design boutiques with a northern Californian flair. **4505 Meats** is hugely popular for Chef Ryan Farr's butchery classes, as well as for his smoked artisan hotdogs, sausages, and *chicarrones*.

While such world-class food shopping may whet the appetite, more immediate satisfaction can be found in the building's more casual dining spots. **DELICA** offers beautifully-prepared Japanese fusion foods, from signature sushi rolls to savory croquettes. Grab a seat with the FiDi lunch crowds filling the picnic tables at **Mijita** (run by Traci Des Jardins of Jardinière) to enjoy some Oaxacan chicken tamales or Baja-style fish tacos. Or, take a stool at the bar of the **Hog Island Oyster Company**, whose fresh bivalves are plucked from the Tomales Bay in Marin County—this is a great spot to sit, slurp, and take in the view. Still perhaps the most decadent takeout option may be from **Boccalone Salumeria**, where one can find a comprehensive selection of charcuterie that are available for purchase by the platter, pound, or layered in a single-serving "cone" for an unapologetically carnivorous treat. On Tuesday and Saturday mornings, join the chefs and crowds at the **Ferry Plaza Farmers Market** for organic produce, mouthwatering baked goods, fresh pasta, and more.

On market days, stands and tents soak the sidewalk in front of the building and rear plaza that overlooks the bay. Clusters of FiDi office workers head to the Embarcadero Center (spanning five blocks in the heart of the commercial district with reduced parking rates on weekends) to get their midday shopping fix in the sprawling three-story indoor mall and to grab a quick lunch in one of the complex's 30-some eateries. These food respites range from chain restaurants to little noodle shops. Here you'll also find two longtime local favorites, **See's Candies** and **Peet's Coffee**. Any serious shopper in San Francisco makes a pilgrimage to Union Square, the area bordering the formal park (named on the eve of the Civil War) on the FiDi's western edge. Here, upscale department stores like Saks and Neiman Marcus preside over the square. While fashionistas flock to the designer boutiques, foodies come for the area's profusion of gourmet restaurants. Restaurants in this area are also favored by drama lovers, since they are conveniently located near some of the city's most beloved theaters.

Anzu

Fusion

222 Mason St. (bet. Ellis & O'Farrell Sts.)

Phone: 415-394-1100 — Lunch & dinner daily
Web: www.restaurantanzu.com
Prices: $$$

By the look of its stodgy dress and FiDi digs in the Nikko Hotel, Anzu calls to mind the Mac v. PC commercials wherein a creative type squares off with a corporate suit. Yet in a Clark Kent–style twist, Anzu sheds its uptight guise to reveal powerfully artistic "Euro-Japanese" cuisine guaranteed to impress.

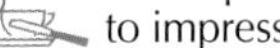

Sample the popular signature sushi, bold with aromatics like shiso or ponzu, while the imaginative and flavorful fusion entrées reveal the menu's true inspiration. Smoky, caramelized, and nearly sweet fresh cod arrives glazed with miso alongside silky pork belly and a crisp daikon cake—the aromas of ginger and barbecue conspire to wake the senses. Also try hamachi with Spanish chorizo and albariño sauce, or yuzu ginger chicken with *kabocha* risotto.

Barbacco

220 California St. (bet. Battery & Front Sts.)

Phone: 415-955-1919 — Lunch Mon – Fri
Web: www.barbaccosf.com — Dinner Mon – Sat
Prices: ⊜

Barbacco's style is matched only by its efficiency. This younger sister of Perbacco (next door) stretches its long, lean interior with the *oomph* of an Italian sports car—think Ferrari red and yellow accents, shiny stainless steel, and contemporary photos with a dizzying sense of motion. Busy FiDi regulars appreciate that the staff is equipped with hand-held POS systems to keep them on the go.

Bustling at lunch, dinner, and for drinks in between, Barbacco serves impeccable trattoria fare as well as takeout bites. Light nibbles include crispy bruschetta topped with smoked *lonza* and marinated Tuscan kale, while pickled peppers, olives, and house-cured *salumi* make a hearty butcher's salad. As at Perbacco, the rustic homemade pastas are perfection.

Bocadillos

710 Montgomery St. (at Washington St.)

Phone: 415-982-2622 — Lunch Mon – Fri
Web: www.bocasf.com — Dinner Mon – Sat
Prices: 

A fiery shade of *piment d'espelette* heats the walls at beloved Bocadillos, Chef/owner Gerald Hirigoyen's tiny tapas bar that pays homage to a *pequeño* Spanish sandwich loaded with big, sunny flavors. At lunch, FiDi suits file in for the $10 duo and choose from hot and cold varieties such as chorizo with walnut spread and parsley; 18-month Serrano rubbed with fleshy tomato; and mini lamb burgers mingled with fresh shallot.

High stools around the polished wood bar are a laid back perch to enjoy a glass of Spanish wine, while assorted tapas and crisp salads round out the offering at supper. Come nightfall, votives illuminate a snug, uncluttered space where the tables are loaded with baskets of utensils and small plates for sharing.

Boulette's Larder

Californian 

D3

1 Ferry Building (at The Embarcadero)

Phone: 415-399-1155 — Lunch Sun – Fri
Web: www.bouletteslarder.com
Prices: $$

"Boulette" is the owner's Hungarian sheepdog, and if this is its pantry, then that dog sure can cook. Buried in the bustling Ferry Building, this is a foodie's version of an apothecary displaying everything from wild Italian fennel and rose petal sugar, to squab sauce and Japanese specialty items—freeze-dried yuzu anyone?

The menu changes per the proffering of local farmers and fisherman, but by day Boulette doles out ingredients for sophisticated cooks as well as salads, soups (silky butternut squash), and heartier fare (braised beef short ribs). By night, Chef Amaryll Schwertner transforms the tiny spot into an intimate chef's table with elegant place settings and candlelit floral arrangements that sit pretty next to a sweet lemon meringue tart.

Bourbon Steak

Steakhouse 

A2

335 Powell St. (bet. Geary & Post Sts.)

Phone: 415-397-3003 Dinner nightly
Web: www.michaelmina.net
Prices: $$$$

If the name Bourbon Steak has you warmed and salivating at the dream of a luscious cut of meat, then cheers!—you have come to the right place. Those seeking the refinement of Michael Mina, which once graced this same grand dining room, will also find reason to toast.

Chef/owner Mina has transformed his Westin St. Francis home and infused it with an elegant gentlemen's club vibe. Cork-topped tables are well suited to swirling glasses of deep red wine, and butterscotch leather and ambient lighting further exalt the richness. Here the hungry and well-heeled satisfy their cravings with starters like a Hudson Valley foie gras terrine or tempura-fried squash blossoms filled with *burrata*. Save room: the dry-aged ribeye and salt-baked potato are not to be missed.

Café de la Presse

French XX

B2

352 Grant Ave. (at Bush St.)

Phone: 415-398-2680 Lunch & dinner daily
Web: www.cafedelapresse.com
Prices: $$

After a fashionable stroll through nearby Union Square, Café de la Presse is a lovely spot to brush up on your French with an après-shopping glass of viognier. The sunny streetfront café is dotted with bistro tables and stocked to the rafters with international newspapers and magazines; if you desire to actually speak French, the restaurant's manager is happy to oblige.

Framed reproductions of vintage French posters dress the slightly more formal wood-paneled dining room where Francophiles from near and far nosh on authentic dishes such as a Niçoise salad heaped with flaked white tuna, haricot verts, olives, and hard-boiled eggs atop butter lettuce; or traditional steak frites seasoned simply with salt and cracked black pepper. *Bon appétit*!

Campton Place ✿

Contemporary

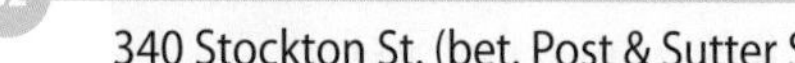

B2

340 Stockton St. (bet. Post & Sutter Sts.)

Phone: 415-955-5555 Lunch & dinner daily

Web: www.camptonplacesf.com

Prices: **$$$$**

Taj Campton Place

From its home in the boutique Taj Campton Place, this refined scene is set with the dining room's dramatic chandelier in the shape of oversized blown-glass blossoms. But that nod to whimsy is equally matched by the sophisticated staff's approach throughout the stately, cream-colored restaurant. For full effect, skip the bistro tables by the wood-paneled bar, and stay for a multi-course meal in the dining room, whether or not you choose the chef's degustation.

Chef Srijith Gopinathan's menu seamlessly blends contemporary preparations with global influences. A cucumber and Dungeness crab salad with diced blood oranges might be followed by a rich lobster curry with rice crisps, cilantro foam, and hearts of palm. Other dishes reveal pan-seared gnocchi in a tomato purée over roasted turnips, butternut squash, and parsnips; or a pan-seared duck breast, topped with melting slices of foie gras, spiced-pear preserves, and ginger-infused duck jus.

If you finish with a roasted white chocolate crémeux, topped with tarragon ice cream and black currant purée, you might even find yourself gazing at the ceiling's crystal flowers, and reflect on the height of inspiration that each dish can attain.

Chiaroscuro

Italian XX

C1

550 Washington St. (bet. Montgomery & Sansome Sts.)

Phone: 415-362-6012 — Lunch Mon – Fri
Web: www.chiaroscurosf.com — Dinner Mon – Sat
Prices: $$

Set across from the dramatic Transamerica pyramid, Chiaroscuro takes its aesthetic cues from stark architectural forms and the neighborhood's Italian heritage. Austere white walls, dotted minimally with art, rise to a vaulted ceiling; while a concrete banquette with fluffy pillows provides Chiaroscuro with its namesake point of contrast.

The stellar team of chefs takes most of their inspiration from *bella Roma*: Italian specialties from the open kitchen include homemade carbonara and *spaghetti all'Amatriciana* with *guanciale* and San Marzano tomato sauce. Begin with fresh-baked bread paired with flavored butters and the *insalata di fragole*—a mix of greens, pistachios, and fresh strawberries in balsamic vinaigrette. *Viva* the friendly service!

Colibrí

Mexican XX

A2

438 Geary St (bet. Mason & Taylor Sts.)

Phone: 415-440-2737 — Lunch & dinner daily
Web: www.colibrimexicanbistro.com
Prices: $$

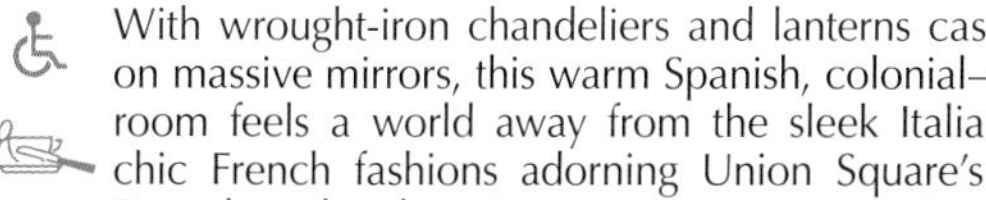

With wrought-iron chandeliers and lanterns casting a glow on massive mirrors, this warm Spanish, colonial–style dining room feels a world away from the sleek Italian suits and chic French fashions adorning Union Square's boutiques. But when the shopping set craves a margarita, it heads to the mahogany bar at Colibrí, a high-end Mexican bistro displaying an impressive array of tequilas and vintage Latino films.

The front of the house buzzes with theatergoers grabbing a bite before a show; at back, larger tables are ideal for leisurely meals. Begin with guacamole mixed tableside then sink your teeth into tender poblano chicken with a chocolaty mole. Cooler days call for a fortifying bowl of *posole verde* with braised chicken, plump hominy, and green chili.

Credo

Italian XX

C2

360 Pine St. (bet. Montgomery & Sansome Sts.)

Phone: 415-693-0360 — Lunch Mon – Fri
Web: www.credosf.com — Dinner Mon – Sat
Prices: **$$**

At Credo, located in the heart of the Financial District and named for the Latin term "I believe," pinstriped suits can roll up their sleeves. The industrial, loft-style space features clean white walls, scrawled with philosophical quotes, and handmade salvaged wood tables—a refreshing addition to the modern, business-savvy neighborhood.

The Italian trattoria menu of thin-crust pizzas, salads, and rustic pastas lends to the warm downtown vibe. And with relatively low prices, hungry execs can indulge in a feast. Look for a flavorful albacore tuna and cannellini bean salad, and pies topped with spicy Tuscan sausage and smoked mozzarella. The dense, flourless chocolate cake is well above average and the bar is ideal for dining solo or post-work drinks.

E&O Trading Company

Asian XX

B2

314 Sutter St. (bet. Grant & Stockton Sts.)

Phone: 415-693-0303 — Lunch Mon – Sat
Web: www.eotrading.com — Dinner nightly
Prices: **$$$**

Just steps from the dramatic 1970s Chinatown Gate, E&O Trading Company serves a taste of Southeast Asia in an interior that reflects both exotic flavors and Union Square chic. Mammoth glowing lanterns take center stage in the dramatic dining room where Asian artifacts and green bamboo create a steamy vibe that lures both neighborhood professionals for lunch or happy hour as well as tourists at dinner.

The spicy menu offerings are as far reaching as the soaring ceilings. In addition to the notable house infusions, the cocktail crowds sample such appetizers as lemongrass-scented Thai rock shrimp cakes and chicken and pork dumplings with tangy citrus-chili sauce. Entrées, like roasted *char siu* black cod, may lack the zest of their creative small plates.

Farallon

A2

450 Post St. (bet. Mason & Powell Sts.)

Phone: 415-956-6969 Dinner nightly
Web: www.farallonrestaurant.com
Prices: $$$

Some build castles in the air, while others create underwater fantasies. This vastly lauded seafood respite brings ocean to land only feet from Union Square in a spectacular space where every detail captures the life aquatic with octopus stools, jelly fish light fixtures, and shell motifs. Snake through elaborate dining nooks to the stunning pool room, bathed in intricate mosaic and beloved by an operatic set dressed to the nines.

Beneath sea urchin chandeliers, glimpse the flawless symphony between kitchen and staff. Then dive into a menu featuring seared ahi slices fanned over a salad of lentils, frisée, and tapenade; grilled Alaskan salmon made pungent with Chinese black bean sauce; and bittersweet chocolate mousse crested with tequila cream.

Fish & Farm

American XX

A2

339 Taylor St. (bet. Ellis & O'Farrell Sts.)

Phone: 415-474-3474 Dinner nightly
Web: www.fishandfarmsf.com
Prices: $$

Don't be put off by Fish & Farm's address inside FiDi's Mark Twain hotel; rather, let the evocation of Americana lure you in. Two large canvases depicting aquatic and pastoral scenes dominate the dark wood dining room, and tufted leather banquettes are a comfortable place to settle in. Fish & Farm brings a simply delightful surf and turf experience.

Locally sourced, organic ingredients star in many of the dishes, from oysters on the half shell with malt vinegar mignonette to Southern-style fried Petaluma chicken served with mashed potatoes, wilted collard greens, and cornbread madeleines. Steak lovers will relish the ribeye with corn and chanterelles, while the all-American sweet tooth can sate itself on velvety ricotta cheesecake in a jar.

Fleur de Lys

French

777 Sutter St. (bet. Jones & Taylor Sts.)

Phone: 415-673-7779 Dinner Tue – Sat
Web: www.fleurdelyssf.com
Prices: $$$$

Bill Milne/Fleur de Lys

A first-class destination on SF's culinary map since 1986, Fleur de Lys is like classical music or a Renaissance painting: studied and opulent for those who seriously appreciate it and a bit stodgy for those who don't. As with art, fine dining is subjective; but whatever your state of mind, there is no denying that Fleur de Lys has earned its place among the masters.

Sitting in the dining room, one can imagine it as a jewelry box—soft and draped with rich fabrics overhead, highlighting a dramatic Murano glass chandelier and floral arrangements. While these trappings are no longer de rigueur, Fleur de Lys wears its patina as a mark of the test of time. The service also evokes bygone hospitality, where a choreographed company of waiters anticipates your every need.

This is all thanks, of course, to the thoughtful artistry of Chef/owner Hubert Keller, whose exquisite craft is apparent in every French dish. Served in three-, four- and five-course prix-fixe offerings, dinners might bring Petrale sole and Dungeness crab atop olive oil mashed potatoes; sinfully tender Kobe beef cheeks spiced with mustard seed; and veal sweetbread meunière. Ask the sommelier for just the perfect pairing.

Georges

Seafood

415 Sansome St. (bet. Commercial & Sacramento Sts.)

Phone: 415-956-6900 — Lunch Mon – Fri
Web: www.georgessf.com — Dinner Mon – Sat
Prices: $$

Housed in the historic Fugazi building–an Italian bank during the Gold Rush Era–Georges adheres to a philosophic purity in tune with the mod Bay Area. The restaurant takes great pride in its locally sourced ingredients and sustainable fare, while the atmosphere is warmed by recycled design—envisage tables made of reclaimed Asian rosewood flooring.
A window display of fresh fish and shellfish is a not-so-subtle hint of what's to come from the sleek, open kitchen: octopus carpaccio with lemon, capers, and arugula; plump blue nose sea bass with rosemary-roasted fingerling potatoes; and ice cold oysters, ceviche, and clams at the raw bar. A glass wall of wine is mighty alluring, though a sweet *tartufo* chocolate tempts one to a hasty finish.

Gitane

Mediterranean

6 Claude Ln. (bet. Bush & Sutter Sts.)

Phone: 415-788-6686 — Dinner Tue – Sat
Web: www.gitanerestaurant.com
Prices: $$

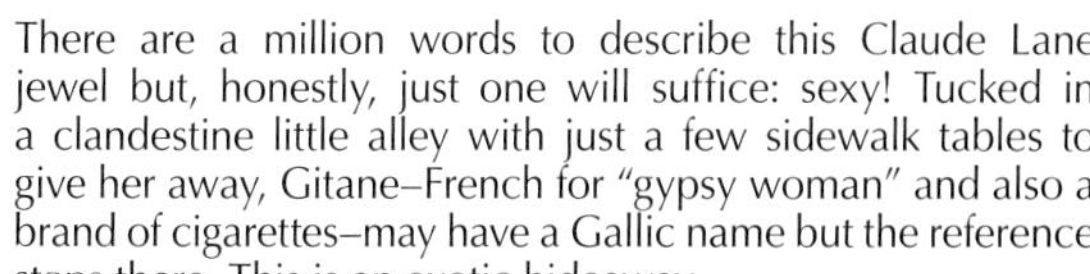

There are a million words to describe this Claude Lane jewel but, honestly, just one will suffice: sexy! Tucked in a clandestine little alley with just a few sidewalk tables to give her away, Gitane–French for "gypsy woman" and also a brand of cigarettes–may have a Gallic name but the reference stops there. This is an exotic hideaway.
Wrought-iron chandeliers and red lamps cast a dim light on mirrored walls, which reflect rich textiles and cushioned banquettes. Sound sultry? The cuisine is equally seductive. You'll salivate for Catalan-style flatbread with cilantro, caramelized onions, and merguez sausage; flaky pan-seared opah with herbed yogurt and seasoned chickpea stew; and a chicken tagine with green olives, almonds, and saffron-tomato broth.

Katanya

Japanese

430 Geary St. (bet. Mason & Taylor Sts.)

Phone: 415-771-1280 — Lunch & dinner daily
Web: N/A
Prices:

In the heart of what locals fondly call the "Splenderloin," this Tenderloin neighborhood noodle house has all the trappings of a favorite haunt in a gritty locale: questionable décor and a line of mixed patrons loitering outside the door.

That's right, those in the know aren't put off by Katanya's gaudy gilded artwork or well-worn furnishings. Rather, they are in a hurry and here for lunch, which promises rewarding bowls of piping hot ramen. Start with tempura, plump *gyoza*, or offerings from the sushi bar before getting to the good stuff: belly-warming bowls of the house specialty noodles come laden with fried chicken and potatoes as well as corn, egg, and barbecued pork. Even the most tired taste buds will perk up for the kimchi-flavored broth.

La Mar

Peruvian

D2

Pier 1 1/2 (at The Embarcadero)

Phone: 415-397-8880 — Lunch & dinner daily
Web: www.lamarsf.com
Prices: $$

This spacious waterfront Peruvian favorite is ideal for boisterous groups in the mood for fresh fare and Bay Bridge views...and for anyone else seeking a truly evocative San Francisco spot. Located next to the iconic Ferry Building on the palm-lined Embarcadero, La Mar is so flawlessly fun that it verges on formulaic, but competent food and a stellar location make it a beloved destination.

Latin music fills the massive interior, where a raw bar overflows with fresh citrus; and pans in the dramatic open kitchen send flames several feet into the air. It's all a bit theatrical, but service is spot on and the cuisine is consistent. Try the *cebiche mixto,* loaded with mahi mahi, calamari, and octopus in *ají amarillo*; and *choclo,* or Peruvian corn empanadas.

Michael Mina ✿

Contemporary XXX

C2

252 California St. (bet. Battery & Front Sts.)

Phone: 415-397-9222 — Lunch Mon – Fri
Web: www.michaelmina.net — Dinner nightly
Prices: $$$$

Mina Group

When one thinks of prominent SF chefs, a few names always rise to the top: Michael Mina is undoubtedly one of them. And in a new home on California Street where Aqua used to be, Mina is enjoying a fresh lease on life in the heart of the Financial District.

The new home is grand in scale yet retains a sense of casual Californian warmth, with oversized mirrors picking up the reflection of massive floral arrangements and dark denim-clad mixologists shaking drinks and pouring wines into Spiegelau stemware at the polished concrete bar. Proximity to luxury hotels guarantees the restaurant is packed with an affluent clientele who appreciates a setting that strikes the right balance between relaxed and refined—Michael Mina is ideal for truly enjoying the food that's to come.

The chef is best known for punctuating local, seasonal ingredients with Mediterranean and Asian accents; the result is at once creative, contemporary, and comforting. À la carte meals may include bundles of *lardo*-wrapped Dungeness crab legs resting against pillowy gnocchi; a duo of crispy fish presented with a rich lobster and coconut sauce; and vanilla-poached rhubarb with Straus Family Creamery's ricotta cream.

Millennium

Vegan XX

A2

580 Geary St. (at Jones St.)

Phone: 415-345-3900 — Dinner nightly
Web: www.millenniumrestaurant.com
Prices: $$

Millennium was lauded for its exceptional vegan food long before it was cool to be vegan. Even fervid carnivores trade their steaks for tofu here inside the Hotel California, where the friendly staff is eager to advise on the area's best organic markets.

Influenced by countless cultures, Millennium's gourmet vegan made at the hands of Chef Eric Tucker personifies flavor and creativity. Sustainable products star in dishes like roasted Peruvian & huckleberry potato salad with purslane and chicories; Kaffir lime and chile-glazed portobellos with red coconut curry; and roasted wild mushrooms with fennel and seitan "sausage."

Dishes are so tasty that this place is packed nightly, so reserve ahead or pray for a seat at the first-come, first-served bar.

Palio d'Asti

Italian XX

C2

640 Sacramento St. (bet. Kearny & Montgomery Sts.)

Phone: 415-395-9800 — Lunch Mon – Fri
Web: www.paliodasti.com — Dinner Mon -Sat
Prices: $$

Named for Il Palio, a bareback horserace in the Italian town of Asti that harks back to the Middle Ages, this FiDi favorite does not stray from its theme. Equestrian art gallops around concrete columns and across walls, while courtly banners and vibrant coats of arms trumpet contemporary Italian meals of enormous proportions.

The fare hails from various Italian regions and is available in two-, three-, and four-course prix-fixe menus that largely appeal to neighborhood businessmen. Aromatic, authentic, and generous dishes might include hand-rolled penne pasta with herb-rich tomato sauce and Berkshire pork *guanciale*; fennel sausage pizza with smoked mozzarella; or a steaming fisherman's stew with spicy saffron-lobster broth and grilled sourdough.

Perbacco

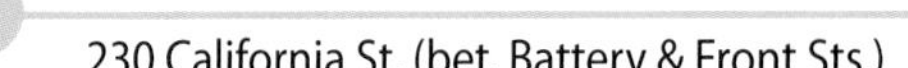

Italian

C3

230 California St. (bet. Battery & Front Sts.)

Phone: 415-955-0663 — Lunch Mon – Fri
Web: www.perbaccosf.com — Dinner Mon – Sat
Prices: $$

Perbacco loosely translates to "good times" in Italian and that's exactly what you'll have when you come here. From the cool marble bar to the sleek furnishings, Perbacco has city chic written all over it. It is urban and up-to-the-minute, and its smartly dressed and sophisticated crowd knows it.

The highly professional and knowledgeable staff makes this a tightly run ship, while the country Italian cooking is sure to please. The food focuses on Piemonte, with a little bit of Liguria, and even Provence thrown in for good measure. It is comfort food for city slickers and may include truffle herb ricotta gnocchi, rabbit-stuffed agnolotti, pappardelle topped with short rib ragù, and slow-roasted veal—all at palatable prices.

Rotunda

Californian

B3

150 Stockton St. (at Geary St.)

Phone: 415-362-4777 — Lunch daily
Web: www.neimanmarcus.com
Prices: $$$

Upon entering Neiman Marcus from Union Square, cast your eyes skyward to the four-story Belle Époque rotunda. This marvelous architectural opus was crowned the City of Paris department store and built in 1908 on this site. Highlighted in cream and gold with carvings of Poseidon, the soaring stained glass dome bears a nautical theme. During lunch, the eponymous restaurant that sits under the rotunda is drowned by the clickety-clack of stilettos on the polished marble floors of ladies who lunch.

Tradition calls for light, ladylike, and complimentary starters including consommé, flaked puffed turnovers, and sweet strawberry butter. While Rotunda's menu leans towards salads and sandwiches, a selection of hearty entrées is sure to satiate the men in tow.

Sanraku

Japanese

704 Sutter St. (at Taylor St.)

Phone: 415-771-0803 — Lunch Mon – Sat
Web: www.sanraku.com — Dinner nightly
Prices:

When it comes to consuming raw fish, it's easy to judge a sushi bar by its cover: sleek can be a misleading synonym for fresh. But San Francisco sushi connoisseurs know that the most outstanding seafood hides out in unassuming corners. Welcome to Sanraku, a no-frills favorite with quick, inexpensive, and quality Japanese bites.

Dressed in bare light walls and blonde wood tables, Sanraku isn't much to look at. But natural light and spunky service keep things upbeat, and ample portions do not disappoint the Western palate. Santa Barbara uni is fresh and creamy, and the sashimi platter is loaded with flavorful fluke, Spanish mackerel, and salmon. With small salads and bowls of miso soup, lunch specials appeal to the local working set.

Scala's Bistro

Italian

B2

432 Powell St. (bet. Post & Sutter Sts.)

Phone: 415-395-8555 — Lunch & dinner daily
Web: www.scalasbistro.com
Prices: $$

Historic charm radiates from this casually elegant bistro, adjacent to the venerable Sir Francis Drake Hotel a block from Union Square. Classy but not stuffy, Scala's tuxedo-clad servers, original murals, and art deco ceiling conjure the best of the Old World. An open kitchen provides a brick backdrop dangling with antique copper cookware.

Here, the men (and women) manning the stoves infuse Italian country cuisine with Californian flair in turkey tortellini in a Parmesan *brodo* with vegetables and tarragon *pistou*. *Secondi* may feature a tender braised Wagyu short rib with creamy celery root purée, gremolata, and parsnip crisps; or *mezzaluna* ravioli stuffed with braised lamb *agrodolce*. Mini portions of selected desserts allow a last sweet bite.

Silks

Contemporary

222 Sansome St. (bet. California & Pine Sts.)

Phone: 415-986-2020 — Lunch Sun – Fri
Web: www.mandarinoriental.com — Dinner Tue – Sat
Prices: $$$$

Gold and white linens top the tables at Silks, the resident restaurant at the magnificent Mandarin Oriental. Here you'll find coppery silk drapes and honey silk hanging lamps, as well as luxurious armchairs and booths rich with blue velvet. The effect is a subtly exotic background for Californian cuisine with a distinct Asian inflection.

Prosperous patrons flood the gorgeous space in anticipation of dishes such as a classic green papaya salad, beautifully plated on contemporary whiteware, with the bright colors and vibrant flavors of pink grapefruit and dried red pepper. Confit of Sonoma duck leg has a perfectly rendered, crispy skin that locks in serious moisture; and for a decadent finish, sweet tooths should try the coconut sorbet.

The Slanted Door

Vietnamese

1 Ferry Building (at The Embarcadero)

Phone: 415-861-8032 — Lunch & dinner daily
Web: www.slanteddoor.com
Prices: $$

Faraway from the heat of Vietnam, Charles Phan's forever sacred Slanted Door embodies a fortuitous marriage of local bounty kissed with Californian flair and faithful Vietnamese flavors. A virtual emperor of a Bay Area empire, his branches ooze verve and vivacity. Superbly set in the cuisine-centric Ferry Building, the hype still sates at this swank and scenic space.

Cypress tables cradle earthenware parading a litany of Viet delights. Tinged with clean, fresh flavors are tiger shrimp in chili sauce; classic spring rolls; squid sautéed with sweet peppers and jalapeño; lemongrass chicken drenched in roasted chili paste; and cellophane noodles rippling with crab.

The bar lures boisterous beauties with a bevy of beers, cocktails, and teas.

Tadich Grill

Seafood

240 California St. (bet. Battery & Front Sts.)

Phone: 415-391-1849 Lunch & dinner Mon – Sat
Web: www.tadichgrill.com
Prices: $$

Tadich Grill is as much a spot for history buffs as it is for local foodies: opened in 1849, San Francisco's oldest restaurant retains its antique charm. While there are a few tables, regulars prefer a niche at the long wood bar where they can catch up with fellow barflies and watch the white-coated staff up close.

Try not to fill up on sliced sourdough—the simple dishes are hearty. Mainstays include a creamy Boston clam chowder; large Dungeness crab cakes with steamed baby bok choy; and fresh seafood entrées that may be broiled, pan-fried, sautéed, poached, deep-fried, or baked *en casserole*. Don't forget about the delightful daily specials, which may include seafood cioppino with garlic bread; broiled lobster tail; and corned beef hash.

Wayfare Tavern

Gastropub

558 Sacramento St. (bet. Montgomery & Sansome Sts.)

Phone: 415-772-9060 Lunch Mon – Sat
Web: www.wayfaretavern.com Dinner nightly
Prices: $$

What was once beloved Rubicon is now Wayfare Tavern, and the address is just about the only thing they both have in common. These days, find the space dressed in celebrity chef Tyler Florence's signature style: breezy, masculine and just a bit raucous, with renovations including white subway-tiled walls and a billiards room upstairs.

The man himself can often be spotted in what is now a seriously bustling exhibition kitchen. Grab a seat at the antique bar for the best view as servers whir past with plates of deviled eggs, made with mustard crème fraîche; fresh oysters; and the Wayfare burger "Le Grand," with Mt. Tam cheese and a Petaluma egg on brioche. The tri-level space is constantly packed, so make your reservations well in advance.

Wexler's

American

568 Sacramento St. (bet. Leidesdorff & Montgomery Sts.)

Phone: 415-983-0102 Lunch Mon – Fri
Web: www.wexlerssf.com Dinner Tue – Sat
Prices: $$

Blink and you might just miss Wexler's. This diminutive spot has just a sprinkling of tables and a few seats at the bar, but those who plan ahead and make reservations are generously rewarded with inspired Southern-influenced cooking.

Inside, it feels like the simple dining room of a slightly quirky art student. Stark white walls are offset by two red chandeliers, while simple metal chairs and stools sit at blonde wood tables.

Dishes exemplify the restaurant's slightly offbeat, but gourmet approach to barbecue-inspired American cuisine. Expect the menu to highlight smoked and roasted flavors in dishes such as barbecue Scotch eggs wrapped in short ribs and served with sweet tea gastrique; pork plate with creamy grits; and smoked collard greens risotto.

Sunday brunch plans?
Look for the !

Marina

Japantown · Pacific Heights · Presidio

If San Francisco were a university campus, the Marina would be Greek Row, for what it lacks in diversity and substance, it makes up with a nod to those with "new money." The Marina's more sophisticated sister, Pacific Heights, thrives on serious family money and couldn't care less about being edgy. When the tanned denizens of this beautiful bubble aren't jogging with their golden retrievers at Crissy Field, or sipping aromatic chocolate from the **Warming Hut**, they can be seen pushing designer baby strollers in boutiques or vying for parking in Mercedes SUVs.

Cafe Culture

Perhaps surprisingly, fine dining is not a hallmark of the Marina. Rather, this socialite's calling card is the quick-bite café **La Boulange** or **The Grove**; the gastropub, à la **Liverpool Lil's** or the **Balboa Café**; and the pickup joint **Perry's**, said to have been among the world's first. In truth, quality cuisine has little to do with a Marina restaurant's success: The locals are delightfully content to follow the buzz to the latest hot spot, whose popularity seems mandated by the number of pretty people sitting at its tables. However, in the Presidio, where Lucasfilm H.Q. rules, creatives and tech geeks opt for convenience at nearby **Presidio Social Club** and **La Terrasse**. "Off the Grid-Fort Mason" features a collection of food trucks who gather every Friday evening proffering fantastic street eats. For the Marina's physically fit and diet-conscious residents, food is mere sustenance to the afternoon shopper and a sponge for the Champagne and chardonnay flowing at plentiful watering holes. In other words, it's all about the bar scene, baby, and there's a playground for everyone. Oenophiles save the date for the annual ZAP Zinfandel Festival in January. Preppy post-collegiates swap remembrances of European semesters abroad at **Ottimista Enoteca-Café**, **Bacchus Wine Bar**, and **Nectar**. Guys relive their frat house glory days at

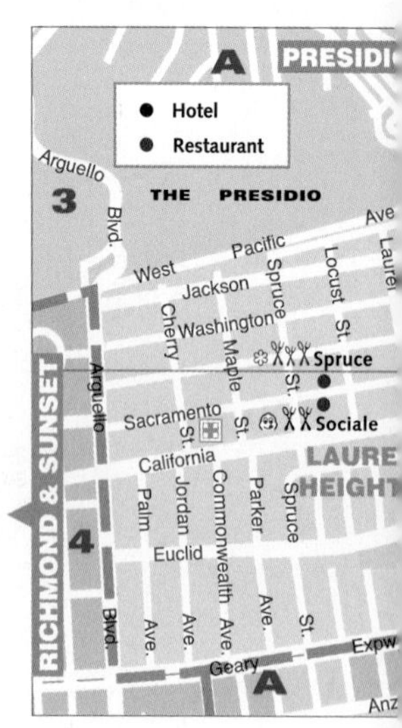

Harry's Bar, and singles on the hunt for marriageable meat opt for the fireplace at the posh **MatrixFillmore**. With a burgeoning Asian culture, Japantown is the exception to the rule. Hotel Tomo got a cool J Pop overhaul and serves all-you-can-eat shabu-shabu at **Mums Restaurant and Bar**. **O Izakaya Lounge** riffs on the Japanese novelty for baseball; and the fabulous **Sundance Kabuki Cinema** serves a range of treats in their two full bars. Also in abundance here are hugely sought after Japanese cultural events, local shopping, and scores of schools.

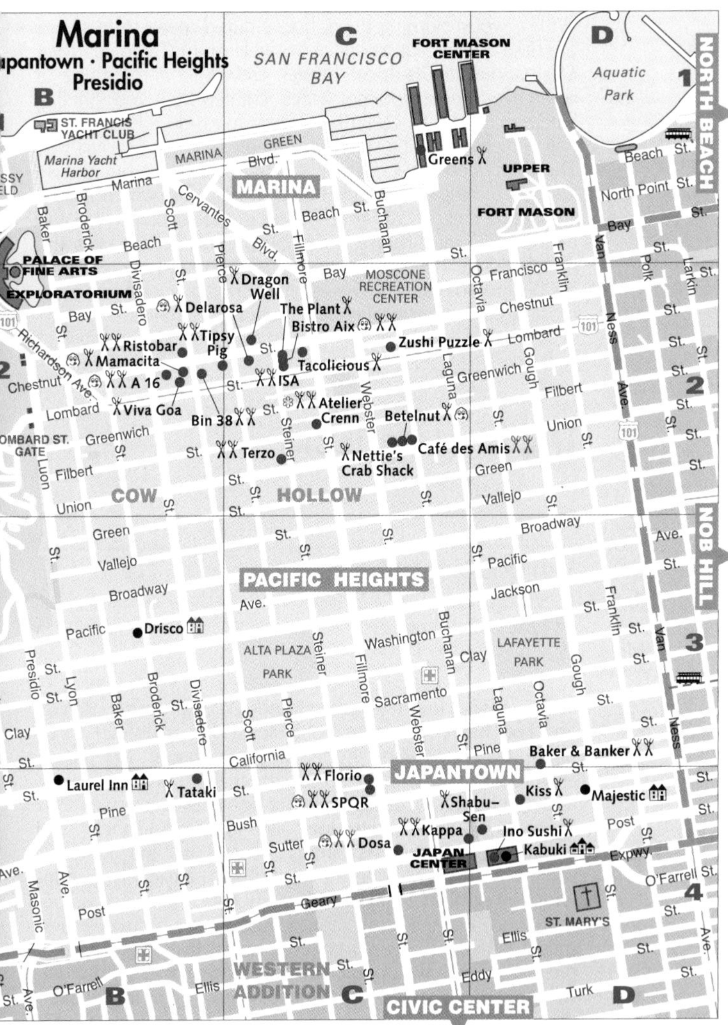

A 16

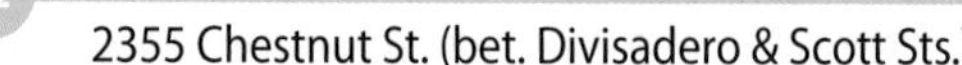

B2

2355 Chestnut St. (bet. Divisadero & Scott Sts.)

Phone: 415-771-2216 — Lunch Wed – Fri
Web: www.a16sf.com — Dinner nightly
Prices: $$

With a wood-burning oven, house-cured meats, and swags of chili hanging out to dry, A 16 feels more Campania than Marina despite its local hipster crowd. Pour in a list of seductive Southern Italian wines, curated by owner Shelley Lindgren, and A16 could be a cozy roadside retreat on the Italian highway that inspired its name.

The team of chefs successfully steers the laid-back but precise kitchen, turning out soulful Southern Italian fare with northern Cali influences. Pizzas are blistered to a delectable crisp and heaped with mushrooms and smoked mozzarella; pastas and meatballs are divine; and entrées like roasted stuffed quail are big crowd pleasers. Dessert may bring a fig and raspberry *crostata* with ricotta gelato and crunchy pistachios.

Baker & Banker

Californian

D3

1701 Octavia St. (at Bush St.)

Phone: 415-351-2500 — Lunch Sun
Web: www.bakerandbanker.com — Dinner Tue – Sun
Prices: $$

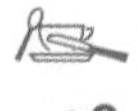

A true labor of love for husband-and-wife team Jeffrey Banker and Lori Baker, this casual-chic space has a distinct bistro bend. Envisage wood floors and furnishings, low lights, espresso leather banquettes, chalkboards listing beers, wines, and other specials, and the picture becomes clear.

Baker & Banker's love for, and loyalty to, local and sustainable produce is amply evident in the kitchen's shining dishes. Moving beyond bistro basics is bacon-wrapped pork loin ladled with tangy cabbage and a juniper reduction. Braised lamb atop a mélange of crispy veggies, mushrooms, and parsnip gnocchi; and a lush Meyer lemon pie topped with whipped cream, candied thyme, surrounded by wonderfully sticky-sweet black olives crown this market-driven deal.

Atelier Crenn ✿

Contemporary XX

C2

3127 Fillmore St. (bet. Filbert & Pixley Sts.)

Phone: 415-440-0460 Dinner Tue – Sat
Web: www.ateliercrenn.com
Prices: **$$$**

Atelier Crenn

Every fig leaf, willow branch, and firefly-like filament light bulb was designed to evoke a warm sense of nature at Atelier Crenn. The serenity is palpable as foodies and sophisticates wax poetic over the menu. At the same time, the passionate staff is informative, friendly, and effervescent with enthusiasm for the food and wine they serve.

From behind the glass-walled kitchen and while visiting each table, Chef Dominique Crenn expresses clear dedication to her craft while flaunting an edgy demeanor on her person and plate.

Frozen and dehydrated elements, pastes, foams, oils, and powders underscore the very contemporary nature of this ambitious cuisine. At the same time, its elegance is paramount in dishes like new potato *memoire d'enfance* cooked in goat fat, accompanied by peas, sprouts, mint, basil, and crisps in a creamy goat cheese sauce that brings spectacular interplay and balance between ingredients. The "tastes of the forest" is its own midsummer-night dream–earthy mushrooms, sweet pine meringue, crushed hazelnuts, chestnuts, micro-greens, and chickpea crisps–so evocative of woodland flavors that Puck is probably a regular. You need to see the carrot cake to believe it.

Betelnut

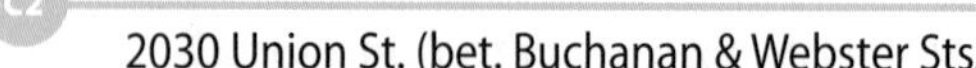

C2

Asian

2030 Union St. (bet. Buchanan & Webster Sts.)

Phone: 415-929-8855 — Lunch & dinner daily
Web: www.betelnutrestaurant.com
Prices: $$

This bustling open kitchen cranks out great Far Eastern street-food delicacies, with a focus on small plates designed for sharing and pairing with perhaps a Tsing Tao or Elephant beer. Sample grilled pancakes with hand-pulled Mongolian hoisin pork; *bien pow* chicken with dried Sichuan chilies and almonds; Sri Lankan clay pot curried fish; and myriad other options for those with an asbestos palate.

Its mysterious vibe, sultry lighting, and lazy bamboo fans over streetfront Dragonfly Lounge earn this Marina favorite major points for ambience, though service is often lukewarm. Nevertheless, a red lacquered bar is a sleek spot for creative cocktails and the upstairs dining room is constantly packed with festive revelers—reservations are recommended.

Bin 38

B2

American

3232 Scott St. (bet. Chestnut & Lombard Sts.)

Phone: 415-567-3838 — Dinner nightly
Web: www.bin38.com
Prices: $$

It's tragic that most people come to Bin 38 only for a glass of wine. These folks are missing out on some serious talent behind the stoves. While the aura exuded is all wine bar, the small plates in the dining room scream delicious restaurant. Under a clear sky, join the swank Marina set on the back patio by the fire pit for a comforting bowl of ricotta-packed agnolotti combined with caramelized pancetta, a quivering egg, and spring onion slivers.

With such a creative selection of food and wine, sipping and snacking here is oh-so-enjoyable. And, between the lamb trio (mini chops, grilled merguez, and crispy lamb bacon) drizzled with a green garlic purée; and a pristine olive oil cake licked with lavender ice cream, you are bound to leave beaming.

Bistro Aix

Mediterranean

3340 Steiner St. (bet. Chestnut & Lombard Sts)

Phone: 415-202-0100 Dinner nightly
Web: www.bistroaix.com
Prices: $$

New and improved Bistro Aix, with its glorious glass ceiling and well-tread bar (carved from discarded marble) pouring delicious libations, now lures loyalists from far and wide with the scent of an oak-burning grill. A reclaimed and warming redwood banquette lines the back dining room where solid tables are topped with cotton dishcloth napkins; the back atrium is sunny, framing a decade-old olive tree, giving Aix the au naturel aroma of Provence.

Southern French fare has a Californian accent; and from the expert kitchen, expect such luscious dishes as a white bean crostini with tender squid and flavorful *persillade*; fresh salmon *a la plancha* perfectly prepared; and a high-quality dark chocolate cloud cake with whipped crème fraîche and toasted almonds.

Café des Amis

French

2000 Union St. (at Buchanan St.)

Phone: 415-563-7700 Lunch & dinner daily
Web: www.cafedesamissf.com
Prices: $$

Lovers of the sometimes-stereotypical but ever-charming French café will be easily won over by *très chic* Café des Amis. Here petite tables are topped with white linen and laden with excellent renditions of brasserie classics, such as *moules frites*, with PEI mussels steamed in a fragrant broth of fine herbs, shaved fennel, and a splash of Pernod; or satisfying cassoulet.

Word to the wise: the well-heeled neighborhood is partial to this stylish spot, so a fire-warmed seat beneath the glittering chandelier on the mezzanine requires a reservation. Without one, find yourself dining amongst the plebeians at the bar, or in the marble-floored street-level dining room. Either way, we are all one at dessert—look for decadent profiteroles, *naturellement*.

Delarosa ☺

Italian

2175 Chestnut St. (bet. Pierce & Steiner Sts.)

Phone: 415-673-7100 — Lunch & dinner daily
Web: www.delarosasf.com
Prices: $$

Pizza and beer prove their very happy (and economy-proof) marriage at this posh neighborhood darling from the owners of Beretta and Starbelly. The challenging parking is a boon to the deep-pocketed local hipsters, who walk here in droves to keep the small place packed.

Inside the modern space in gray and tangerine hues, trendsters hoping to see and be seen line the blonde wood communal tables. A selection of 15 draught beers complements the Roman-style crispy pizzas festooned with house-cured meats. The ever-popular Margherita is worth the upgrade to their silky *burrata* cheese for a few bucks more.

The kitchen also turns out an array of *antipasti* including beet carpaccio and crab *arancini*; and Italian gelato spiked with grappa.

Dosa ☺

Indian

C4

1700 Fillmore St. (at Post St.)

Phone: 415-441-3672 — Lunch Wed – Sun
Web: www.dosasf.com — Dinner nightly
Prices: $$

Regulars to Dosa's Mission home will hardly recognize this second location, across from the Kabuki Theater, where owners Emily and Anjan Mitra are bringing their South Indian flavors to a vast, contemporary interior decked in eco-friendly materials, mismatched chandeliers, and a palette inspired by the spices in the kitchen.

In fact, spice lovers will find much to love. Begin with the complimentary fennel-studded *pappadum,* then try a crispy fish *pakora* marinated in cumin, ginger, and chili, and paired with cilantro chutney. Of course, this is also a worthy start for an introduction to *dosas*—thin pancakes with plentiful fillings including habañero-mango or the more classic masala with spiced potatoes. Exotic cocktails flow at the bustling bar.

Dragon Well

Chinese X

2142 Chestnut St. (bet. Pierce & Steiner Sts.)

Phone: 415-474-6888 Lunch & dinner daily
Web: www.dragonwell.com
Prices: $$

Sandwiched between the posh boutiques and trendy eateries of Chestnut Street, Dragon Well is a modest favorite for fresh Chinese served continuously from 11:30 A.M. until 10:00 P.M. The cozy space sports well-worn wood floors, close tables, and skylights that shed light onto butter-yellow walls. Scenes from China overlook the fully Western clientele who pack the house at lunch to feast on somewhat Americanized fare.

Made with the freshest ingredients, dishes include flavorful tea-smoked duck with plump steamed buns and hoisin sauce; stir-fried chicken and black beans with red bell pepper and chili sauce; and a crisp "bird's nest" of scallops, calamari, and prawns with sugar snap peas, carrots, and ginger. Dragon Well is also terrific for takeout.

Florio

Italian XX

1915 Fillmore St. (bet. Bush & Pine Sts.)

Phone: 415-775-4300 Dinner nightly
Web: www.floriosf.com
Prices: $$

On a tree-lined avenue bursting with trendy retailers, this European-style bistro tips its hat to an earlier time, when neighborhood haunts served soul-warming classics with a smile of genuine hospitality. Expect to see the well-stocked bar at the front of the house filled with familiar residents ordering "the usual." In the back, parchment paper lines wooden tables and conversation bubbles over the low cling clang rising from the semi-open kitchen.

The menu offers first-class travel between Italy and France, featuring such traditional fare as butternut squash ravioli with fresh thyme and earthy chanterelles, or juicy rosemary steak in tarragon béarnaise with crispy frites. New- and old-world varietals as well as wines by the carafe offer good value.

Greens

Vegetarian

Building A, Fort Mason Center

Phone: 415-771-6222 — Lunch Tue – Sun

Web: www.greensrestaurant.com — Dinner nightly

Prices: **$$**

This jewel in the crown of vegetarian restaurants procures her products solely from small, local farms including her own Green Gulch farm in Marin. This can only mean inventive, organic vegetarian cuisine featuring the freshest seasonal vegetables, herbs, and fruits. Greens' Zen philosophy extends to its dining room complete with stunning views of the marina and Golden Gate Bridge.

The chefs at the helm are in charge of crafting these fine ingredients into flavorful dishes like grilled Knoll Farm figs on rosemary skewers gleaming with Andante Dairy goat cheese; fire roasted ancho chili with corn, poblanos, grilled onions, cheddar, and tomatillo salsa; and pappardelle with slow-roasted Juliette tomatoes, spinach, torpedo onions, and Grana Padano.

Ino Sushi

Japanese

22 Peace Plz., Ste. 510 (bet. Buchanan & Laguna Sts.)

Phone: 415-922-3121 — Dinner Tue – Sat

Web: N/A

Prices: **$$**

Japantown locals and film buffs headed to the Kabuki Theater rub elbows (literally) in this teeny authentic sushi joint on the second floor of the neighborhood's Miyako mall. A true mom-and-pop place, Ino serves all combinations of fresh nigiri, maki, and sashimi prepared by a stern, seasoned chef and served by his exceedingly polite wife.

A minimum order applies ($20 for a table, $30 at the counter), but it shouldn't be a problem—sushi aficionados know that even little bits of seafood add up. Start with an assorted nigiri platter piled with Spanish mackerel, tai snapper, *unagi*, toro, and more, spiked appropriately with wasabi. Still hungry? The neat salmon and avocado roll ought to hit the spot. Can't decide? Let the chef do so for you.

ISA

C2

3324 Steiner St. (bet. Chestnut & Lombard Sts.)

Phone: 415-567-9588 Dinner nightly
Web: www.isarestaurant.com
Prices: $$

ISA's new owners, Elias and Sameera Memon, were wise to keep this quaint Marina eatery just as it was before, with a petite candlelit interior that houses just a few tables, an L-shaped bar, and a romantic back patio covered in climbing ivy. People-watching from the front windows is a popular evening pastime but, really, the best thing about ISA is its weekday prix-fixe.

The Californian-French cuisine comes with extensive choices to make up a three-course meal—as you swirl a glass of delicious wine, sink your teeth into grilled squid with a brush of honey and dusting of sweet cinnamon and cloves; pan-roasted free-range chicken with zesty herbs stuffed beneath its crispy skin; and amaretto semifreddo garnished with crunchy cookies.

Kappa

1700 Post St. (at Buchanan St.)

Phone: 415-673-6004 Dinner Mon – Sat
Web: www.kapparestaurant.com
Prices: $$$$

Kappa necessitates a call ahead: not only will you need precise directions to find this obscure Japantown hole-in-the-wall, but the chef only cooks for expected guests. The omakase–an $85 tasting suggested for novices of traditional *koryori* cooking–must be ordered a day in advance. A true mom-and-pop shop, Kappa specializes in intricate small plates with homespun Japanese style.

Served by the lady of the house, who dons a traditional kimono, expect such dishes as bonito atop roasted eggplant in dashi; high grade sashimi; and fried corn fritters. The à la carte menu, penned in Japanese calligraphy, is tough to discern even in English. Thankfully, the husband-wife duo is happy to guide your experience, with the hope that you will become a regular.

Kiss

Japanese

D4

1700 Laguna St. (at Sutter St.)

Phone: 415-474-2866 Dinner Tue – Sat
Web: N/A
Prices: **$$$**

Shaded by the 100-foot-tall Peace Pagoda, Japantown seems the obvious go-to for authentic Japanese cuisine. But, amid the quirky magazine shops, hardware and garden stores, where to eat isn't immediately obvious. Walk a few blocks, and tucked in the corner of a building, find Kiss.

Like its noodle shop neighbors, Kiss doesn't make much of a first impression: the mom-and-pop shop has little décor and even less seating. A keen foodie though will notice that there's not a vacant seat in the house. Book in advance and make like the regulars who order the daily omakase, a multi-course feast of traditional dishes like smoky sardine salad; fresh nigiri; and *chawan mushi* studded with halibut and gingko nuts. You will never again wonder where to eat in Japantown.

Mamacita

Mexican

B2

2317 Chestnut St. (bet. Divisadero & Scott Sts.)

Phone: 415-346-8494 Dinner nightly
Web: www.mamacitasf.com
Prices: **$$**

The name is Mexican and, despite major Californian influence, so is the cuisine's inspiration. Still, Mamacita is a bona fide gringo hangout for affluent Marina youngsters, hipsters, players, and cougars who pose among them. Upbeat, loud, and festive with starry lanterns and photos of Mexican life, these close quarters are a non-issue for the boisterous crowd fueled by top-shelf margaritas.

That said, Mamacita's creative combinations and bold flavors are legitimately delicious. Seared ahi tuna "tacos" arrive in clever jicama wraps with persimmon-apple *pico de gallo*. Mixed into the towering heap of house-made chips, even the ubiquitous *chilaquiles* are fresh with pulled roasted chicken, sautéed spinach, and poblano *rajas* tossed in chipotle cream.

Nettie's Crab Shack

Seafood

C2

2032 Union St. (bet. Buchanan & Webster Sts.)

Phone: 415-409-0300 — Lunch Wed – Mon
Web: www.nettiescrabshack.com — Dinner Wed – Sun
Prices: $$

A far cry from the aquatic kitsch that's drowning Fisherman's Wharf, Nettie's Crab Shack is an homage to east coast sensibilities, with a towering palm, solarium-like front, and surfer-chic interior filled with weathered cottage chairs and New England expats pining for home.

More to the point, this crab house is all about the crab (often Dungeness), whether grilled, steamed, half or whole, in a deviled egg, cake, or roll. On Sundays, don't wear your best but do grab a bib for an old-school, seasonal crab feed with salads, boiled potatoes, and artichokes. Those who feel like branching out can try the clam chowder or Anchor Steam-battered cod and chips. Home-style desserts like ginger cake are a sweet indulgence before moving on to the area's chic shops.

The Plant

Vegetarian

C2

3352 Steiner St. (bet. Chestnut & Lombard Sts.)

Phone: 415-931-2777 — Lunch & dinner daily
Web: www.theplantcafe.com
Prices:

The name has changed from Lettus Café Organic, but the concept remains the same at this eco-friendly eatery that aims to keep both their (mostly feminine) patrons and the planet healthy. Vegetarian and vegan options abound, beginning with a breakfast stack of blueberry pancakes. Lunch and dinner bring sandwiches, veggie burgers, shiitake mushroom spring rolls, and an array of smoothies. The menu also remembers those craving meatier choices, with the likes of mango-lime chicken panini.

The Plant is popular with business people, families, and single diners, who can opt to sit in the simple dining room, at the counter, or sidewalk tables. If rushed, grab a pre-packed meal from the to-go cooler. Also try waterfront dining at their Pier 3 location.

Ristobar

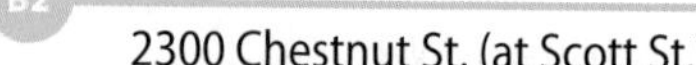

B2 — Italian XX

2300 Chestnut St. (at Scott St.)

Phone: 415-923-6464
Web: www.ristobarsf.com
Prices: $$

Lunch Sat – Sun
Dinner nightly

The name says it all at this fashionable Marina newcomer. Ristobar is part restaurant, part bar, and all chic. The corner location, with a sidewalk patio perfect for people-watching, can't be beat. Don't fret if the chilly San Francisco summer has forced you inside, since the stylish interior is furnished with clusters of wood tables, cushioned banquettes, and a long bar; but those lovely, eye-catching painted ceilings are what captures everyone's attention.
The solid menu is designed for sharing, so snack happy on everything like absolutely delicious cracker-thin crust pizzas; tender and juicy roasted pork tenderloin with crunchy Sicilian pistachios swirled into a rich jus; and creamy, espresso-soaked tiramisu doused with a shot of sambuca.

Shabu-Sen

D4 — Japanese X

1726 Buchanan St. (bet. Post & Sutter Sts.)

Phone: 415-440-0466
Web: N/A
Prices: ⊜

Lunch & dinner daily

Founded in 1906, San Francisco's Japantown is among the oldest in America; on this district's main street is Shabu-Sen. With a modest décor and prices to match, the restaurant keeps decision-making to a minimum by focusing on two styles of dishes: shabu-shabu and *sukiyaki*. These preparations derive from the Japanese practice of families gathering in front of a fire to share a meal together.
To join in this experience, order from the half-dozen combinations of beef, pork, chicken, tiger prawns, sushi-grade scallops, and premium beef. Then, cook your ingredients with seasonal vegetables or noodles in a pot of rich, aromatic broth boiled right at the table. Homemade sesame and ponzu dipping sauces are served by helpful and amiable Japanese waitresses.

Sociale

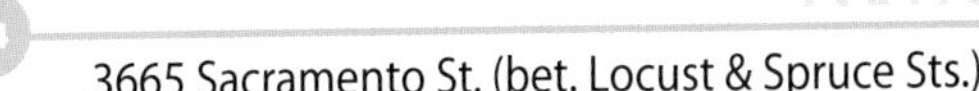

Italian XX

A4

3665 Sacramento St. (bet. Locust & Spruce Sts.)

Phone: 415-921-3200
Web: www.caffesociale.com
Prices: $$

Lunch Tue – Sat
Dinner Mon – Sat

Burrowed behind a wisteria corridor fringed with flowers and shops, Sociale is *the* destination for family feasts and frolicking with friends. A dandy dining room pleases patrons with peach banquettes and walls warmed with black-and-white photos. Augmenting the space is an attractive arch, but their gorgeous garden rules the roost.

Frenzy-free, the patio is an idyllic roost for relishing Italian classics crafted with crazy Cali flair. Laughter rises up in the air as tickled diners dive into such sophisticated surprises as yellow wax beans tossed with strawberries, pancetta, and goat cheese; *malfaddini* flirting with clams, *grechetto*, chili, and spinach; and a chocolate oblivion cake crowned with olive oil, sea salt, and amaretti cookies.

SPQR

Italian XX

C4

1911 Fillmore St. (bet. Bush & Pine Sts.)

Phone: 415-771-7779
Web: www.spqrsf.com
Prices: $$

Lunch Sat – Sun
Dinner nightly

SPQR may be reason enough to move to the Fillmore, where proximity is an advantage for scoring a table at one of SF's most buzzed about eateries. Just put down your name and go home to watch Glee. Don't worry, there's time.

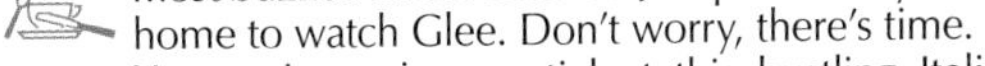

Yes, patience is essential at this bustling Italian hot spot, which is like the Forum for Pac Heights foodies—once you're in, you'll want to stay. Seats at the Carrara marble counter provide a view of the semi-open kitchen, which churns out fresh and flavorful offerings. Look for crispy pig's ear with pickled vegetables; rigatoni with melting *burrata* in spicy tomato ragù; and local quail with chestnut-farro stuffing. At brunch, dishes lean more Californian but, hey, who can complain about farm eggs with fennel sausage?

Spruce 

Mediterranean 

A4

3640 Sacramento St. (bet. Locust & Spruce Sts.)

Phone: 415-931-5100 — Lunch Mon – Fri
Web: www.sprucesf.com — Dinner nightly
Prices: $$$

Frankie Frankeny

If you've ever walked into a place and instantly thought it looked like a movie set or a catalog shoot, then you'll love Spruce. This stylish restaurant has the "easy-breezy-beautiful cover girl" look—maybe that's because it was designed by Williams-Sonoma Home. Those faux (of course, we are in California after all) ostrich chairs and those decadent chocolate brown mohair walls look perfect and pristine. Where's a good supermodel when you need her? Probably dining a few tables down. The food at Spruce is terrific enough to make a diehard dieter skip a night.

It might have been meant for wedding vows, but for richer or poorer fits right in line here. Go for broke with the osetra caviar, or start with the more parsimonious potato and cabbage soup. There's agnolotti with wild nettle; foie gras with hot and cold pineapple; and seared sweetbreads with foraged mushrooms. The menu is heavy on seafood (butter poached lobster, roasted bass, and cod persillade), but there's also Berkshire pork tenderloin, squab breast *a l'orange*, and sage roasted chicken.

And just when you thought they'd thought of everything, check out the coffee list with six varieties hailing from different countries.

Tacolicious

C2

2031 Chestnut St. (bet. Fillmore and Steiner Sts.)

Phone: 415-346-1966 — Lunch & dinner daily
Web: www.tacolicioussf.com
Prices:

Marina dwellers craving Mexican street food head to Tacolicious and gratify a juicy temptation. Evocative prints, votive candles, and wrestling figurines add local flavor to the "bar" vibe. Once just a taco stand, it unfolds a throng of inventive tacos in the former Laiola space.

Free your forks and with your fingers plunge into fleshy tacos with the freshest ingredients. The shot-and-a-beer chicken tacos; the taco of the week with fried chicken or grilled filet mignon aside caramelized onions, arugula, and poblano salsa; and tuna tostadas with chipotle mayonnaise and avocado are kissed with spice and all things nice.

A lick from the homemade salsa spectrum (chipotle, tomatillo, habañero) and a sip from the slew of tequilas will keep grown-ups jaunty.

Tataki

Japanese

B4

2815 California St. (bet. Broderick & Divisadero Sts.)

Phone: 415-931-1182 — Lunch Mon – Fri
Web: www.tatakisushibar.com — Dinner nightly
Prices: $$

In an area famed for organic eats, Tataki puts the rest to eco-shame and takes sustainable cuisine to new heights. Not only are the rolls and sashimi perfectly pristine, but the kitchen makes it a point to respect the sanctity and fragility of the environment by sourcing only the freshest fish for their menu. Tataki may have eliminated the mercury-high *maguro*, but after slurping up shrimp ceviche with yuzu on futomaki chips; crab croquettes; sea change salad with jellyfish and tobiko; and a comforting soba bowl, you will start to reel from (and feel) the effects of an intensely flavorful journey. Tataki also pays it forward with take-home sustainability guides from the Monterey Bay Aquarium. This is a bite-size gem with big heart and a tiny footprint.

Terzo

C2 Mediterranean XX

3011 Steiner St. (bet. Filbert & Union Sts.)

Phone: 415-441-3200 Dinner nightly
Web: www.terzosf.com
Prices: $$

The third time's a charm as the saying goes and Terzo, the third restaurant from the group that owns Rose Pistola and Rose's Café, gets it right. Filament bulbs cast a cool light over the dark contemporary interior where chocolate leather covers the banquettes and a central communal table bustles with noshing regulars. Wall-mounted racks display a good selection of global wines, with many available by the glass—de rigueur for washing down these Mediterranean-inspired small plates.

Start with grilled Monterey Bay calamari with lentils, fennel, and a dusting of pimentón; or try the vegetarian hummus and beet salad. Hearty appetites should look for larger entrées like roasted mahi mahi with garbanzo beans and almonds. Terzo is romantic, so do bring a date.

Tipsy Pig

B2 Gastropub XX

2231 Chestnut St. (bet. Pierce & Scott Sts.)

Phone: 415-292-2300 Lunch Wed – Sun
Web: www.thetipsypigsf.com Dinner nightly
Prices: $$

Despite its silly name, Tipsy Pig is beloved by the beautiful people in the Marina. By constantly researching and re-inventing the allure of British pub culture and putting their own Californian spin on things, this has become quite the hipster den, so make sure you knock back a few to better tolerate the noise.

Escape to the oasis of the back patio to enjoy playful dishes like deviled eggs with candied bacon and a lemon cucumber relish. The smoked mac and cheese gets a lot of ink; while the pretzel braid with a cheddar-beer dip begs for more beer—choose from either a piglet, pint, or the 20-ounce tipsy pig. Despite all the bar trappings, there is a kid's menu for your toddlers to enjoy as they count the number of pigs adorning the room.

Viva Goa

Indian 𝕏

B2

2420 Lombard St. (bet. Divisadero & Scott Sts.)

Phone: 415-440-2600 — Lunch & dinner daily
Web: www.vivagoaindiancuisine.com
Prices: $$

Cardamom, curry, and the strums of an Indian sitar hang in the air at Viva Goa, the Lombard Street eatery that offers a rich culinary experience thanks to Goa's coastal life where Portuguese influences mingles with the local cuisine. Once you find parking–this neighborhood can be tricky–slide into a burgundy booth and order a Goan specialty—both the seafood curry and stuffed-and-fried whole pomfret are unexpected standouts.

Indian food lovers will also find tasty executions of the classics: fried chicken lollipops drenched in a peppery red sauce; spicy *vindaloo*; aromatic *biryani*; *tikka masala*; savory *samosas*, and blistered garlic naan. Spice junkies can ask for extra hot, while budget diners will appreciate the $8.99 buffet at lunch.

Zushi Puzzle

Japanese 

C2

1910 Lombard St. (at Buchanan St.)

Phone: 415-931-9319 — Dinner Mon – Sat
Web: www.zushipuzzle.com
Prices: $$

This packed Lombard Street *sushi-ya* may have the oddest name on the block, but its success is no puzzle: a fish is flown in fresh from Japan each day and dozens of specialty maki–including the soft shell and snow crab Dynasty roll–are both beautifully plated and among the tastiest around. The Best Hand Roll isn't just the flourish of a confident chef, but earns its superlative name.

In fact, Chef Roger Chong is a friendly, funny guy from his post at the back counter. Make a reservation (you'll need one) for a view of the master at work. Adventurous types can relinquish the menus and let the chef steer your course, while safer palates find comfort in bowls of soba and udon noodles. Seafood addicts should check the dry erase board for the day's catch.

Mission

Bernal Heights · Potrero Hill

The sun always shines in the Mission, a bohemian paradise dotted with palm trees and home to artists, activists, and a vibrant Latino community. Graffiti murals line the walls of funky galleries, thrift shops, and bookstores; and sidewalk stands burst with Mexican plantains, nopales, and the juiciest limes this side of the border.

The markets here are among the best in town: **La Palma Mexicatessan** brims with homemade *papusa*, chips, and fresh Mexican cheeses. **Lucca Ravioli** stocks imported Italian goods, while **Bi-Rite** is a petite grocer popular for fresh flowers and prepared foods. Across the street find **Bi-Rite Creamery**, a cult favorite for ice cream. From cheese and ice cream, turn the leaf to hipster coffee hangout, **Ritual Coffee Roasters**. What's so stellar about their coffee? Join the line outside the door, order one of their special roasts from the Barista, and you will start to get the picture.

Countless bargain *mercados* and dollar stores might suggest otherwise, but the Mission is home to many an avant-garde hangout. **Dynamo Donuts** on 24th Street is the place for delectable flavors like apricot-cardamom, chocolate-star anise, and maple-glazed bacon apple. **Walzwerk** charms with East German kitsch and is *the* go-to for Deutsch delights. Mission pizza reigns supreme–thin crust lovers wait in line at **Pizzeria Delfina**–they serve a wicked pie with crispy edges blistered just so. Carb addicts cannot (and should not) miss the exceptional breads, pastries, and pressed sandwiches at **Tartine Bakery**. To best experience the flavors of the Mission, forgo the table and chairs and pull up at a curb on Linda Street, where a vigilant street food scene has incited a revolution of sorts. The **Magic Curry Kart** plates $5 steaming rice dishes, while the **Crème Brûlée Cart** torches fresh custards, some spiked with Bailey's Irish Cream, *à la minute*. The alley buzzes with locals noshing homemade pastries, empanadas, and Vietnamese spring rolls until the grub runs out.

The city's hottest 'hood also offers a cool selection of sweets. A banana split is downright retrolicious when served at the Formica counter of 90-year-old **St. Francis Fountain**. The sundaes are made with **Mitchell's Ice Cream**, famous in SF since 1953. Modish flavors–think foie gras and salted licorice–are in regular rotation at the newer **Humphrey Slocombe**. **Mission Pie** is a neighbhood jewel that lures people far and wide for their sumptuos selection of savory and sweet pies. Their menu dances to the season; pays homage to the environment (by using only local, sustainable produce sourced from nearby farms); and unveils light savory treats, baked goods, and a terrific mélange of pies. Dance off your indulgences on Salsa Sunday at **El Rio**, the dive bar with a bustling back patio, or join the hip kids for DJs and live bands at **Elbo Room** and **12 Galaxies**. The lesbian set shoots pool at the **Lexington Club**. On the late night, growling stomachs brave harsh lighting at numerous taquerias, many of which are open till 4:00 A.M. Go see for yourself: Try the veggie burrito at **Taqueria Cancun**; tacos at **La Alteña**; and mind-blowing meats (*lengua* or *cabeza*?) at **El Farolito**. During the day, **La Taqueria**'s carne asada burrito is arguably the best. And **El Tonayense** taco truck, to quote one blogger, is of course "da bomb!"

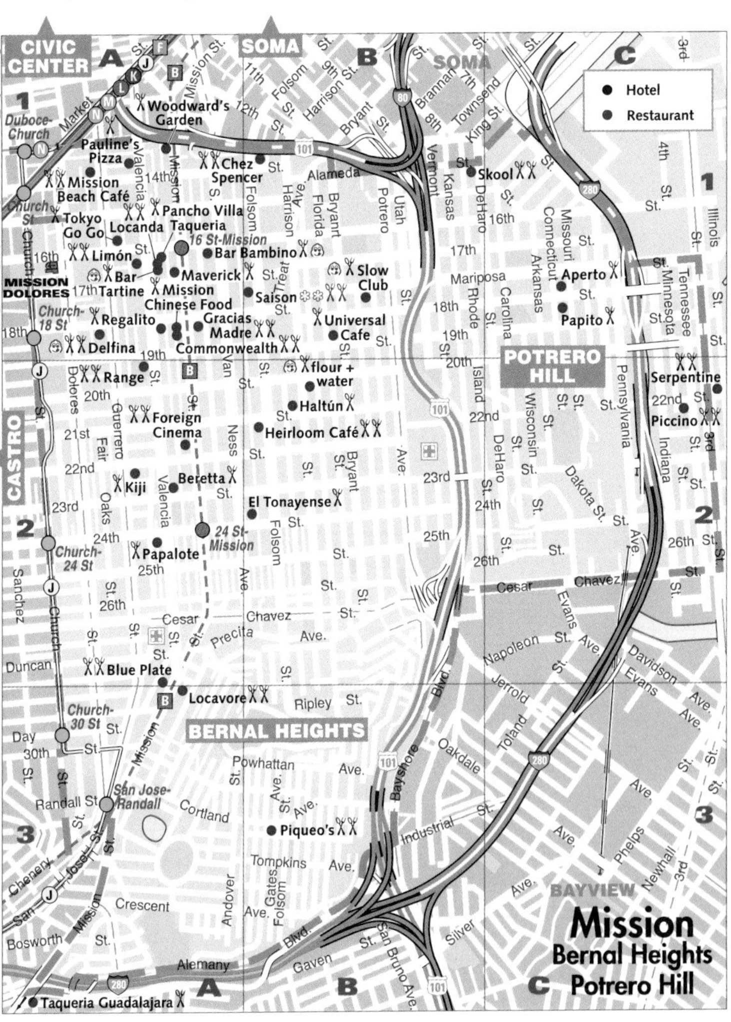

Aperto

Italian

1434 18th St. (at Connecticut St.)

Phone: 415-252-1625 — Lunch & dinner daily
Web: www.apertosf.com
Prices: $$

There is no resisting the open arms and warm kitchen at Aperto, the Potrero Hill spot whose apt name is Italian for "open." A casual neighborhood vibe and daily chalkboard specials set the tone for convivial Italian meals that might include chicken liver pâté on grilled bread drizzled with olive oil, or *radiatore* (spiral pasta) tossed with osso buco ragù of braised pork. Seasonal pastas and *secondi* change regularly with Californian flourishes appearing throughout.

Like its East Bay sister restaurant Bellanico, Aperto is also open to children: a five dollar kids' special features any shape pasta, either plain or with three choices of simple sauce. The wine list is equally accommodating with more than 15 good value varietals available by the glass.

Bar Bambino

Italian

A1

2931 16th St. (bet. Mission St. & Van Ness Ave.)

Phone: 415-701-8466 — Dinner Mon – Sat
Web: www.barbambino.com
Prices: $$

This polished little refuge in a rather dank Mission alcove holds some of the area's hottest tables. Inside the pleasant wine bar, hooks await your coat and more than 35 European wines by the glass are ready to erase the day. Try for a seat at the white marble bar or heated back patio, as you remember that this bite-sized spot is a SF favorite, so reservations would have been a good idea.

The menu offers shareable plates of artisanal cheese, house-made *salumi*, daily *antipasti* such as fried olives stuffed with prosciutto and pecorino; or a chicken panino with roasted butternut squash. Stylish couples and small groups of friends pack the zinc tables, while singles find conversation at the long communal table, lit by a recycled wine bottle chandelier.

Bar Tartine

Eastern European

561 Valencia St. (bet. 16th & 17th Sts.)

Phone: 415-487-1600
Web: www.bartartine.com
Prices: $$

Lunch Sat – Sun
Dinner Tue – Sun

Bar Tartine may be one of the most recognizable of San Francisco's foodie mainstays, but even regulars to this Mission favorite are likely to find a surprise in store. Sure, there's still a line out the door to snag a seat at the long counter in the snug, wood-clad dining room, but a new chef behind the stoves is putting a fresh accent on things—a Hungarian intonation, to be exact.

Eastern European influences abound in pickled starters; fennel pork sausage with plum mustard; and goat meatballs with wilted amaranth and roasted green strawberries. Loyalists, however, will be happy to find the bakery's artisan breads and desserts still on the menu—look for a savory farmer's cheese tart with a buttery crust and trickle of caraway honey.

Beretta

Italian

1199 Valencia St. (at 23rd St.)

Phone: 415-695-1199
Web: www.berettasf.com
Prices: $$

Lunch Sat – Sun
Dinner nightly

Beretta delivers a bang-up performance with its thin-crust pizzas and shared Italian dishes. This well-loved spot is perpetually jamming with Mission hipsters who pack the place for its relaxed vibe and fantastic food at reasonable prices. From meatballs like *Mamma* used to make to tender lamb chops and daily entrée specials, there's plenty on the menu, but pizzas always emerge as the champion.

The quarters are tight (elbow-to-elbow at the bar and communal tables), but it's all part of the friendly spirit. Besides, the menu is designed for sharing. Just make sure you call dibs on the last slice of wild mushroom and spicy *coppa* topped pizza.

Call ahead for a coveted spot on the waiting list, since reservations are for large groups only.

Blue Plate

A2 — American XX

3218 Mission St. (bet. 29th & Valencia Sts.)

Phone: 415-282-6777 — Dinner nightly
Web: www.blueplatesf.com
Prices: $$

Despite San Francisco's outdoorsy image, there is nary a restaurant patio in sight on the dawn of a rare warm day. That's why Missionites have been heading to Blue Plate for more than a decade, where potted plants and blossoming fruit trees overhang café tables in the garden and the kitchen serves mostly organic Cal-Med cuisine inspired by the season. Inside, the narrow space is cool, casual, and ambient with local art lining the walls and skinny-jeaned regulars chowing tasty comfort fare. Chef/owner Cory Obenour's Mediterranean flavor combinations shine in dishes such as grilled Monterey Bay squid with lemon juice and sorrel chiffonade; and slip-from-the-bone pork osso buco cooked in red wine with wilted chard, porcini, and seasoned walnuts.

Chez Spencer

B1 — French XX

82 14th St. (bet. Folsom & Harrison Sts.)

Phone: 415-864-2191 — Lunch Sun
Web: www.chezspencer.net — Dinner Tue – Sun
Prices: $$$

Not an easy find (camouflaged by warehouses and workshops), Chez Spencer is considered a darling of the Mission. Upon entering, guests walk through a large wooden gate, followed by a gorgeous garden terrace and covered patio, until reaching the lofty dining room. Under the skylights and soaring arched wooden beams, two kitchens and a wood-burning oven are as integral to the space as the patrons.

Named for his son, Spencer, and owned by Chef Laurent Katgely, Chez Spencer offers both a lengthy tasting menu and à la carte choices including creamy cauliflower veloute dressed with a crispy Parmesan chip; wood-roasted sturgeon; roasted rack of lamb; or possibly Arctic char baked in parchment.

For French food fast, look for the Spencer on the Go "mobile bistro."

Commonwealth

Californian XX

2224 Mission St. (bet. 18th & 19th Sts.)

Phone: 415-355-1500 Dinner Tue – Sun
Web: www.commonwealthsf.com
Prices: **$$**

In about the most seedy part of the Mission, come to find some of the most inventive dishes in town. Commonwealth is their name (and game) as they aspire to reign supreme in the food world through turning techniques and ambitious dishes into charitable offerings—a portion of their nightly tasting menu goes to charity. The surrounding dilapidation is hard to digest, but frosted windows, hickory floors, and white-brick walls help keep the cheer.

Find foodies clamouring for more of such avant-garde plates as potato gnocchi sautéed with mushrooms, spinach, and truffles; charred octopus perked with sea beans and smoked potatoes; and a baton of peanut butter semifreddo. Faithful to the theme is a focused wine list and frosty cocktails made with liquid N2.

Delfina

3621 18th St. (bet. Dolores & Guerrero Sts.)

Phone: 415-552-4055 Dinner nightly
Web: www.delfinasf.com
Prices: **$$**

Some things, like the popularity of Delfina, never change. This Italian joint is as busy as ever. Delfina relies heavily on Californian ingredients and sensibilities, but the menu is strictly Italian from start to finish. The casual space and warm staff make you feel like an old pal; they even fuss over you with attentive service. Eating solo? The long counter overlooking the dining room is the perfect spot.

You don't need a lot of dough to enjoy the delicious dishes. Chicken liver crostini with *giardiniera*, risotto Milanese with oxtail sugo, and mint tagliatelle topped with fresh porcini mushrooms are just some of the goods you'll sup and sample. The next door pizzeria bustles with the same energy as its more sophisticated sister Delfina.

El Tonayense

Mexican

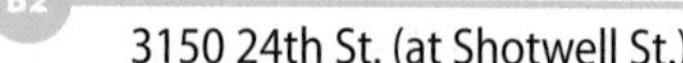

B2

3150 24th St. (at Shotwell St.)

Phone: 415-550-9192 — Lunch & dinner daily
Web: www.eltonayense.com
Prices: ⊜

Devout local foodies often chow down in the curbside shadow of one of El Tonayense's popular taco trucks. But those who prefer to dine at simple wood tables and worn rattan chairs visit the original El Tonayense, perhaps the city's best taqueria.

Prepare your palate for the bold wallop of deep flavors and spice that elevates these corn tortillas, piled high with tender, intensely seasoned meats. Try the smoky carne asada with roasted red chile salsa, or juicy *al pastor* with fresh cilantro and onions. Four varieties of their outstanding homemade salsas are available at the bar, though most have already found nirvana in the amount splashed atop their order. While the tacos really shine here, burrito junkies relish a variety of enormous wraps.

flour + water

Italian

B2

2401 Harrison St. (at 20th St.)

Phone: 415-826-7000 — Dinner nightly
Web: www.flourandwater.com
Prices: $$

In Italian cooking, it all just amounts to flour and water, the two basic ingredients in homemade pasta and pizza dough. Both are cooked to perfection at this hipster haunt where artsy twenty-somethings are cool with waiting an hour for a blistered pie.

Join the crowd in the standing room bar for a glass of nebbiolo as you look around. Concrete floors and a redwood bar lend a requisite industrial vibe, but seafoam walls, aquatic art and fossilized curiosities keeps things oddly warm. The narrow space gets loud, with regulars chirping over crispy trotter with pine nut relish; nightly tastings of fresh pasta such as Aleppo pepper and rabbit sausage; and fire-licked pizzas topped with the likes of bone marrow and horseradish or nettles and garlic.

Foreign Cinema

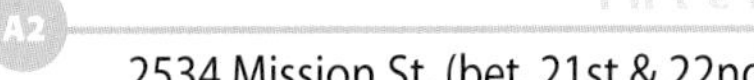

International XX

A2

2534 Mission St. (bet. 21st & 22nd Sts.)

Phone: 415-648-7600 — Lunch Sat – Sun
Web: www.foreigncinema.com — Dinner nightly
Prices: $$

Date night is a wrap at Foreign Cinema, the Mission's art house eatery that projects international films and cult classics onto a white brick wall on the heated courtyard patio. After dinner, get your contemporary art fix in the adjoining gallery and finish with a nightcap at László, the Soviet-themed annex bar.

Subtle, modish accents keep the films in focus, but Foreign Cinema's global translation of Mediterranean fare is worthy of center stage. At dinner, couples share tuna tartare tossed in ginger-lime vinaigrette or moist swordfish with wilted greens and herb-rich *gremolata*. At brunch, locals give fried eggs deglazed with balsamic or the Champagne omelet two thumbs up.

Speaking of which, check out baby sis Show Dogs on Market St. for a fab breakfast.

Gracias Madre

Vegan XX

A1

2211 Mission St. (bet. 18th & 19th Sts.)

Phone: 415-683-1346 — Lunch & dinner daily
Web: www.gracias-madre.com
Prices: $$

Gracias Madre is one of those Mission eateries that conjures everything San Francisco, with a communal vibe, covered patio, dining counter, open kitchen, and organic vegan cuisine that attracts young hipsters with kids. Local art for sale on the walls? But of course.

Skeptics of vegan "Mexican" food will be wise to keep an open mind. While nut-based cheeses and creams aren't exactly authentic, Madre's dishes are fresh, spicy, and delicious. Don't miss the organic guacamole perked up with cilantro and lime to scoop up with purple heirloom corn tortillas; and wickedly spicy *gorditas* with black beans, cilantro, and spicy cashew cream. The house-made *horchata* is certainly tasty, but its premium price tag strays from this otherwise budget-friendly menu.

Haltún

Mexican

B2

2948 21st St. (at Treat Ave.)

Phone: 415-643-6411 — Lunch & dinner daily
Web: www.haltunsf.com
Prices:

This Mission spot might be Mexican, but don't expect the typical quesadilla and burrito affair. Instead, Haltún specializes in Mayan dishes not often seen on other menus. Need to get out of a snit? The cheery dining room with bright orange walls and tiled floors as well as the warm, friendly service will definitely banish bad moods.

The authentic, home-style food is flavorful, fresh, and filling, so even though chips and salsa arrive right away, don't stuff yourself just yet. Save your appetite for dishes like *pol-can,* fried corn dumplings stuffed with lima beans and crushed pumpkin seeds, or *diabla* shrimp in chile chipotle sauce. *Pollo pibil,* chicken marinated and glazed with annatto seed sauce, is finger-licking good.

Heirloom Café

Californian 

B2

2500 Folsom St. (at 21st St.)

Phone: 415-821-2500 — Dinner Mon – Sat
Web: www.heirloom-sf.com
Prices: $$$

San Francisco foodies may have a new mecca in Heirloom Café, a recent favorite melding the Mission's indie spirit with a vintage interior aesthetic: think wallpaper, worn wood floors, and natural light. The open kitchen lends to a feeling of warmth and bustle, and the limited menu feels a bit like dinner at home—that is, if you happen to be a highly skilled chef.

Seasonal dishes are perfectly prepared and might include house-cured gravlax with grilled artisan bread; pillowy gnocchi atop sweet corn and fennel sausage; and roasted halibut with mushrooms, English peas, and creamy cauliflower purée. At dessert, black pepper syrup jazzes up moist olive oil cake with compote of *fraise du bois.* Order a Châteauneuf-du-Pape from the expertly curated wine list.

Kiji

Japanese

A2

1009 Guerrero St. (bet. 22nd & 23rd Sts.)

Phone: 415-282-0400 — Dinner Tue – Sun
Web: www.kijirestaurant.com
Prices: $$

Less is more at Kiji, a super-simple neighborhood sushi joint on a busy stretch of Guerrero Street, in the heart of the Mission. With just a handful of tables and a tiny sushi counter, Kiji is perennially packed: have patience–a table will turn over soon–or make like the locals and call in your order to-go.

While an array of maki are available for Americanized tastes, the menu is best represented by traditional Japanese fare such as hamachi *kama*, a broiled yellowtail collar served with ponzu sauce; and a nightly list of nigiri that may include melt-in-your-mouth *aji*, *tai*, escolar, and ocean trout. Everything here is fresh and good, rather than fancy. Try the Kiji roll, stuffed with snow crab and asparagus and topped with tuna, *tobiko*, and spicy sauce.

Limón

Peruvian

A1

524 Valencia St. (bet. 16th & 17th Sts.)

Phone: 415-252-0918 — Lunch & dinner daily
Web: www.limon-sf.com
Prices: $$

When a fire closed Limón's doors in 2009, regulars satiated their cravings for flavorful Peruvian fare at newly opened sister restaurant, Limón Rotisserie. The offshoot remains popular for juicy rotisserie chicken, particularly at lunch, but loyalists are thrilled to be back in Limon's bi-level space painted a zesty lime green.

The draw of Limón has long been its attention to detail, from skillfully prepared plates down to a notably dishy staff. But the real spice is in the bold cuisine, which ranges from traditional ceviches to flaky empanadas stuffed with braised sirloin and chopped hard-boiled eggs. Entrée delights include a plump fillet of fish and shrimp cooked in garlicky *aji amarillo*; don't miss the crispy fried yucca drizzled with *chimichurri*.

Locanda

A1 Italian XX

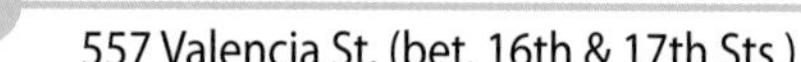

557 Valencia St. (bet. 16th & 17th Sts.)

Phone: 415-863-6800 — Dinner nightly
Web: www.locandasf.com
Prices: $$

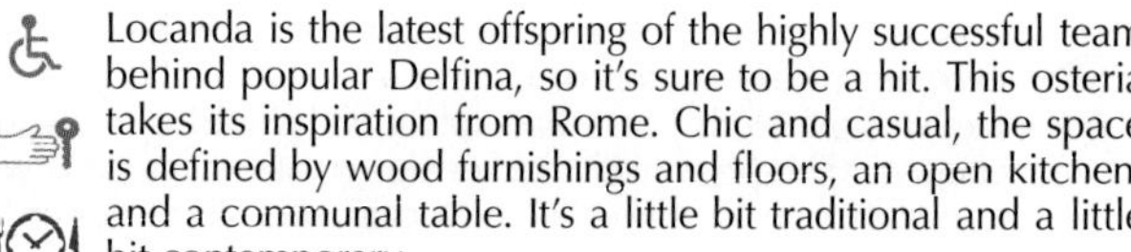

Locanda is the latest offspring of the highly successful team behind popular Delfina, so it's sure to be a hit. This osteria takes its inspiration from Rome. Chic and casual, the space is defined by wood furnishings and floors, an open kitchen, and a communal table. It's a little bit traditional and a little bit contemporary.

Antipasti like shaved raw artichoke with grilled ricotta and a refreshing salad with endive, crème fraîche, and cured salmon, are a great way to begin before moving on to heartier pastas and charcoal-grilled dishes. Don't be fooled by the simple-sounding menu, since there's also a selection of offal plates like chilled tongue with salsa verde, tripe with tomato, mint, and pecorino, or fried sweetbreads and artichokes.

Locavore

A3 American XX

3215 Mission St. (bet. Fair & Virginia Aves.)

Phone: 415-821-1918 — Lunch Sat – Sun
Web: www.locavoreca.com — Dinner Tue – Sat
Prices: $$

Talk about eating local: Locavore is *the* go-to for residents who call this part of the Mission home. The rustic communal tables are filled with regulars who come for American fare made with, you guessed it, locally sourced ingredients. The vibe is homespun in Mission style: raw concrete floors, reclaimed wood, and a petite bar area at the back.

At lunch, come for house-made sausages including a Portuguese number with roasted kumquat relish. Dinner brings a small, but more refined offering: a pickled beet and fennel salad is a fresh and tangy start, while a roulade of roasted chicken is served with earthy kale and velvety cauliflower purée. The service is laid-back and can be a tad slow—all the more time to relish your tasty grapefruit curd tart.

Maverick

American

3316 17th St. (at Mission St.)

Phone: 415-863-3061 — Lunch Sat – Sun
Web: www.sfmaverick.com — Dinner nightly
Prices: $$

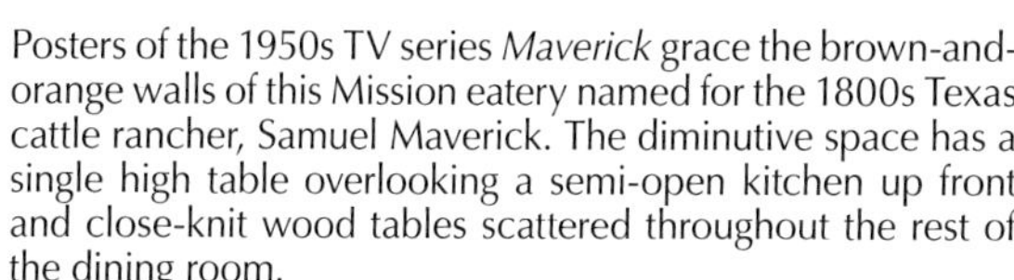

Posters of the 1950s TV series *Maverick* grace the brown-and-orange walls of this Mission eatery named for the 1800s Texas cattle rancher, Samuel Maverick. The diminutive space has a single high table overlooking a semi-open kitchen up front and close-knit wood tables scattered throughout the rest of the dining room.

The culinary vibe is hipster American and the patrons are mostly from the neighborhood. Familiar comfort food may include a crispy corn tostada with shrimp, black beans, and slaw; and a grilled Berkshire pork chop glazed in honey and bourbon served with cornbread stuffing and candied pecans. And is there a better way to cap a night than with warm cookies dipped in cool milk?

Love all things ham and oysters? Check out sibling Hogs & Rocks.

Mission Beach Café

198 Guerrero St. (at 14th St.)

Phone: 415-861-0198 — Lunch daily
Web: www.missionbeachcafesf.com — Dinner Mon – Sat
Prices: $$$

Heard the buzz about the amazing homemade pies? We bet you did. But lucky for locals (and us) there's even more to this delightful neighborhood fave than fantastic pastries. Dive right into the delectable goodness with crispy lemon-saffron risotto cakes, topped with tea-smoked albacore, fried quail eggs, and caviar, drizzled with chili-crème fraîche and basil oil.

Catch the pot pie menu every Tuesday night with offerings that may include a heart-warming rabbit pot pie with turnips and baby parsnips; or beef short rib pot pie with earthy trumpet mushrooms. The seafood pot pie boasts fresh shellfish and fennel. Can't decide on sweet? Get spoiled with a trio of desserts—lavender-honey cheesecake; strawberry rhubarb pie; and pear-plum pie.

Mission Chinese Food

Asian

A1

2234 Mission St. (bet. 18th & 19th Sts.)

Phone: 415-863-2800 Lunch & dinner Thu – Tue
Web: www.missionchinesefood.com
Prices: $$

Only in a hipster culinary capital will you find a pop-up restaurant within a restaurant, where renegade chefs are perfectly content to prepare their vittles in someone else's kitchen. Well, for the time being. Such is the case with the much buzzed about Mission Chinese Food, a guerilla cult eatery housed inside the Mission's more established (and banal) Lung Shan.

While Lung Shan is the house, Mission Chinese packs in the crowds for its inventive and wacky creations. Here, braised Mongolian beef cheeks are a spicy take on the classic with fermented chilies and chili oil; salt and pepper shrimp are wok-fried in pork fat and fennel; and tongue-numbing *ma po* tofu becomes exceptional when enriched with garlic-braised Kurobuta pork shoulder.

Pancho Villa Taqueria

Mexican

A1

3071 16th St. (bet. Mission & Valencia Sts.)

Phone: 415-864-8840 Lunch & dinner daily
Web: www.panchovillasf.com
Prices: $$

Choice is chief at Pancho Villa, so scope the menu and come ready to make brisk decisions. This masterful Mexican taqueria presents a parade of burritos, tacos, quesadillas, nachos et al. With wrapper and protein in hand, select a refreshing beverage. Then, an immaculate and colorful salsa bar with myriad condiments will spin you right round like a record.

There is no table service here, so grab the first seat in sight. As the mariachis gently lilt, dive into a fit-for-a-family super burrito, jammed with rice, beans, *chile verde* chicken, *pico de gallo*, cheese, guacamole, and sour cream; classic chips made divine with a mélange from the salsa bar; and a side order of fried *flautas* filled with chicken and bathed in a tomato-chile sauce.

Papalote

Mexican

A2

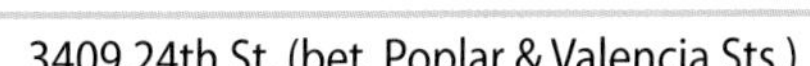

3409 24th St. (bet. Poplar & Valencia Sts.)

Phone: 415-970-8815 Lunch & dinner daily
Web: www.papalote-sf.com
Prices: $

With a cheerful dining room awash in primary hues and playful kites (*papalotes*) flying overhead, this is the kind of taqueria your mom has always wished for—one that garnishes its menu with fresh ingredients and truly healthy choices. The art-filled Mexican grill may find critics among Mission locals who prefer gritty authenticity, but sometimes breaking tradition just tastes good.

Here, taqueria mainstays have a northern Californian soul: vegetarian burritos share table space with spicy-sweet mole chicken, fresh fish, and carne asada tacos, all topped with crisp romaine lettuce, guacamole, ripe Roma tomatoes, and even refreshing jicama. Vegans are also welcome; Papalote offers soy chorizo and grilled tofu as lightweight alternatives to meat.

Papito

Mexican

C1

317 Connecticut St. (at 18th St.)

Phone: 415-695-0147 Lunch & dinner daily
Web: www.papitosf.com
Prices: $

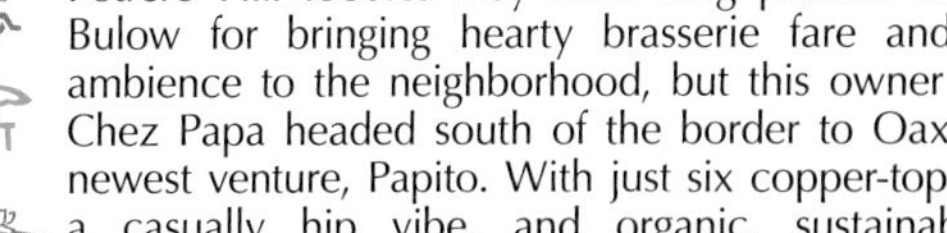

Potrero Hill foodies may have long praised Chef Jocelyn Bulow for bringing hearty brasserie fare and charming ambience to the neighborhood, but this owner of favorite Chez Papa headed south of the border to Oaxaca for his newest venture, Papito. With just six copper-topped tables, a casually hip vibe, and organic, sustainably-sourced ingredients, this Connecticut Street eatery is a far cry from the city's taquerias.

Yet tacos are the order of day, piled high with fresh toppings including crispy *pollo*, purple cabbage slaw, and chipotle rémoulade. Also find fat and flavorful quesadillas; chunky (and pricey) guacamole; and *camaron costeno*, sautéed shrimp with fixings atop an organic corn tortilla. Space is limited so locals often place orders to-go.

Pauline's Pizza

Pizza

260 Valencia St. (bet. Duboce Ave. & 14th St.)

Phone: 415-552-2050 Dinner Tue – Sat
Web: www.paulinespizza.com
Prices: $$

Along busy Valencia Street, recognize Pauline's by the crowds sitting on the interior benches, hungry for a delectable pizza and a free table (this budget-friendly hot spot takes no reservations).
Thin and crisp yet doughy inside, these handmade crusts may be strewn with "eccentric" toppings ranging from andouille or linguiça sausage to Kalamata olives and French goat cheese. Fans of Pauline's crust can even buy a three pack of frozen shells to-go. The restaurant's Berkeley garden and Star Canyon Ranch provide a year-round supply of greens and vegetables that comprise the fresh salads.
Local enthusiasts know to check online after 3:00P.M. to hear the nightly specialty pizzas and salads, before walking over—thus avoiding the challenging parking.

Piccino

Pizza

1001 Minnesota St. (at 22nd St.)

Phone: 415-824-4224 Lunch & dinner Tue – Sun
Web: www.piccinocafe.com
Prices: $$

First impressions do matter and with Piccino, you'll be charmed at first sight. Housed on the first floor of a Victorian building painted bright yellow with green trim, Piccino isn't as cutesy inside as it is on the outside. Instead, this chic restaurant employs raw wood planked floors, sleek chocolate brown chairs, and Eames stools at the counter to rather cool effect.
Headed by Chef Rachel Sillcocks, the kitchen turns out Italian food with California punch. Thin-crust crispy pizza is the shining star, though panini and pastas are a close second. Refreshing salads whet your appetite for the deliciously chewy and crispy pizzas, served on wooden, parchment paper-lined boards. For dessert try the *affogato* made with Pink Squirrel ice cream.

Piqueo's

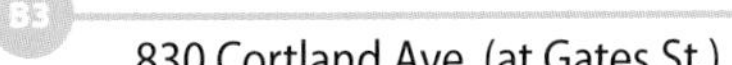

Peruvian XX

B3

830 Cortland Ave. (at Gates St.)

Phone: 415-282-8812 Dinner nightly
Web: www.piqueos.com
Prices: $$

Big flavor comes in tiny packages at Píqueo's, a small eatery in a Bernal Heights bungalow with cozy candlelight and walls the shade of ripe avocado. Neighborhood types sit at the counter for a view of the open kitchen where Chef/owner Carlos Altamirano deploys unusual Peruvian produce in dishes that seem to burst in the mouth.

Adventurous diners new to these enticing flavors will enjoy the learning experience. For the full effect, sample an array of small plates including crunchy wontons filled with creamy minced shrimp; fried white bean cake with sliced plantain and silky egg; and a roast beef sandwich with garlicky *aji* and sweet potato fries. Wash it down with a *chicha morada*, a drink made from the pulp of Peruvian purple maize.

Range

Contemporary XX

A2

842 Valencia St. (bet. 19th & 20th Sts.)

Phone: 415-282-8283 Dinner nightly
Web: www.rangesf.com
Prices: $$

Tucked in a block of small Mission boutiques, Range is just what every neighborhood bistro should be. The minimally decorated, narrow space is cozy with close-knit tables, candlelight, a tiny bar crowded with foodies, and just a few large floral arrangements adding color to dark furnishings and chocolate leather banquettes. Guests are focused on their conversations–which can get loud–and, of course, the food.

Contemporary American meals might begin with sautéed chanterelles with a poached farm egg over wheatberries and sunchoke purée; or entrées like braised daube of beef over a flavorful combination of roasted Brussels sprouts, caramelized whole *cipollini* onions, and roasted mushrooms. People-watchers vie for tables overlooking Valencia Street.

Regalito

Mexican

3481 18th St. (at Valencia St.)

Phone: 415-503-0650 — Lunch Sat – Sun
Web: www.regalitosf.com — Dinner Tue – Sun
Prices: $$

Spanish for "little gift," Regalito Rosticeria has a polish unique to the Mission, where Mexican food is synonymous with humble taquerias and markets. Here, Regalito is *the* neighborhood spot for market-driven fare in a stylish atmosphere, clean and bright with chartreuse accent walls and vibrant art.

A long wood counter peeks into the open kitchen, where seasonal food is carefully crafted from mostly organic produce and free range meats. A roasted half chicken is sublimely tender and smothered in nutty mole *negro,* while habañero salsa and fresh avocado garnish smoky, grilled *carnitas*. Flavors are more refined than bold, but these premium ingredients are prepared with skill, as if to enhance the pure flavors and complement the contemporary space.

Serpentine

Californian

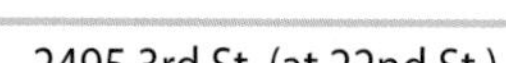

2495 3rd St. (at 22nd St.)

Phone: 415-252-2000 — Lunch daily
Web: www.serpentinesf.com — Dinner Mon – Sat
Prices: $$

Serpentine is every bit a product of its environment. The Dogpatch eatery fuses finely with the neighborhood's cool architecture and sense of recycled design with a wide cement bar, steel accents, and wooden furnishings in a sun-filled space. The dining room snakes comfortably throughout the lofty venue, with ample tables for large parties, and fewer bar tables perfect for sharing small plates.

Service is intimate and warm, and the cuisine is equally pleasant. A seasonal grilled artichoke arrives halved, charred, and laden with Dungeness crab salad; while a delectable risotto rests beneath an abundance of snap peas, Chantenay carrots, and fiddlehead ferns. For dessert, the spongy buttermilk cake with huckleberry purée and Meyer lemon curd is a hit.

Saison 

B1

2124 Folsom St. (bet. 17th & 18th Sts.)

Phone: 415-828-7990 Dinner Tue – Sat
Web: www.saisonsf.com
Prices: **$$$$**

Naseema Khan

Tucked behind an inconspicuous gate that could easily be the threshold to a private country estate, Saison is an urban culinary retreat that feels at once exclusive and yet as welcoming as home. Make your way to a paved brick courtyard and take a nice deep breath: freshness is *key* at Saison.

In fact, the restaurant is one of few in San Francisco where al fresco dining is pleasant year-round, with an airy dining room dotted with throw pillows and pashminas. Here you'll find tender herbs growing in the planters and an open hearth where meats come alive. The interior is equally appealing with a lofty industrial-cottage vibe, natural furnishings, and Chef/owner Joshua Skenes' chic open kitchen dressed in both nostalgic butcher blocks and modern stainless steel.

Skenes' multi-course, prix-fixe dinners are adventurous and superbly delish, so make a reservation and expect to be charmed. The offering changes regularly, but one may expect such enchantments as crustaceans in Meyer lemon cream with bright sunflower petals; explosively flavorful brassicas greens in savory bonito broth; and *nuvola di pecora* cheese, which oozes from toasted brioche glazed in honey and dusted with 24-karat gold.

Skool

Seafood XX

B1

1725 Alameda St. (at De Haro St.)

Phone: 415-255-8800 Lunch & dinner daily
Web: www.skoolsf.com
Prices: **$$**

The "k" is just the first indication that Skool is no old-fashioned seafood restaurant. Located in the SF Design Center, this sunny, contemporary interior has no nautical knickknacks to speak of. Rather, high ceilings, reclaimed materials and industrial-chic lines welcome the well-heeled sort to refuel as they peruse their fabric swatches; on gorgeous days, there's no better spot to dine than on Skool's garden patio.

Both Californian and Japanese inflections are to be found in the light, bright fare turned out from the open kitchen. Nosh on house-cured salmon pastrami Benedict with yuzu-hollandaise sauce; a modern Niçoise salad with sesame-crusted tuna and cucumber-anchovy vinaigrette; or mussels and smoked bacon in Point Reyes blue cheese broth.

Slow Club

Californian X

B1

2501 Mariposa St. (at Hampshire St.)

Phone: 415-241-9390 Lunch daily
Web: www.slowclub.com Dinner Mon – Sat
Prices: **$$**

With a somewhat obscure address and an urban-warehouse air, Slow Club is a bona fide hipster hangout. Chicly underdressed with polished concrete floors, exposed metal eye beams, and unremarkable wood furnishings, the Potrero Hill joint would border on ubiquity, but for its aura of having coined the look first. The reasonable prices are unexpected for the well-executed fare sent from the tiny open kitchen.

At lunch, eco-chic locals and business types nosh on baby spinach salads with caramelized bacon and grated tangy apple, or sandwiches that run from a basic-but-tasty burger to roasted turkey, avocado, and garlic aïoli on a warm torpedo roll. Dinner is a more ambitious foray, with dishes such as grilled pork loin with savory nettle bread pudding.

Taqueria Guadalajara

Mexican

4798 Mission St. (at Onondaga Ave.)

Phone: 415-469-5480 — Lunch & dinner daily
Web: N/A
Prices: ⚭

Sitting at a carved wood table inside this Outer Mission favorite, imagine yourself at the center of a Guadalajaran town square: Mexican architectural façades loom in floor-to-ceiling murals on three walls, while the aromas of flavorful grilled meats waft from the open kitchen.

Queue up at the counter and order the inexpensive, fresh, and generously portioned menu. Tacos may be filled with adobo-marinated pork or grilled carne asada along with minced white onion and cilantro. Intrepid eaters should dare to try the chicken super burrito, overloaded with the works. With a focus more on grilled meats than on accoutrement, the self-serve salsa bar is a popular stopover. Complement meals with perhaps the city's best *horchata*, redolent with cinnamon and rice.

Tokyo Go Go

Japanese

3174 16th St. (bet. Guerrero & Valencia Sts.)

Phone: 415-864-2288 — Dinner nightly
Web: www.tokyogogo.com
Prices: **$$**

Welcome to Tokyo Go Go, where blazing lights, thumpin' techno beats, and palate-pleasing bites draw in a hip and stylish set from around the Mission. Toss aside any expectations of traditional Japanese and get motoring for innovative flavorsome fusion instead. Sure, you can have your beloved nigiri, but opt for one of the splendid specialty rolls too, like the *kamikaze* (spicy tuna and crunchy asparagus rolled and topped with albacore tuna, scallions, and tangy ponzu), or the fish taco roll (battered fish, avocado, cilantro, onion, tomato, jalepeño, and chipotle aïoli).

Brought your battalion of buddies? Fill the table with "shared plates" like smoky miso-marinated black cod; tempura sweet onion rings; Tokyo garlic shrimp; or the Kobe beef *tataki*.

Universal Cafe

Californian 

2814 19th St. (bet. Bryant & Florida Sts.)

Phone: 415-821-4608 — Lunch Wed – Sun
Web: www.universalcafe.net — Dinner Tue – Sun
Prices: **$$**

Universal Café is one of those contagiously cute places where everyone seems to chill out and be cheerful. The sunny dining room has a bustling open kitchen, a few counter seats ideal for solo diners, and a rustic-urban feel that suits its industrial-cum-residential neighborhood. One could call the spot a bit European, but with a market-driven daily menu and on-the-ball staff, this café is très San Francisco.

First rate organic ingredients shine in simple preparations. At lunch, seasonal fare hinges on crisp grilled flatbreads and entrée salads, laden with the likes of hearty avocado and winter citrus. Dinner brings the hugely popular steak frites, but brunch is Universal's true claim to fame. Bring your morning paper and enjoy the wait outdoors.

Woodward's Garden

American 

1700 Mission St. (at Duboce St.)

Phone: 415-621-7122 — Dinner Tue – Sat
Web: www.woodwardsgarden.com
Prices: **$$$**

Woodward's Garden may sit on the site of San Francisco's first amusement park in a location that, frankly, has little curb appeal–views to the 101!–but this hidden gem somehow manages to retain a vintage charm that lures a coterie of locals questing a quiet meal on the town. The mainstay feels just a bit like your grandma's house, with peeling paint, comfortable worn furnishings, and an antique chandelier.

The old-fashioned ambience sets a sweet stage for home-style fare that changes with the season. Savor farmer's market-fresh ingredients in dishes such as herbed polenta served in an iron crock with tender mushrooms, fresh thyme, and oozing Taleggio; and red wine-braised Sonoma duck leg aromatic with stewed Bing cherries and earthy turnips.

Peter L. Wrenn/MICHELIN

Nob Hill

Chinatown · Russian Hill

In company with the Golden Gate Bridge and Alamo Square's "Painted Ladies," Nob Hill is San Francisco at its most iconic. Historic cable cars chug up the dramatic grades that lead to the top, with familiar chimes tinkling in the wind, and brass rails checking tourists who dare to lean out and take in the sights. The Powell-Mason line offers a peek at Alcatraz; and the California Street car stops right at the gilded doors of Grace Cathedral.

Once a stomping ground for Gold Rush industry titans, this urbane quarter–sometimes dubbed "Snob Hill"–echoes of mighty egos and ancestral riches. It is home to white-glove buildings, ladies who lunch, and opulent dining rooms. Named for the 1800s railroad magnates, the **Big Four** is a stately hideaway known for antique memorabilia and nostalgic chicken potpie. Extravagant **Top of the Mark** is beloved for bounteous brunches and panoramic vistas. **Le Club**, a lush supper room and cocktail lounge inspired by the private clubs of yore, is a VIP haunt in an exclusive residential high-rise. For a total departure, kick back with a Mai Tai (purportedly invented at Oakland's Trader Vic's in 1944) at the **Tonga Room & Hurricane Bar**, a tiki spot with a live thunderstorm inside the Fairmont Hotel.

Russian Hill

Downhill, toward Polk Street, the vibe mellows as heirloom splendor gives way to Russian Hill, chockablock with boutiques, dive bars, and casual eateries that cater to regular groups of mostly twenty-something singles. Good, affordable fare abounds at haunts like **Rex Cafe**, and **Street**. **Nick's Crispy Tacos**, the tacky taqueria turned nighttime disco, is a perennial fave. For dessert, try the sinful chocolate earthquake from **Swensen's Ice Cream** flagship parlor, which is still *so* 1948.

A handful of haute foodie shops whet the palate of resident young professionals. **Cheese Plus** stocks more than 300 international cultures, artisan charcuterie, and chocolate. Across the street, the **Jug Shop** is a mecca for micro-brew beers and southern hemisphere wines. Dining at the eternally delish and inexpensive **House of Nanking** is a rare experience. Don't bother ordering from the menu—the owner often takes menus out of diner's hands and orders for them.

Chinatown

For a change of pace, head to Chinatown, whose authentic markets, dim sum palaces, and souvenir emporiums spill down the eastern slope of Nob Hill in a wash of color and Cantonese characters. Here you'll find some of the city's finest and crave-worthy barbecue pork buns at the area's oldest dim sum house, **Hang Ah Tea Room**, and a bevy of quirky must-sees. Fuel up on oven-fresh 95 cent custard tarts at **Golden Gate Bakery**, but save room for samples at **Golden Gate Fortune Cookie Company**, where you can watch the prophetic little sweets in the making. The Mid-Autumn Moon Festival brings mooncakes, a traditional pastry stuffed with egg yolk and lotus seed paste. Gastronomes should unwind (and take home a taste of Chinatown) at the family-owned and operated Wok Shop for unique Asian cookware, linens, and tools. Their stock of rare products encompasses nearly every facet of Asian cooking.

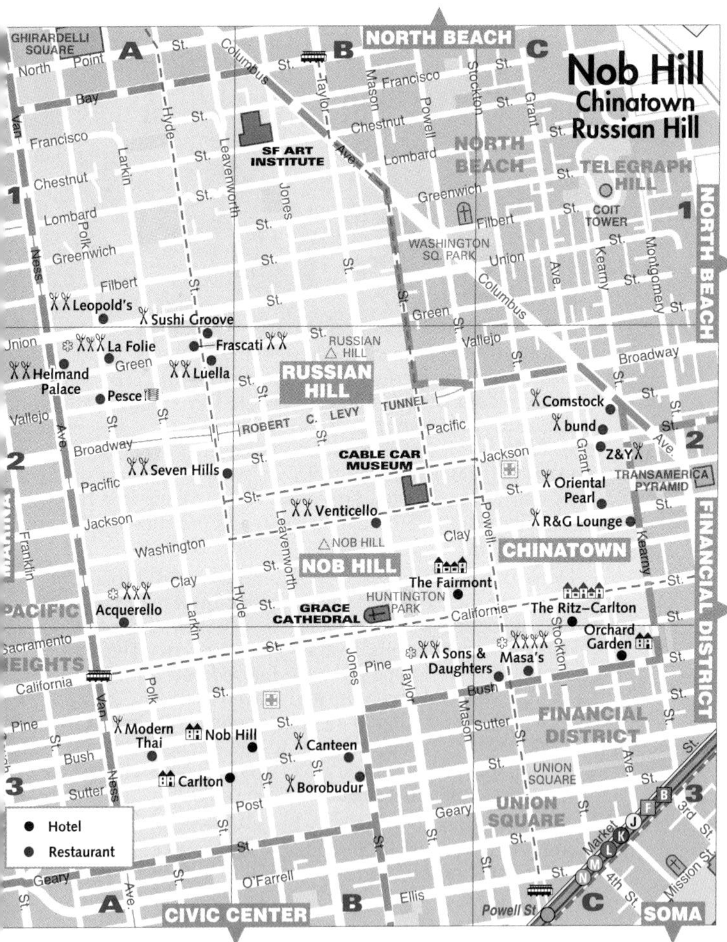

Acquerello

Italian 

A2

1722 Sacramento St. (bet. Polk St. & Van Ness Ave.)

Phone: 415-567-5432 Dinner Tue – Sat
Web: www.acquerello.com
Prices: $$$$

Marty Kelly

Upon reflecting that this restaurant occupies a former chapel, it seems perfectly appropriate to drop to your knees to give thanks for Acquerello. Located in a neighborhood that was rundown but is now shabby-chic, Acquerello saves its magic for its interiors. Vaulted wood ceilings have elaborate gilding and the walls are painted in warm shades of dusty rose, salmon, and gold. Two wrought-iron beams span the width of the dining room and enhance the Italian chapel look.

Don your Sunday best to fit in among power brokers and moneyed locals converging for Italian-by-way-of-California fine dining. Feast on dishes like a succulent ragù of guinea hen and duck with feather-light gnocchi. The potato cannelloni enveloping red wine-braised beef with intensely fragrant vegetable *brunoise* and shaved truffles is, in a word, revelatory. In addition to the regular menu, the chef's tasting menu offers a front row seat to the kitchen's talents. Be sure to peruse the impressive wine list and cheese cart showcasing different regional Italian selections.

The professional and attentive black-suited staff adeptly offer suggestions and deliver seamless service that elevates the exceptional experience.

Borobudur

Indonesian

700 Post St. (at Jones St.)

Phone: 415-775-1512 — Lunch & dinner daily
Web: www.borobudursf.com
Prices: 💲💲

Named for a Javanese Buddhist megasite, Borobudur is an appropriately obscure San Francisco eatery specializing in Indonesian cuisine. Walking down Post Street, just look for the sheer orange draperies and potted orchids in the windows.

Once you do manage to find this hidden gem, you'll be treated to an inviting little dining room where white cloths top the tables and comfortable cushioned booths line the quiet room. You're likely to dine in the company of few, but rest assured they are connoisseurs of the cuisine. Settle in for spicy-sweet flavor profiles in such dishes as sautéed tempeh and tofu in delicate soy sauce, or barbecue chicken in decadent coconut milk. Particularly hungry? Try the *rijsttafel*, which is Dutch for an Indonesian smorgasbord.

bund

Chinese

640 Jackson St. (bet. Kearny St. & Wentworth Pl.)

Phone: 415-982-0618 — Lunch & dinner daily
Web: N/A
Prices: 💲💲

On chilly San Francisco days, Chinatown savants (and a few tourists who wandered in the right direction) slurp belly-warming juicy buns, aka soup dumplings, at bund. Though these particular morsels want an extra kick of ginger, the tender pork and quality dough remind us why they command a cult following. The dining room here is cleaner than its neighbors', the friendly owners are ever-present, and the Shanghainese cuisine is a nice departure from the neighborhood's ubiquitous Cantonese menus. Such dim sum options as a flaky turnip puff make for divine snacking, and vegetarians will rejoice in a spinach stir-fry with fresh bamboo shoots.

Reasonable prices, generous portions, friendly service, and tasty food make bund a no-brainer.

Canteen

Californian

817 Sutter St. (bet. Jones & Leavenworth Sts.)

Phone: 415-928-8870 — Lunch Sat – Sun
Web: www.sfcanteen.com — Dinner Tue – Sat
Prices: $$

Sit yourself down at the lime green counter and watch Chef Dennis Leary work his magic before you in an open kitchen. Sublime, seasonal dishes are concocted right before your eyes, in a mesmerizing display of choreographed chaos. The diner-like space is tiny–four booths and a few seats at the forever packed counter–so waits can be lengthy, but, it's worth it.

Steaming Parker house rolls start things off right, while tasty bites like halibut gravlax (thinly sliced and salt-cured, beneath diced green tomatoes, avocado, and celery) hit the spot. Twirl your tongs around carbonara—capellini noodles, diced ham, chopped herbs, egg yolk, Parmesan, and chili pepper; and as a special treat, try their deliciously warm chocolate *pot de crème*.

Comstock

Gastropub 

155 Columbus Ave. (at Pacific Ave.)

Phone: 415-617-0071 — Lunch Mon – Fri
Web: www.comstocksaloon.com — Dinner nightly
Prices: $$

Named for the legendary Comstock Lode–the mining jackpot that launched the 19th century Gold Rush–Comstock is a historically correct homage to Americana and the classic cocktails–think Sazerac and Manhattan–that are legendary in their own right. The saloon has served as a watering hole since 1907, and its refreshed pressed-tin ceilings and carved wood bar feel like they've been there as long.

Comstock is a bar first and foremost but, in the San Francisco foodie tradition, also serves quite good pub grub. Soak up the suds with salty fried fava beans tossed in chili oil; plump corn and jalapeño fritters; and, at dinner, the much loved chicken-fried rabbit. If the booze and bites don't take you back, take a gander at the antiques and old-time portraits.

Frascati

Mediterranean

1901 Hyde St. (at Green St.)

Phone: 415-928-1406 — Dinner nightly
Web: www.frascatisf.com
Prices: $$

Named for a bucolic hilltop town overlooking Rome, Frascati is a charming and friendly neighborhood treasure. Sidewalk tables enjoy the chimes of passing cable cars, while lovers prefer romantic mezzanine seating on cooler nights. The interior bursts with boisterous Russian Hill regulars who nosh on seasonal Mediterranean fare paired with wines from California and Italy.

Begin with plump and beautifully grilled sardines accented with Meyer lemon aïoli and micro-greens, or sample wild mushroom bruschetta with goat cheese fondue and bacon. Entrées focus on proteins, such as pan-seared *branzino* with herbed polenta and candy cap mushrooms.

Frascati is a popular spot and parking is near impossible. Fortunately, the cable car stops right out front.

Helmand Palace

2424 Van Ness Ave. (bet. Green & Union Sts.)

Phone: 415-345-0072 — Dinner nightly
Web: www.helmandpalace.com
Prices: $$

In a neighborhood where appearances are everything, Helmand Palace is a reminder that beauty is more than skin deep. On a bus-choked stretch of Van Ness Avenue behind a non-descript façade, this local favorite serves Afghan recipes in an interior as rich as the food. Exotic red carpets and royal blue-cushioned armchairs make a cozy atmosphere for warming up with spicy fare. Newbies can trust that the murals depicting Afghani life are a promise of authenticity.

Here meals begin with hearty oven-fresh bread served with a trio of dips, then go on to include traditional appetizers such as *kaddo*, baked pumpkin with spicy ground beef and yogurt-garlic sauce; or tasty *seek kabab*, a charbroiled leg of lamb with sautéed eggplant, tomato, and raisins.

La Folie ✿

French

A2

2316 Polk St. (bet. Green & Union Sts.)

Phone: 415-776-5577 Dinner Mon – Sat
Web: www.lafolie.com
Prices: **$$$$**

Dan Peak

Caught at the crossroads of the Marina and Pacific Heights, La Folie is what's for dinner among well-heeled neighborhood types who want to check their Beemers at valet and then be waited on hand and foot.

With traditionally professional service comes serious ambience too, and La Folie doesn't skimp in this department. A somewhat old-school interior is warm with rusty hues and heavy drapes, while linen-covered tables are carefully set with only the best: Bernardaud Limoges china, flickering candles, and Speigelau stemware thirsty for suggestions from an eager sommelier. Such a pretty table wants a gorgeous meal—sip and swirl while you wait for the main event.

Chef/owner Roland Passot is a French master and is typically on hand to direct each and every dish of your three-, four- and five-course prix-fixe dinner. Meals at La Folie are consistently artful and succulent: look for butter-poached lobster with English pea *raviolo*, truffle *beurre* fondue, and shaved black truffle; and a signature rabbit trio that takes root vegetables from earth to simply divine. By the time you finish your cherry and apricot clafouti, the valet will have your chariot ready for a triumphant ride home.

Leopold's

Austrian XX

2400 Polk St. (at Union St.)

Phone: 415-474-2000 Dinner nightly
Web: www.leopoldssf.com
Prices: $$

Beer lovers are saying *Prost*! to Leopold's, an authentic Austrian *gasthaus* that opened in 2011 and is already the toast of the town. And it's no wonder: two-, three- and five-liter beer steins and boots hold lots of liquid to cheers with. Word to the wise: non-diehards coming for the food should slip in before it gets too crowded. Reservations? *Nein*.

With Alpine décor and all manner of fried, cheesy, and meaty fare, Leopold's is an honest restaurant ideal for the genuinely hungry. Dinner might include rich *kasespatzle* gratin seasoned with nutmeg, garnished with crisp onions, and served with a warm cabbage and bacon salad; and the extra-hearty *choucroute garnie* platter laden with smoky pork and bratwurst with sauerkraut and caraway-roasted potatoes.

Luella

Mediterranean XX

1896 Hyde St. (at Green St.)

Phone: 415-674-4343 Dinner nightly
Web: www.luellasf.com
Prices: $$

The parking can cause heartburn, but the food and service at Luella make it worth the frustration. Better yet, hop aboard the Powell & Hyde Street cable car for a little old-fashioned, and stress-free, commute.

Ben and Rachel de Vries run the show at this charming, if often boisterous, place. From Coca-Cola-braised pork shoulder and ahi tuna tacos with mango salsa to beef Wellington, this menu covers it all. The food is seriously delicious, but casual pizzas, pastas, and a children's menu prove that this place doesn't take itself too seriously. Dessert is worth saving room for with selections like miniature banana cream pies with Valrhona chocolate sauce and orange and sweet ricotta fritters. The three-course prix-fixe is a real deal.

Masa's ✿

Contemporary XXXX

C3

648 Bush St. (bet. Powell & Stockton Sts.)

Phone: 415-989-7154 Dinner Tue – Sat
Web: www.masasrestaurant.com
Prices: $$$$

Masa's

The service is professional and the scene is formal; in fact, the only thing to warm the atmosphere is soft jazz playing in the background. Still, Masa's dark walls, white tablecloths, deep-red chandeliers, and tall bronze sculpture of interlocking figures are dramatic, stylish, and fitting of this contemporary cuisine with classical twists.

The extensive wine list is a force to be reckoned with here, so consider seeking the counsel of the house's knowledgeable sommelier.

When the warm, cheesy *gougères* or amuse-bouche of uni custard topped with a generous dollop of Ostetra caviar arrive at your table, know that you are in for a feast. Dishes focus on seasonal offerings with global touches, as in a starter of crisp and plump soft-shell crabs with precise rectangles of black sesame paste and drops of pale-red aïoli, kicking a bit of spicy heat. Offerings go on to include agnolotti filled with stinging nettle and a touch of white polenta; or meatier options like a pan-seared ribeye of pork wrapped in bacon with *pommes fondants* so buttery that their ability to hold a shape defies gravity. Treat yourself to a dessert timbale of chocolate mousse with charred cinnamon ice cream.

Modern Thai

Thai

1247 Polk St. (at Bush St.)

Phone: 415-922-8424 Lunch & dinner daily
Web: www.modernthaisf.com
Prices: 

In the cheery, colonial-style dining space, shades of raspberry sherbet and lime vivify stark white walls, while colorful Gerber daisies adorn glass-topped tables. An enclosed porch affords sunny street side views and a great spot to tuck into some cheap and tasty Thai. Pumpkin lovers rejoice—this gourd is prepared in all kinds of delicious ways, whether shredded and deep-fried with sesame and coconut, or cubed in a luscious, creamy curry. Specialties like crispy calamari with cashews or roasted duck with lychee curry are equally worthy, as are the fishcakes—golden crispy pancakes of minced fish, silver rice noodles, and shiitake mushrooms.
Exotic desserts like blueberry *roti* or the MT sundae with purple yam and coconut ice cream are a perfect finale.

Oriental Pearl

760 Clay St. (bet. Grant & Kearny Sts.)

Phone: 415-433-1817 Lunch & dinner daily
Web: www.orientalpearlsf.com
Prices: 

At Portsmouth Square, Chinese elders gather to play cards or dominos, smoking cigarettes amid hovering crowds. Across the way, a gem of an eatery lures in those locals, where gracious servers clad in red bow ties serve up authentic, delicious Hong Kong-style Chinese at budget-friendly prices. With no dim sum cart in sight, everything is ordered straight off the menu and served fresh from the kitchen. Dim sum menus are for two or more so eating turns into a team sport tackling delights like lightly fried chive, spinach, and shrimp dumplings. The house special meatball—a blend of chicken, shrimp, mushrooms, and Virginia ham wrapped "dumpling style" in a poached egg white, all tied together with a thin green onion, is something of a little treasure.

Pesce

2227 Polk St. (bet. Green & Vallejo Sts.)

Phone: 415-928-8025 Dinner nightly
Web: www.pescesf.com
Prices: **$$**

Long a mainstay on this bustling stretch of Polk Street, Pesce is an easygoing seafood bar where the locals get along swimmingly. Serving Italian small plates known as *cicchetti*, the restaurant is particularly beloved among neighborhood types who like to catch up over a quick glass of wine and a snack–think plump grilled sardines with pickled root vegetables–at the long zinc bar.

For those who've come to stay a while, simple wood furniture, penny tile floors, and that ever-friendly service make for a comfortable vibe in the narrow ambient space. Look for popular dishes like grilled Monterey calamari with caramelized fennel and spicy *pomodoro* sauce; Dungeness crab with cucumber and avocado; squid ink risotto; and fresh oyster shots spiked with horseradish.

R & G Lounge

C2

631 Kearny St. (bet. Clay & Sacramento Sts.)

Phone: 415-982-7877 Lunch & dinner daily
Web: www.rnglounge.com
Prices:

Deceptively large R & G Lounge is a true standout, especially in comparison to its sketchier Chinatown neighbors. The wood-paneled subterranean dining room is uncommonly clean and lined with tanks full of the freshest seafood around. During the lengthy season, whole salt-and-pepper Dungeness crab is the signature dish, while *kung pao* prawns please the lunch crowd year-round. Landlubbers enjoy familiar classics such as hot and sour soup or lemon chicken.

The menu is extensive and service is especially prompt, but newbies should stand their ground and take time to peruse the offerings. Solo diners should beware that they may be seated among strangers at the round communal tables. At dinner, parking is validated in the Portsmouth Square garage.

Seven Hills

Italian

1550 Hyde St. (at Pacific Ave.)

Phone: 415-775-1550 Dinner Tue – Sun
Web: www.sevenhillssf.com
Prices: $$

Shrouded by the rustling trees of Hyde Street and the ding-ding of the passing cable car, Seven Hills is an obscure Italian eatery that is beginning to get noticed. And how could locals not flock to this bambino-sized *ristorante* where a cozy ambience, jovial service, and just four seats at the bar make Seven Hills a perfectly low-key neighborhood haunt.

Two petite wood-clad dining rooms host a consistent crowd where those in the know opt for pasta, the specialty of the house, in either half- or whole portions. Seasonal recipes might include delish scallop ravioli with sweet corn and English peas. Other delightfully unembellished fare may include seared calamari with tangy caponata to start, and house-made ricotta studded with candied pistachios to finish.

Sushi Groove

1916 Hyde St. (bet. Green & Union Sts.)

Phone: 415-440-1905 Dinner nightly
Web: www.sushigroove.com
Prices:

This fishbowl of a Hyde Street space is forever packed with friends who crave raw seafood in creative preparations. The soft glow of the sunset behind neighboring homes casts a warm spell, and the intimate space may be boisterous with groups catching up after work. Parking is a trick, so call ahead to see about valet.

Sushi Groove also has a popular location in sleek SoMa, so the place must be doing something right. A fresh ahi *poke* salad is layered with thinly sliced cucumber, mango, and papaya; translucent *hirame* nigiri drapes over cool rice; and the maki are tantalizing—try the tuna *caliente* with garlic, jalapeño, and *tobiko*. Those looking for cooked fare can find comfort in a glass of sake and try to enjoy the party.

Sons & Daughters ❀

Contemporary XX

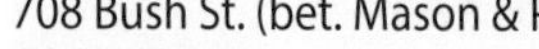

C3

708 Bush St. (bet. Mason & Powell Sts.)

Phone: 415-391-8311 Dinner nightly
Web: www.sonsanddaughterssf.com
Prices: $$

Sara Kraus

Adorned with Ball jars stuffed with spices and black-and-white prints of culinary oddities, Sons & Daughters might feel like a homespun tribute to gastronomic tradition. Take a second look at the tattooed chefs toiling over an open flame in the tiny kitchen and you may get the sense that the restaurant is poised for a takeover: old masters, beware.

Maverick Chefs Matt McNamara and Teague Moriarty burst onto the scene in 2010 with a fresh, hip space and wicked food. Architectural moldings and chandeliers cap a chic room with leather chairs and bare wood tables. Service is on point but not fussy because, well, Sons & Daughters is just cooler than that. This place takes its food, but not itself, seriously.

Avant-garde foams and gels are part and parcel to any meal but the chefs are down-to-earth, sourcing produce from a family garden in Los Altos. One of the chef's moms delivers ingredients throughout the week. Compose your own four-course dinner from plates like lamb tartare with potato chips, grapefruit, and beets; plump sweetbread with fresh crab; and braised lamb cheeks topped with abalone and burdock root foam. Pair with a wine from the concise but beautifully curated list.

Venticello

Italian

1257 Taylor St. (at Washington St.)

Phone: 415-922-2545 — Dinner nightly
Web: www.venticello.com
Prices: **$$$**

Concierges in the Nob Hill luxury hotels eagerly recommend this charming restaurant, whose name is Italian for "little breeze." Indeed, this place is a breath of fresh air, from the rustic, cozy dining room in terra-cotta hues that conjures a Tuscan farmhouse, to the menu of well-made Italian favorites. This cuisine adheres to the restaurant's decidedly Italian philosophy: *chi mangia bene, vive bene* (he who eats well, lives well). True to this philosophy, everyone is well-fed after polishing off *pizzette* fresh from the cobalt blue-tiled wood-fired oven; plates of homemade pasta dishes like spaghetti carbonara or cheese ravioli; as well as outstanding specials.

Parking spaces are precious in this neighborhood, so use the valet or take the cable car.

Z & Y

655 Jackson St. (bet. Grant Ave. & Kearny St.)

Phone: 415-981-8988 — Lunch & dinner daily
Web: www.zandyrestaurant.com
Prices: **$$**

This precious Chinatown pearl is loved and lauded for its bold-flavored, tasty Chinese food. Attention spice addicts: when Z & Y's menu indicates that a dish will be chili-hot, *trust* them—fiery flavors aren't toned down for gun shy American palates. By virtue of its tempting Chinese, this long and slender restaurant with tight-knit tables aglow with red Chinese lanterns, is forever packed.

Nailing the red-hot motif are brusque servers robed in red and carrying savory dishes like golden brown scallion pancakes sprinkled with sesame seeds; tender pork strips bathing in a garlic sauce pungent with dried Sichuan chilies; and Mongolian beef flavored with oyster and soy sauce. Also joining the fan faves is a deliciously sticky black sesame rice ball soup.

North Beach

Fisherman's Wharf · Telegraph Hill

Nestled between bustling Fisherman's Wharf and the steep slopes of Russian and Telegraph hills, North Beach owes its lively nature to the Italian immigrants who settled here in the late 1800s. Many of these were fishermen from the Ligurian coast; the seafood stew they made on their boats evolved into the quintessential San Francisco treat, cioppino—a must-order in this district. Though Italians are no longer in the majority here, dozens of pasta places, pizzerias, coffee shops, and bars in North Beach attest to their idea of the good life. At the annual North Beach Festival in mid-June, a celebrity pizza toss, Assisi Animal Blessings, and Arte di Gesso (chalk art) also nod to the neighborhood's Italian heritage. **Fog City Diner** remains a popular stop for tourists after a ferry to Alcatraz, or a walk along The Embarcadero.

Today the majority of North Beach's restaurants and bars lie along Columbus Avenue. Be sure to check out the quarter's Italian delis, like **Molinari's**, whose homemade salami has been a local institution since 1896. Pair some imported meats and cheeses with a bottle of wine for a perfect picnic in nearby Washington Square Park. Hanging out in North Beach can be a full-time job, which is what attracted a ragtag array of beret-wearing poets to the area in the 1950s. These so-called beatniks–Allen Ginsberg and Jack Kerouac among them–were eventually driven out by busloads of tourists. Bohemian spirits linger on at such landmarks as the City Lights bookstore, and next door at **Vesuvio**, the original boho bar.

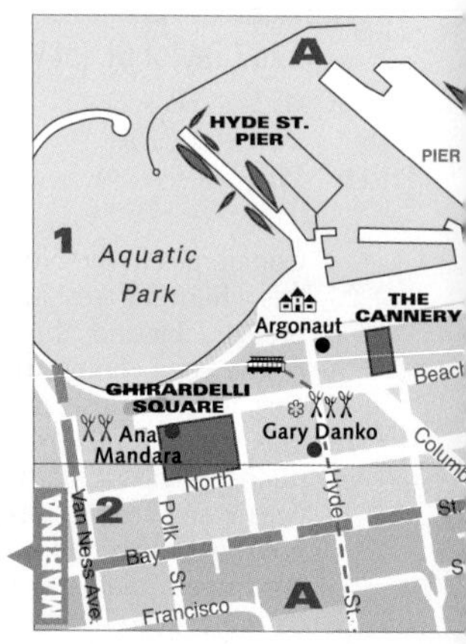

Feasting in Fisherman's Wharf

You won't find many locals here, but Fisherman's Wharf, the mile-long stretch of waterfront at the foot of Columbus Street, ranks as one of the city's most popular tourist attractions. It may teem with souvenir shops, street performers, rides, and other attractions, but you should go—if only to feast on a sourdough bread bowl soaked in clam chowder, and fresh crabs cooked in huge steamers right on the street. Sample a piece of edible history at **Boudin Bakery**. This old-world bakery may have bloomed into a large modern operation–complete with a museum and bakery

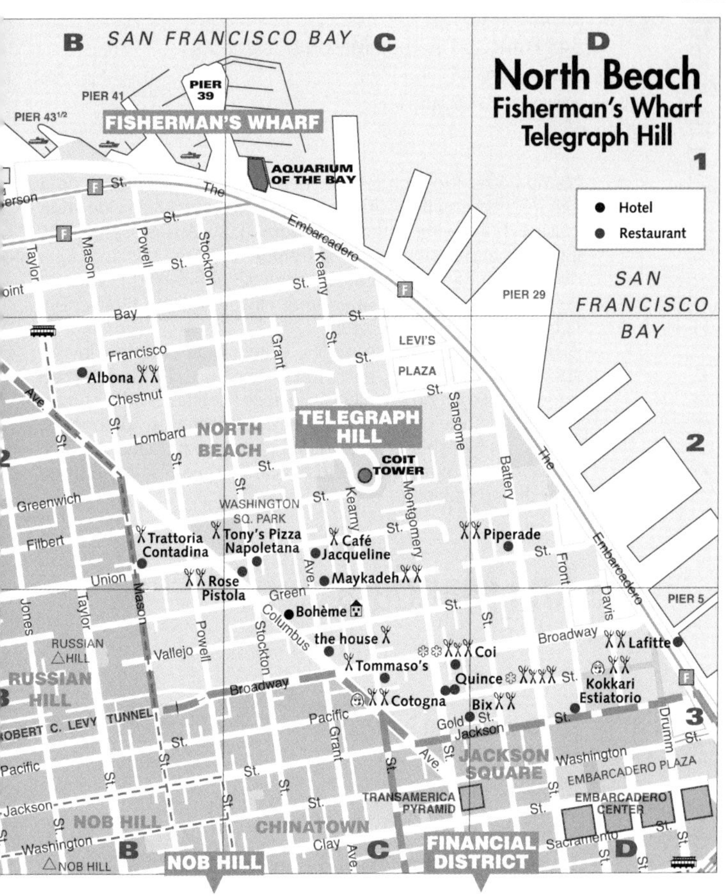

tour–but they still make their sourdough bread fresh every day, using the same mother first cultivated here from local wild yeast in 1849. Nearby on North Point Street, Ghirardelli Square preserves another taste of old SF. This venerable chocolate company, founded by Domingo Ghirardelli in 1852, now flaunts its delectable wares at the **Ghirardelli Ice Cream and Chocolate Manufactory**. Here you can ogle the original chocolate manufacturing equipment while you enjoy a decadent hot-fudge sundae. Don't leave without taking away some sweet memories in the form of their chocolate squares.

Albona

Italian XX

B2

545 Francisco St. (bet. Mason & Taylor Sts.)

Phone: 415-441-1040 — Dinner Tue – Sun
Web: www.albonarestaurant.com
Prices: $$

Named after the picturesque town that is perched high on a cliff overlooking the Adriatic Sea, Albona specializes in Istrian cuisine borrowing influences from Italy, Austria, Hungary, Greece, and other parts of Central Europe. Located in a discreet building, the atmosphere inside feels old-fashioned yet charming with a scattering of closely-spaced tables, low lighting, and smiling servers.

A beloved spot for date nights, watch local couples devour such interesting and flavorful dishes as pan-fried potato gnocchi in a brown sirloin sauce spiked with cumin; homemade ravioli stuffed with three cheeses, pine nuts, raisins, and freshly ground nutmeg; or an aromatic Adriatic seafood stew of red wine and balsamic-tomato sauce poured over grilled polenta.

Ana Mandara

Vietnamese XX

A1

891 Beach St. (at Polk St.)

Phone: 415-771-6800 — Lunch Mon – Sat
Web: www.anamandara.com — Dinner nightly
Prices: $$

Located in the crowded and commercial Ghirardelli Square area is Ana Mandara; and as the names suggests, she is indeed a "beautiful refuge." Colonial Vietnam comes alive in its Southeast Asian temple décor, replete with silk lanterns, rattan furnishings, trickling fountains, and leafy palms. On the weekends, visit the upstairs Cham bar & lounge for live jazz tunes and a lovely perspective of the scene below.

Servers dressed in traditional silk gowns are courteous and efficient delivering a mélange of delicacies with soothing names. Whether you're feasting on Hands of the Child (Vietnamese spring rolls); or Whispering Waves which reveal crispy lobster ravioli floating in a mango and coconut sauce, rest assured that you will leave fulfilled.

Bix

American XX

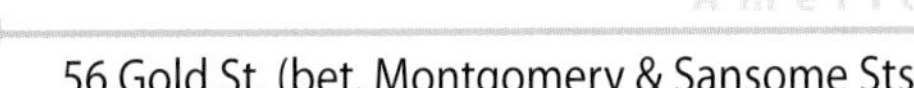

D3

56 Gold St. (bet. Montgomery & Sansome Sts.)

Phone: 415-433-6300 — Lunch Fri
Web: www.bixrestaurant.com — Dinner nightly
Prices: **$$$**

Pass through the nondescript brick façade, follow the cryptic entry, and find yourself in the bygone supper club era, paying homage to jazz great Bix Beiderbecke. The dining room exudes fanciful charm with lofty columns, rich mahogany panelling, and a baby grand. Lull at the bar where tenders satiate with much shaking and stirring; then sweep up the staircase and into a scenic booth.

Elegant servers enhance the throwback tone, reciting–perhaps to the backdrop of live jazz shows–a menu of revived classics like hearty onion and oxtail soup; crisp golden cakes of chicken hash drizzled with a mascarpone sauce; and syrupy banana bites on ice cream. Deviled eggs with truffles and chives, and Maine lobster spaghetti add to the delicious nostalgia.

Café Jacqueline

French X

C2

1454 Grant Ave. (bet. Green & Union Sts.)

Phone: 415-981-5565 — Dinner Wed – Sun
Web: N/A
Prices: **$$$**

This petite bistro specializes in soufflés—and what incredibly light and flavorful soufflés they are. Her space may not dazzle with tables packed like sardines, but Café Jacqueline's faithful French treats certainly will.

Not ideal for large gatherings or groups-on-the-go as a meal here may take hours, the café is patronized by those who have time on their hands and delicious, fluffy soufflés on their mind. You may start with the staple French onion soup, but with such a surfeit of savory soufflés on display, it seems only right to follow suit with a towering chanterelle mushroom rich with Gruyère; or lobster soufflé that is at once decadent and fresh. Moving on—the warm dark chocolate soufflé is so plush and moist, you may wonder how you lived before it.

Coi ✿✿

C3 — Contemporary ✗✗✗

373 Broadway (bet. Montgomery & Sansome Sts.)

Phone: 415-393-9000 — Dinner Wed – Sat

Web: www.coirestaurant.com

Prices: $$$$

Dwight Eschliman

There is a sense of fun and hint of naughty in this neighborhood; but inside, Coi's style is minimal, organic, and elegant. From beneath rice-paper panels diffusing soft light throughout the intimate room, earthy gray and brown tones flow from small tables to banquettes seating a casually cool clientele. Servers may appear hip and mod, but are professional and very courteous as they offer flawless descriptions of each dish.

In keeping with the attractive design, the menu quickly stirs intense curiosity, with deeply gratifying results. Single bites deliver myriad sensations, from sharp to velvety smooth, in superb oysters "under glass" sheets of yuzu-steeped gelatin with radish-fennel *brunoise* and Vietnamese cilantro. A single dish highlighting "earth and sea" proves Chef Daniel Patterson's mastery of complex and delicate flavors in a steamed tofu mousseline with mushroom dashi, yuba, fresh seaweed, and root vegetables. Even a humble cheesecake can be an eye-opening experience here, when goat cheese, graham crackers, nasturtium, and Niabell grape sorbet combine with tangy-sweet results.

The recently refurbished lounge is more casual but offers the same 11-course prix-fixe menu.

Cotogna

Italian XX

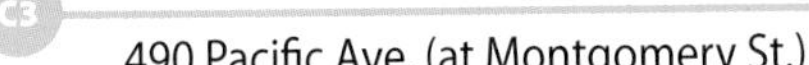

C3

490 Pacific Ave. (at Montgomery St.)

Phone: 415-775-8508
Web: www.cotognasf.com
Prices: $$

Lunch Mon – Sat
Dinner nightly

Lack the funds to fork over for dinner at Quince? Head to Chef Michael Tusk's latest, less expensive outpost just next door. Cotogna is a rustic Italian eatery aimed at the Roman heart. Here you'll find straightforward, well-prepared fare such as salt-and-pepper Monterey squid over chopped *puntarella* salad; pillowy beet *tortelloni* with poppy seeds in butter; and skirt steak with grilled radicchio and balsamic.

Grab a $10 glass of *vino* at the copper-topped bar and swirl while you spy the goings-on in the kitchen. Here find the pizza furnace and green oven fired by almond wood where the staff labors over grilled meats and esoteric Neapolitan pies (like sea urchin and cauliflower). Take a seat at one of the communal tables for a quieter experience.

the house

C3

1230 Grant Ave. (bet. Columbus Ave. & Vallejo St.)

Phone: 415-986-8612
Web: www.thehse.com
Prices: $$

Lunch Mon – Sat
Dinner nightly

At the heart of Italian North Beach stands a tiny Asian eatery known for colorful fusion flavors and known simply as the house. Blonde wood furnishings and a minimalist décor create a pleasant vibe without detracting from the cuisine, while efficient servers recount the daily specials. Listen closely before making hasty decisions.

The meal begins with tangy marinated cucumbers and appetizers like steamed shrimp-and-chive Chinese dumplings on a vibrant bed of carrots, beets, and radishes. Slurp a bowl of udon with grilled chicken and toasted nori or sample more unique fare: wasabi noodles topped with teriyaki-glazed grilled salmon are a house specialty and worth the wait for a table. The house also offers a nice choice of tea, beer, and wines by the glass.

Gary Danko ✿

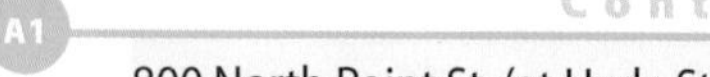
Contemporary XXX

A1

800 North Point St. (at Hyde St.)

Phone: 415-749-2060 Dinner nightly
Web: www.garydanko.com
Prices: $$$$

Gary Danko

Fine dining at Gary Danko seems to bring together all things San Franciscan. It's perched on a hill above Fisherman's Wharf. Cable cars whiz past the front door. And did we mention celebrated California chef, Gary Danko? It's like a perfect little package of San Francisco tied with a golden (gate) ribbon.

This is indeed a nice place to be seen, but the blackened windows keep things intimate. It's the ultimate date place, with well-dressed couples celebrating anniversaries or kids flying the nest for college, but business types also love it for impressing clients and bosses. The staff is old-school professional, trained to the hilt, and work as a well-oiled machine.

Three-, four-, and five-course menus, in addition to an extensive chef's tasting menu, showcase Danko's deft culinary abilities and contemporary flair. Dishes are refined and masterful, as in beautifully roasted Guinea hen with a delicious hash of sweet potatoes and caramelized bacon. And don't forsake the farmhouse and artisanal cheeses presented with a variety of fruit compotes, unless it is to save room for desserts like the sweet orange biscuit with passion fruit curd and elderflower-orange sherbet.

Kokkari Estiatorio

Greek XX

D3

200 Jackson St. (at Front St.)

Phone: 415-981-0983
Web: www.kokkari.com
Prices: $$

Lunch Mon – Fri
Dinner nightly

Easily one of San Francisco's most sensuous dining destinations, Kokkari lures guests back again and again with a roar in the cavernous wood-burning fireplace, plush mismatched armchairs, and an exhibition kitchen in the taverna-style back room. Ambient lighting and moderate space between tables make Kokkari a prime spot for dates and special occasions, so reservations are highly recommended.

Standout Greek and Mediterranean specialties include grilled lamb riblets with lemon and oregano; flaky *spanakotiropita* stuffed with spinach, feta, leek, and dill; and tender pan-roasted halibut steak with sweet corn, peppers, zesty olives, and herbs. Finish the evening with a stone-ground Greek coffee heated in a traditional copper urn over piping hot sand.

Lafitte

French XX

D3

Pier 5, The Embarcadero (at Broadway)

Phone: 415-839-2134
Web: www.lafittesf.com
Prices: $$

Lunch Tue – Sat
Dinner nightly

Open the dictionary to industrial chic and you may find a picture of Lafitte. Revered for bringing pulse to this Central Piers Historic District, Lafitte's space feels airy and features high ceilings, concrete floors, granite tables, exposed ductwork, timber shelves showing a fully stocked bar, and a display kitchen.

There's a palpable energy about this place even without the surrounding echoes of French music and jazz tunes. Farm fresh California meets funkified French here, so don't come expecting anything but surprises like short rib Bourguignon; roast trout glistening with uni butter; and spicy merguez sausage with mussels. The adjoining (enclosed) porch offers waterfront dining with views of the Coit Tower and San Francisco Queen riverboat.

Maykadeh

C2 Persian XX

470 Green St. (bet. Grant Ave. & Kearny St.)

Phone: 415-362-8286 Lunch & dinner daily
Web: www.maykadehrestaurant.com
Prices: $$

At Maykedeh–a name referring to Persian taverns of yore where poets and mystics converged to dine and drink–gracious service and generous portions abound. A burgundy-and-gold awning crowns the entrance; while inside, Middle Eastern songs and scents linger amid banquettes and linen-draped tables that accommodate crowds savoring the foods of their homeland.

Meals start with a plate of raw onion, fresh basil, and feta cheese—trust in these new refreshing combinations, salads, and dips laced with alluring Middle Eastern flavors. Sample the rich *kashke bademjan*, an eggplant and garlic spread with warm pita, then a tender skewer of *koobideh*, fresh ground lamb and beef with warm Persian spices. Valet the car to avoid the Telegraph Hill parking conundrum.

Piperade

D2 Basque XX

1015 Battery St. (bet. Green & Union Sts.)

Phone: 415-391-2555 Lunch Mon – Fri
Web: www.piperade.com Dinner Mon – Sat
Prices: $$

Soft Spanish melodies soothe the air at Piperade, where the brick façade, weathered oak floors, and communal shepherds' table evoke a Basque boarding house of yore. This cozy spot is home to Chef Gerald Hirigoyen, who hails from the French Basque country but cooks with both San Franciscan and Northern Spanish sensibilities.

Since "Hiri" oversees every detail, expect a top notch experience. The namesake *pipérade*, or pepper stew, arrives with Serrano ham and poached egg, while scrambled eggs accent an aromatic garlic soup with shrimp and lardons. Merguez sausage and tender braised fennel accompany expertly prepared and sublimely juicy lamb chops. Peruse and sample from their 200 carefully selected wines while enjoying patio seating on a warm evening.

Quince ✿

Italian

470 Pacific Ave. (bet. Montgomery & Sansome Sts.)

Phone: 415-775-8500 Dinner Mon – Sat
Web: www.quincerestaurant.com
Prices: **$$$$**

Marion Brenner

Whoever the who's-who may be, expect to see them dining at Quince. (And yes, those are their limos lined up in front of the kitchen's picture window.) The stylish and sophisticated clientele is matched by the restaurant's atmosphere, which features a contemporary lounge and soft-gray dining room with plush banquettes, Murano glass chandeliers, dramatic floral arrangements, and archways that lead to a popular bar for pre-dinner cocktails. This is all overseen by an extraordinary service team that continues to be among the best in San Francisco.

The Italian menu may offer dishes like a springtime starter of delicate white asparagus with melting lumps of creamy *burrata*, smoky speck, and a deep-fried egg that, once pierced, brings velvety richness to the entire plate. However, pastas remain the highlight here, with excellent preparations that may include sweet, fresh lobster meat encased in tender sheets of pasta, with a luscious and buttery sauce of fava beans, chives, and nasturtium flowers.

A cheese course makes a lovely finale, although you may want to save room for desserts such as the crisply sugared polenta cake with silky olive oil ice cream and delicious Meyer lemon curd.

Rose Pistola

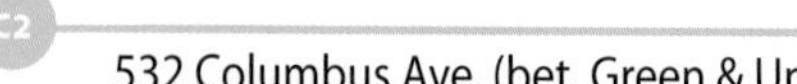

Italian XX

C2

532 Columbus Ave. (bet. Green & Union Sts.)

Phone: 415-399-0499 Lunch & dinner daily
Web: www.rosepistolasf.com
Prices: $$$

An unmistakable North Beach favorite, Rose Pistola pays tribute to the Ligurian Coast immigrants who once settled the neighborhood. Here, expect to feast on Northern Italian cuisine that focuses on seafood from independent and local fisherman, imported and house cured *salumi*, as well as meats from the rotisserie grill. The menu changes often but might include cracker-crisp pizza topped with salty prosciutto and fresh mozzarella; and nicely seasoned grilled octopus with Tuscan white beans, fennel, and arugula.

A large open kitchen and wood-burning oven warm the comfortable dining room with blue-and-white tile floors and an elegant bar mixing plenty of drinks. Service is typically friendly and sidewalk tables are preferred among locals with pets.

Tommaso's

Italian X

C3

1042 Kearny St. (bet. Broadway St. & Pacific Ave.)

Phone: 415-398-9696 Dinner Tue – Sun
Web: www.tommasos.com
Prices: $$

California pizza kitchens love to celebrate the bounty of the season, turning out pies with toppings that would boggle a red-blooded Italian (snow peas and sauerkraut?). Not so at Tommaso's, the family-friendly North Beach mainstay where the wood-fired pizzas hail straight from the old country. The chewy thin-crust pies are heaped with sausage, meatballs, salami, and *Prosciutto di Parma*. Fancy pants can sample garlic and clams or chicken and artichoke.

Set against a bright mural depicting the Bay of Naples, dinners at Tommaso's might also include a meaty antipasto plate loaded with rosemary ham and *bresaola*, or classic tiramisu. A fixture in the neighborhood since 1935, this fortress is a refreshing escape from seedy North Beach nightlife.

Tony's Pizza Napoletana

C2

1570 Stockton St. (at Union St.)

Phone: 415-835-9888 Lunch & dinner Wed – Sun
Web: www.tonyspizzanapoletana.com
Prices: $$

Tony's is a North Beach institution that churns out a large menu of Neapolitan-, Sicilian-, and American-style pizzas; it is also well-liked by locals and tourists who flock here not just for the pizza, but also for the buzzing social scene. You may think you've done well by arriving early, yet find herds waiting for a coveted seat in this casual pizzeria.

The bar is fair game and flanked by crowds hungry for the prized Margherita, a wood-fired crust slathered with San Marzano tomatoes, mozzarella, and basil. Tony's boasts a pizza for every palate, so come with friends to sample selections like the coal-fired New Yorker (pepperoni, sausage, and ricotta); or Californian style: "Fear and Loathing" with tamarind-glazed pork, jalapeños, and agave drizzles.

Trattoria Contadina

B2

1800 Mason St. (at Union St.)

Phone: 415-982-5728 Dinner nightly
Web: www.trattoriacontadina.com
Prices: $$

Look no further than the corner of Mason and Union streets for a neighborhood trattoria where the décor is rustic, the vibe is lively, and the staff is welcoming. Inside, witness a homey vibe with families and regulars mingling amidst linoleum floors and signed photos of celebrities; while outside you can hear the clanging of cable cars on the Powell-Mason line.

The wave of smaller portions has not affected the plates here—the food is still honest and appealing. Preparations of veal and chicken remain classic, but count on a few daily specials to round out the selection. Your *nonna* will not be worried about you as you fill up on fusilli with chicken, prosciutto, sun-dried tomatoes, and cream. After all, the dish is called Pavarotti for a reason.

Richmond & Sunset

Here in the otherworldly outer reaches of San Francisco, the foggy sea washes up to the historic Cliff House and Sutro Baths; in spring, cherry blossoms blush at the breeze in Golden Gate Park; and whimsical topiaries wink at pastel row houses in need of fresh paint. Residents seem inspired by a sense of zen not quite found elsewhere in town, whether you happen upon a Japanese sushi chef or a Sunset surfer dude. A melting pot of settlers forms the culinary complexion of this quiet urban pocket. The steam wafting from bowls of piping hot *pho* is nearly as thick as the marine layer, while many of the neighborhoods' western accents hail from across the pond.

New Chinatown

The Richmond, however, has earned the nickname "New Chinatown" for a reason. A bazaar for the adventurous cook, Clement Street bursts with cramped sidewalk markets where clusters of bananas sway from the awnings and the spices and produce are as vibrant as the nearby **Japanese Tea Garden** in bloom. While the Bay Area mantra "eat local" doesn't really apply here, sundry international goods abound—think kimchi, tamarind, eel, live fish, and pork buns for less than a buck. Curious foodies find global delicacies: this is *the* place to source that 100-year-old egg. A gathering place for sea lovers, **Outerlands** is perfect when in need of warmth, food, shelter, and "community." There is a mom-and-pop joint for every corner and culture. The décor is nothing to write home about and, at times, feels downright seedy, but you're here for the cuisine, which is usually authentic: Korean barbecue at **Brothers Restaurant**; Burmese at **B Star Bar**; *siu mai* at **Shanghai Dumpling King** and **Good**

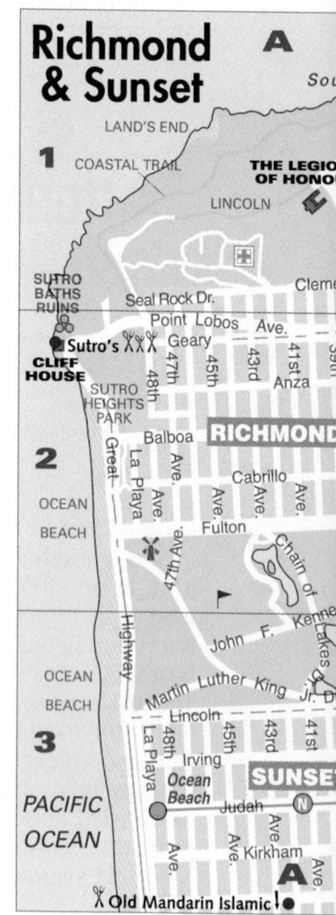

Luck Dim Sum; as well as an intoxicating offering of tequila and mescal at **Tommy's Mexican Restaurant**. For dessert, it's Asian kitsch: **Polly Ann Ice Cream** has served such flavors as durian, jasmine tea, and taro for years; while young club kids nibble Hong Kong–style sweets late night at **Kowloon Dessert Café**.

Sunset

A touch more gentrified than neighboring Richmond, Sunset–once a heap of sand dunes–retains a small-town vibe that's groovy around the edges. In the early morning, locals line up for fresh bread and pastries at **Arizmendi Bakery**, then wash down their scones at the **Beanery** around the corner. **Katana-Ya** and **Hotei** offer soul-warming bowls of handmade noodles for lunch. While tourists taking in the sights at the DeYoung Museum or the Academy of Sciences, might grab a bite at the **Academy Café**, loyalists to **L'Avenida Taqueria** take their burritos to the park. Finally, don't miss dinner at the **Moss Room**, boasting a plethora of unique (and delicious) dishes made with seasonal and healthy ingredients.

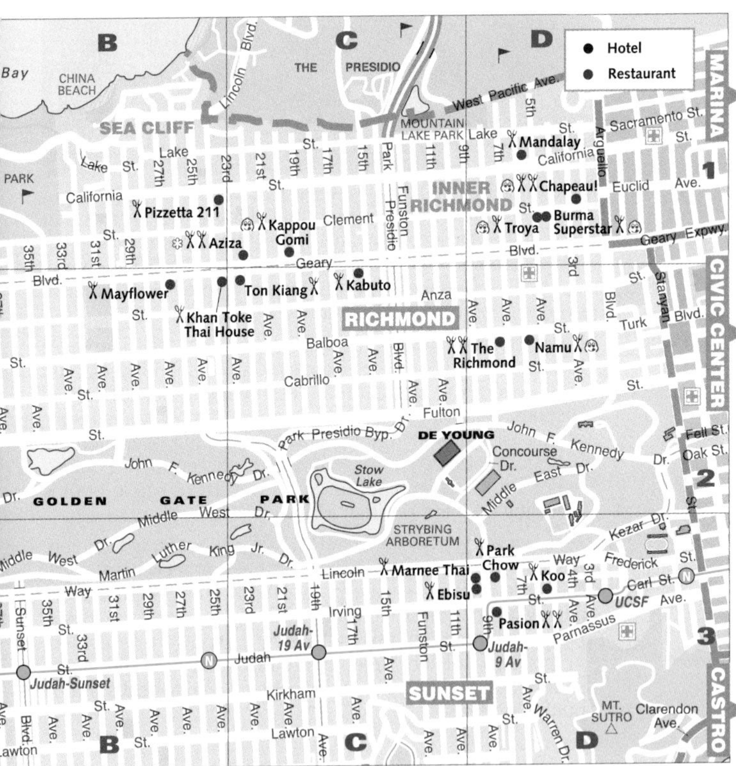

Aziza ✿

C1 Moroccan XX

5800 Geary Blvd. (at 22nd Ave.)

Phone: 415-752-2222 Dinner Wed – Mon
Web: www.aziza-sf.com
Prices: $$$

Amy Snyder

The brick building that houses Aziza may be plain-Jane, but there is a dusky sensuality about this Moroccan star that only ignites as lights dim and the night wears on. Everything about Aziza is swanky and sultry; the crowd includes darling couples and small groups congregating to celebrate special events at this romantic retreat.

Before being whisked away by the stately staff, take a moment to feast your eyes upon glorious red glass chandeliers, blue tinted windows, and ceramic tiles gilding a bar that pours specialty cocktails. Through Moorish archways, glimpse photos of majestic Arabian stallions peering over intimate banquette nooks. And if that isn't exotic enough, hanging lamps bestow a mysterious glow over azure suede booths revealing intricate wooden inlays.

An onyx votive is the only frill on tables robed in white linen, and doesn't distract from the fine-tuned and contemporary Moroccan fare—imagine prawns with crunchy puntarelle; and Wagyu carpaccio crested with jalapeño shavings. Honest ingredients (and inspiration) are powerfully evident in perfectly plated squab with huckleberries and nettle soubric; and a beet sorbet with yogurt *granité* and candied pumpkin seeds.

Burma Superstar

Burmese

D1

309 Clement St. (bet. 4th & 5th Aves.)

Phone: 415-387-2147 — Lunch & dinner daily
Web: www.burmasuperstar.com
Prices:

Any foodie worth their cilantro in San Francisco has made the trek to Clement Street to jot their name on a clipboard and wait it out at Burma Superstar, the now cult classic with everything going for it. Seriously, Chinatown restaurants wish they were this cool.

The massive menu wants for large parties that like to share—narrowing down the options can be a bit of a task. Have faith, an uber-friendly staff is on hand to help. You'll find a mix of Asian flavors, but seek out the genuine Burmese recipes noted by asterisks on the menu. Mild-mannered fare includes a tea leaf salad with roasted peanuts and fish sauce. The star of Superstar is the *mohinga*—a divine noodle soup with ground catfish and Asian veggies spiked with lemon and lemongrass.

Chapeau!

French

D1

126 Clement St. (bet. 2nd & 3rd Aves.)

Phone: 415-750-9787 — Dinner Tue – Sat
Web: www.chapeausf.com
Prices: $$

Upon arriving at Chapeau!, stylish women are welcomed with a kiss-kiss from Monsieur and Madame Gardelle, the husband-wife team that runs a strictly French ship. A long banquette and close-knit tables span the boisterous dining room that, with an ambient amber glow, is equally romantic and spirited for date nights.

Chef/owner Phillipe Gardelle is as often shaking hands in the dining room as he is in the kitchen, where he prepares such classic Gallic cuisine as porcini-crusted sweetbreads, fresh seafood bouillabaisse, and hearty *cassoulet de Toulouse*. At the end of a meal, the chef may even turn up tableside for a round of applause. On weekdays, early birds put their hands together for the under $30 prix-fixe from 5:00 P.M. to 6:00 P.M.

Ebisu

D3 — Japanese

1283 9th Ave. (at Irving St.)

Phone: 415-566-1770 — Lunch & dinner Tue – Sun
Web: www.ebisusushi.com
Prices:

Steps away from Golden Gate Park, the well-tread Ebisu is run by Steve Fujii and his wife Koko. This *sushi-ya* (in business for nearly 30 years) is loved both for its chic and contemporary style (featuring a long, sleek sushi bar and wood accents throughout), as well as its creative maki. While some purists are wary, fresh fish fans know this is the place to experiment. With names like Potato Bug (cucumber and freshwater eel inside-out roll); Tootsie Roll (deep-fried halibut wrapped in soybean paper); and deliciously innovative starters (scallop carpaccio with blood orange vinaigrette or steamed monkfish liver), these inventions clearly push the limits of tradition. To get your slurp on, sip on a premium sake from their impressive collection.

Kabuto

C2 — Japanese

5121 Geary Blvd. (bet. 15th & 16th Aves.)

Phone: 415-752-5652 — Lunch Mon – Sat
Web: www.kabutosushi.com — Dinner nightly
Prices: $$

Named for a helmet worn by the noble samurai, Kabuto is dead serious about sushi. Seafood arrives from Japan daily to land beneath the deft blade of these *itamae,* whose skills command respect. Check the whiteboard for the day's freshest catch and watch quietly at the blonde wood counter as the chef transforms simple fish into an artful sushi experience.
Each bite is a complete flavor adventure, so please, heed the occasional "no soy sauce" decree—sushi is best enjoyed without a scowl from the chef. With such clever concoctions, this advice is worth obeying. Sample *hirame* "Jerry" with Japanese clover, ponzu jelly, and wasabi cream; tempura-coated albacore wrapped in a crêpe with crispy nori; or sliced fresh hamachi with cilantro and jalapeño slivers.

Kappou Gomi

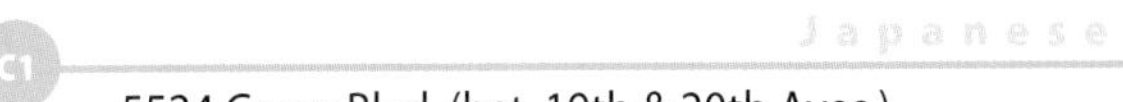

Japanese

C1

5524 Geary Blvd. (bet. 19th & 20th Aves.)

Phone: 415-221-5353 Dinner Tue – Sun
Web: N/A
Prices: $$

Kappou Gomi feels a world away from the city's popular Japanese eateries and, as a sign in the window makes clear, seekers of bento boxes and trendy maki need not apply. This is one of San Francisco's rare *kappou* restaurants, which specializes in more delicate and authentic food.

The small, subdued space features an extensive menu organized by ingredients and intricate preparations that draw a house full of Japanese diners. Look for such exotic dishes as *namayuba,* a salad of fresh favas in creamy soy skin; raw *tai* with pickled celery in chrysanthemum blossom dressing; and whole *aji tataki.* Once you've finished the fillets, the kitchen will deep-fry the head, bones, and tail for a crunchy finish. You won't find that at your local sushi hot spot!

Khan Toke Thai House

Thai

B2

5937 Geary Blvd. (bet. 23rd & 24th Aves.)

Phone: 415-668-6654 Dinner nightly
Web: N/A
Prices: $$

Word on the street is that Khan Toke offers *the* most unique Thai in SF. Surely this isn't a stretch given that guests relinquish their shoes at the door as is customary; and the "House's" décor screams authenticity by way of low carved tables frilled with diners seated on floor cushions, dangling their legs in sunken wells beneath. Wood paneling and carvings adorn the walls and faithful artifacts complete the exotic backdrop. In the same vein, diners can look forward to classic, shareable fare like *sur rong hai* (deliciously tender beef tips marinated in tamarind and finished with cilantro); *gaeng kheaw wan* (spicy green chicken curry with potatoes, sweet basil, and lush coconut); and *moo ga prou* (pork sautéed with scallions and splashed with chili sauce).

Koo

Japanese

408 Irving St. (bet. 5th & 6th Aves.)

Phone: 415-731-7077 Dinner Tue – Sun
Web: www.sushikoo.com
Prices: $$

Koo is praised and preferred for its delicate tempura and pristine nigiri, but this local darling also advertises an array of maki which, although mighty innovative, are created for an American palate. Enter the pleasant wood-trimmed dining room, dotted with tight-knit tables and hints of classic Japanese architecture, to find a cool Richmond set engrossed in their traditional nightly specials.

Take your cue from here, and order off of the list of fresh fish before the droves in line deplete such specials as *saba tataki*, thin slices of mackerel dressed with scallion and ponzu; top-notch nigiri topped with expertly cut and sourced fish; and an U2 roll filled with lacy shrimp tempura, creamy avocado, and crowned with spicy tuna and tobiko beads.

Mandalay

4348 California St. (bet. 5th & 6th Aves.)

Phone: 415-386-3895 Lunch & dinner daily
Web: www.mandalaysf.com
Prices: 

Mandalay lays claim to being the oldest Burmese restaurant in the city. The cuisine draws inspiration from their borders with China and India; and the flavors will leave you wholly fulfilled. Crowding a large, kitschy dining room (read: holiday decorations hang year-round) are familiar fans, so be prepared to wait for a table.

An expansive menu puts you in the mood for similar food. Lovers of the subcontinent will find plenty to please their palates here, reveling in such tantalizing creations as a tea leaf salad—a virtual cacophony of flavor with tea leaves, toasted lentil seeds, ground shrimp, garlic, peppers, and peanuts. For something completely unique, try the Rainbow salad made up of twenty intriguing ingredients.

Marnee Thai

Thai

D3

1243 9th Ave. (bet. Irving St. & Lincoln Way)

Phone: 415-731-9999 Lunch & dinner daily
Web: N/A
Prices: $$

The city's food field may be packed, but Marnee Thai stands tall with its authentic array of affordable, fresh, and creative Thai tidbits. Within an earshot of Golden Gate Park, stroll past the anonymous façade and into a snug dining room coupled with gracious service and creative food. Dodge the rumbling open kitchen by grabbing a seat in the back where curvy orange tabletops with dainty orchids evoke a bit of Siam.

The exotic menu includes mildly spiced angel wings with a chili-garlic sauce; golden triangles laden with pumpkin, potato, and curry in crispy wrappers; and palate-pleasing *pad kee mao,* pan-fried noodles tossed with thinly sliced beef, chili, garlic, tomato, and basil. Vegetarians frolic in the inventive and tasty selection of dishes.

Mayflower

Chinese

B2

6255 Geary Blvd. (at 27th Ave.)

Phone: 415-387-8338 Lunch & dinner daily
Web: www.mayflower-seafood.com
Prices: $$

A mostly Asian clientele attests to the authenticity of Mayflower, a Cantonese dim sum house that sits opposite the golden dome of the Holy Virgin Russian Orthodox Church. Westerners beware: authenticity in Chinese cuisine brings recipes that may challenge the uninitiated palate—think goose webs; fish maw; and plump marinated duck tongues meant to be devoured, soft bones, cartilage and all.

Yet timid eaters should fear not, for there are plenty of delectable familiar options, as in crispy spring rolls; barbecue pork buns; and shrimp-and-pork *siu mai.* Deep-fried squid and soft-shell crab dusted with a spicy salt are only moderately adventurous. Given the many aquariums, know that the seafood is fresh and these hearty portions won't break the bank.

Namu 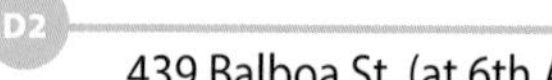

D2 — Asian

439 Balboa St. (at 6th Ave.)

Phone: 415-386-8332 — Lunch Sat – Sun
Web: www.namusf.com — Dinner nightly
Prices: $$

It's all "A" game here at Namu, where Chef Dennis Lee, together with siblings Dan and Dave, run a heck of an enterprise, combining a serious work ethic with healthy doses of creativity and tradition. The innovative menu highlights the family's Korean roots, and here things get a tasty twist.

Kimchi is more than just fermented cabbage; it transforms Korean "tacos" into heavenly bites when combined with barbecued short rib meat over rice, remoulade, *kalbi demi glace*, and daikon salsa wrapped in nori. Luxurious handmade ramen noodles with pork miso broth, pork shoulder, and a deep-fried egg are made in limited supply, so get here early for the goodies.

"Namu" is Korean for tree, inspired by their 14-foot bar carved of reclaimed Cypress from Golden Gate Park.

Old Mandarin Islamic

A3 — Chinese

3132 Vicente St. (bet. 42nd & 43rd Aves.)

Phone: 415-564-3481 — Lunch Fri – Mon & Wed
Web: N/A — Dinner nightly
Prices: ⊜

On cool days, these interior windows perspire from the steam coming off the Beijing-style hot pots; this popular spot is guaranteed to help shake off any chill.

In keeping with what is Halal, or permissible to eat under Islamic law, these bubbling pots may be filled with slices of beef and lamb or fish, but no pork. Feel free to add vegetables like spinach, cabbage, and rice noodles, all simmering in a pot of broth placed over an open flame, making this the perfect meal for a group. Intrepid eaters should try the *na si mi*, "extremely hot pepper," a dish so brazenly fiery that it is hailed as the spiciest in the city. Beyond hot pots, the menu covers a world of offerings; those in the know go for the lamb dishes, or beef and green onion pancakes.

Park Chow

D3

1240 9th Ave. (bet. Irving St. & Lincoln Way)

Phone: 415-665-9912 Lunch & dinner daily
Web: www.chowfoodbar.com
Prices: $$

Welcome to Park Chow, the inner Sunset neighborhood joint where you can truly have it your way. In the mood for spicy Thai noodles tossed with cilantro and peanuts? You got it. Wild mushroom *pizzette* with chewy crust and thyme? Sure thing. Pork chops, deviled eggs, and home-baked coconut cream pie? (You get the picture.)

With such a diverse menu and an equally eclectic staff, Park Chow succeeds at pleasing everyone. A crackling fire warms the homey, two-story spot where a retractable roof lets the sunshine in. Daily sandwiches come with soup or fries for just $10 at lunch, and healthy salads are bountiful. There's even a menu of pint-sized burgers and chicken strips for the kiddos to fuel up before a walk in Golden Gate Park, just a block away.

Pasion

D3

737 Irving St. (bet. 8th & 9th Aves.)

Phone: 415-742-5727 Lunch Sat – Sun
Web: www.pasionsf.com Dinner nightly
Prices: $$

In a neighborhood loved for authentic international flavors, Pasion is causing a stir with Latin American ingredients and an ambience as fiery as the food. But while the name suggests a sultry vibe, couples seeking romance may be met with a boisterous after-work scene: squeeze into the bar for an alluring drink and get ready to make a night of it. Luckily, the kitchen has just the thing to pair with that pisco sour.

Helmed by Chef/owner Jose Calvo-Perez of the popular Peruvian restaurant Fresca, Pasion serves zesty ceviches alongside more creative items. Belly up to bold lamb *albondigas* with Manchego cheese and chilies in a savory foie gras broth, or a double-cut pork chop in mango-cilantro sauce. Duck confit empanadas are ideal for sharing at the bar.

Pizzetta 211

B1 Pizza

211 23rd Ave. (at California St.)

Phone: 415-379-9880 Lunch & dinner daily
Web: www.pizzetta211.com
Prices: ⊜

Thin-crust devotees continue to pack this quaint, stripped-down pizzeria hideaway, with limited indoor seats at a premium on a cool day—though a few sidewalk tables help accommodate overflow.

No one is pampered here: place an order at the counter, pick up your own utensils, napkins, and grab a seat during the five short minutes before the pizza arrives. Artisanal pies change daily and veer from the cerebral (squash blossom, cherry tomato, chive, goat cheese, and citrusy *agrumato*) to the humble Margarita. The daily menu prides itself on supporting local, organic producers, so check the appetizer, salad, and calzone specials, as well as the fresh-baked dessert display. Get the pizza chef to crack a smile and you'll become the talk of the Outer Richmond.

The Richmond

D2 American

615 Balboa St. (bet. 7th and 8th Aves.)

Phone: 415-379-8988 Dinner Mon – Sat
Web: www.therichmondsf.com
Prices: **$$**

Its far-flung locale makes quaint and unassuming The Richmond a no-brainer for neighborhood types, but John and Thu Ha's thoughtful cuisine puts the restaurant on the map for any SF foodie seeking fine dining on a dime.

After visiting the de Young Museum or Academy of Sciences in Golden Gate Park a few blocks south, head to The Richmond for a five-course tasting menu for less than $50. À la carte offerings are available for those who prefer to steer their own course, including crab cakes with smooth avocado purée or poached yellowfin tuna. A highball of coffee semifreddo is a sweet and speedy cap to the meal. Pine wine crates that double as wall panels and bar tops remind of the rewards of dining here: good wines by the glass start around $7.

Sutro's

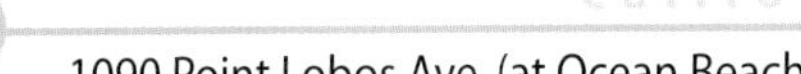

A2

1090 Point Lobos Ave. (at Ocean Beach)

Phone: 415-386-3330 — Lunch & dinner daily
Web: www.cliffhouse.com
Prices: $$$

San Francisco literally begins at Sutro's, perched on the city's westernmost tip with a legacy to rival its bird's eye view of the spectacular Pacific Coast. Housed in the third incarnation of the 1909 Cliff House, Sutro's is named for the nineteenth century Sutro Baths, whose neighboring ruins can still be explored. Today, antiques and memorabilia such as old-fashioned swimwear fill the downstairs dining room in salute to the area's storied past.

Sutro's seafood-rich Californian cuisine lives happily in the present and has finally grown worthy of its sensational setting. Such dishes as portobello-stuffed chicken breast, and Loch Duart salmon over plump hummus ravioli are enough to distract from the surfers and crashing waves at Ocean Beach nearby.

Ton Kiang

C2

5821 Geary Blvd. (bet. 22nd & 23rd Aves.)

Phone: 415-752-4440 — Lunch & dinner daily
Web: www.tonkiang.net
Prices:

Upstairs or down, the focus here is on dim sum and Hakka cuisine. The Hakka people migrated across their country from Northern China, many of them settling in the Guangdong Province near the Ton Kiang, or East River.

Once seated at a round table, equipped with a lazy Susan for sharing dishes, you'll be bombarded by a flurry of female servers proffering steamed, fried, blanched, and roasted miniature delights with little explanation (though there is a diagram on each table to help you identify your choices). The density of the crowd, which gets chaotic on weekends, dictates the level of service.

No prices are posted for dim sum, but never fear; the total bill here may well add up to less than what you'd pay for just an entrée elsewhere.

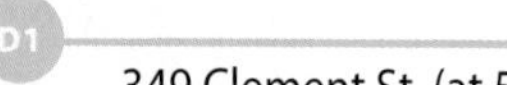

Troya

D1 — Mediterranean

349 Clement St. (at 5th Ave.)

Phone: 415-379-6000 — Lunch & dinner daily
Web: www.troyasf.com
Prices: $$

The face that launched a thousand ships also inspired one of San Francisco's great Mediterranean eateries. Troya is named in honor of the fabled city Troy and the icons that perished in her wake. This incarnation is a touch less dramatic, with simple Greek and Turkish cuisine served in a sunny corner space with classical-style art.

A six-seat bar offers a welcoming break from the battles of the day. Relax with beautifully golden and flavorful falafel set atop hummus, *tzatziki*, and spicy tomato sauce; tender lamb shish kebabs; or, on a foggy day, a steaming crock of moussaka topped with a béchamel brûlée. In lieu of the expected baklava, try the flaky nightingale's nest: a walnut-stuffed phyllo pastry with vanilla ice cream, pistachios, and honey.

Feast for under $25 at all restaurants with ☺.

Peter L. Wrenn/MICHELIN

SoMa

Peek behind the unassuming doors of the often-gritty façades prevalent in SoMa, the neighborhood South of Market, and discover a trove of creative talent. While you won't find a flood of sidewalk cafés and storefronts ubiquitous to more obviously charming enclaves, SoMa divulges gobs of riches (from artistic diamonds in the rough to megawatt culinary gems) to the tenacious urban treasure seeker.

Residential Mix

A diverse stomping ground that defies definition at every corner, SoMa is often labeled "industrial" for its hodgepodge of converted warehouse lofts. Or, with a mixed troupe of artists, photographers, architects, dancers, and designers now occupying much of SoMa's post-industrial real estate, you might also call it "artsy." In reality, dynamic SoMa wears many faces: Youths in concert tees navigate their skateboards around the pitfalls of constant construction, fueled by "Gibraltars" from cult classic **Blue Bottle Café**. Sports fans of a different sort converge for Giants baseball and **Crazy Crab'z** sandwiches at AT&T Park. In the Sixth Street Corridor, an immigrant population enjoys tastes of home at such authentic dives as **Tu Lan**, the Vietnamese hole-in-the-wall favored by the late Julia Child. Just blocks away, a towering crop of luxury condominiums draws a trendy yuppie set keen to scoop up modern European furnishings at the SF Design Center and dine at equally slick restaurants—think of **Roe**, which doubles as an after-hours nightclub.

Arts and Eats

Since SoMa is perhaps most notable for its arts scene–this is home to the San Francisco Museum of Modern Art, countless galleries, Yerba Buena Center for the Arts, and the Daniel Libeskind-designed Contemporary Jewish Museum–neighborhood foodies crave stylish culinary experiences to match their well-rounded worlds. Art and design play a key role in the district's most unique dining and nightlife venues; and naturally, the neighborhood is fast welcoming new and avant-garde restaurant concepts. Not far from the Jewish Museum, is **Mint Plaza**—step into this charming gathering spot for a bite, perhaps a respite, or to simply read a book.

Post-dinner, art evangelists hit **111 Minna**, a gallery turned late-night DJ bar, or the wine bar at **Varnish Fine Art**. Down the street, **Ducca** plays on a Venetian theme with a lush lounge and whimsical paintings of the ducal couple. Speaking of Ducca, the restaurant inside the Westin Market Street, hip hotel restaurants and bars are prolific in SoMa, in part because of its proximity to the Moscone Convention Center. While there are a myriad of upscale watering holes to choose from, a batch of casual joints have sprung up of late. **Custom Burger/Lounge**, at Best Western Americana, piles gourmet toppings such as Point Reyes Blue Cheese and black olive tapenade onto patties of Kobe beef, salmon, and lamb. **Perry's**, the "meet market" made famous in Armistead Maupin's *Tales of the City*, is enjoying a second home in the Hotel Griffon on Steuart Street. At the InterContinental San Francisco, **Bar 888** pours more than 100 *grappe* to taste.

SoMa is home to a veritable buffet of well-known restaurants with famous toques at the helm. But the fact that these boldface names can also be found in the food court at the mall is testament to the area's democratic approach to food: there is high-quality cuisine to be here had at workaday prices. Here, wondrous things can be found between two slices of bread. Tom Colicchio's **'wichcraft** is a popular lunch spot among area professionals, and former Rubicon star Dennis Leary can actually be spotted slinging sandwiches at **The Sentinel**.

Chef Charles Phan has expanded his empire of Asian eateries in the neighborhood to include **Out the Door**, in Westfield San Francisco Centre, that dishes up tantalizing Vietnamese fare in a flash. For budget gourmands, SoMa brims with cheap eats. Westfield Centre houses an impressive food court with plenty of international options. Nearby, museumgoers can refuel with a fragrant cup of tea at **Samovar** or try a micro-brew beer at **Thirsty Bear Brewing Company**. Take a peaceful stroll around South Park, and make sure you stop by **Mexico au Parc**, where the *sopes* run out by noon. Ballpark denizens get their burger fix at brewpub **21st Amendment**, and **Citizen's Band** is renowned for its casual vibe and seasonal American fare.

Nightlife

This is all to say little of SoMa's buzzing nightlife, whose scene traverses the red carpet from sports bars to DJ bars, hotel lounges to ultra-lounges, and risqué dinner theater—think drag (at **AsiaSF**) to Dutch (the Amsterdam import **Supperclub** that serves a racy mixed plate of performance art and global cuisine in bed.) Oenophiles should definitely pop by **Terroir**, the witty little wine bar on Folsom that stocks more than 700 organic and old-world varietals. For more boisterous imbibing, **Bossa Nova** bursts with the flavors of Rio. Soak up your *cachaça*, SoMa-style, with a Nutella banana pancake from the 11th Street trailer, **Crêpes a Go-Go**.

SoMa
Hotel
Restaurant
NOB HILL
MARINA
CIVIC CENTER
MISSION
CHINATOWN
UNION SQUARE
TENDERLOIN
CIVIC CENTER
ASIAN ART MUSEUM
CITY HALL
SF PUBLIC LIBRARY
UN PLAZA
SF WAR MEMORIAL & PERFORMING ARTS CENTER
OLD MINT
MOSCONE CENTER WEST
Four Seasons
Palomar
Fifth Floor
Tropisueño
The Mosser
Lark Creek Steak
Chez Papa Resto
54 Mint
Luce
InterContinental
Heaven's Dog
Una Pizza Napoletana
Basil Canteen
Bar Agricole
Manora's Thai Cuisine
Sushi Zone
Powell St
Civic Center
Van Ness
TUNNEL
MUNI
Jackson
Washington
Clay
Sacramento
California
Pine
Bush
Sutter
Post
Geary
O'Farrell
Ellis
Eddy
Turk
Golden Gate Ave.
McAllister
Fulton
Grove
Hayes
Fell
Oak
Page
Market
Polk
Hyde
Leavenworth
Jones
Taylor
Mason
Powell
Stockton
Grant Ave.
Kearny
Larkin
Van Ness Ave.
Franklin
Gough
Octavia
Stevenson
Jessie
Mission
Tehama
Clementina
Folsom
Russ
Howard
Harriet
Langton
Rausch St.
Minna
Natoma
Dore
Kissling
Brady
McCoppin St.
Otis St.
Plum St.
Valencia
Harrison
Bryant
Duboce Ave.
Division St.
4th
5th
6th
7th
8th
9th
10th
11th
12th
101
80
A
B
1
2
3
4

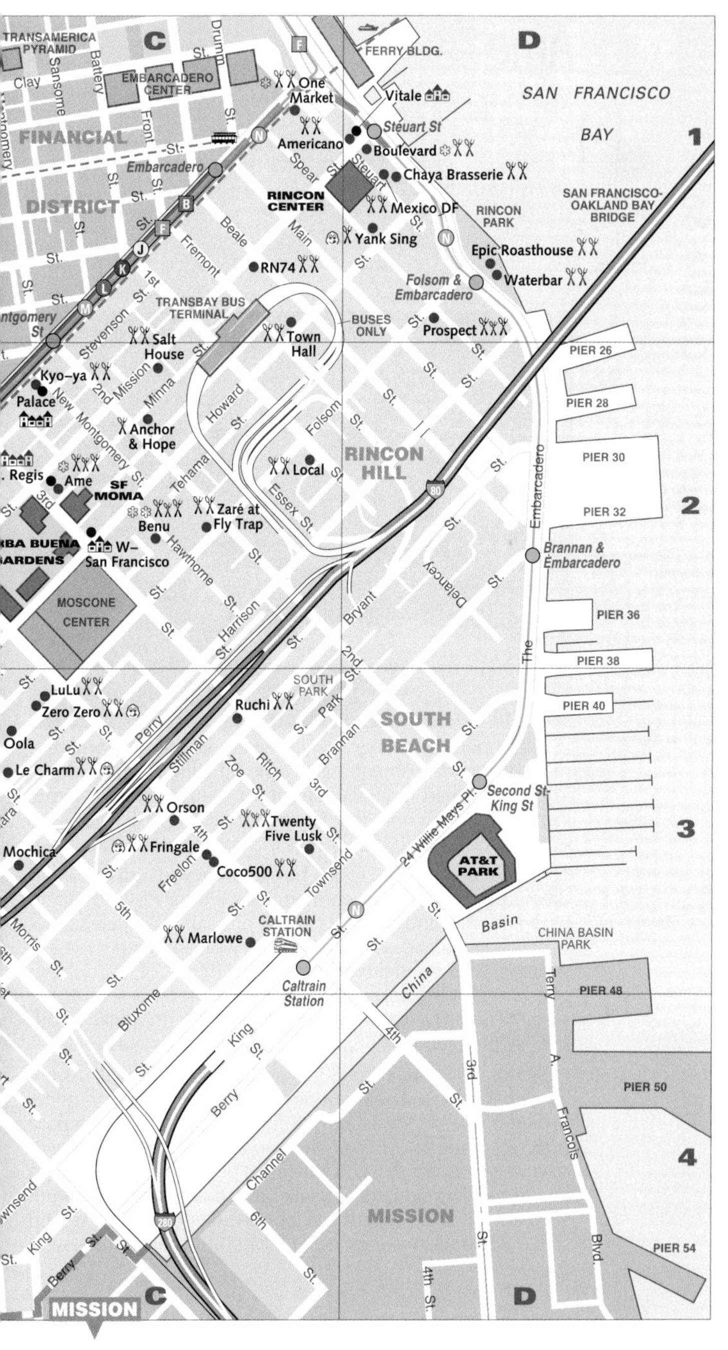

C
D
TRANSAMERICA PYRAMID
EMBARCADERO CENTER
FERRY BLDG.
SAN FRANCISCO BAY
FINANCIAL DISTRICT
One Market
Vitale
Americano
Steuart St
Boulevard
Chaya Brasserie
RINCON CENTER
Mexico DF
RINCON PARK
SAN FRANCISCO-OAKLAND BAY BRIDGE
Yank Sing
Epic Roasthouse
RN74
Waterbar
Folsom & Embarcadero
TRANSBAY BUS TERMINAL
BUSES ONLY
Town Hall
Prospect
Salt House
Kyo-ya
Palace
Anchor & Hope
PIER 26
PIER 28
PIER 30
PIER 32
RINCON HILL
Local
Regis
Ame
SF MOMA
Zaré at Fly Trap
Benu
W-San Francisco
YERBA BUENA GARDENS
MOSCONE CENTER
Brannan & Embarcadero
PIER 36
PIER 38
PIER 40
SOUTH PARK
SOUTH BEACH
LuLu
Zero Zero
Ruchi
Oola
Le Charm
Orson
Twenty Five Lusk
Second St-King St
Mochica
Fringale
Coco500
AT&T PARK
CHINA BASIN PARK
Marlowe
CALTRAIN STATION
Caltrain Station
PIER 48
PIER 50
PIER 54
MISSION
1
2
3
4

Ame 

Contemporary XxX

C2

689 Mission St. (at 3rd St.)

Phone: 415-284-4040 Dinner nightly
Web: www.amerestaurant.com
Prices: **$$$**

Joe Fletcher

In a competitive culinary world where keeping up with the neighbors is key, Ame (housed inside the impossibly chic St. Regis hotel) had its work cut out for it. Just a stone's throw from SFMOMA and the Contemporary Jewish Museum, Ame keeps up with the Joneses in sophisticated style.

The L-shaped dining room has a moneyed urbane vibe, dressed to the nines in earthen hues with stylish end-grain wood flooring and sculptural fabric pendants. A single scarlet wall is a jazzy accessory to an otherwise subdued space. In keeping with its deluxe mien, Ame thinks of everything: guests without a reservation may be offered a seat at the sashimi bar. The dining room, meanwhile, is stocked with suits sipping full-bodied pinots from Spiegelau glasses.

Helmed by chefs Hiro Sone and Lissa Doumani, Ame's kitchen poses a contemporary take on Japanese cuisine, served à la carte or as an $85 four-course menu. Tempura *poke* is composed of nori-wrapped *tombo* tuna topped with sesame seeds, *tobiko*, and Hawaiian pink salt, while Alaskan black cod is marinated in sake and floated in miso broth with a fresh twist of yuzu. Wines are worldly, but sake and stellar cocktails make for more adventuresome pairings.

Americano

Italian XX

8 Mission St. (at The Embarcadero)

Phone: 415-278-3777 — Lunch Mon – Fri
Web: www.americanorestaurant.com — Dinner Mon – Sat
Prices: $$$

Follow the trajectory from frat pack to the FiDi corner office and you'll eventually land in the circular lounge at Americano, the Hotel Vitale hub for happy-hour-seeking young execs. A lengthy bar and gorgeous outdoor patio boasting views of the Bay Bridge and Embarcadero make this the neighborhood's most conducive restaurant for cocktailing.

Though the setting emphasizes libations and a trendy, contemporary vibe, do not overlook the very solid Italian fare served in the earth-toned dining room. Crafted with superior seasonal ingredients, the menu might include tasty crowd pleasers like grilled bruschetta piled with creamy white bean purée and silky duck confit; a delightfully crisp-crusted pizza; or perfectly grilled ribeye with an earthy porcini rub.

Anchor & Hope

Seafood 

83 Minna St. (bet. 1st & 2nd Sts.)

Phone: 415-501-9100 — Lunch Mon – Fri
Web: www.anchorandhopesf.com — Dinner nightly
Prices: $$$

A maritime theme hangs in the salty air and conjures an east coast seaside shack at Anchor & Hope, sister restaurant to Salt House and Town Hall. This converted early 1900's auto shop now echoes a warehouse on the wharf, with thick ropes hanging from the high-pitched ceiling while a mounted garfish keeps a watchful eye. Like any bustling pier, Anchor & Hope is a boisterous place to dock.

Still, everyone is here for seafood. Blackboards boast the day's fresh oysters and shellfish, while a classic shrimp cocktail or apple-ginger cured salmon tartare are tasty starts. At lunch, try a tuna melt with Gruyère and tomato confit or Smithwicks beer-battered cod with rosemary potato wedges. To drink, dive into a massive list of imported and draught beers.

Bar Agricole

Californian

B4
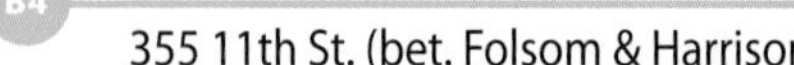

355 11th St. (bet. Folsom & Harrison Sts.)

Phone: 415-355-9400 — Lunch Sun
Web: www.baragricole.com — Dinner nightly
Prices: $$

Anyone looking for the latest SF foodie buzz should head to SoMa's Bar Agricole. This newest addition to the city's highly designed scene is as popular for its industrial-chic vibe as it is for its tasty Californian small plates.

Start in the redwood-sided patio, where tables for alfresco dining surround the chef's fresh herb garden. Inside, the modern space features backlit sculptural fixtures hanging from soaring ceilings; a second, more intimate dining area is sunken off the main room. The concrete bar proudly offers a selection of unusual cocktails, though some may entice more from the page than the glass. For dinner, expect dishes like spaghetti with chanterelles and duck ragù, or smoky pork sausage with sauerkraut and lobster mushrooms.

Basil Canteen

Thai

B4

1489 Folsom St. (at 11th St.)

Phone: 415-552-3963 — Lunch Mon – Fri
Web: www.basilthai.com — Dinner nightly
Prices:

Craving Bangkok street food? Make your way to Basil Canteen settled in the industrial confines of the former 1912 Jackson Brewery building. The spacious interior reflects a classic SoMa aesthetic with exposed brick, steel beams, and chalkboards listing daily specials; while the menu, more exotic than piquant, is a veritable blend of casual dishes and complex flavors.

Grab a seat at the communal table and sip on an enticing cocktail while chowing on *satays* that far outshine the more conventional chicken-on-a-stick. Chinese sausage and star anise-plum sauce add zest to a blue crab roll; and pork lovers will not want to miss the *khao moo daeng*, crispy slices of house-cured pork belly with star anise gravy. Fiery condiments are available for heat seekers.

Benu ✿✿

22 Hawthorne St. (bet. Folsom & Howard Sts.)

Phone: 415-685-4860 Dinner Tue – Sat
Web: www.benusf.com
Prices: **$$$$**

Benu

Graced with Japanese maples and high grass in a trellised courtyard on Hawthorne St., Benu scores automatic points for a Zen-like vibe in the heart of bustling SoMa. Hand your keys to the valet and, before heading in, peek through the glorious arched windows for a view of the immaculate kitchen.

With the Museum of Modern Art just around the corner, Benu's interior is fittingly contemporary and of strict high design thanks to architect Richard Bloch, whose angled beams make for an interesting, if fragmented, space. Dressed in gray and beige with deep carpeting and dark-wood tables, Benu's severe, minimalist dining room provides plenty of quiet for reflecting on serious cuisine. Thankfully, a perfectly polished and friendly staff achieves a comfortable balance.

Chef/owner Corey Lee exacts his modern Asian dishes with precision, plating such wonders as whole Japanese sea cucumber stuffed with pork belly, shrimp, and fermented pepper on delicate, custom-made Korean porcelain. Here dignified business types wheel and deal over creative recipes such as lily bulb soup flecked with apple, gingko, and fresh-water eel; and black truffle-scented risotto topped with pristine sea urchin fillets.

Boulevard ✿

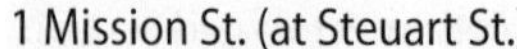

Californian XX

D1

1 Mission St. (at Steuart St.)

Phone: 415-543-6084 — Lunch Mon – Fri
Web: www.boulevardrestaurant.com — Dinner nightly
Prices: $$$

Boulevard

Embracing a unique Belle Epoque style from its waterfront location in the historic Audiffred Building, Boulevard makes the most of each and every handsome detail. Pale brick arched ceilings, iron beams, parquet floors, stained glass, and leafy plants dress a dining room that faces three different streets yet manages to remain convivial. Neat and polite servers tend tables populated by diners young and old. At lunch, local business folk come to say "you're hired!" Dinner is quieter with couples canoodling.

Despite the popularity and enormous scope of this space, the kitchen maintains excellent consistency in putting forth its widely appealing California-inspired fare. Bowls of crisp-seared yet pillowy gnocchi with rich buffalo short rib Bolognese and fresh Italian *burrata* melt together with exceeding pleasure. Perfectly grilled wild Coho salmon with *pommes fondantes* and wilted Napa cabbage highlights the chef's solid technique.

But save room, because desserts can be showstoppers, as in the *fromage blanc* cheesecake, with a crust of pistachio *feuillantine*, curls of candied lemon zest, tangy Meyer lemon sherbet, and crème Chantilly flecked with tart pomegranate granita.

Chaya Brasserie

132 The Embarcadero (bet. Howard & Mission Sts.)

Phone: 415-777-8688 — Lunch Mon – Fri
Web: www.thechaya.com — Dinner nightly
Prices: $$

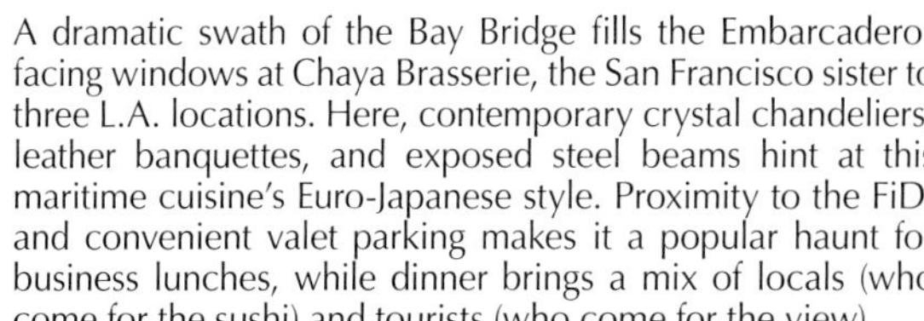

A dramatic swath of the Bay Bridge fills the Embarcadero-facing windows at Chaya Brasserie, the San Francisco sister to three L.A. locations. Here, contemporary crystal chandeliers, leather banquettes, and exposed steel beams hint at this maritime cuisine's Euro-Japanese style. Proximity to the FiDi and convenient valet parking makes it a popular haunt for business lunches, while dinner brings a mix of locals (who come for the sushi) and tourists (who come for the view).

A bright exhibition kitchen plates specialty sushi rolls like the vegetarian caterpillar with refreshing daikon and pickled burdock; and flavorful entrées like Hawaiian butterfish with sautéed mushrooms and tomato. Desserts can miss their mark, but happy hour is typically happening.

Chez Papa Resto

Mediterranean

414 Jessie St. (bet. Market & Mission Sts.)

Phone: 415-546-4134 — Lunch Tue – Sat
Web: www.chezpaparesto.com — Dinner nightly
Prices: $$

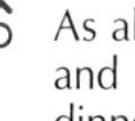

Just the sort of unflagging French bistro that an armchair traveler dreams of, Chez Papa is constant in its timeless Gallic fare, moody interior mixing black Venetian chandeliers and deep velvets with bright silks and light rattan chairs—even the upbeat soundtrack is *en français*. Everyone seems genuinely happy to be here, among animated servers happily discussing the bistro fare in telltale French accents.

As always, this local favorite is packed for weekend brunch, and its Mint Plaza patio remains particularly popular after dinner among the *Gitanes*-smoking set. Come for the poached egg frisée salad served with crispy duck confit, pancetta, and mustard vinaigrette; stay for the warm cocoa nib profiteroles with pistachio gelato and toasted almonds.

Coco500

Californian XX

C3

500 Brannan St. (at 4th St.)

Phone: 415-543-2222 — Lunch Mon – Fri
Web: www.coco500.com — Dinner Mon – Sat
Prices: $$

This effortlessly hip SoMa spot continues to draw hefty crowds for lunch and dinner, and they've been doing it for over five years. Imagine a loud buzz from happy patrons in the minimalist setting. Think chocolate, blue, and caramel tones coloring a room decked with work by local artists, and a handsome teak-and-Italian glass-tile bar beckoning with freshly-squeezed juice cocktails, and you will get the rest.

Chef/owner Loretta Keller has cobbled a Californian menu with many meant-to-be-shared dishes like crispy green beans or a duck liver terrine. California-sourced and Mediterranean-inspired starters like grilled Monterey squid with tangerine and olives are a perfect prelude to bigger things like wood-fired pizzas and milk-braised pork shoulder.

Epic Roasthouse

Steakhouse XX

D1

369 The Embarcadero (at Folsom St.)

Phone: 415-369-9955 — Lunch Thu – Sun
Web: www.epicroasthousesf.com — Dinner nightly
Prices: $$$

With a name like Epic, it's a safe bet that this ravishing roasthouse is a thrilling endeavor. Situated on the iconic Embarcadero with matchless views of the Bay Bridge, Epic is a massive and pricey tourist attraction. Exposed pipes and ductwork are inspired by a saltwater pump house that battled the fires of the 1906 quake; however, leather banquettes, plush carpets, and a fireplace lend an air of classic comfort.

This is just the ambience you'd want for imbibing a full-bodied merlot with your filet of beef, seasoned with salt and pepper and garnished with glazed baby carrots. Don't forget the sides! Garlic oil and red chili flakes add smoke to grilled *broccolini*, and the scent of truffle adds that *je ne sais quoi* to buttery whipped potatoes.

Fifth Floor

Contemporary

B2

12 4th St. (at Market St.)

Phone: 415-348-1555 Dinner Tue – Sat
Web: www.fifthfloorrestaurant.com
Prices: $$$$

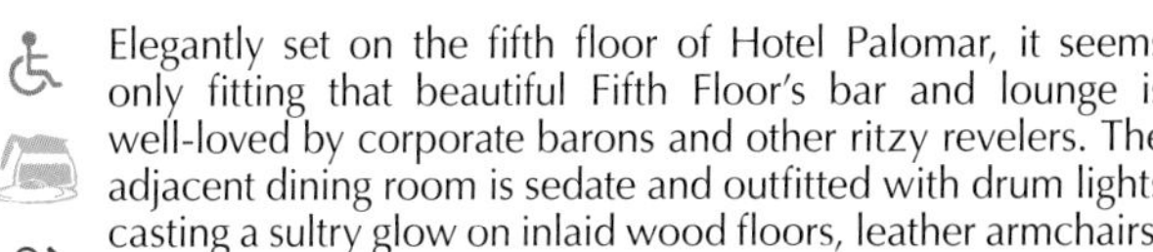

Elegantly set on the fifth floor of Hotel Palomar, it seems only fitting that beautiful Fifth Floor's bar and lounge is well-loved by corporate barons and other ritzy revelers. The adjacent dining room is sedate and outfitted with drum lights casting a sultry glow on inlaid wood floors, leather armchairs, and a lavish wine cellar.

A casual dining experience can be had amidst the refined servers and wood tables dressed with sparkling silverware. Such flush accessories keep fine company with contemporary plates of Mendocino uni flan lush with lobster "fondue" and saffron; Brillat-Savarin ravioli with mushrooms and ricotta twirling in a sage-brown butter sauce; and crisp-skinned duck breast set atop roasted sunchokes and threaded with candied kumquats.

54 Mint

Italian

B2

16 Mint Plaza (at Jessie St.)

Phone: 415-543-5100 Lunch & dinner Mon – Sat
Web: www.54mint.com
Prices: $$

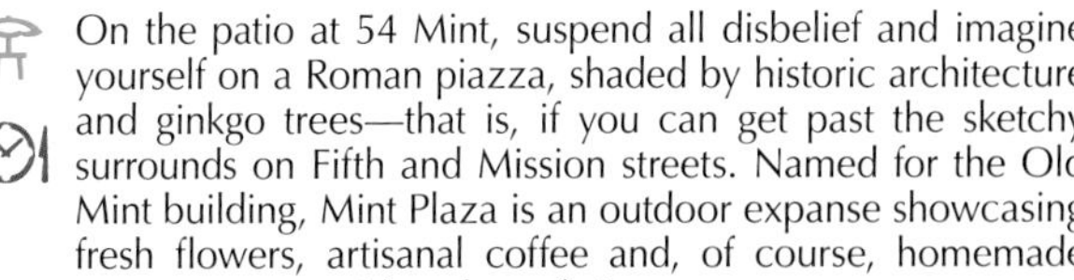

On the patio at 54 Mint, suspend all disbelief and imagine yourself on a Roman piazza, shaded by historic architecture and ginkgo trees—that is, if you can get past the sketchy surrounds on Fifth and Mission streets. Named for the Old Mint building, Mint Plaza is an outdoor expanse showcasing fresh flowers, artisanal coffee and, of course, homemade pastas to savor with a glass of *vino*.

This casual trattoria serves rustic fare made from primo ingredients: organic potato gnocchi are tossed in a hearty and aromatic beef ragù ; while a char-grilled skirt steak is served with sauteed broccoli rabe and a drizzle of olive oil. Those impressed with the ingredients may take some home; the space is stocked with mouthwatering Italian groceries for purchase.

Fringale

C3 French

570 4th St. (bet. Brannan & Bryant Sts.)

Phone: 415-543-0573 Lunch Tue – Fri
Web: www.fringalesf.com Dinner nightly
Prices: $$

Housed in a cheery yellow building on SoMa's restaurant-lined Fourth Street, unassuming Fringale is just the sort of intimate bistro this neighborhood needs: petite, hospitable, utterly charming, and delicious every time. The menu satisfies with authentic Basque cuisine and a decidedly French accent. A perfect beginning is found in the foie gras terrine—velvety and delicate with warm sliced brioche, a pineapple chutney quenelle, and sprinkling of fleur de sel. Other bistro favorites include crispy duck confit with French lentils, bacon, drizzled with a tangy red wine sauce; sautéed prawns in Pastis; and wonderful daily specials like bœuf Bourguignon.

For dessert, try Mme. Angèle's gâteau Basque, a buttery almond torte filled with custard cream.

Heaven's Dog

B3 Chinese

1148 Mission St. (bet. 7th & 8th Sts.)

Phone: 415-863-6008 Dinner nightly
Web: www.heavensdog.com
Prices: $$

This somewhat desolate stretch of Mission Street may seem an odd destination for happy hour, but Heaven's Dog brings it with a quirky vibe–think sleek banquettes and canine art–and inventive alcoholic creations such as the Shanghai Buck, a piquant concoction of Pompero Aniversario rum with fresh pressed ginger.

Cocktailers, of course, will need a bite to eat and few will complain about the contemporary Asian fare dreamed up by Chef/owner Charles Phan—that's right, of Slanted Door fame. Phan's clever take on Chinese cooking brings wonderfully sticky-salty, hoisin-glazed pork tossed in a steamed bun, as well as sweet-and-sour-and-spicy tiger prawns with Thai basil and a fresh twist of pineapple. On warm nights, check out the streetfront patio.

Kyo-ya

Japanese 

C2

2 New Montgomery St. (bet. Jessie & Market Sts.)

Phone: 415-546-5090 Lunch & dinner Mon – Fri
Web: www.sfpalacerestaurants.com
Prices: $$$

At home in downtown's Palace Hotel, Kyo-ya's chic, simple dining room and straightforward Japanese fare are more down-to-earth than the lavish surrounds. The mood is tranquil with a few vibrant works of art and a long sushi bar overlooking sparse tables dotted with fresh flowers. Efficient service pleases the mostly corporate clientele who arrive here to conduct midday business.

An ample selection of sake complements the chef's nigiri omakase, which features very fresh, unadorned fish. Savor delicious toro, crab, and salmon simply garnished with only a bit of spicy wasabi. Large sushi pieces are something of a mouthful and, with few fireworks, Kyo-ya's prices can seem high. The quality of the fish, however, out-swims most competitors.

Lark Creek Steak

Steakhouse 

845 Market St. (bet. 4th & 5th Sts.)

Phone: 415-593-4100 Lunch & dinner daily
Web: www.larkcreeksteak.com
Prices: $$$

Easily the best steak you will find in a mall (yes, in a mall!), Lark Creek Steak is set off the rotunda on the fourth floor of the Westfield Centre, and allures savvy shoppers who come to splurge on sales (and great steak). Farm-fresh American fare and a wine list add up to this perfect respite from rifling through the racks at Nordstrom.

Local farms and ranches provide many of the ingredients for the kitchen's seasonal à la carte menu, among which the hearty grass-fed beef and free-range chicken are best. Starters like filet mignon tartare with capers lead into heavier mains like prime rib, blackened pork chops, and hearty steakburgers. A decadent butterscotch pudding will furnish the sugar rush needed for a few more hours of shopping.

Le Charm

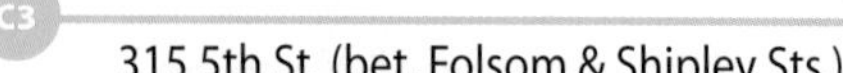

French XX

C3

315 5th St. (bet. Folsom & Shipley Sts.)

Phone: 415-546-6128 Lunch Tue – Fri
Web: www.lecharm.com Dinner Tue – Sun
Prices: $$

Le charm of this high-ceilinged spot with a sun-sprinkled patio rife with umbrellas and walls lined with trellised vines; mini copper bar set off the foyer; and large, wiry chandelier is truly everlasting. Flocks of butcher paper-topped tables cluster together in a small dining room dressed with persimmon and caramel walls, and the open kitchen offers a perfect respite to both French expats on a budget and novices to the cuisine that everyone will appreciate.

Ubiquitous offerings may include baked escargot with garlic-parsley butter; braised veal *paupiette* with cabbage and mushrooms; and a light, flaky tarte Tatin. There's more variety? Opt for the 3-course dinner for $32.

Live jazz on the patio every Thursday night merely adds to the charm of Le Charm.

Local

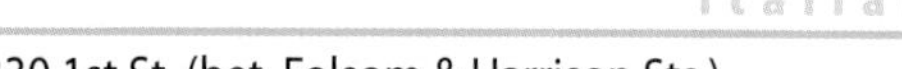

Italian XX

C2

330 1st St. (bet. Folsom & Harrison Sts.)

Phone: 415-777-4200 Lunch Sun – Fri
Web: www.sf-local.com Dinner Tue – Sun
Prices: $$

Local elevates the humble pizza joint. This contemporary loft-like space finds European inspiration in its urban minimalist décor comprised of polished concrete floors, aluminum chairs, Carrara marble tiles, and Mondrian-inspired doors. Only in San Francisco could a spot named "local" look so utterly cool.

Local has a small wine shop and shelves of gourmet items at the front, but it is the California-influenced Italian fare that draws in the crowds. The menu focuses on perfectly browned, crispy, wood-burning oven-fired, thin-crust pizza dough. Even the rustic pasta dishes come served with a round of flash baked pizza dough—ideal for soaking up those last flavorful bits of spicy wine and tomato sauce left in a deep bowl of their *linguini allo Scrigno.*

Luce 

Contemporary 

B3

888 Howard St. (at 5th St.)

Phone: 415-616-6566 Lunch & dinner daily
Web: www.lucewinerestaurant.com
Prices: $$$

Rien van Rijthoven

Those who enter off the street–rather than from inside the Hotel InterContinental–behold the rather icy wall of bluish-tinted windows before experiencing this exceptional cuisine. No matter the word on the street, this lofty, modern dining room with marble inlaid floors, a creamy palette, and orbital chandeliers rarely sees a local.

Luce's appeal to out-of-towners may relate to its rather corporate ambience and hit or miss service, but San Franciscans are sadly missing out on this open kitchen's carefully prepared and fantastic food. With just a sip of grappa at Bar 888 or sampling of wine from the gleaming glass cellar tower, and you no longer notice any hiccups or missteps in light of the promise of what is to come.

Under the helm of a new chef, Luce's fare is more contemporary, composed of Californian ingredients and prepared with French fundamentals. Dinner might bring elegant, silky ocean trout crudo with cucumber, tangy kumquat, and *piment d'Espelette*; hoisin-lacquered roast guinea hen with white asparagus and earthy morels; and for dessert, a playful construction of pumpkin seed and praline sponge cake arranged with mushroom caps and diced persimmon to resemble a forest floor.

LuLu

Mediterranean XX

C3

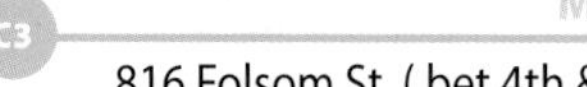

816 Folsom St. (bet 4th & 5th Sts.)

Phone: 415-495-5775 Lunch & dinner daily
Web: www.restaurantlulu.com
Prices: $$

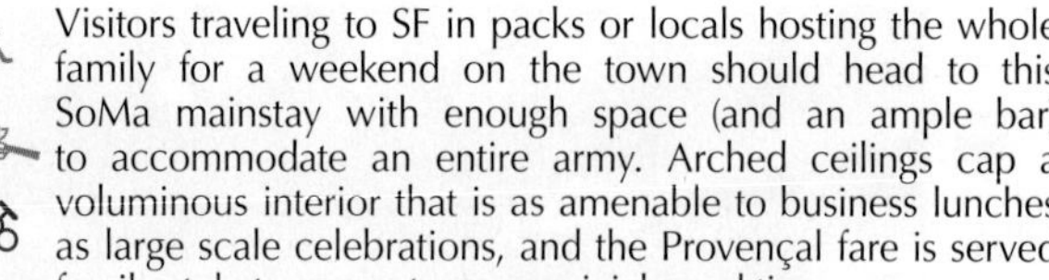

Visitors traveling to SF in packs or locals hosting the whole family for a weekend on the town should head to this SoMa mainstay with enough space (and an ample bar) to accommodate an entire army. Arched ceilings cap a voluminous interior that is as amenable to business lunches as large scale celebrations, and the Provençal fare is served family style to guarantee a convivial good time.

A roaring rotisserie and wood-burning pizza oven draw the eye into the exhibition kitchen, where seasonal ingredients are king. Thin-crust pizzas may be topped with slices of spring asparagus, while fresh field greens with tangy vinaigrette accompany a bison burger on a green onion bun. Don't miss out on such hearty side dishes as earthy, roasted *kabocha* squash.

Manora's Thai Cuisine

Thai X

A4

1600 Folsom St. (at 12th St.)

Phone: 415-861-6224 Lunch Mon – Fri
Web: www.manorathai.com Dinner nightly
Prices: ⊜

Large appetite, small budget? Grab your loose change and get your growling belly to Manora's, where bountiful portions of tasty Thai keep locals coming in herds. Quick service and super cheap specials (soup, fried rice, and two main courses for under 9 bucks) make this a go-to spot for lunch, though dinner lingers in this league. Start off with a bowl of creamy *gai tom ka*, a tangy, traditional Thai soup of coconut milk, lemon, and cilantro quivering with tender chunks of stewed chicken. Next, order up a plate of scrumptious garlic pork–marinated and char-grilled to tender perfection–or the *gai kraprao*, a stir-fry of ground chicken, chili, garlic, and fresh basil.

Quench your thirst with a tall glass of creamy Thai iced-tea—a cool remedy for a warm day.

Marlowe

Californian XX

C3

330 Townsend St., Ste. 230 (bet. 4th & 5th Sts.)

Phone: 415-974-5599 Lunch Mon – Fri
Web: www.marlowesf.com Dinner Mon – Sat
Prices: $$

Locals who lamented the loss of Aussie wine bar South are now making merry at Marlowe, the rustic-chic bistro that opened in its place. Reimagined with white penny-tile floors, faux-ostrich banquettes, and a wall of front windows inscribed with whimsical food and wine quotes, the tiny Townsend Street spot is already packed with regulars, so do plan in advance.

If there is a wait, hit a barstool and nurse a crisp glass of Riesling—it will pair well later with a "snack" of sea-salty Brussels sprout chips, or seared black cod smeared with sautéed spinach and spring vegetables. Marlowe's market-driven menu has much to crave, including a decadent burger. Finish with an upside-down apple crisp beneath bourbon ice cream and a crumbled oatmeal cookie.

Mexico DF

Mexican XX

D1

139 Steuart St. (bet. Mission & Howards Sts.)

Phone: 415-808-1048 Lunch Mon – Fri
Web: N/A Dinner nightly
Prices: $$

Revolving digital artworks, rich textiles, and low lighting are just the first clues that Mexico DF is a world away from San Francisco's beloved taquerias. The vibe here is contemporary and the cuisine a bit westernized, but top-notch ingredients guarantee that DF is anything but run-of-the-mill.

Friendly service echoes the warmth of brick walls, velvet, and leather accents in the streetfront lounge, where the SoMa set shares small plates over rounds of mojitos and margaritas at happy hour. For those who stay to dine, meals are festive and flavorsome. Soft corn tacos may be heaped with moist, ancho chile-braised leg of lamb, while the *huarache de Costilla*, a griddled masa cake laden with smoky short ribs and *cotija* cheese, is quite simply delicious.

Mochica

Peruvian XX

C3

937 Harrison St. (bet. 5th & 6th Sts.)

Phone: 415-278-0480 — Lunch & dinner Wed – Mon
Web: www.mochicasf.com
Prices: **$$**

Mochica is the first of Chef Carlos Altamirano's three prized and popular Peruvian eateries in the Bay Area. Rich hues, slate floors and well-set communal tables offer a tasty glimpse through over-sized windows.

The belly-sating cuisine is nearly always perfectly prepared, flavorful, with tastes of authenticity in each bite. Meals here may begin with dishes such as the buttery corn cake, *pastelito choclo,* made with potato, *queso fresco,* and crunchy bits of Peruvian corn alongside salsa blanca and *sarsita d'choclo*; or *causa limena,* a ring of creamy mashed potatoes flavored with *aji amarillo* and lime juice topped with cilantro-marinated tiger shrimp. Tasty endings include a sweet *arroz con leche* drizzled with a deliciously dark purple fruit sauce.

Oola

C3

860 Folsom St. (bet. 4th & 5th Sts.)

Phone: 415-995-2061 — Lunch Sun – Fri
Web: www.oola-sf.com — Dinner nightly
Prices: **$$**

Night owls lounging in high-backed suede booths, ambient light, and pounding club music set the scene at this chic and sophisticated SoMa hot spot. The restaurant actually takes its moniker from Chef/owner Ola (pronounced ooh-la) Fendert, who turns out bold Californian cuisine with superlative ingredients from start to finish.

With an urban vibe and well-executed fare–think moist salmon with fennel confit or baby back ribs that slip right off the bone–Oola lures large crowds to its chic open dining room and loft upstairs. Call ahead for a reservation or chance a seat at the backlit bar. But be warned: with dinner served until midnight or even 1:00 A.M, Oola is usually a popular choice for a post-party snack. Doors close at 2:00 A.M.

One Market

C1

1 Market St. (at Steuart St.)

Phone: 415-777-5577
Web: www.onemarket.com
Prices: $$

Lunch Mon – Fri
Dinner Mon – Sat

John A. Benson

There is nothing but one love for One Market. This corner restaurant, marked by a brick and glass façade, shows off towering windows that look upon the Ferry Building and historic streetcar passing. Yet what makes this gorgeous getaway so memorable is the fact that its kitchen churns out consistent product with grand results.

Hedging the busy FiDi and sleek SoMa, One Market is most beloved for business lunches. Here, more deals are sealed than romantic rendezvous. Courteous service is the rule in the big, bright, and bustling dining room. Tables may feel snug and neighboring conversations might drown yours, but look to the open kitchen and lofty ceilings for order and inspiration.

No matter your location (perhaps at one of the plush booths), well-versed servers sate with sophisticated dishes like lightly-smoked Tasmanian Ocean trout "mi cuit" set upon a golden-brown potato rösti and poached egg, drizzled with a pancetta vinaigrette; or rice flake-crusted petrale sole sauced with a rosy shrimp jus. There may be no other terrifically rustic way to end such indulgence than with a flaky Frog Hollow Warren pear tart licked with a sweet hazelnut cream and a tangy apple-pear gastrique.

Orson

C3 Contemporary XX

508 4th St. (at Bryant St.)

Phone: 415-777-1508 Lunch Tue – Sun
Web: www.orsonsf.com Dinner Tue – Sat
Prices: $$

With a name like Orson (as in Welles), this SoMa haunt has both the grit and glam of classic film noir. Chef/owner Elizabeth Falkner, a former film student, directs the scene: Orson is a cultural and culinary show starring hip thirty-somethings, inventive cocktails, and edgy movies projected on the wall.

In a lofty space on a slightly seedy block, Orson's urban palette is accented with vibrant artworks, a single crimson table, and a sculptural chandelier. Falkner's cuisine is equally modern whether enjoyed at a table or in the lounge. Look for Dungeness crab salad spiked with candied Buddha's hand citron or filet mignon with tangy garlic yogurt. Falkner is best loved for desserts; don't miss her Breakfast of Champions with bourbon-fried French toast.

Prospect

D1 American 

300 Spear St. (at Folsom St.)

Phone: 415-247-7770 Lunch Sun
Web: www.prospectsf.com Dinner nightly
Prices: $$$

From the creators of Michelin-starred Boulevard comes this pleasing Prospect—a spacious and sophisticated urban haunt, encased in a luxury glass high-rise, without any of the pomposity one might expect. In fact, heavy wooden doors hint at a slightly earthy interior: dark wood and warm browns blanket the SoMa hot spot, where cocktails at the communal table are as coveted as a banquette for two.

The contemporary menu is at once familiar and fabulous, with well-executed favorites such as yellowtail crudo with pickled cucumbers atop airy rice crackers; savory chicken roulade with maple-roasted sweet potatoes and spiced polenta fondue; and petit peppermint s'mores with cocoa nibs and caramel corn. Regulars here know that the service is always spot-on.

RN74

Californian XX

301 Mission St. (at Beale St.)

Phone: 415-543-7474 Lunch Mon – Fri
Web: www.rn74.com Dinner nightly
Prices: $$$

Named for Burgundy's main *route nationale*, Michael Mina's RN74 is an intoxicatingly sleek spot for a singular wine experience. Beckoning from an old-school train station schedule board is a handful of rare labels, while vaulted ceilings, iron rafters, and antique lanterns further invoke an aura of journeys. When a wine sells out, letters flip to reveal another bottle. Market wines are displayed on additional boards, where white lights signal the vintages that guests are drinking.

Drawing crowds to this chic space is a concise and carefully considered menu which may reveal grilled Monterey Bay sardines with capers and aged balsamic; leg of lamb and merguez adorned with chanterelles and farro; or warm beignets with fragrant nutmeg and chicory caramel.

Ruchi

Indian XX

474 3rd St. (bet. Bryant & Stillman Sts.)

Phone: 415-392-8353 Lunch & dinner Mon – Sat
Web: www.ruchisf.com
Prices:

The name literally means "taste," so it's not surprising that Ruchi delivers a powerful lip-smacking punch to the taste buds. The focus is on Southern Indian flavors at this SoMa newcomer. *Dosas*, those thin, lacy, crispy little tastes of heaven, are a "don't miss." Try the Mysore masala *dosa* with crushed potato filling and spicy chutney on the side—yum! Stews and curries account for most of the menu, but this isn't anything like your *nani* used to make. Instead, the stews are pungent and flooded with rich flavors and tender, juicy meats.

Nab a table in the back and watch the action in the open kitchen. With all of those bubbling pots of curries and other concoctions, it may look a bit more like a coven, but there's nothing evil about these tasty treats.

Salt House

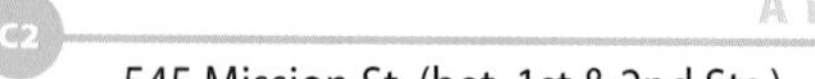

American

545 Mission St. (bet. 1st & 2nd Sts.)

Phone: 415-543-8900 — Lunch Mon – Fri
Web: www.salthousesf.com — Dinner nightly
Prices: $$

It's a little bit country, a little bit rock and roll here, where amusing yet chic country touches abound (find milk bottles used for water and jars in place of dessert plates) and everyone seems to be having fun. From the communal counter and lively bar to the bustling open kitchen, Salt House has a palpable energy. The service is efficient and professional, yet manages to make everyone in the crowd feel cosseted. However, this house is packed, so reservations are a good idea.

The menu has an appealing mix of citified comfort food. Your country cousin surely never cooked like this, with dishes that may include a refreshing salad of smoked trout with beets and tart grapefruit, or a modern interpretation of roasted pork pozole in chile broth.

Sushi Zone

Japanese

A4

1815 Market St. (at Pearl St.)

Phone: 415-621-1114 — Dinner Mon – Sat
Web: N/A
Prices: $$

Sushi connoisseurs looking for the city's best aren't likely to find it at Sushi Zone, but that doesn't stop locals from lining the sidewalk to wait for one of a handful of tables or an old chrome stool at the counter. Situated at the spot where SoMa, the Mission, and Hayes Valley collide, Sushi Zone is a convenient spot for dinner after work.

Check the board for nightly specials, which may include hot items like baked mussels with spicy mayo and scallions or baked seabass with mango. Sushi meanwhile is fresh and simple: albacore, yellowtail, mackerel and salmon nigiri are above average and served over well-prepared rice; sweet papaya balances smoky *unagi* in a simple roll; and spicy hamachi maki is studded with avocado, jalapeño, and lime.

Town Hall

American

342 Howard St. (at Fremont St.)

Phone: 415-908-3900 — Lunch Mon – Fri
Web: www.townhallsf.com — Dinner nightly
Prices: $$

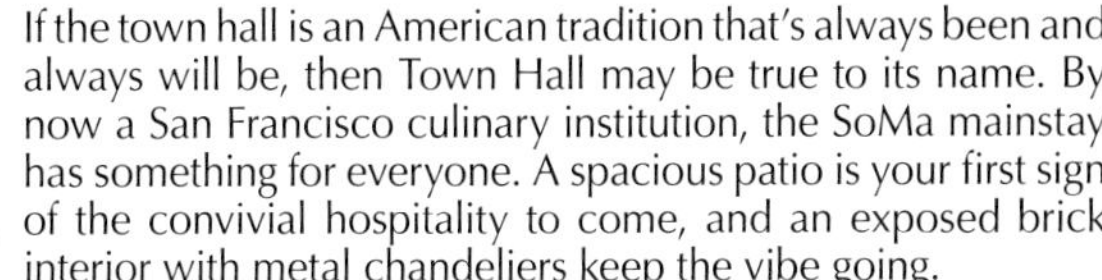

If the town hall is an American tradition that's always been and always will be, then Town Hall may be true to its name. By now a San Francisco culinary institution, the SoMa mainstay has something for everyone. A spacious patio is your first sign of the convivial hospitality to come, and an exposed brick interior with metal chandeliers keep the vibe going.

The flavor of the kitchen is American, of course, with unassuming yet crave-worthy fare. Crispy artichokes and Meyer lemon dress up a Dungeness crab salad; fresh cilantro and shaved radish garnish flavorful pulled pork enchiladas with goat cheese and *tomatillo* salsa; and warm beignets, with espresso ice cream and chicory streusel, beg you to order dessert—even when you couldn't possibly.

Tropisueño

75 Yerba Buena Ln. (bet. Market & Mission Sts.)

Phone: 415-243-0299 — Lunch & dinner daily
Web: www.tropisueno.com
Prices: ©©

Shaded by the dramatic, blue steel wing of the Contemporary Jewish Museum, Yerba Buena Lane is becoming a foodie destination for local art junkies and tourists alike. Tropisueño has something for everyone. At lunch, a taqueria-style counter serves tacos and tortas to professionals on the run; for those with time for a knife and fork, the super burrito *mojado* is a saucy siesta-inducer.

The restaurant dresses up a bit for dinner, delivering Latin American dishes like ceviche and tender chicken with *mole poblano*. A small salsa bar brims with jalapeños, sliced radishes, and tangy tomatillo salsa to pile on the mercifully thin chips.

But that's nothing compared to the expansive mahogany bar that oozes fine tequila and top-shelf margs.

Twenty Five Lusk

Contemporary

C3

25 Lusk St. (bet. 3rd & 4th Sts.)

Phone: 415-495-5875 — Lunch Sun
Web: www.25lusk.com — Dinner nightly
Prices: $$$

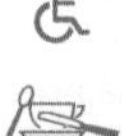

Well-known architect Cass Calder Smith gave this contemporary alley hideaway a high-industrial makeover and his professional hand shows at every turn, from the glassed-in exhibition kitchen and wine cellar to the suspended modular fireplaces that inspire stylish cocktailers to get cozy after work.

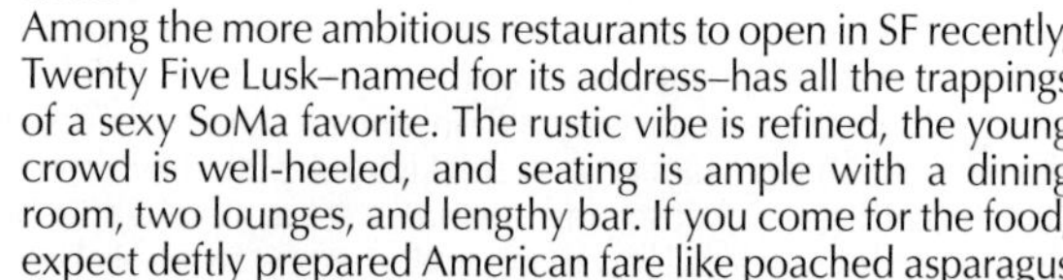

Among the more ambitious restaurants to open in SF recently, Twenty Five Lusk–named for its address–has all the trappings of a sexy SoMa favorite. The rustic vibe is refined, the young crowd is well-heeled, and seating is ample with a dining room, two lounges, and lengthy bar. If you come for the food, expect deftly prepared American fare like poached asparagus terrine with gravlax and smoked salmon caviar, or roast quail with olives and black rhubarb sauce.

Una Pizza Napoletana

Pizza

A4

210 11th St. (at Howard St.)

Phone: 415-861-3444 — Dinner Wed – Sat
Web: www.unapizza.com
Prices: $$

You get what you pay for at Una Pizza Napoletana, the New York to SoMa transplant that serves purely authentic pies at import prices. But, a bevy of regulars who race in to claim their tables clearly believe that Una Pizza is worth the premium.

There is no decor to speak of unless you count the assemblage of pizzas a product of high design. Make do with white walls and concrete floors, and don't expect your pizza to get any fancier. Just a few choices of 12-inch rounds come fire-licked and lightly topped. Try the Margherita with San Marzano tomatoes, basil, and buffalo mozzarella; or the smoky Ilaria, topped with arugula and cherry tomatoes, and named for the chef's own wife. Finish with an intense Neapolitan coffee served with a hunk of dark chocolate.

Waterbar

Seafood XX

D1

399 The Embarcadero (at Harrison St.)

Phone: 415-284-9922 — Lunch & dinner daily
Web: www.waterbarsf.com
Prices: $$$

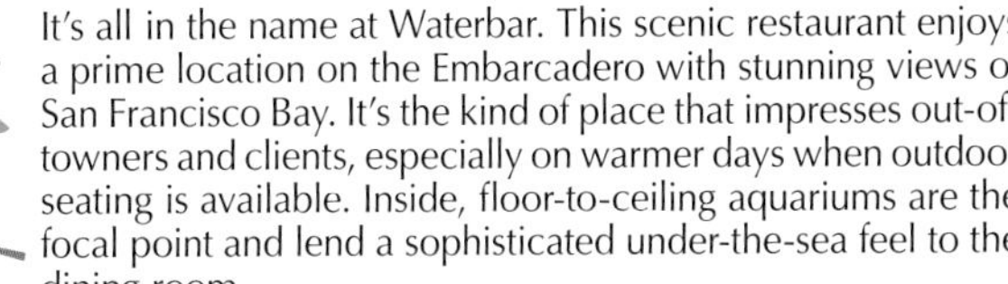

It's all in the name at Waterbar. This scenic restaurant enjoys a prime location on the Embarcadero with stunning views of San Francisco Bay. It's the kind of place that impresses out-of-towners and clients, especially on warmer days when outdoor seating is available. Inside, floor-to-ceiling aquariums are the focal point and lend a sophisticated under-the-sea feel to the dining room.

Of course, seafood anchors the comprehensive bill of fare, which even includes a separate daily shellfish menu featuring selections from across the country as well as fantastic desserts. Prix-fixe lunch and oyster specials are reasonable ways to sample the goods, and the bar menu has small plates all day. Not hungry? Just drink in the view at the swanky bar.

Yank Sing

Chinese X

D1

101 Spear St. (bet. Howard & Mission Sts.)

Phone: 415-957-9300 — Lunch daily
Web: www.yanksing.com
Prices: $$

Two tiny words will rouse any San Franciscan on Saturday morning: dim sum. The city's soup dumplings are legendary, and no one does them quite like Yank Sing, where Shanghai dumplings are stuffed with moist ground pork and a burst of juicy broth. Lengthy weekend waits are testament to each morsel's yummy goodness.

In the airy urban space, carts manned by servers wired with earpieces and mikes are loaded with steamed and fried delights then wheeled up to tables in rapid fire. Barbecue pork buns are smoky and tender; caramelized pot stickers are a standout; and sesame balls filled with sweet mung paste are a sticky, lovely finish. Over-ordering is a hazard here; mind that prices add up quickly.

Take heart in validated parking in the subterranean garage.

Zaré at Fly Trap

Middle Eastern XX

C2

606 Folsom St. (bet. 2nd & 3rd Sts.)

Phone: 415-243-0580 — Lunch Mon – Fri
Web: www.zareflytrap.com — Dinner Mon – Sat
Prices: $$

Nearly 20 years since Hoss Zaré emigrated from Iran and found a job at the Fly Trap to help pay for medical school, the chef/owner is still pursuing his passion in the kitchen he has long called home. A red awning marks the SoMa favorite where the spice-hued interior is as warm as the food.

Zaré himself can be found in the dining room nearly every evening, often serving his flavorful Medi-Middle Eastern fare himself, much to the delight of his regulars. The chef's kitchen turns out such mouthwatering dishes as braised duck with walnuts and pomegranate; lamb shank with black-eyed peas; and the best baklava in San Francisco. Having at last succumbed to the demand of his fans, Zaré now offers a Grill & Grain lunch menu of light salads, soups, and wraps.

Zero Zero

Pizza XX

C3

826 Folsom St. (bet. 4th & 5th Sts.)

Phone: 415-348-8800 — Lunch & dinner daily
Web: www.zerozerosf.com
Prices: $$

A modish neighborhood pizza newcomer, Zero Zero is named for the imported Neapolitan flour that gives these crusts their character. But for a taste of these bubbling Italian masterpieces, be prepared to wait and brave the din: reservations are elusive; and the bar (known for creative and carefully crafted drinks) is inevitably packed.

If you make it to a table beneath the colorful mural in the close-knit upstairs dining room, take advantage of the opportunity to feast. Start with antipasti or local squid à la plancha, then meander through a range of pies, many of which are named after San Francisco streets. The Margherita "Extra" is heaped with buffalo mozzarella, while the Fillmore forgoes the sauce in favor of leeks, fontina, and garlic.

MICHELIN

MICHELIN

East Bay

East Bay

Berkeley is legendary for its liberal politics and university campus that launched the 1960s Free Speech Movement. Among foodies, this is a Garden of Eden that sprouted American gastronomy's leading purist, Alice Waters, and continues to be a place of worship. Waters' Chez Panisse Foundation has nurtured the Edible Schoolyard, an organic garden and kitchen classroom for students; she also founded Slow Food Nation, the country's largest festival of slow and sustainable foods. Since Waters is credited with developing Californian cuisine, her influence can be tasted in myriad restaurants.

But, one needn't look much further than Berkeley's "gourmet ghetto." The North Shattuck corridor is aromatic with fresh-roasted joe from **Village Grounds** and fab take out from **Grégoire** and **Epicurious Garden**. This strip houses Co-ops like the **Cheese Board Collective**; the **Cheese Board Pizza Collective**; and the **Juice Bar Collective**. On Thursday afternoons, the **North Shattuck Organic Farmers Market** is crammed with local produce. **La Note**'s brioche *pain perdu* is lovely; **Tomate Café** proffers a Cuban breakfast on a pup-friendly patio; and **Caffe Mediterraneum** is the SF birthplace of the caffe latte. Berkeley is also home to **Acme Bread Company** and Chef Paul Bertolli's handcrafted **Fra'Mani Salumi**. Oakland doesn't quite carry the culinary panache of neighboring Berkeley, but the workaday city has seen a revival of its own with new businesses and condos. **Jack London Square** has stunning views of the bay, and crows the area's chief tourist destination for dining, nightlife, and a **Sunday Farmers and Artisan Market**. **Fentons Creamery** has served ice cream for 115 delicious years. Taco junkies congregate on International Boulevard for a taco feast; **Tacos Sinaloa** and **Mariscos Sinaloa** are known for chorizo and fish tacos, respectively. Downtown, crowds nosh on Po'boys at **Café 15**; in Temescal, **Bakesale Betty** serves crispy chicken sandwiches atop ironing board tables. After work, the **Trappist** pours over 160 Belgian and specialty beers.

On Sundays, oyster mongers line up at **Rudy Figueroa's** at the **Montclair Farmer's Market** for bivalves shucked to order. In August, the Art & Soul Festival brings a buffet of world flavors, as does the Chinatown Streetfest with curries galore and barbecue meats. In Rockridge, the quaint shopping district between Oakland and Berkeley, boutiques and eateries abound.

Tara's Organic Ice Cream serves unique flavors (imagine chile pistachio or basil) in compostible cups. **Market Hall** is a gourmet shopper's paradise with sustainable catch at **Hapuku Fish Shop**, specialty groceries at the **Pasta Shop**, a bakery, produce market, and coffee bar.

East Bay
Danville
Hotel
Restaurant
LAFAYETTE, WALNUT CREEK, DANVILLE
DANVILLE
BERKELEY
OAKLAND
ALBANY
EMERYVILLE
ROCKRIDGE
PIEDMONT
LAFAYETTE
WALNUT CREEK
DANVILLE
UNIV. OF CALIFORNIA BERKELEY
ALAMEDA NAVAL COMPLEX
COAST GUARD I.
BERKELEY AQUATIC PARK
MT. DIABLO STATE PARK
Rivoli
Fonda
China Village
Vanessa's Bistro
Bangkok Jam
Lalime's
César
Chez Panisse
Café Gratitude
Bistro Liaison
Corso
Zatar
Slow
La Rose Bistro
eVe
Ippuku
Zabu Zabu
Gather
FIVE
Tacubaya
Zut!
O Chamé
Anchalee
Sea Salt
900 Grayson
Kirala
Claremont Resort & Spa
Café Colucci
Wood Tavern
Riva Cucina
Addie's Pizza Pie
Zachary's Chicago Pizza
Oliveto
Á Côté
Uzen
Chu
Pizzaiolo
Hong Kong East Ocean
Barlata
Doña Tomás
Sahn Maru
Adesso
Ohgane
Dopo
Bay Wolf
Commis
Brown Sugar Kitchen
Camino
Boot & Shoe Service
Picán
Hawker Fare
Ikaros
Plum
Grand Avenue Thai
Sidebar
Hibiscus
Bellanico
Marzano
Lake Chalet
Tamarindo
Legendary Palace
Battambang
Champa Garden
Encuentro
Miss Pearl's Jam House
Bocanova
Metro Lafayette
Artisan Bistro
Lafayette Park
Chevalier
Elevé
Prima
Walnut Creek Yacht Club
Sasa
Va de Vi
Thai House
Bridges
The Peasant & The Pear
Esin
Laurus
BLACKHAWK MUSEUM
SAN FRANCISCO BAY
Inner Harbor
North Berkeley
Downtown
Ashby
Rockridge
MacArthur
19 St-Oakland
Oakland City Center-12 St
West Oakland
Lake Merritt
Walnut Creek
Lafayette

À Côté

B3 Mediterranean

5478 College Ave. (bet. Lawton & Taft Aves.), Oakland

Phone: 510-655-6469 Dinner nightly
Web: www.acoterestaurant.com
Prices: **$$**

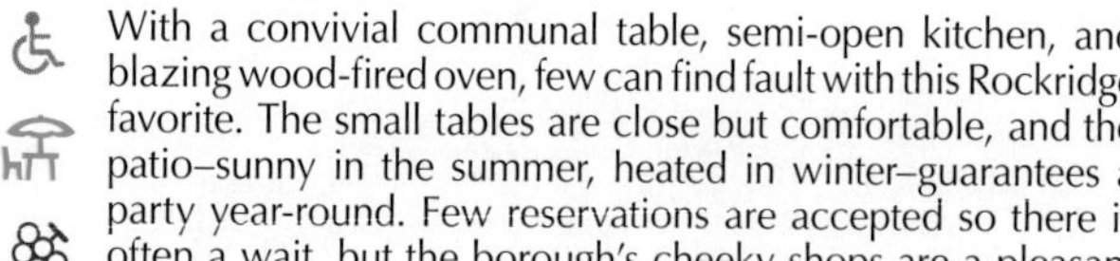

With a convivial communal table, semi-open kitchen, and blazing wood-fired oven, few can find fault with this Rockridge favorite. The small tables are close but comfortable, and the patio–sunny in the summer, heated in winter–guarantees a party year-round. Few reservations are accepted so there is often a wait, but the borough's cheeky shops are a pleasant way to pass the time. Singles might score seats at the bar.
Seasonal Mediterranean small plates are both simple and satisfying. Dip into a steaming *bollito* of sliced braised beef brisket soaking in rich broth or sample chunks of grilled lamb with pomegranate glaze. Finish with fluffy ricotta fritters, crisp gold and served with a trio of sweet sauces. Forty wines by the glass make pairing a snap.

Addie's Pizza Pie

B2 Pizza

3290 Adeline St. (at Alcatraz Ave.), Berkeley

Phone: 510-547-1100 Dinner Mon – Sat
Web: www.addiespizzapie.com
Prices: **$$**

Flourishes of graffiti and bars on nearby windows are telltale signs of this Berkeley neighborhood's rough-and-tumble past, but recent gentrification has brought promise to the East Bay alcove. As the Romans know, with civilization comes pizza, and there's no local shop doing it better than Addie's Pizza Pie, a festive joint with live music Thursdays in a historic Beaux-Arts building.
Sister to Temescal's Doña Tomas, Addie's red vinyl booths are a kitschy counterpoint to high arched windows and soaring painted columns. But the focus is on New York-style pies, piled high with toppings on puffed-up thin-crusts. Try the Southside, laden with spicy sausage, fennel, black olives, and quality mozzarella; team it with a Chef's salad for healthy good measure.

Adesso

Italian

B3

4395 Piedmont Ave. (at Pleasant Valley Rd.), Oakland

Phone: 510-601-0305 — Dinner Mon – Sat
Web: www.dopoadesso.com
Prices: $$

No matter what you call these salty delights (charcuterie, *salumi*, or…ahem…cold cuts), when it's good, it's good. And here at Adesso, carnivores come to ogle the 30 different varieties of superb, house-made *salumi*. This is truly an ode to meat with gifts like pâté paired with blood orange; tissue-thin ham slices; or the namesake "adesso" (Sicilian fennel seed pork salami) just begging to be wrapped over crunchy bread. A relation to nearby Dopo, Adesso attracts an after-work bunch with its wraparound bar (stocked with original cocktails), flatscreens, and foosball table. In addition to *salumi*, this cool watering hole also shows a nice, tasty selection of small plates including *antipasti* and panini all quickly served, and priced to please.

Anchalee

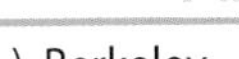

A2

1094 Dwight Way (at San Pablo Ave.), Berkeley

Phone: 510-848-4015 — Lunch & dinner daily
Web: www.anchaleethai.com
Prices:

A casual dining room with olive green walls, wood floors, exposed brick, and paintings of the Buddha himself (whose eyes are set in deep meditation) gives Anchalee an air of authenticity that sets it apart from other ethnic eateries crowding Berkeley. Stay clear of the lonely tables by the door—for what you gain in breeze, you lose in ambience. Instead make your way towards the cozy gas fireplace which cuts the chill on foggy days.

Tiny pendant lights cast a flattering glow on Anchalee's fresh, flavorful food. The ample selection of vegetarian choices keeps hungry herbivores (and Berkeley's college set) happy; while creative Thai entrées like basil, squid, and salmon fried rice make for exciting picks alongside trusty standbys like pad Thai and *satays*.

Artisan Bistro ☺

B1 French XX

1005 Brown Ave. (at Mt. Diablo Blvd.), Lafayette

Phone: 925-962-0882 Lunch & dinner Tue – Sun
Web: www.artisanlafayette.com
Prices: $$

Hearts carved into the exterior shutters are your first clue that this Craftsman cottage is an ideal hideaway for canoodling lovers. Duck into the cluster of cozy dining rooms where warm Dijon walls, local artwork, and a stone hearth work together to set the mood; or, on sunny days, bask on the umbrella-shaded patio.

No matter the season, Chef/owner John Marquez's Cal-French cuisine is right on cue. At lunch, roasted lamb shoulder and grilled portobello mushrooms make for fancy sandwiches; dinners are swankier. One might begin with a creamy foie gras mousse or vibrant baby beets, endives, and apples made decadent with herbed goat cheese. Entrées are hearty—think rabbit three ways or roasted chicken with terrine of leg, apples, and mustard.

Bangkok Jam

B1 Thai XX

1892 Solano Ave. (bet. Fresno Ave. & The Alameda), Berkeley

Phone: 510-525-3625 Lunch & dinner daily
Web: N/A
Prices: ☺☺

Taking up residence in Boran Thai's former digs, this ritzy replacement kicks it up a notch with fresh, creative twists on classic Thai. Vibrant paintings and vivid photos brighten the walls, while milky glass chandeliers illuminate a chic, modern space. If those luscious scents of coconut, basil, and lemongrass don't have your mouth watering, sate your buds with a "wrap and bite"—roasted coconut, peanuts, lime, ginger, and diced shrimp cradled in lettuce leaves, served with a savory ginger sauce. Or tuck into crispy shrimp and cream cheese "wontons," dress up prawns aside pineapple sweet and sour sauce.

Fresh produce and organic ingredients weave their way into a menu of salads, curries, noodle, and rice dishes; and affordable prices to boot.

Barlata

Spanish

B3

4901 Telegraph Ave. (at 49th St.), Oakland

Phone: 510-450-0678 Dinner nightly
Web: www.barlata.com
Prices:

Settled in the restaurant-rich Temescal neighborhood, Barlata's modest space is dressed up with funky can-inspired artwork, hanging hams, and quaint scooters. Canned food gets a bad rap, so in the tradition of so-wrong-it's-right, Barlata celebrates the *lata* which is, you guessed it, a can.

Yet, there's nothing lowbrow about Chef/owner Daniel Olivella's Spanish tapas. Happy hour delivers a flight of drink specials and $5 tapas courtesy of the Catalan native who conjures the Iberian Peninsula with small plates that include *lata de pulpo* featuring octopus and potatoes in adobo oil; *boquerones* with pears and Idiazabal cheese; paella; and the ubiquitous *patatas bravas*. Food stuffs like tuna, *pimenton*, and anchovies (canned of course) are available to-go.

Battambang

Cambodian

B4

850 Broadway (bet. 8th & 9th Sts.), Oakland

Phone: 510-839-8815 Lunch & dinner daily
Web: N/A
Prices:

Named for Cambodia's second largest city, Battambang is beloved by foodies with a taste for authentic cooking—which, oddly, is tough to find among the area's many Asian eateries. Fresh orchids and perky yellow walls enliven the modest room, where charming servers are proud and knowledgeable of the cuisine. Thai and Vietnamese influences are evident across the extensive menu; though these well-seasoned dishes are less spicy, that jar of garlic-chili sauce on each table allows self-spice gratification.

Expect the likes of charbroiled meats, pan-fried lemongrass catfish, and the vegetarian favorite *trorb aing* (smoky roasted eggplant in spicy lime sauce), as well as specialties that some may find intimidating, but others are sure to find delicious.

Bay Wolf 

Californian XX

B3

3853 Piedmont Ave. (at Rio Vista Ave.), Oakland

Phone: 510-655-6004 Dinner nightly
Web: www.baywolf.com
Prices: **$$**

In a wood-shingled house on Piedmont Avenue, Bay Wolf has been an Oakland icon since the 1970s. Even then, this quaint little haunt was at the forefront of the Slow Food movement and today still serves the kind of seasonal Californian fare that warms the soul: a rustic duck pâté is spread on toasty Acme bread with capers and cornichons, and celery root purée lends a little sweetness to grilled steelhead trout and crispy onions.

Chef/owner Michael Wild continues to run this show, greeting neighborhood regulars who crowd the heated patio and dining room, which is split in two by a small, central bar. Simple desserts are a pleasant cap to the meal. With layers of lemon curd and champagne gelée, the lime panna cotta is a mandatory indulgence.

Bellanico 

Italian XX

C4

4238 Park Blvd. (at Wellington St.), Oakland

Phone: 510-336-1180 Lunch & dinner daily
Web: www.bellanico.net
Prices: **$$**

A small wonder in Glenview, Bellanico is a kid- and foodie-friendly eatery tucked into a former flower shop with a new open kitchen and a warm palette. The Italian cuisine is both rustic and elegant: seasonal starters may include a savory goat cheese and pink peppercorn panna cotta with tomatoes and peaches, or juicy pork saltimbocca with fresh sage, prosciutto, and fig *agrodolce*. Entrée prices are a hearty welcome for budget-conscious gourmands.

For petite gourmands, bambino-sized pasta dishes are available with a choice of toppings. Parents can thank the owners' own tots, whose combined names form the amalgamation Bellanico. There is also a four-course dinner tasting menu for $26 that will appease the indecisive.

Bistro Liaison

French XX

B2

1849 Shattuck Ave. (at Hearst Ave.), Berkeley

Phone: 510-849-2155 — Lunch Sun – Fri
Web: www.liaisonbistro.com — Dinner nightly
Prices: $$

Pleasing droves for over a decade now, Bistro Liaison paints the very picture of a bistro with its handsome curved bar, open kitchen, luxurious banquettes, and a dining room done in yellow walls and burgundy accents highlighted by French posters and paintings.

Aluminum bins of fresh produce are a sign of what to expect from Chef Todd Kneiss, a former protégé of Roland Passot—French food for the soul made with a creative hand. Classics like *crevettes antibes* (sautéed prawns with garlic, cherry tomatoes, chilies, and arugula); and petrale sole stuffed with crab and licked with a shrimp and Cognac-cream sauce are sure to lift the spirits of any expat.

Dessert and cocktail choices are rubber-stamped on the white butcher paper that covers each table.

Bocanova

Latin American 

B4

55 Webster St. (at Jack London Square), Oakland

Phone: 510-444-1233 — Lunch & dinner daily
Web: www.bocanova.com
Prices: $$

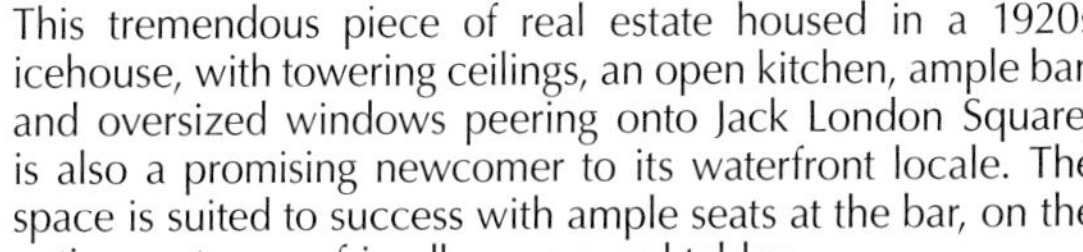

This tremendous piece of real estate housed in a 1920s icehouse, with towering ceilings, an open kitchen, ample bar, and oversized windows peering onto Jack London Square, is also a promising newcomer to its waterfront locale. The space is suited to success with ample seats at the bar, on the patio, or at group-friendly communal tables.

The pan-American cuisine focuses heavily on ocean dwellers and old-world tastes mixed with New World creativity. Flavors are bright in such dishes as halibut ceviche with cilantro and *ají amarillo*, and bowls of Yucatan seafood stew are perfectly prepared, yet other offerings are still finding their sea legs. Save room for dessert: the roasted banana cake with cashew brittle and red pepper sauce is a triumphant end.

Boot and Shoe Service

Pizza X

3308 Grand Ave. (bet. Lake Park Ave. & Mandana Blvd.), Oakland

Phone: 510-763-2668 Dinner Tue – Sun
Web: www.bootandshoeservice.com
Prices: $$

Can't get a table at Oakland's popular Pizzaiolo? Well, you may not have much luck at sister pizzeria, Boot and Shoe Service, either. Nevertheless, it's still well worth the wait. On a bustling stretch of Grand Avenue, this crammed casual eatery is also a favorite among East Bay locals looking for a quality pie in a low-key, family-friendly atmosphere.

Here you'll find exposed brick walls, laid-back service, and seats at a counter or bare tables that provide unassuming space for comforting Italian meals. Get your greens on in the form of tender asparagus with poached farm egg; then dig into signature seasonal pizzas topped with rapini and house-made fennel-pork sausage, or black olive and tomato with spicy arugula and shaved Grana Padano.

Bridges

International 

44 Church St. (at Hartz Ave.), Danville

Phone: 925-820-7200 Lunch Mon – Fri
Web: www.bridgesdanville.com Dinner nightly
Prices: $$

Robin Williams' fans may remember Bridges' cameo appearance in the 1993 hit *Mrs. Doubtfire*, but this Danville starlet stakes its true claim to fame in a consistent appeal to an East Bay audience. The cinematic setting is geared to special occasions with tangled vines and a trickling waterfall weaving romance on the patio. Inside, a mural of grand bridges spans one of the few walls not occupied by soaring windows.

Neighborly hospitality lends a small town vibe. The cuisine, however, explores the globe from Europe to Asia and back home again. Start with a hearty salad or a shrimp and avocado quesadilla; then, journey on with sautéed mahi mahi dressed in tangy pineapple salsa. The creamsicle parfait is a dressed-up end to a most enjoyable ride.

Brown Sugar Kitchen

American

A3

2534 Mandela Pkwy. (at 26th St.), Oakland

Phone: 510-839-7685 — Lunch Tue – Sun
Web: www.brownsugarkitchen.com
Prices: **$$**

Southern folks looking for a taste of home will find it in an unlikely spot: the industrial park that Chef Tanya Holland calls "Sweet West Oakland." In her Brown Sugar Kitchen, the French-trained chef whips local, organic ingredients into down-home goodness—think buttermilk fried chicken atop cornmeal waffles with brown sugar butter and apple cider syrup.

Grab a counter seat overlooking the kitchen and let the hunger seep in. Soulful breakfasts include cheddar grits with poached eggs, while lunches offer fried oyster Po'boys or baby back ribs glazed with brown sugar and pineapple. Wash it all down with a glass of wine from one of their many African-American producers. Don't miss the dessert counter brimming with snickerdoodle cookies and red velvet cake.

Café Colucci

6427 Telegraph Ave. (at 65th St.), Oakland

Phone: 510-601-7999 — Lunch & dinner daily
Web: www.cafecolucci.com
Prices:

Looks can be deceiving and such is the case with Café Colucci, an Ethiopian eatery with an Italian name. First-timers will find another world where red wall coverings and colorful tables carry the fragrance of foreign spices, many blended in house. Novices need not fret: a friendly, all-Ethiopian staff has your back.

The menus also offer a glossary of sorts, chock-full of enticing delicacies: *shouro fitfit*, or shards of crêpe-like *injera* bread with tomato and jalapeño in olive oil and spicy dressing; *kitfo*, lean raw beef with cardamom in spicy *mitmita*; and *doro wot*, delicate chicken simmered in a classic and delicious *berbere* sauce. Vegetarians and meat lovers can put aside their differences: with no utensils to speak of, we're all in this together!

Café Gratitude

Vegan

1730 Shattuck Ave. (at Virginia St.), Berkeley

Phone: 415-824-4652 — Lunch & dinner daily
Web: www.cafegratitude.com
Prices: ⊜

Picture a Berkeley café in the 1960s, where hippies sang Beatles tunes and bookshelves were stocked with spiritual tomes, and you have a clear image of Café Gratitude—the vegetarian eatery where you are likely to have your palm read as you sip a wheatgrass smoothie on the patio.

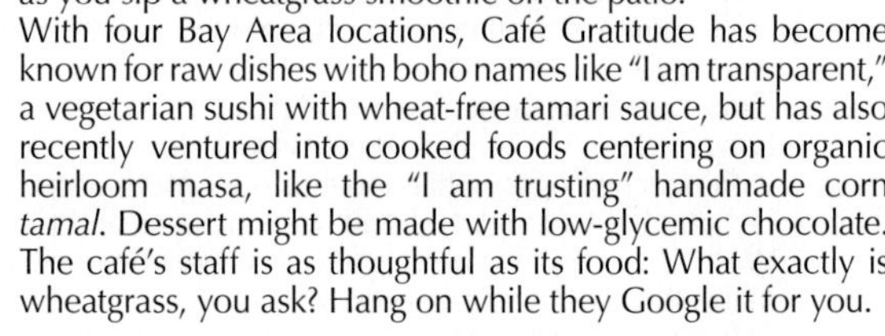

With four Bay Area locations, Café Gratitude has become known for raw dishes with boho names like "I am transparent," a vegetarian sushi with wheat-free tamari sauce, but has also recently ventured into cooked foods centering on organic heirloom masa, like the "I am trusting" handmade corn *tamal*. Dessert might be made with low-glycemic chocolate. The café's staff is as thoughtful as its food: What exactly is wheatgrass, you ask? Hang on while they Google it for you.

Camino

Californian

3917 Grand Ave. (at Sunny Slope Ave.), Oakland

Phone: 510-547-5035 — Lunch Sat – Sun
Web: www.caminorestaurant.com — Wed – Mon dinner only
Prices: $$

Escape from Oakland's Grand Avenue into Camino, a lofty Basque-style dining hall where pressed-tin ceilings and wrought-iron chandeliers hang above exposed brick and salvaged redwood communal tables lit by candles and lined with vintage church pews.

Mammoth bowls laden with fresh produce are a clue to what's on the menu: with 20-year Chez Panisse vet Russell Moore at the fire, you can count on perfectly rustic, seasonal fare. The menu is concise but has something for everyone. Watch from the butcher-block counter as cooks in flannel shirts grill Dungeness crabs; bake Tomales Bay oysters in absinthe; and turn out juicy duck breast from the wood-fired oven. Finish with moist bread pudding crowned by huckleberries, almonds, and crème fraîche.

César

Spanish

B1

1515 Shattuck Ave. (bet. Cedar & Vine Sts.), Berkeley

Phone: 510-883-0222 — Lunch & dinner daily
Web: www.barcesar.com
Prices: $$

While Chez Panisse remains a Berkeley big ticket, don't underestimate this lively neighboring tapas bar next door with all the Californian influence, indie soul, and simple cooking with Alice Waters alums running the show. Amusingly, the eatery is named for filmmaker Marcel Pagnol's character César, a café owner who sets about reuniting the estranged family of Honoré Panisse.

Spanish-style tapas may begin with *patatas rellenas*, potatoes stuffed with spicy chorizo and bathed in *queso Urgelia*, continuing with fresh fish or beef *a la plancha*, or *bocadillos*. The seasonal paella may be slow to develop but is rich in reward. Be sure to cap off meals with a selection from their black book of sherries, Madeiras, and ports.

A larger Latino sib is in nearby Oakland.

Champa Garden

Asian

B4

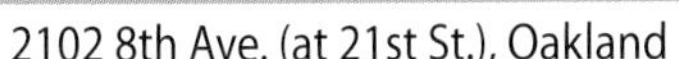

2102 8th Ave. (at 21st St.), Oakland

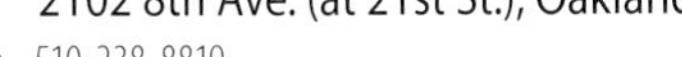

Phone: 510-238-8819 — Lunch & dinner daily
Web: www.champagarden.com
Prices: ⊖

Attention San Antonio area residents: Curious about the sumptuous scents wafting about the 'hood? Follow them straight to Champa Garden, where Thai, Vietnamese, and Laotian cuisines are served with authenticity. Inside, a small bar with indoor awning serves inexpensive beer and a full menu, while the deep rust dining room is equipped with a disco ball and TV monitor in the corner (karaoke anyone?).

Those overwhelmed by the options can begin with the fried rice ball salad–a tasty pile of crispy fried rice, crumbled pork, green onions, dried chilies, and lime juice, served with Romaine lettuce, mint, and cilantro–just wrap 'em up and enjoy the symphony of textures and flavors. Or rely on tasty dishes of old favorites, like the classic pad Thai.

East Bay

Chevalier

French XX

B1

960 Moraga Rd. (at Moraga Blvd.), Lafayette

Phone: 925-385-0793 Dinner Tue – Sun
Web: www.chevalierrestaurant.com
Prices: **$$**

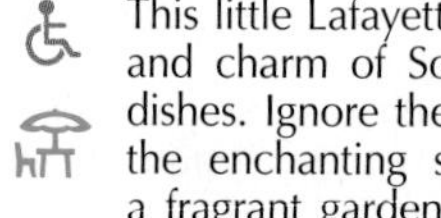

This little Lafayette neighborhood spot captures the warmth and charm of Southern France in its delightful seasonal dishes. Ignore the strip mall location and request a seat on the enchanting semi-circular patio, which winds around a fragrant garden stocked with herbs, flowers, and hedges for privacy. With white-clothed tables and soft French background music, the patio encourages romantic dinners on a warm evening.

The chef's passion fires the authentic fare, with appetizers of silky and tender *escargots de Bourgogne* in a pool of buttery garlic and parsley. Entrées may include roasted Colorado lamb with a spicy chorizo ragout and tarragon-lamb jus, followed by traditional desserts such as tarte Tatin, rich with the flavors of caramel and butter.

Chez Panisse

Californian XX

B1

1517 Shattuck Ave. (bet. Cedar & Vine Sts.), Berkeley

Phone: 510-548-5525 Dinner Mon – Sat
Web: www.chezpanisse.com
Prices: **$$$$**

For Californian cuisine, Chez Panisse has been the mother of invention for over 40 years now. The culinary icon, opened by Chef/owner Alice Waters in 1971, launched a cuisine as well as the careers of many top Bay Area chefs. The jewel of Berkeley's gourmet ghetto is shiny as she ever was: mature vines cover her wooden façade and patio, while antiqued mirrors and copper accents lend her interior a golden hue.

Chez Panisse is still packed to the hilt with locals and a few tourists eager to devour dishes made with organic produce fresh from local farms. Curious eaters may spy at the open kitchen for a view of the nightly fare, which might include a wonderful asparagus salad with roast pork or tea-smoked Sonoma duckling with morels and spring vegetables.

China Village

1335 Solano Ave. (at Pomona Ave.), Albany

Phone: 510-525-2285 Lunch & dinner daily
Web: www.chinavillagesolano.com
Prices: 

Chinese dwellers dominate this authentic Albany spot lauded for its faithful and fiery Mandarin- and Sichuan-style cuisines. If you're a heat-loving gourmand, China Village will happily oblige. While classics like *kung pao* share the stage with more esoteric offerings like thousand chili chicken or boiled kidney, save space for spectacles like the West Sichuan-style fish fillet bedecked with a startling number of dried red chilies. Don't be afraid as the server will filter them out, leaving a moderately piquant soup of delicate whitefish and cellophane noodles in a tasty broth.

The modest space–divided into a few banquet-style dining rooms with artfully decorated tables and tanks of live Dungeness crabs–is ideal for large groups and families.

Chu

5362 College Ave. (bet. Bryant & Manila Aves.), Oakland

Phone: 510-601-8818 Lunch Mon – Sat
Web: www.restaurantchu.com Dinner nightly
Prices: $$

A universe away from Oakland's grittier Chinatown, Chu serves urbane Chinese fare in Rockridge style. Dramatically dressed in black and white with high ceilings and sleek leather chairs, the restaurant draws its aesthetic influence from contemporary Chinese art.

Owners Dana and Philip Chu, also the proprietors behind Berkeley's Kirin, take an equally modern approach to cuisine. The open kitchen conceives such exotic fare as green onion pancakes laden with thin slices of flavorful smoked salmon, cilantro, and hoisin sauce; *ching hua* chili prawns laced with tongue-tingling Sichuan pepper; and expertly refined versions of classics such as pot stickers and spring rolls. In lieu of dessert, try a lychee oolong tea beautifully presented in an iron pot.

Commis ✿

B3 **Contemporary** XX

3859 Piedmont Ave. (at Rio Vista Ave.), Oakland

Phone: 510-653-3902 Dinner Wed – Sun
Web: www.commisrestaurant.com
Prices: $$$

Aaron Stienstra

While many San Franciscans attest that the best food is found within the city's walls, Commis proves that progressive cuisine knows no boundaries. This Oakland eatery opens up a new world of dining to foodies who want to try something different and head for the hinterlands (for those urbanites who believe that anything outside of the Mission is a foreign country).

Here, everyone's focal point is the showpiece kitchen taking center stage in the middle of the dining room. Reserve a seat at the bar if you don't want to miss one spoon's worth of action, or sit among the hip twenty- and thirty-somethings who populate the black leather chairs and light wood tables.

Commis gets right to the point with one of the most concise menus around. It's multi-course and there is little wiggle room when ordering, but quell your high-maintenance ways and be rewarded with a tasty array of contemporary cuisine. Dishes includes the likes of delicate oysters poached in unfermented apple cider, adorned with velvety sunchoke cream; or roulades of pressed guinea fowl that have been cured, braised, and deliciously crisped. Even better, opt for the menu with special wine pairings for each course—even dessert.

Corso

Italian

B2

1788 Shattuck Ave. (bet. Delaware & Francisco Sts.), Berkeley

Phone: 510-704-8004 Dinner nightly
Web: www.trattoriacorso.com
Prices: $$

Wining and dining her way through Tuscany was hard work for Wendy Brucker, who now shows off the fruits of her labor at Corso in Berkeley. Mementos of her Florentine travels can be found in framed souvenir menus, an all-Italian wine list–poured by taste, glass, or carafe–and in the traditional *bistecca alla Fiorentina*, named for the Renaissance city's Trattoria Sostanza. Nosh on Dungeness crab toast; butternut squash and potato gnocchi; then perhaps panna cotta for dessert. Most menu items are under $20.

True to Tuscany, Corso's dining room is simply set. The best seats may be at the granite kitchen counter where meat lovers will enjoy the view of dangling, house-cured *salumi*. Movie buffs can dig into black-and-white Italian films over the bar.

Doña Tomás

Mexican 

B3

5004 Telegraph Ave. (bet. 49th & 51st Sts.), Oakland

Phone: 510-450-0522 Dinner Tue – Sat
Web: www.donatomas.com
Prices: $$

Follow the freshly fashioned Yupsters through revitalized Temescal, which is fast becoming Oakland's own up and coming arts community, to this Mexican highlight of the local culinary scene. Upbeat Latin music pulses through the dining room, and the later it gets, the higher the volume climbs. Evenings may begin with a margarita at the small corner bar and end with coffee in the inviting back courtyard.

Regional Mexican and Californian cuisines offer seasonal flair, fusing into favorites like *antojitos* featuring *sopes* with poblano cream, chanterelle, and cremini mushrooms; or *entradas* of plump chile rellenos stuffed with raisins, pinenuts, and *queso*.

While the price tag is higher than the neighborhood taqueria, quality is what stands out here.

Dopo

B3

4293 Piedmont Ave. (at Echo St.), Oakland

Phone: 510-652-3676 — Lunch Mon – Fri
Web: www.dopoadesso.com — Dinner Mon – Sat
Prices: $$

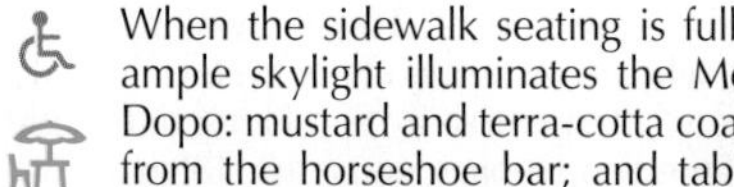

When the sidewalk seating is full on sunny afternoons, an ample skylight illuminates the Mediterranean colors inside Dopo: mustard and terra-cotta coat the walls; azure tiles glint from the horseshoe bar; and tables are made of platinum blonde pine wood.

With California in the heart and Italy on the mind, Chef/owner Jon Smulewitz, a veteran of nearby mainstay Oliveto, relies on fresh ingredients grown close to home for simply satisfying meals at lunch and dinner. Locals gravitate to *antipasti* and Neapolitan pizzas like the namesake Dopo, with oregano, chili flakes, and Pecorino Romano; calzones stuffed with basil, ricotta, and chanterelles; and a selection of crudi at dinner. *Salumi* junkies should also try sister restaurant Adesso, down the street.

Élevé

Vietnamese

C1

1677 N. Main St. (1677 N. Main St.), Walnut Creek

Phone: 925-979-1677 — Lunch Tue – Fri
Web: www.eleverestaurant.com — Dinner Tue – Sun
Prices: $$

Across from City Hall in Walnut Creek, Élevé has broad portrait windows that invite the hungry wanderer. Inside, where natural light and a stunning quartzite bar lend a welcoming, modern vibe, cocktail hounds appreciate such creative pours as the "Sleepy Head," a concoction of brandy, ginger, and mint; while burled wood tabletops are a warm surface for family-style Vietnamese meals.

The fusion cuisine is laden with crisp flavors in entrées such as spicy steak salad with watercress, daikon radish, and jalapeños; and chicken *zao lan* with yellow coconut curry, mushrooms, and sweet onion. Vegetarians will find plenty of dishes to satisfy them, including garlic tofu and spicy root curry. Noodle lovers must also try sister restaurant Pho84 in Oakland.

Encuentro

Vegetarian

202 2nd St. (at Jackson St.), Oakland

Phone: 510-832-9463 Dinner Tue – Sat
Web: www.encuentrooakland.com
Prices: 

While many Bay Area restaurants go hog wild for meaty menus showcasing charcuterie and *porchetta,* the chef's club at Encuentro continues to practice the art of high vegetarian cuisine. Lauded in San Francisco as a vegetarian's haven, this is a welcome addition to the burgeoning neighborhood of Jack London Square.

Natural light fills the tiny corner spot where rugs warm the concrete floors and a handful of tables and wine counter seating yield a cozy getaway from the din of the square. Amidst a simple yet welcoming setting, vegans may feast on pâtés made from nuts and truffled mushrooms, while others take their time and their tomato bread pudding with a regal crown of Humboldt Fog cheese. The wine bar is a mellow spot for deviled eggs and roasted nuts.

Esin

Mediterranean

750 Camino Ramon (at Sycamore Valley Rd. W.), Danville

Phone: 925-314-0974 Lunch & dinner daily
Web: www.esinrestaurant.com
Prices: **$$**

From its plot in Danville's Rose Garden marketplace, Esin feels fresh with soft yellow walls and dark wood trim, as if it just sprouted yesterday. In fact, Esin is actually a transplant that flourished for 10 years in San Ramon.

Here, it continues to please crowds with well-executed, homey fare that takes a cue from the Turkish roots of Chef/owner Esin deCarion, whose name means "inspiration." Working together with her husband and co-owner, this kitchen team turns out such Cal-Med dishes as apple-cured gravlax with grilled bread and caperberry butter; and a fillet of petrale sole cooked meunière-style with lemon-caper beurre blanc. Desserts are tasty and homemade, like the rich and subtly sweet banana cream pie with a dark chocolate cookie crust.

eVe

Contemporary XX

B2

1960 University Ave. (bet. Martin Luther King Jr. Way and Milvia St.), Berkeley

Phone: 510-868-0735 Dinner Tue – Sat
Web: www.eve-berkeley.com
Prices: $$

The choices may be limited but everything is worth a taste at eVe, a sleek University Avenue eatery. This ultimate neighborhood spot stays simple with black leather banquettes, bare tables, and a minimalist display of art. The clean stainless steel kitchen is a gallery for well-edited cuisine—just four starters and three entrées each night.

The open workspace is home to Chef/owners Veronica and Christopher Laramie, who turn out two-course prix-fixe dinners perhaps including squid ink risotto with tender calamari, black radish, and kumquat compote; or seared butcher's steak with seasonal garnish. Two desserts and a cheese course are also available. Look for an excellent dark chocolate *cremeaux* infused with Peruvian *lucuma* fruit and Thai tea ice cream.

FIVE

American XX

B2

2086 Allston Way (at Shattuck Ave.), Berkeley

Phone: 510-845-7300 Lunch & dinner daily
Web: www.five-berkeley.com
Prices: $$

Housed in the sparkling Hotel Shattuck Plaza, a glossy checkered floor leads the way to FIVE's charismatic dining room—a stylish feast for the eyes with towering columns and discreet red jewel tones that illuminate the bright space. The sophisticated setting is relaxed and comfortable, but taste is assured, as American favorites are deliciously reimagined.

Expect to enjoy flavorful comfort food that is beautifully evident in dishes such as braised pork belly with cider vinegar glaze and apple-walnut salad; short rib pot roast with horseradish-Yukon Gold purée and red wine jus; or creamy macaroni and cheese starring orzo and braised morel mushrooms topped with tangy tomato jam. Be sure to save room for freshly made, homespun desserts.

Fonda

Latin American

1501 Solano Ave. (at Curtis St.), Albany

Phone: 510-559-9006 — Lunch Sat – Sun
Web: www.fondasolana.com — Dinner nightly
Prices: $$

Part of the restaurant empire of Haig and Cindy Krikorian, this festive Albany hot spot showcases creative Latin American cuisine and drinks to match. A long inviting bar offers views of the open kitchen, while the upstairs mezzanine sports a comfortable, lounge-y feel with its upholstered chairs. Mavens of the late-night scene drop in for happy hour, which starts here after 9:00 P.M. every night.

The original menu spotlights favorites such as Veracruz-style seafood cocktail with Caribbean white shrimp, mahi mahi, and avocado; or grilled skirt steak with Manchego-flavored onion rings and mojo Colorado. Drop in for an afternoon "siesta" menu featuring rum cocktails and a selection of tapas, or go earlier for their weekend brunch.

Gather

Californian

2200 Oxford St. (at Allston Way.), Berkeley

Phone: 510-809-0400 — Lunch & dinner daily
Web: www.gatherrestaurant.com
Prices: $$

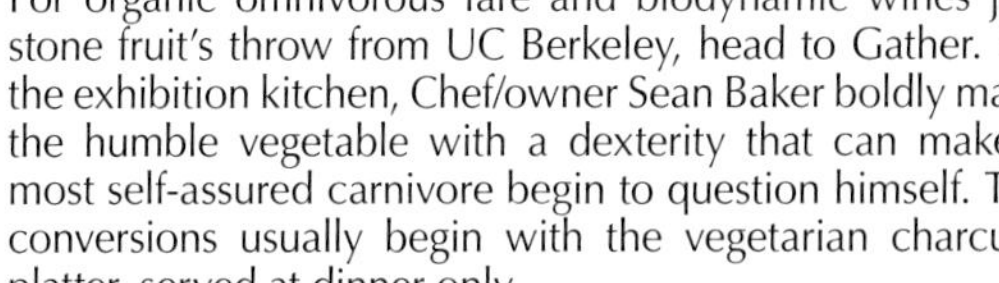

For organic omnivorous fare and biodynamic wines just a stone fruit's throw from UC Berkeley, head to Gather. From the exhibition kitchen, Chef/owner Sean Baker boldly masters the humble vegetable with a dexterity that can make the most self-assured carnivore begin to question himself. These conversions usually begin with the vegetarian charcuterie platter, served at dinner only.

This is campus territory where a festive collegiate vibe rules and the organic specialty cocktails flow freely. Vegetarians may opt for the stinging nettle pizza, topped with smoked mozzarella and olive caper sauce, while meat lovers relish the young chicken "under a brick."

The pumpkin cheesecake may be a crowdpleaser, but its pistachio crust is a revelation.

Grand Avenue Thai

Thai

384 Grand Ave. (bet. Perkins St. & Staten Ave.), Oakland

Phone: 510-444-1507 — Lunch Mon – Sat
Web: www.grandavenuethai.com — Dinner nightly
Prices: $$

Dying to appease your hunger pangs after a jog around Lake Merritt? What's better than Grand Avenue Thai with its chic and cheery décor showing bright walls, splashes of color from fresh flowers on every table, and evocative artwork created by the chef's friend?

A comfy space for sampling contemporary Thai cuisine, Grand Avenue fills daily with the Oakland workaday crowd looking for a lunchtime pick-me-up. Spice lovers may be disappointed (the kitchen turns down the heat to suit Western palates), but dishes are nonetheless packed with flavor. House favorites include roast duck in red coconut curry studded with basil and veggies; grilled marinated rack of lamb gleaming with a spicy garlic sauce; and a tasty array of Thai noodle and barbecue dishes.

Hawker Fare

Asian

2300 Webster St. (at 23rd St.), Oakland

Phone: 510-832-8896 — Lunch Mon – Fri
Web: www.hawkerfare.com — Dinner Thu – Sat
Prices: $$

Street carts often dole out some of the tastiest food you can find, but who wants to stand on a street corner as you nibble and nosh? Salvation can be found at Hawker Fare. This Oakland newcomer brings the flavors of Southeast Asian street carts inside to a funky, but friendly, space filled with graffiti-decorated walls and stained concrete floors.

Mostly Thai in influence, the inexpensive menu features appetizers and main course rice bowls topped with everything from lemongrass chicken and pork belly to *issan* sausage and beef short ribs. Tasty salads like the beef *larb* with grilled beef and fish sauce-lime vinaigrette; and the Hawker *affogato*, made with condensed milk-flavored soft-serve ice cream and a shot of Thai coffee, are especially refreshing.

Hibiscus

Caribbean

B4

1745 San Pablo Ave. (at 18th St.), Oakland

Phone: 510-444-2626 — Lunch Fri
Web: www.hibiscusoakland.com — Dinner Wed – Sun
Prices: $$

Something special is brewing in Sarah Kirnon's kitchen. The Barbados-raised chef wields her island-inspired talent like a fiery wand, transforming locally sourced products into plates of Caribbean and Creole-style deliciousness. Island grooves flow through the dining room, where smoky brown walls display floral paintings while white linens and rattan seating create a warm elegance. Begin with rock shrimp and egg salad featuring chopped romaine, pimiento-stuffed olives, and hearts of palm in a sugarcane vinaigrette. Next, nosh on Miss Ollie's Fried Chicken—tender pieces snuggled between zesty potato salad on one side and sautéed kale and sweet corn on the other.

Refresh with homemade ginger limeade, and save room for panna cotta with drunken cherries.

Hong Kong East Ocean

Chinese

A3

3199 Powell St., Emeryville

Phone: 510-655-3388 — Lunch & dinner daily
Web: www.hkeo.us
Prices: 

Cantonese dishes, fresh seafood, and dim sum are the main reasons crowds flock to this massive pagoda-roofed restaurant that flanks the Bay. Here, diners enjoy fantastic views of the nearby marina, Bay Bridge, and San Francisco skyline through the large windows that define the space.

This place is meant for family-style dining, so bring a few relatives or friends and try the special set menu available for four, six, or eight. Or choose from the regular bill of fare, which includes fish from the massive tanks along one wall. At lunchtime, opt for dim sum; check off a sampling of items from the written list, and moments later they parade from the kitchen one by one.

Plenty of banquet rooms accommodate groups from business meetings to birthday parties.

East Bay

Ikaros

Greek XX

B4

3268 Grand Ave. (bet. Mandana Blvd. & Santa Clara Ave.), Oakland

Phone: 510-899-4400 Lunch & dinner daily
Web: www.ikarosgr.com
Prices:

While there are no white, sandy beaches here, the soothing Grecian vibe, Greek patrons, and scrumptious bites will take you at least part of the way to the Greek Isles. Inside, Mediterranean blues and whites color the high-arched ceiling, where a long skylight evokes that sublime island feel; framed photos of the coast, white stone sculptures, and Greek music seal the deal.

Sit down to an order of tangy *dolmades* (stuffed grape leaves), packed with rice and fresh herbs, served with a thick yogurt sauce. Next sink your teeth into a gyros stacker—chunks of seasoned lamb and chicken, served with pita, thick steak fries, sliced red onion, tomato, and *tzatziki*. The classic spanakopita filled with spinach, dill, and feta, is crispy and delicious.

Ippuku

Japanese X

B2

2130 Center St. (bet. Oxford St. & Shattuck Ave.), Berkeley

Phone: 510-665-1969 Dinner nightly
Web: www.ippukuberkeley.com
Prices: **$$**

East Bay *shochu* lovers belly up to the bar at Ippuku, a Berkeley yakitori spot celebrating that indigenous Japanese libation. Evenings here begin with Shochu School, offered nightly from 5:00 to 6:00 P.M., with half-priced drinks for novices and aficionados alike. Plan to take the BART—the station is across the street.

Yet this is an *izakaya*, with equal focus on its excellent, very authentic Japanese small plates and listing of yakitori specials. A recommendation from a hip young server may include delights such as bacon-wrapped *mochi*, while simple souls appreciate crispy chicken wings flecked with sea salt. White meat chicken tartare may sound bizarre, but with sesame, spicy *togarashi* and daikon sprouts, this eggy oddity is surprisingly delicious.

Kirala

2100 Ward St. (at Shattuck Ave.), Berkeley

Phone: 510-549-3486 — Lunch Mon – Fri
Web: www.kiralaberkeley.com — Dinner nightly
Prices: 

Situated only a stone's throw from Berkeley Bowl (the area's market mecca), Kirala is a favorite neighborhood haunt. The dining room is fittingly restrained and echoes such eclectic beats as reggae, jazz, and Latin; and with a spectrum of over 30 sake varieties, Kirala is a natural selection for Japanophiles around the Berkeley way.

Nature plays a pivotal role in the form of fresh seafood, and daily market specials are displayed on a whiteboard above the bar, which is staffed by experts who take great care while preparing perfectly steamed sticky rice, topped with hamachi or crimson *maguro*; bowls of steaming soba and udon; and grilled items like skewered baby lobster tails, lamb chops, bacon-wrapped asparagus, and chicken-stuffed mushrooms.

Lake Chalet

1520 Lakeside Dr. (bet. 14th & 17th Sts.), Oakland

Phone: 510-208-5253 — Lunch & dinner daily
Web: www.thelakechalet.com
Prices: **$$**

In a remodeled boathouse on Lake Merritt, Lake Chalet impresses with refined American classics that promise to inspire its beach-destination competitors with large portions of carefully prepared, familiar fare in a setting that is infinitely "travel-friendly" but never touristy.

The tremendous space hosts tables upstairs and down, as well as on the picturesque pier in the company of gulls and geese. On a sunny day, the serene view from the 80-foot marble bar is attractive to out-of-towners looking for an escape from urban Oakland. The menu depends on where you sit (more formal in the dining room, casual outdoors), but expect such favorites as fresh oysters; petrale sole *piccata* with fried capers and spicy cress; and a luscious coconut cream pie.

Lalime's

International

A1

1329 Gilman St. (bet. Neilson & Peralta Aves.), Berkeley

Phone: 510-527-9838 — Dinner nightly
Web: www.lalimes.com
Prices: $$

Owners Haig and Cindy Krikorian still know how to throw a party. Like sister restaurants Sea Salt and T-Rex Barbecue, Lalime's is a local favorite, drawing an affable crowd of regulars who congregate upstairs for lively meals near the bar, fireplace, and semi-open kitchen. Couples and quiet types prefer the downstairs dining room where citrus-hued walls add a friendly vibe and storefront windows offer a view of the neighborhood.

The staff is attentive and knowledgeable of the cuisine, which marries diverse cultural influences with California's seasonal-organic philosophy. Dishes may include squab with apple, chestnut, and bacon bread pudding; Idaho pork "prime rib" with honey mustard glaze; and Maine lobster cake with satsuma oranges and curry aïoli.

La Rose Bistro

French

B2

2037 Shattuck Ave. (at Addison St.), Berkeley

Phone: 510-644-1913 — Lunch Mon – Fri
Web: N/A — Dinner nightly
Prices: $$

Painted with pastel hues and pastoral murals, La Rose is equally good for a casual lunch, family get-together, or romantic evening out. This laid back bistro is located in Berkeley's theater district (on the one way, north bound bit of Shattuck), attracting drama lovers as well.

A meal here begins with fresh-baked French bread and an herbaceous cilantro pesto for dipping. Then come consistently well-prepared French classics, such as *entrecôte frites* and duck confit with Madeira sauce. Californian touches stand out in succulent roasted medallions of pork with honeyed apples and rosemary jus.

Lunch may offer sandwiches such as the *pain bagnat* stuffed with tuna, olives, anchovies, and egg, as well as a full complement of main courses.

Laurus

Mediterranean XX

3483 Blackhawk Circle Dr. (at Tassajara Ranch Dr.), Danville

Phone: 925-984-2250 — Lunch Tue – Fri
Web: www.laurussf.com — Dinner nightly
Prices: $$

Dressed in hues of olive and bay leaf, draped in tawny curtains that open to koi ponds and fountains, Laurus is a Mediterranean oasis situated in buzzing Blackhawk Plaza. A wall of windows illuminates the spacious dining room where the Green Fairy, contained in an absinthe dispenser, flutters on a curved stone bar.

The clipboard menu is served all day, perhaps featuring braised wild boar Bolognese atop al dente tagliatelle to pair with wines selected from Italy, Spain, and France. Truffled honey mustard glazes a crispy half chicken served with a sophisticated mac 'n' cheese made with *cavatelli*. Like much of the menu, desserts are kid-friendly, as in flaky apple tart topped with granola, aged cheddar, and caramel gelato.

Legendary Palace

Chinese XX

708 Franklin St. (at 7th St.), Oakland

Phone: 510-663-9188 — Lunch & dinner daily
Web: N/A
Prices: ⊜

A bright red and gold color scheme greets guests at Legendary Palace, in the heart of Oakland's Chinatown. Everything is large at Legendary—imagine rambling dining rooms with 600 guests spread over two floors. Yet, this literal palace of Chinese cuisine keeps the quality. Inside, the décor is surprisingly elegant with plush red chairs, twinkling chandeliers, and gold curtains framing floor-to-ceiling windows.

During dim sum hour, carts circulate amid close-knit tables unveiling a treasure trove of tasty gems including shrimp and water chestnut dumplings; chicken feet with black bean sauce; sliced barbecued pork; and egg custard tarts. An à la carte selection spotlights Cantonese specialties and seafood fresh from the aquarium tanks in the back.

Marzano

Pizza

4214 Park Blvd. (at Glenfield Ave.), Oakland

Phone: 510-531-4500 — Lunch Sat – Sun
Web: www.marzanorestaurant.com — Dinner nightly
Prices: $$

This Oakland eatery takes its name from the town located on the volcanic slopes that produce the world's best tomatoes, and Marzano strives to honor this legacy. Gothic chandeliers and hand-blown glass wine casks illuminate the timber beams and brick walls, while an 800-degree fire in the wood-burning pizza oven casts a glow on the kitchen. Tip your hat to the *pizzaiolo*: his blood and sweat are your tears of joy.

Charred and chewy Neapolitan pies are pure perfection whether you choose the simple Margherita or a specialty topped with calamari, pecorino, and spicy tomato. Begin with *gnocchi alla Romana* set on goat cheese and wilted spinach or fire-roasted winter squash with *burrata* cheese and marjoram. The close-knit bar is ideal for antipasti and *vino*.

Metro Lafayette

Californian

3524 Mt. Diablo Blvd. (bet. 1st St. & Oak Hill Rd.), Lafayette

Phone: 925-284-4422 — Lunch & dinner daily
Web: www.metrolafayette.com
Prices: $$

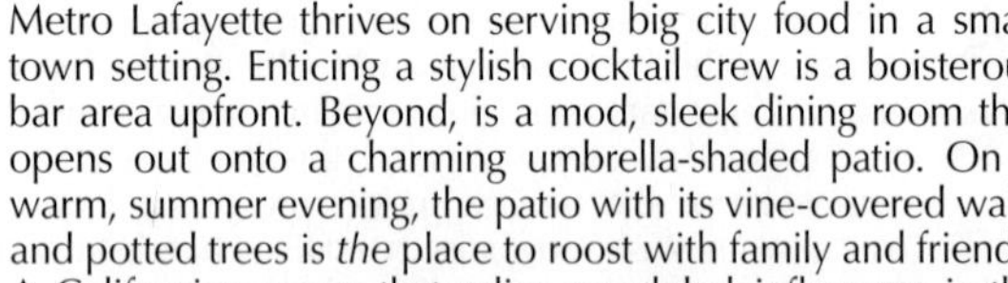

Metro Lafayette thrives on serving big city food in a small town setting. Enticing a stylish cocktail crew is a boisterous bar area upfront. Beyond, is a mod, sleek dining room that opens out onto a charming umbrella-shaded patio. On a warm, summer evening, the patio with its vine-covered walls and potted trees is *the* place to roost with family and friends.

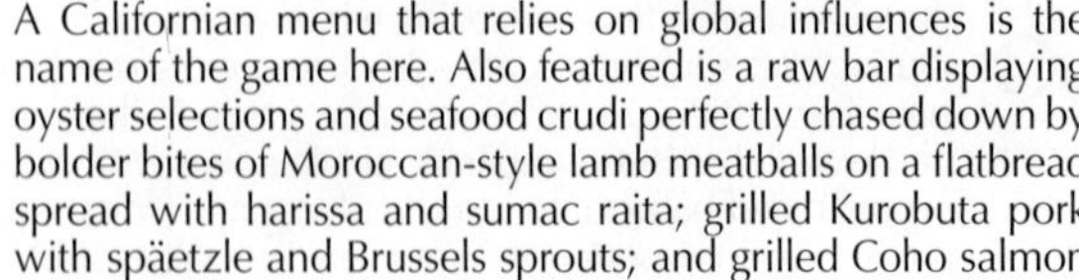

A Californian menu that relies on global influences is the name of the game here. Also featured is a raw bar displaying oyster selections and seafood crudi perfectly chased down by bolder bites of Moroccan-style lamb meatballs on a flatbread spread with harissa and sumac raita; grilled Kurobuta pork with späetzle and Brussels sprouts; and grilled Coho salmon topped with spinach and mushrooms.

Miss Pearl's Jam House

Caribbean XX

1 Broadway (at The Embarcadero), Oakland

Phone: 510-444-7171 — Lunch & dinner daily
Web: www.misspearlsjamhouse.com
Prices: $$

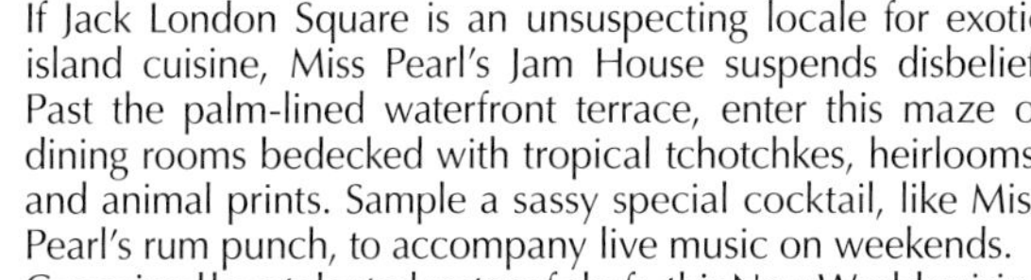

If Jack London Square is an unsuspecting locale for exotic island cuisine, Miss Pearl's Jam House suspends disbelief. Past the palm-lined waterfront terrace, enter this maze of dining rooms bedecked with tropical tchotchkes, heirlooms, and animal prints. Sample a sassy special cocktail, like Miss Pearl's rum punch, to accompany live music on weekends.

Conceived by a talented roster of chefs, this New World cuisine is both fun and familiar. Flavors of Cuba, the Caribbean, and the Bahamas tickle the palate at Miss Pearl's, which might also be the pearly gates for fried food aficionados—look for fried Louisiana catfish beside Cajun tartar sauce; or Creole shrimp poppers and crisp sweet plantains with creamy lime sauce. Jerk chicken lovers are also in heaven.

900 Grayson

American

900 Grayson St. (at 7th St.), Berkeley

Phone: 510-704-9900 — Lunch Mon – Sat
Web: www.900grayson.com
Prices: ⊜

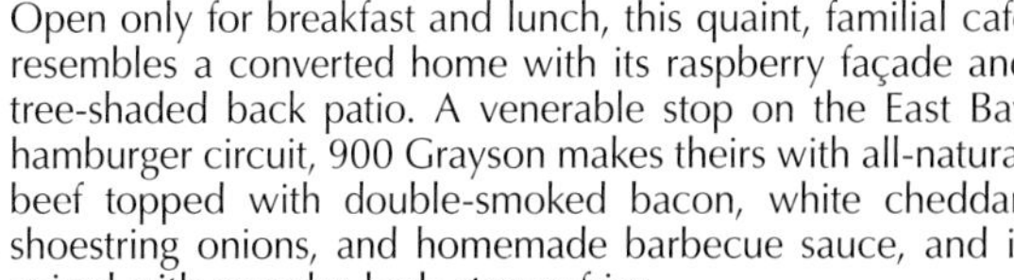

Open only for breakfast and lunch, this quaint, familial café resembles a converted home with its raspberry façade and tree-shaded back patio. A venerable stop on the East Bay hamburger circuit, 900 Grayson makes theirs with all-natural beef topped with double-smoked bacon, white cheddar, shoestring onions, and homemade barbecue sauce, and is paired with crunchy, herb-strewn fries.

If that isn't decadent enough for you, their spin on fried chicken and waffles (the Demon Lover) headlines boneless chicken paillard in a peppery breading accompanied by a crispy buttermilk waffle and your choice of country-style gravy or Vermont maple syrup. With a few bottles of hot sauce to perk things up, vegetarians are just as happy to substitute seitan for the chicken.

O Chamé

Asian

1830 4th St. (bet. Hearst Ave. & Virginia St.), Berkeley

Phone: 510-841-8783 — Lunch & dinner daily
Web: N/A
Prices: **$$**

The piping hot bowls of soba and udon soup at this high-end noodle house are a go-to treat for shoppers in Berkeley's Fourth Street neighborhood. On sunny days, the patio is an ideal perch for people watching; those on the go will takeout a bento box, although it may have lost some of its caché when it officially became a menu item and no longer the exclusive domain of in the know foodies.

Inside, peaceful scenes of the Orient are etched into honey-hued walls, and earthenware dishes are heaped with the likes of sweet corn and green onion pancakes, grilled local sardines, and seared tuna sashimi with braised leeks and horseradish sauce. Try the tender beef tongue with grilled artichoke hearts or save room for a unique dessert, like sherry custard.

Ohgane

3915 Broadway (bet. 38th & 40th Sts.), Oakland

Phone: 510-594-8300 — Lunch & dinner daily
Web: www.ohgane.com
Prices:

A mix of Korean businessmen and local families flock to Oakland's Ohgane with one intention—to devour their gargantuan (and constantly refilled) lunch buffet prettily priced at $10. Clearly an authentic holding cell for all things Korean, foodies come to savor such terrific treats as fried mackerel; buckwheat noodles; *bi bim bap*; and a flurry of barbecued meats served with soups, salads, noodles, rice, and kimchi—think crunchy daikon, fiery with vinegar, red chili paste, and garlic.

On Monday, Tuesday, and Wednesday nights, the barbecued meats dinner buffet takes center stage. Cooked over mesquite wood or prepared by the diners themselves on table-top grills, these hearty delicacies are especially beloved by the local Korean cliques.

Oliveto

5655 College Ave. (at Shafter Ave.), Oakland

Phone: 510-547-5356 Lunch Mon – Fri
Web: www.oliveto.com Dinner nightly
Prices: **$$$**

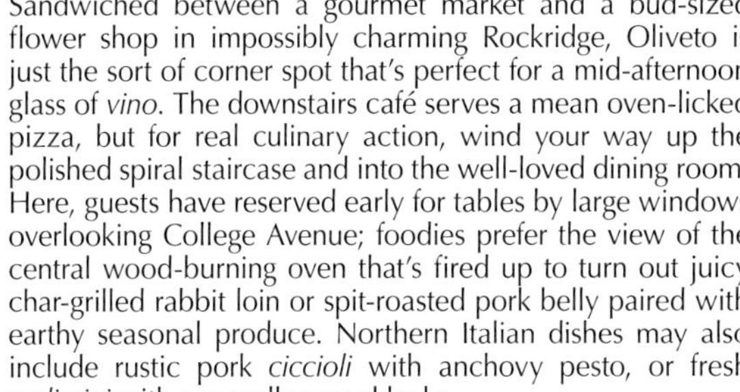

Sandwiched between a gourmet market and a bud-sized flower shop in impossibly charming Rockridge, Oliveto is just the sort of corner spot that's perfect for a mid-afternoon glass of *vino*. The downstairs café serves a mean oven-licked pizza, but for real culinary action, wind your way up the polished spiral staircase and into the well-loved dining room. Here, guests have reserved early for tables by large windows overlooking College Avenue; foodies prefer the view of the central wood-burning oven that's fired up to turn out juicy char-grilled rabbit loin or spit-roasted pork belly paired with earthy seasonal produce. Northern Italian dishes may also include rustic pork *ciccioli* with anchovy pesto, or fresh *tagliarini* with sea scallops and leeks.

Picán

2295 Broadway (at 23rd St.), Oakland

Phone: 510-834-1000 Lunch Sun – Fri
Web: www.picanrestaurant.com Dinner nightly
Prices: **$$**

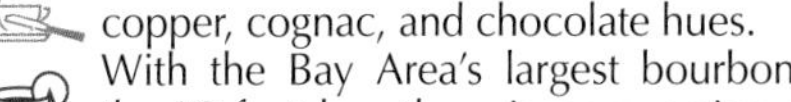

Having made it big as a trailblazing African-American executive, Michael LeBlanc set his sights upon a more delicious dream: bringing a taste of the South to uptown Oakland. Picán is dreamy indeed, with an interior that echoes of New Orleans' French Quarter, gussied up in copper, cognac, and chocolate hues.

With the Bay Area's largest bourbon selection poured at the 30-foot bar, there is no guessing at the drink of choice here; a Bourbon Room is open for private events. The menu follows suit with a jazzy repertoire of Cajun, Creole, and low country eats, with contemporary Southern favorites, like fried chicken and waffles with truffled honey or a pimento-bacon cheeseburger. After dinner, catch a show at the nearby art deco Paramount Theater.

Pizzaiolo

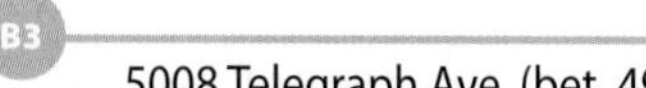

B3 Pizza

5008 Telegraph Ave. (bet. 49th & 51st Sts.), Oakland

Phone: 510-652-4888 Dinner Mon – Sat
Web: www.pizzaiolooakland.com
Prices: $$

Couples and small groups descend upon Pizzaiolo's main room (set with wood floors and whitewashed brick walls) while solo diners line the polished wood bar at this perennial East Bay pet. All come for the blistered, thin-crust pizzas, perhaps teamed with wine or a signature cocktail. Piled with toppings that personify California, pizza creations may pair Manila clams, green garlic, and Calabrian peppers; or potato, pancetta, fontina, and rosemary.

A peek into the open kitchen reveals colorful wall tiles, a wood-burning oven that turns out those mesmerizing pies, and a young, spunky staff. Outside, two spacious patios are just right for basking.

For more of his comfort food, stop by Charlie Harewell's Boot and Shoe Service pizzeria in Oakland.

Plum

B4 Californian

2214 Broadway (at 22nd St.), Oakland

Phone: 510-444-7586 Lunch & dinner daily
Web: www.plumoakland.com
Prices: $$

Just a glance into this dark, plum-y interior, where tatted-up hipsters wield plates for under $20 beneath massive plum still-lifes, and Daniel Patterson devotees will know we're not at Coi anymore. The chef who made his name for fine dining in San Francisco is going back to his roots, serving up more approachable fare at rough-hewn communal tables in Oakland.

Of course the chef's mastery can be seen in every morsel, categorized on the menu by Snacks, To Start, Vegetables & Grains, Animal, Cheese, and Sweet. Even Patterson diehards will find such straightforwardness nice for a change! Standouts include velvety rabbit pâté with whole grain mustard; smoked farm egg over farro and onion consommé; and dark chocolate crunch with rosemary-caramel ice cream.

Prima

Italian

1522 N. Main St. (bet. Bonanza St. & Lincoln Ave.), Walnut Creek

Phone: 925-935-7780 — Lunch Mon – Sat
Web: www.primaristorante.com — Dinner nightly
Prices: $$$

Prima's prime location (in Walnut Creek's downtown shopping district crowded with boutiques and cafés) makes it a fave among the Italian-loving locals. Whether you linger in the front area anchored by a wood-burning oven, or next to the wine cellar, or at the back bar, sultry touches like fireplaces, skylights, and candles are sure to lure.

What's all the fuss about? Try an item from the "Salumeria" (maybe *finocchiona* pork *salame* with fennel and black pepper; or *mortadella* studded with pistachios) and all doubt will vanish. A market-fresh menu unveils the likes of Monterey Bay calamari sautéed with ginger; *linguini di Mare*; and sheets of spinach pasta filled with herb-seasoned ground lamb. Exceptional and vast, the wine list revels in Italian reds.

Riva Cucina

Italian

800 Heinz Ave. (at 7th St.), Berkeley

Phone: 510-841-7482 — Lunch Mon – Fri
Web: www.rivacucina.com — Dinner Tue – Sat
Prices: $$

Translated as the point where land and water meet, Riva marries Italian hospitality with Berkeley industrial chic. The interior echoes a former spice factory with exposed brick and ductwork, but owners Massi and Jennifer Boldrini have warmed the space with citrusy paint and velvet curtains. The Northern Italian fare is crafted with mostly local, organic ingredients—even the restaurant's patio is redolent with fresh herbs and vegetables. (The planters also serve as lessons in healthy eating for the nearby preschool.) If this sounds very California, it is; these influences can be seen in such dishes as free range chicken in Dijon, lemon, and herbs.

For a more authentic taste of Italy, opt for handmade pastas like tagliatelle with *ragù alla Bolognese*.

Rivoli

A1

1539 Solano Ave. (bet. Neilson St. & Peralta Ave.), Berkeley

Phone: 510-526-2542 Dinner nightly
Web: www.rivolirestaurant.com
Prices: **$$**

Recycled cork wainscoting and parchment lanterns lend an earthy, Japanese vibe to Rivoli, which backs up to a lush "secret" garden framed by dramatic windows. The potted plants, climbing ivy, and fronds are a pretty, natural contrast to the interior's white linen-topped tables, which provide a clean backdrop for northern Californian fare with a shake of Italian seasoning.

Start with a "napoleon" of butter-poached shrimp and crab flavored with Pernod lobster sauce and a crisp puff pastry garnish, then dive in deeper with a fillet of salmon grilled and perched atop potato and celery root purée. Save room for the light and tangy mascarpone cheesecake with shortbread cookie crust, sautéed apples and pears, and a drizzle of sweet rhubarb sauce.

Sahn Maru

Korean

B3

4315 Telegraph Ave. (bet. 43rd & 44th Sts.), Oakland

Phone: 510-653-3366 Lunch & dinner Wed – Mon
Web: N/A
Prices: **$$**

In Korean, Sahn Maru means "top of the mountain" and literally, this paragon of Korean cuisine towers over the rest for her unique and quality food. She may be pricey, but homey Sahn Maru captivates with a fine assortment of *banchan* (think dried fish in chili sauce, and bean sprouts in sesame oil) that is served faithfully with every meal.

Impressing locals are the quality ingredients and singular recipes—proof is in the soft tofu served in a stoneware pot topped with oysters, shrimp, and clams; and black goat stew paired with a pungent dipping sauce. Further proof lies in the fact that most diners converse with the servers in Korean; and, as if to finally reinforce her authenticity, local TV plays in the background, and Korean trinkets adorn the walls.

Sasa

Japanese

1432 N. Main St. (bet. Cypress St. & Lincoln Ave.), Walnut Creek

Phone: 925-210-0188 Lunch & dinner daily
Web: www.sasawc.com
Prices: $$

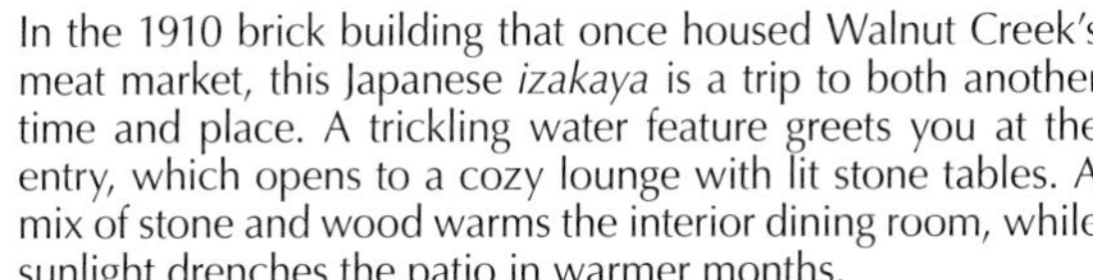

In the 1910 brick building that once housed Walnut Creek's meat market, this Japanese *izakaya* is a trip to both another time and place. A trickling water feature greets you at the entry, which opens to a cozy lounge with lit stone tables. A mix of stone and wood warms the interior dining room, while sunlight drenches the patio in warmer months.

The tradition of Japanese hospitality is palpable, with several small plates and sake samplers to bolster conversation. Snack on fresh sushi from Tokyo's Tsukiji fish market or on such cooked items as seafood *kara-age*, a mixed fry of tender calamari, ice fish, asparagus, and jalapeños. At lunch, nosh on classic combos like chicken teriyaki with crunchy shrimp and vegetable tempura, sashimi, and miso soup.

Sea Salt

Seafood

2512 San Pablo Ave. (at Dwight Way), Berkeley

Phone: 510-883-1720 Lunch & dinner daily
Web: www.seasaltrestaurant.com
Prices: $$

A relaxed seaside vibe reigns at this Berkeley favorite where, thanks to a recent expansion and remodel, the look is cool with high ceilings, exposed brick walls, and aquatic hues throughout. At happy hour, slurp dollar oysters at the raw bar or alfresco on the large patio; stick around for late night bites till midnight.

From the semi-open kitchen comes an ocean-centric fare perhaps including calamari classically combined with plump butter beans in basil-almond pesto; grilled local sardines; and pan-seared Tsar Nicoulai sturgeon with pork and smoked black pepper aïoli. Regulars loyal to owners Haig and Cindy Krikorian (also of Lalime) relish seasonal desserts like subtly spiced pumpkin cheesecake with a gingerbread crust and licorice anglaise.

Sidebar

Gastropub 

B4

542 Grand Ave. (bet. Euclid Ave. & MacArthur Blvd.), Oakland

Phone: 510-452-9500 — Lunch Mon – Fri
Web: www.sidebar-oakland.com — Dinner Mon – Sat
Prices: $$

Waft into Sidebar along with the breeze from Lake Merritt for artisanal cocktails (need a Corpse Reviver?) and Mediterranean-inspired gastropub dining in a quirky space. Photographs of life on the road add character to the pumpkin-spiced interior, anchored by a U-shaped copper bar. Go with friends and belly up to the communal table or score a seat at the dining counter with views of the open kitchen.
Lunchtime focuses on sandwiches, such as a meaty Cuban with roast pork, Gruyère and jalapeño relish; or the Monte Cristo panini with lighter options including a smoked trout salad. Dinners are hearty and wholesome, featuring the likes of baked pasta dishes or a Basque seafood stew. Wine lovers will find varietals from California, France, and Spain.

Slow

B2

1966 University Ave. (bet. Martin Luther King Jr. Way & Milvia St.), Berkeley

Phone: 510-647-3663 — Lunch & dinner Mon – Sat
Web: www.slowberkeley.com
Prices:

Disposable/compostable dinnerware aside, this Berkeley indie eatery makes you want to take things "slow" and enjoy the afternoon at a picnic table in the restaurant's hidden rose garden. Just remember to order your food at the counter first. Inside the sunny interior, only bar seating is available for such dishes as panzanella salad with sliced plums, artichoke hearts, caper berries, and arugula; linguini with grilled asparagus and earthy mushroom ragout; and seared tempeh with soba noodles, snap peas, bean sprouts, and kiwi. While some dishes may fall a bit flat, others excel with surprisingly good combinations and high nutritional value. Of course, everything here is prepared fresh with local ingredients, but you probably knew that already.

Tacubaya

1788 4th St. (bet. Hearst Ave. & Virginia St.), Berkeley

Phone: 510-525-5160 Lunch & dinner daily
Web: www.tacubaya.net
Prices: 

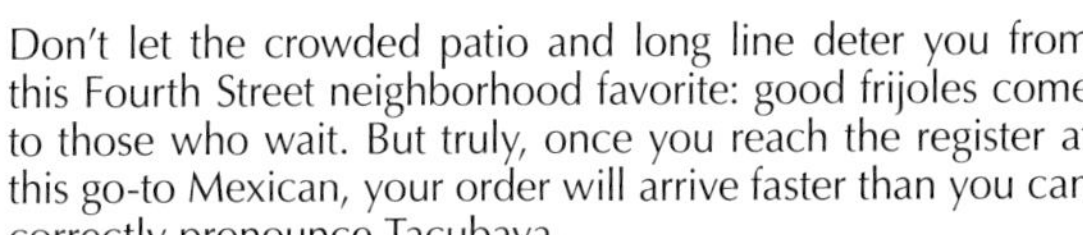

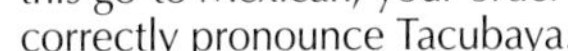

Don't let the crowded patio and long line deter you from this Fourth Street neighborhood favorite: good frijoles come to those who wait. But truly, once you reach the register at this go-to Mexican, your order will arrive faster than you can correctly pronounce Tacubaya.

Sister to Oakland's Doña Tomas, Tacubaya has all the trimmings of a beloved taqueria—festive color scheme, wrought-iron chandeliers, and a communal vibe. But the colorful chalkboard is the object of everyone's focus. Here, find the likes of *tacos al pastor*; seasonal chile relleno; and mushroom quesadillas. Open at 10:00 A.M. for *desayuno*, arrive here early for the *revueltos Norteños*, or scrambled eggs with *nopales*, tomatoes, and black beans. Wash it down with a blood orange aqua fresca.

Tamarindo

468 8th St. (at Broadway), Oakland

Phone: 510-444-1944 Lunch & dinner Mon – Sat
Web: www.tamarindoantojeria.com
Prices: 

Gather a gang of amigos and pop into this sunny spot for a banquet of mouthwatering *antojitos*—small plates, or "little whims." These sharable bites may be small, but they're big on flavor, so park it on the wooden communal table and prepare for a feast. Munch on the likes of Oaxacan tamales steamed in banana leaves; smoky chipotle meatballs; crispy shrimp tacos; or *torta poblana*, a pile of grilled chicken, melted cheese, avocado, and roasted poblano in a fresh torpedo roll spread with black beans and aïoli.

In a space styled in whitewashed walls and tin ceilings, the relatively new Miel tequila bar pours a wealth of *coctels* made with the beloved liquor. Hospitality is first-rate, thanks to Gloria Dominguez and her family, who run the place with heart.

Thai House

B5

254 Rose Ave. (bet. Diablo Rd. & Linda Mesa Ave.), Danville

Phone: 925-820-0635 — Lunch Mon – Fri
Web: www.thaihousedanville.net — Dinner nightly
Prices:

Want to feel like you're dining in the home of your Thai friends? Visit Thai House, a quaint restaurant just off the beaten path in Danville. This retreat is sheltered within a tranquil cottage filled with blooming flowers, antique chandeliers, and hand-carved wood details. The smiling staff makes guests feel warm and comfy in this appropriately named place.

How spicy can you take it? Hopefully a bit more than usual because they have a one- to four-star system, and the heat kicks in at level 2. The menu is huge and can be a bit overwhelming, but just ask for help and you'll be steered in the right direction. Some of the highlights include tender shrimp in a flavorful hot and sour soup, and juicy chicken simmered in coconut milk and *Massaman* curry.

The Peasant & The Pear

International

B5

267 Hartz Ave. (at Linda Mesa Ave.), Danville

Phone: 925-820-6611 — Lunch & dinner Tue – Sun
Web: www.thepeasantandthepear.com
Prices: $$

Danville's The Peasant & The Pear nods to the original Parisian bistro, where simple, slow-cooked foods were served in a modest setting. Within these buttery walls adorned with a few framed photos and dark wood wainscoting, locals get their fill of double cut pork chops and Chianti-braised lamb shank with provolone-studded polenta.

Like a traditional bistro, The Peasant & The Pear feels as familiar as the well-worn dining room of a favorite relative. The petite zinc bar is an easy perch to sip and gab with Chef/owner Rodney Worth as your charming host. When not in the kitchen, he can be found shooting the breeze with regulars who appreciate his American culinary accent in such dishes as prawns *a la plancha* and quesadilla with Brie and spiced-pear chutney.

Uzen

Japanese

B3

5415 College Ave. (bet. Hudson St. & Kales Ave.), Oakland

Phone: 510-654-7753 — Lunch Mon – Fri
Web: N/A — Dinner Mon – Sat
Prices: $$

The ethos of Uzen lies in simplicity. Hardly bigger than a bento box, its decor relies on sunshine from the skylights by day and, at night, pendant lights glistening over fresh fish at the sushi bar. The slanted bar seats fewer than a dozen, still there are more guests than there are menu items. Expect just a few choices of uncomplicated seafood with a happy lack of gimmicky maki.

A couple of cooked teriyaki dishes at times disappoint, though steaming noodle bowls are a treat on cool Oakland nights. But truly, Uzen does sushi best. With deep pink *maguro* and hamachi right from the sea with a dab of wasabi, there is little left to be desired.

Just be sure to keep your eyes peeled in Rockridge: this triangular storefront is equally simple to miss.

Va de Vi

Fusion

C1

1511 Mt. Diablo Blvd. (near Main St.), Walnut Creek

Phone: 925-979-0100 — Lunch & dinner daily
Web: www.vadevi.com
Prices: $$

When on the prowl for fine wine and globally-inspired eats, Walnut Creek denizens head for the hugely hip Va de Vie. The restaurant has an oak-barrel ceiling, dining tables which run its length, and a front bar packed with stylish locals. And with more than 16 wine varietals available by the glass, the taste, or in flights of three, this über popular (yet relaxed) bistro's focus on wine is true to its Catalan moniker.

Dishes like grilled, curried tuna kabobs; crispy potato and chorizo croquettes drizzled with spicy aïoli; and braised beef short ribs atop mashed potatoes and sautéed corn, further demonstrate the menu's international tone and scope.

There is outdoor seating, but the back patio is near majestic with tables surrounding an old oak tree.

Vanessa's Bistro

Vietnamese XX

A1

1715 Solano Ave. (at Tulare Ave.), Berkeley

Phone: 510-525-8300 Dinner Wed – Mon
Web: www.vanessasbistro.com
Prices: $$

There may be no sexier pairing of words than French-Vietnamese, the culinary temptress behind wonders like duck strudel with wild mushrooms and basil risotto. For this tasty fix, head to Vanessa's Bistro, the packed Berkeley spot, run by Chef Vanessa Dang, and begin the night with wicked specialty cocktails at the bamboo-topped bar.

Creative types are wise to listen for the specials; or, go all the way with a four-course tasting menu at just $40. Of course, ordering à la carte does have its perks—small plates are perfectly suited for sharing. Tease your palate with crispy salt-and-pepper prawns with chili-lime dipping sauce, green papaya salad, and banana-raisin-peach bread pudding for dessert. Also look for Vanessa's Bistro in Walnut Creek.

Walnut Creek Yacht Club

Seafood XX

C1

1555 Bonanza St. (at Locust St.), Walnut Creek

Phone: 925-944-3474 Lunch & dinner daily
Web: www.wcyc.net
Prices: $$

Keys to a yacht are not required at this marine-themed restaurant in Walnut Creek, with mahogany and teak fixtures and a boatload of sailing tchotchkes. America's Cup pennants and an authentic jib add to the nautical vibe; if that's not enough, grab a seat at the raw bar for a lesson in oyster shucking.

Chef/owner Kevin Weinberg takes seafood seriously—as did the Mako shark now hanging over the bar. Fish is fresh, never frozen, with nearly a dozen daily selections ready to be grilled and served with simple sides. Other aquatic fare may include seafood cocktails; lobster macaroni and cheese gratin; mahi mahi tacos; or an Idaho trout BLT on ciabatta. Few can resist the Commodore's sundae or warm triple chocolate brownie with vanilla bean ice cream.

Wood Tavern

Californian

6317 College Ave. (bet. Alcatraz Ave. & 63rd St.), Oakland

Phone: 510-654-6607 — Lunch Mon – Sat
Web: www.woodtavern.net — Dinner nightly
Prices: $$

On a block aromatic with fresh produce and just-baked bread, Wood Tavern is like buttah—seriously, those of high cholesterol and crash diets need not apply. Artisan charcuterie and cheese boards are divine for soaking up a glass and you'll find many an Oakland foodie indulging in hearty happy hours. And why not? With lofty ceilings, sage walls, and streetfront windows, Wood Tavern is a quintessential up-market neighborhood joint.

Nab a seat at the chef's counter for a view of the open kitchen, where Mediterranean comfort is the fare du jour. Nosh on crisp pork belly "Lyonnaise" with poached egg and frisée or the favorite pan-roasted half chicken with fingerling potatoes and garlic confit. Save room for the Tavern's beloved root beer float.

Zabu Zabu

Japanese 

1919 Addison St. (bet. Martin Luther King Jr. Way & Milvia St.), Berkeley

Phone: 510-848-9228 — Lunch & dinner daily
Web: www.zabu-zabu.com
Prices: ©©

"All u can shabu-shabu" at Zabu Zabu may sound like a silly Seussian culinary come-on, but try telling that to the budget-conscious UC Berkeley smarty-pants who pack the place. Even if the hot pot meals and group dining concept are a bit novel for the intellectual locale, Zabu Zabu's wide array of thinly sliced meats, vegetables, and choice of seafood are undeniably alluring.

Each table is embedded with a burner where festive DIY diners dip their selections into steaming broth. The method is best suited to sharing among friends, but there are plenty of options for the single diner including briny seaweed salad with a refreshing crunch; creative sushi rolls; noodles; and small plates of golden brown pork *gyoza* with a sweet-spicy dipping sauce.

Zachary's Chicago Pizza

Pizza

5801 College Ave. (at Oak Grove Ave.), Oakland

Phone: 510-655-6385 Lunch & dinner daily
Web: www.zacharys.com
Prices:

In keeping with their reputation of being East Bay's pizza aficionados for over 25 years, Zachary's ensures that their pie is presented with pride at this employee-owned pizzeria. Both locals and lovers of Chicago-style deep dish know that the long wait is part of the deal, and they rest assured in anticipation of the cheesy, calorie-laden Nirvana that is Zachary's signature stuffed pie. Many of the toppings slathered over their tangy tomato sauce are also available on a thin cornmeal crust—though not the favorite spinach and mushroom.

Great for families, this simple spot is always busy (other locations are in Berkeley and San Ramon). To cut down the wait, consider calling ahead to place an order, or take home a "half-baked" pizza to cook in your oven.

Zatar

Mediterranean 

B2

1981 Shattuck Ave. (bet. Berkeley Way & University Ave.), Berkeley

Phone: 510-841-1981 Dinner Wed – Sat
Web: www.zatarrestaurant.com
Prices: $$

Though it is set in Berkeley, Zatar transports diners to the Mediterranean with the colorful murals and collection of hand-painted ceramic platters that adorn the walls. Husband-and-wife team Waiel and Kelly Majid do Berkeley proud in their certified green business by harvesting vegetables from their organic garden, composting raw kitchen scraps, and feeding any vegetarian food remains to their laying hens.

Zatar's name refers to the traditional Middle Eastern spice mixture–made from sesame seeds, oregano, thyme, and sumac–used here in a variety of dishes. The dinner menu recites a litany of vegetable spreads and dolmas to start; grilled leg of lamb, pistachio and spring herb chicken, and sea bass with sesame-*harissa* sauce make satisfying entrées.

Zut!

Mediterranean

1820 4th St. (bet. Hearst Ave & Virginia St.), Berkeley

Phone: 510-644-0444 — Lunch & dinner daily
Web: www.zutonfourth.com
Prices: $$

For ladies looking for a light lunch that won't bog them down while shopping Berkeley's Fourth Street district, *Zut!* answers the call with tuna Niçoise salads, sandwiches, and wraps. But the warm, cherry and pine wood interior sates heartier palates too, serving oven-baked flatbreads and artisanal pizzas all day—try the cremini mushroom pie with bits of Brie and thyme.

Short for *zut alors*, or "shucks" in French slang, *Zut!* is a cozy little spot with copper mirrors, billowing textiles, and a backlit bar. At dinner, the Mediterranean café resembles its mural of a bustling restaurant scene as tables are loaded with the likes of lamb meatballs in tangy tomato sauce; falafel with red pepper and yogurt; and chèvre cheesecake on a gingersnap cookie crust.

Remember, stars (✿✿✿…✿) are awarded for cuisine only! Elements such as service and décor are not a factor.

San Francisco Convention & Visitors Bureau photo by Phil Coblentz.

Marin

Marin

Journey north of the Golden Gate Bridge and entrée the sprawling Marin County. Draped along the breathtaking Highway 1, coastal climates hallow this region with abounding agricultural advantages. Snake your way through this gorgeous county, and find that food oases are spread out. But when fortunate to 'catch' them, expect fresh and luscious seafood, oysters, and cold beer...slurp! Farm-to-table cuisine is the par in North Bay and they boast an avalanche of local food purveyors.

Begin with the prodigious cheese chronicles. Visit the quaint and rustic **Cowgirl Creamery** where "cowgirls" make delicious, distinctive, and artisan cheeses. By producing only farmstead cheese, they help refine and define artisan cheesemaking...respect! The cheese conte continues at **Point Reyes Farmstead Cheese Co**. For a more lush and heady blue cheese, dive into their decadent 'Original Blue.' These driving and enterprising cheesemakers live by *terroir*. Restaurants here follow the European standard and offer cheese before, or in lieu of a dessert course. The ideal is simply magical...end of story! Not sweet enough? Get your candy fix on at **Munchies** of Sausalito; or opt for a more sinful (and creamy) affair at **Noci's** gelato.

From tales of cheese to ranch romances, **Marin Sun Farms** is at the crest. A magnified butcher shop, their heart, hub, and soul lies in the production of local and natural-fed livestock for a sweeping nexus of establishments—from farmers and grocery stores, to a plethora of restaurants. Speaking of marvelous meats, a visit to **Bryan's Fine Foods** is a must. Although petite in comparison, this Corte Madera haunt is an excellent butcher shop.

Ravenous after hours of scenic driving and the ocean waft? Rest at **The Pelican Inn**. Their hearty stew of English country cooking and wide brew of the English 'bar' will leave you craving more of the bucolic. Carry on your hiatus and stroll into foodie paradise, otherwise known as **Spanish Table**. Settled in Mill Valley, gourmand's revel in their selection of Spanish cookbooks, cookware, specialty foods, and rare, palate-pleasing wines. Like most thirsty travelers, let desire lead you to **Three Twins Ice Cream**. A lick of their organically-produced creamy goodness is sure to bring heaven to earth.

Waters off the coast here provide divers with exceptional hunting ground, and restaurants across the country seek the same including lush oysters, clams, and mussels. The difficulty in obtaining a hunting permit, as well as the inability to retrieve the large savory mollusks, makes red abalone a treasured species, especially in surrounding Asian restaurants. Yet, despite such hurdles, seafood is the norm at most restaurants in Marin County. One such gem is **Sam's Anchor Café** known for their superb seafood and glorious views. If seafood isn't your thing, entice your palate with authentic and sumptuous Puerto Rican flavors at **Sol Food**. Turn the leaf to **Western Boat & Tackle** seafood market. Beloved dearly by the fishing community in San Rafael, this seafood shop is outfitted with all things fishy, including a fantastic menu and marine supply store.

Marin County is known for its deluge of local, organic ingredients carried in the numerous farmers' markets. The marriage of food and wine is best expressed at Sausalito's own "Tour de Cuisine" and The Marin County Tomato Festival. Magnificent Marin, with its panoramic views, is one of the most sought after locales and celebrities abound. Thus, some diners may have a touristy mien; however, it is undeniable that restaurants and chefs are blessed with easy access to the choicest food and local food agents.

Arun

Thai

B1

385 Bel Marin Keys Blvd. (near Hamilton Dr.), Novato

Phone: 415-883-8017 — Lunch Mon – Fri
Web: N/A — Dinner nightly
Prices:

Nestled in an area void of Thai treats, Arun's is a fresh little find in meandering Marin. This neighborhood dwelling is beloved by businessmen, software suits, and local families alike who can't help but smile at the sight of such large portions of boldly flavored, well-prepared Thai food.

It may reside in a commercial park, but Arun's handsome floors and furnishings, vibrant accents, Thai relics, and friendly staff ooze oodles of warmth. Strutting a variety of dishes, the menu might also unveil tasty Thai finds like *larb gai,* that tasty plate of ground chicken spiked with fish sauce, lime juice, and chilies; and pumpkin curry lush with prawns, potatoes, and coconut milk. The ginger ice cream is spicy, but a perfect palate-cleanser.

Bar Bocce

Pizza

A3

1250 Bridgeway (bet. Johnson & Turney Sts.), Sausalito

Phone: 415-331-0555 — Lunch & dinner daily
Web: www.barbocce.com
Prices: $$

The only view in Sausalito to rival Bar Bocce's boat-dotted harbor vista is that of its own wood-burning pizza ovens in the exhibition kitchen. Locals and tourists alike are happy to wait for a seat at a simple wooden table, particularly on weekends, for a taste of the artisanal pies.

Bar Bocce finds inspiration both here and there: while a turn at the bocce court is a tribute to Italy, Dungeness crab and Meyer lemon piled atop an avocado and crème fraîche pizza tastes distinctly like home. Additional pies include calamari and clam sprinkled with spicy chili oil, or pork sausage with fennel pollen and onion. Light salads like artichoke, fennel, celery, and pecorino; roasted chicken with lemon and herbs; fudgesicles and winesicles complete the menu.

Boca

Steakhouse XX

B1

340 Ignacio Blvd. (bet. Alameda Del Prado & Enfrente Rd.), Novato

Phone: 415-883-0901 — Lunch Mon – Fri
Web: www.bocasteak.com — Dinner nightly
Prices: **$$**

Decked with timber, rawhide, and leather–oh my!–Boca is just the kind of pared-down yet upscale steakhouse that casual Marinites might keep on their speed dial. And while reservations might be a good idea on Tuesday nights when bottle prices are slashed in half, Boca's interior brick walls and bovine art beg you to just come on down.

Founded by George Morrone, a Jersey boy with Argentine roots, Boca dishes steaks and seafood with sultry Latin appeal. A grass-fed skirt steak is grilled over hardwood and hangs out with a crisp, salty-skinned baked potato. Its Latin flavor comes through in a trio of *chimichurries*. Non-beef eaters can savor the roasted shrimp with spicy cilantro butter, or sample empanadas and *bocadillos* with fabulous duck fat fries.

Brick & Bottle

American XX

C2

55 Tamal Vista Blvd. (bet. Council Crest Dr. & Chicksaw Ct.), Corte Madera

Phone: 415-924-3366 — Lunch & dinner daily
Web: www.brickandbottle.com
Prices: **$$**

Chef Scott Howard has made his mark on a number of restaurants in the Bay Area, but he's finally landed at Brick & Bottle. This Marin native delivers his signature jazzed-up comfort food to this restaurant inside the Marketplace strip mall.

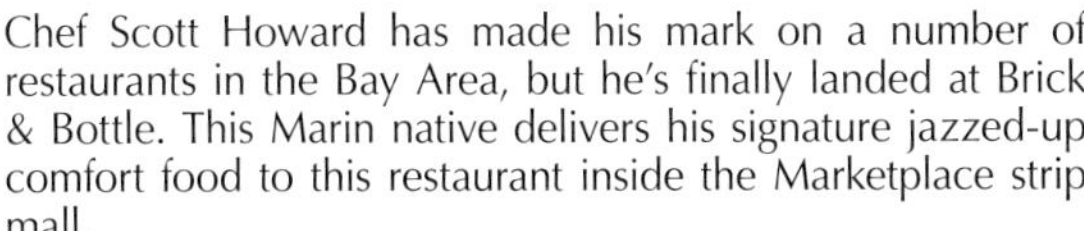

The gleaming copper-topped bar, open kitchen, and warm dining room decked in leather booths, dark wood, and leather paneling are a draw on their own, but looks aren't the only thing at this affable respite. Come armed with an appetite for crowning and creative takes on America's favorite foods, like the white cheddar and braised short rib grilled cheese sandwich. Smoked Gouda orzo mac and cheese is definitely not from a blue box, and pizzas are amped up with duck confit and onions.

Buckeye Roadhouse

American XX

A2

15 Shoreline Hwy. (west of Hwy. 101), Mill Valley

Phone: 415-331-2600 Lunch & dinner daily
Web: www.buckeyeroadhouse.com
Prices: $$

Forget spa food; there are few things more decadent than a succulent, grilled double-cut Berkshire pork chop after an invigorating stomp through the Marin Headlands. Hike over to Buckeye Roadhouse to savor one of the Bay Area's most delicious traditions, perhaps served with a side of creamy chive-mashed potatoes and tangy apricot chutney. Lighter dishes may include house-smoked chicken and local blue cheese jazzing up a salad with green apples, celery, and currants.

True, the Buckeye is located on a Highway 101 on-ramp, but the historic lodge charms with rich wood paneling, deep leather booths, and a roaring fire in the hearth. The sophisticated American fare, delivered by vested servers, pairs well with classic cocktails and enjoys a loyal following.

Bungalow 44

American XX

B2

44 E. Blithedale Ave. (at Sunnyside Ave.), Mill Valley

Phone: 415-381-2500 Dinner nightly
Web: www.bungalow44.com
Prices: $$

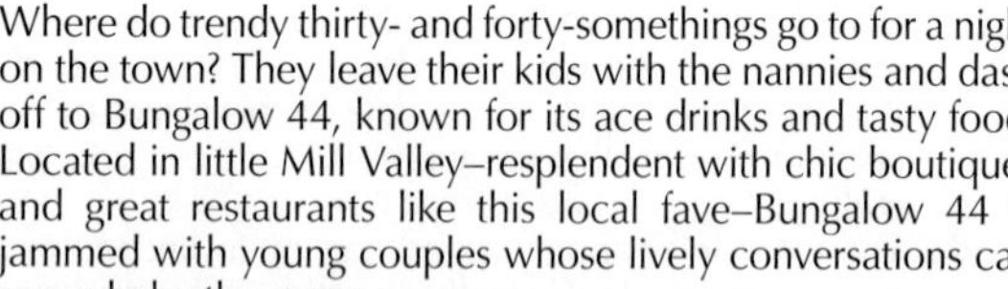

Where do trendy thirty- and forty-somethings go to for a night on the town? They leave their kids with the nannies and dash off to Bungalow 44, known for its ace drinks and tasty food. Located in little Mill Valley–resplendent with chic boutiques and great restaurants like this local fave–Bungalow 44 is jammed with young couples whose lively conversations can overwhelm the space.

On Wednesday nights they molt into a bit of a supper club, so those seeking a quieter evening should aim for a table in the tented dining area or in the main room past the open kitchen. The menu plays with American dishes, so mouths water for wood-grilled calamari; New Orleans barbecue shrimp and grits; Kobe and lamb meatballs; and mini bourbon-biscotti milkshakes.

Cucina

510 San Anselmo Ave. (at Tunstead Ave.), San Anselmo

Phone: 415-454-2942 Dinner Tue – Sun
Web: www.cucinarestaurantandwinebar.com
Prices: $$

For a case of the warm fuzzies along this quaint main strip of San Anselmo, try this charming and welcoming trattoria, courtesy of the folks behind Jackson-Fillmore in San Francisco. Sunny walls, terra-cotta floors, and a blazing wood-burning oven warm the family-friendly dining room, where the staff greets regulars by name and everyone with a smile. Garlicky tomato bruschetta is a tasty start, compliments of the house. The ever-changing menu may feature rustic dishes such as chicken ravioli; or gnocchi with asparagus, fontina cheese, and white truffle oil. These homey preparations are simple, genuine, and uncomplicated. Kids love the pizza margherita, and few can turn down the tiramisu.

The wine bar at back is a perfect post-dinner spot.

El Paseo

American XX

17 Throckmorton Ave. (bet. Blithedale & Sunnyside Aves.), Mill Valley

Phone: 415-388-0741 Dinner nightly
Web: www.elpaseomillvalley.com
Prices: $$$

El Paseo House of Chops isn't cutting any corners when it comes to romancing its diners with a warm and inviting atmosphere. Tucked inside a secluded courtyard that will woo even the most diehard urbanite with its country appeal, it is the go-to spot for date night.

If the Smithsonian had a museum of American cuisine, it would certainly include a good portion of this menu. It has all the hits—Parker house rolls with garlic butter sauce, served in a cute cast-iron dish; BLT deviled eggs with caviar for a spruced up version of that family picnic favorite; even chocolate soufflé (borrowed from the French, but perfectly at home state-side). Of course, as the name suggests, El Paseo specializes in meat, and the 38-day, dry-aged sirloin steak is a winner.

Fish

Seafood

A3

350 Harbor Dr. (off Bridgeway), Sausalito

Phone: 415-331-3474 Lunch & dinner daily
Web: www.331fish.com
Prices: **$$**

To sate a hankering for sustainable seafood and family-friendly feasts served in a bright and airy space overlooking a picturesque Sausalito harbor, go to Fish. Order at the counter and then pick your perch—broad window walls flood the interior with sunlight and aquatic views, while outdoor picnic tables beckon with toe-dipping proximity to the water.

This casual, cash-only joint serves generous portions composed of organic ingredients to satisfy the whole family. Tangy homemade lemonade is a refreshing companion to grilled tilapia tacos with a mound of fresh cilantro or Anchor Steam-battered cod with rustic wedge "chips."

On your way out, check out the small fish market counter where various raw goods are just waiting to be cooked at home.

Frantoio

Italian

A2

152 Shoreline Hwy. (Stinson Beach exit off Hwy. 101), Mill Valley

Phone: 415-289-5777 Dinner nightly
Web: www.frantoio.com
Prices: **$$**

Before meandering off to the shore, sojourn at Frantoio located just a stone's throw from Highway 101. What it lacks in location, it makes up for with its delicious Northern Italian cuisine. Italian for "olive press," Frantoio makes its very own olive oil on-site in November and December, and you can even watch the process behind a large window in the back of the barn-like room.

While lingering at the bar, pick up their floppy leather menu and ogle the ample and fine selection of Italian food. It can get frantic at Frantoio as high ceilings reverberate with animated conversations over spreads like roasted day boat scallops with watercress sauce, potato purée, and truffle oil; pizzas; pastas; and *secondi* like grilled red trout and porcini-dusted ahi tuna.

Hilltop 1892

American XX

850 Lamont Ave. (at Redwood Blvd.), Novato

Phone: 415-893-1892 Lunch & dinner daily
Web: www.hilltop1892.com
Prices: $$

In the case of Hilltop 1892, the name says it all. Set atop a winding driveway above Novato, this turn of the 20th century landmark–first a private home, then a restaurant since the 1930s–has been reimagined by owner Erick Hendricks as a sweeping culinary getaway with dark wood floors, caramel accents, and lazy ceiling fans spinning overhead, all set to the tune of soft jazz.

The urbane dining room is conducive to contemporary nibbles that lean mostly American with a slight international zest. Dishes from the kitchen may include a Dungeness crab dip or smooth and sweet roasted garlic soup to be followed with pan-seared Atlantic salmon with deliciously fresh and bright leek sauce; or smoked baby back ribs with Napa slaw and maple corn bread.

Insalata's

Mediterranean XX

120 Sir Francis Drake Blvd. (at Barber Ave.), San Anselmo

Phone: 415-457-7700 Lunch & dinner daily
Web: www.insalatas.com
Prices: $$

In Italy, cooking is a family affair. And so it is at Insalata's, the charming Sausalito favorite named for Chef/owner Heidi Krahling's late father, Italo Insalata. Today, Krahling pays homage to her beloved *"babbo"* by mixing tender loving care with Mediterranean fare and local, seasonal ingredients that stay close to home.

Insalata's dining room is spacious and perennially packed yet somehow remains cozy, with blonde wood furnishings and art that depicts nature's bounty. Expect Middle Eastern specialties and mezze plates of warm pita, hummus, and *taramasalata*; crispy cigars filled with feta cheese and roasted butternut squash; and Greek-style grilled lamb served with fluffy flatbread. Take a tip from the regulars and spring for valet parking.

Left Bank

B2 French XX

507 Magnolia Ave. (at Ward St.), Larkspur

Phone: 415-927-3331 Lunch & dinner daily
Web: www.leftbank.com
Prices: **$$**

Next time you're in Larkspur, wing over to Left Bank where pressed-tin ceilings, wood furnishings, a long bar, and wraparound dining porch are clues that this is no typical chain restaurant. Tucked inside the town's historic Blue Rock Inn, this authentic French brasserie is one of three Bay Area locations.

Following the Inn's pleasant and relaxed vibe, Left Bank is a low-key spot to enjoy French comfort foods as well as weekend brunch. On chilly days, the rich onion soup with Emmental gratinée is a must; vegetarians will appreciate the eggplant *croque*—a take on the classic prepared with grilled eggplant, bell pepper, and oozing mozzarella. Of course, no bistro meal would be complete without creamy profiteroles drizzled in bittersweet chocolate.

Le Garage

French X

A3

85 Liberty Ship Way, Ste.109 (off Marinship Way), Sausalito

Phone: 415-332-5625 Lunch daily
Web: www.legaragebistrosausalito.com Dinner Mon – Sat
Prices: **$$**

There may be no other picturesque (and tough to find) place for a Gallic lunch than Le Garage, the Sausalito restaurant at the tip of Liberty Ship Way with a bay breeze and view of bobbing yachts and dinghies. Housed in, yes, a real converted garage, the stark and stylish space features crimson retractable doors thrown open to the waterfront air, making this a serene spot for an aperitif and light lunch.

Servers keep with the service station theme in classic mechanics' uniforms, though the accent is French, of both the staff and food. Pull up a wooden bistro chair and order such delights as shrimp Napoleon with avocado mousse and lobster oil, or Tasmanian pepper-crusted steak with house-cut frites. French and Californian wines make for perfect pairing.

Marché aux Fleurs

Mediterranean XX

23 Ross Common (off Lagunitas Rd.), Ross

Phone: 415-925-9200 Dinner Tue – Sat
Web: www.marcheauxfleursrestaurant.com
Prices: $$$

You have not died and gone to the South of France, so don't let your taste buds fool you. It may seem like it, but you are still firmly planted in Marin County in the town of Ross. Named for the celebrated farmer's market in Provence, this French restaurant charms the pants off locals with its farm-fresh cuisine and attractive setting.

Aptly named, since the kitchen works exclusively with products sourced from local farmers, this place turns out consistently delicious Mediterranean-inspired dishes. There's a little bit of cheer on every plate, whether it contains the bacon-wrapped and Grana cheese-stuffed Medjool dates; gnocchi with sweet white corn and foraged mushrooms; or local king salmon with Bloomsdale spinach and green garbanzo beans.

Marinitas

Latin American XX

218 Sir Francis Drake Blvd. (bet. Bank St. & Tunstead Ave.), San Anselmo

Phone: 415-454-8900 Lunch & dinner daily
Web: www.marinitas.net
Prices: $$

Nothing is free in the posh enclave of Marin. Well, except for those delicious and warm homemade tortilla chips with peppery red and green salsas at Marinitas, Heidi Krahling's local tribute to Mexican and Latin American culinary traditions. The lofty cantina makes everyone feel at home with sports on the big screen and a large stone fireplace to keep the taxidermy warm.

Fresh-squeezed juices and sweet-and-sour mixes made in-house highlight the focus on bright flavors and complement a major tequila selection. Sip one of Marinita's killer margaritas and relax while perusing the menu. With options like grilled Atlantic cod tacos, chile relleno stuffed with butternut squash, and daily specials like savory slow-braised carnitas, choosing can be brutal.

Murray Circle

Californian XX

601 Murray Circle (at Fort Baker), Sausalito

Phone: 415-339-4750 — Lunch & dinner daily
Web: www.murraycircle.com
Prices: **$$**

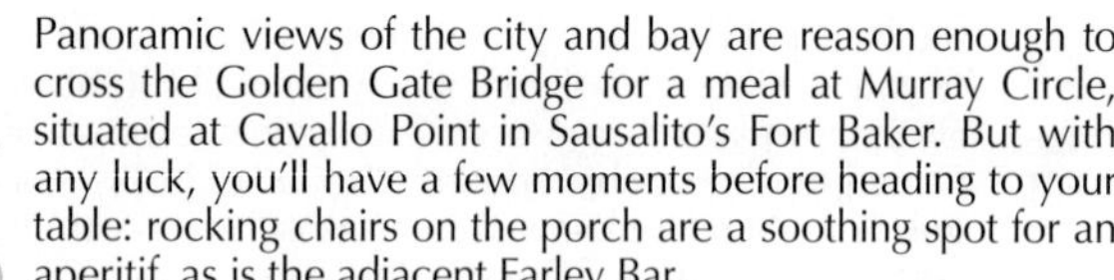

Panoramic views of the city and bay are reason enough to cross the Golden Gate Bridge for a meal at Murray Circle, situated at Cavallo Point in Sausalito's Fort Baker. But with any luck, you'll have a few moments before heading to your table: rocking chairs on the porch are a soothing spot for an aperitif, as is the adjacent Farley Bar.

A trio of dining rooms are warmed by fireplaces and dressed with leather banquettes—the better for couples of a certain age to settle back and imbibe. The new chef has added chilled seafood, 'Ocean on Ice,' to the menu, and a host of house-cured charcuterie. Find dishes like paprika-cured *lomo* with compressed melon; braised beef pavé with horseradish crème fraîche; and a quinoa waffle with rose-geranium ice cream.

Olema Inn

Californian XX

A1

10000 Sir Francis Drake Blvd. (at Hwy. 1), Olema

Phone: 415-663-9559 — Lunch & dinner daily
Web: www.theolemainn.com
Prices: **$$$**

Situated just off the lushly wooded Sir Francis Drake Boulevard, the Olema Inn is a sweet, country-cut outpost ideal for lighthearted dining on a sunny day. Much like a ranch, the inn has a charming porch, and its dining room blurs onto a spacious shaded patio overlooking a grove of fruit trees and gardens. If you must sit inside, wood furnishings and white walls keep with the serene, bucolic vibe.

The relaxed, friendly atmosphere is conducive to easygoing Californian meals. Dishes may reveal a Niman Ranch burger with caramelized onions, smoky bacon, and pungent Point Reyes blue cheese; and flaky halibut perched on tender wax beans, baby potatoes, and roasted cherry tomatoes. Pair your burger with a glass of Pey-Marin pinot noir for a perfect couple.

Om

1518 4th St. (at E St.), San Rafael

Phone: 415-458-1779 — Lunch & dinner Mon – Sat
Web: www.omcuisine.net
Prices:

Om brings to you the warmth and authenticity of Southern India (the owners hail from the Deccan plateau) within a multi-tiered room modestly decorated with a few pictures and one framed portrait of the Mahatma himself. This homely spot will delight your every sense of smell, sight, and taste as evidenced by a barrage of faithfuls devouring the wildly popular and bargain-priced lunch buffet.

Here, food is the focus, so make time to order off the menu. Although ardent, the service is slow, but after a taste of the fragrant *era varuval* (shrimp cooked with chilies, ginger, and garlic); crispy *dosas* made from rice and lentil flour; or an *uttapam* studded with peas, peppers, and paired with sambar and coconut chutney, your agro will be forever forgotten.

Osteria Stellina

Italian 

11285 Hwy. 1 (at 3rd St.), Point Reyes Station

Phone: 415-663-9988 — Lunch & dinner daily
Web: www.osteriastellina.com
Prices: $$$

After slurping oysters at Tomales Bay, cruise down to Point Reyes Station and grab a seat at Osteria Stellina. As befits the tiny charmer of a rural town, Stellina has a rustic aspect and relaxed feel. The osteria is luxuriating in a bit of buzz among area foodies, who come to relish the Italian eatery's local, organic, and seasonal offerings.

Order Hog Island oysters from the raw bar (if you haven't had enough already), or delight in eating your greens: braised collards, chard, and dandelion come with rosemary-infused cannellini beans and a drizzle of olive oil. Pasta lovers will appreciate perfectly al dente fusilli, while meat lovers can dig into a slow-cooked pork osso buco from Niman Ranch. Even if the pork doesn't wow, the mashers are a hit.

Picco

Italian XX

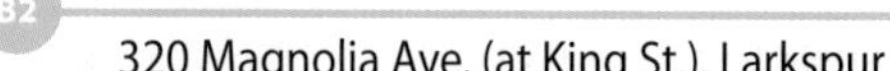

B2

320 Magnolia Ave. (at King St.), Larkspur

Phone: 415-924-0300 Dinner nightly
Web: www.restaurantpicco.com
Prices: $$

If sharing is caring, then Larkspur's Picco is a thoughtful spot indeed. Bruce Hill's popular Italian eatery delivers each small plate right to the center of the table, as friends help themselves, then others, to the likes of local halibut crudo, plated with fennel, blood orange, and jalapeño. Those craving comfort fare will relish cauliflower gratin with cheddar cheese and breadcrumbs; or ever-changing risottos made from scratch each half hour.

Exposed brick, dim lighting, and redwood accents make this a romantic date-night spot. Before heading home, cap the meal with a selection of artisanal cheeses. Locals love Marin Mondays, which showcase the best of North Bay produce. City dwellers can get a taste of Picco at Hill's new SoMa outpost, Zero Zero.

Poggio

Italian XX

A3

777 Bridgeway (at Bay St.), Sausalito

Phone: 415-332-7771 Lunch & dinner daily
Web: www.poggiotrattoria.com
Prices: $$

Having cooked in the Italian regions of Tuscany and Lombardy, Chef Peter McNee brings authenticity to a menu filled with the freshest Californian products. This "special hillside place," housed on the ground level of The Casa Madrona Hotel & Spa, successfully churns out a tandem of Northern Italian indulgences. Mahogany archways, plush booths, terra-cotta tiles, and a buzzing bar makes dining here quite a thrill, especially in warmer months, when French doors swing open to views of the serene Sausalito yacht harbor across the street. Dishes such as roasted octopus with pork belly confit, potato, and poached egg; and Dungeness crab sugo with saffron and Meyer lemon aïoli are enhanced by herbs and greens grown in Poggio's very own terraced garden.

R'Noh Thai

Thai XX

B2

1000 Magnolia Ave. (bet. Frances & Murray Aves.), Larkspur

Phone: 415-925-0599 — Lunch Mon – Sat
Web: N/A — Dinner nightly
Prices:

"Rising sun" is a fitting translation for this serene spot, where a calming vibe, cheery service, and robust flavors uplift and satisfy. The bi-level space rocks rich red walls with framed photos of water lilies on one level, and billowing white fabric under a sunny skylight on the other.

Get your caffeine fix with a creamy Thai iced coffee; when you're ready to chow, choose from any number of delightful curries, salads, soups, noodles, or rice dishes, many of which are prepared with local and organic products. Buttery *samosas* stuffed with chicken, peas, potatoes, and spices are full of flaky golden goodness (note the beautifully carved radish blossom on the side). A small back deck overlooking a marshland and bird sanctuary adds to the tranquility.

Sushi Ran

Japanese XX

A3

107 Caledonia St. (bet. Pine & Turney Sts.), Sausalito

Phone: 415-332-3620 — Lunch Mon – Fri
Web: www.sushiran.com — Dinner nightly
Prices: $$

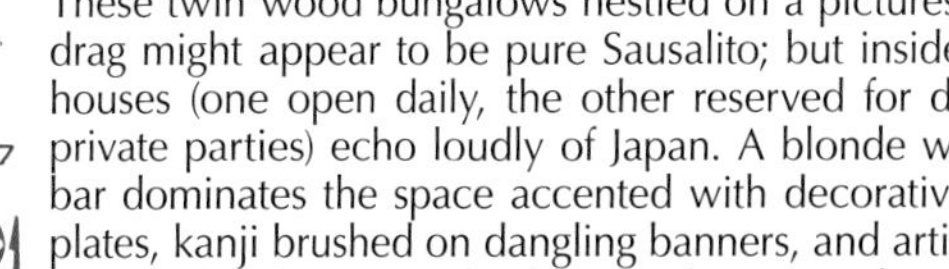

These twin wood bungalows nestled on a picturesque main drag might appear to be pure Sausalito; but inside, the two houses (one open daily, the other reserved for dinner and private parties) echo loudly of Japan. A blonde wood sushi bar dominates the space accented with decorative ceramic plates, kanji brushed on dangling banners, and artistic florals that evoke the minimalist beauty that Japan has honed so well.

Of course, superior sushi and lunchtime bento boxes keep foodies coming back. Innovative maki and tempura reflect influences from California and the Pacific Rim. Don't miss the outstanding seven-piece omakase, which might highlight an excellent flying fish with ponzu and ginger, or a torched barracuda with daikon radish and scallions.

Tavern at Lark Creek

American

234 Magnolia Ave. (at Madrone Ave.), Larkspur

Phone: 415-924-7766 Lunch Sun
Web: www.tavernatlarkcreek.com Dinner nightly
Prices: $$

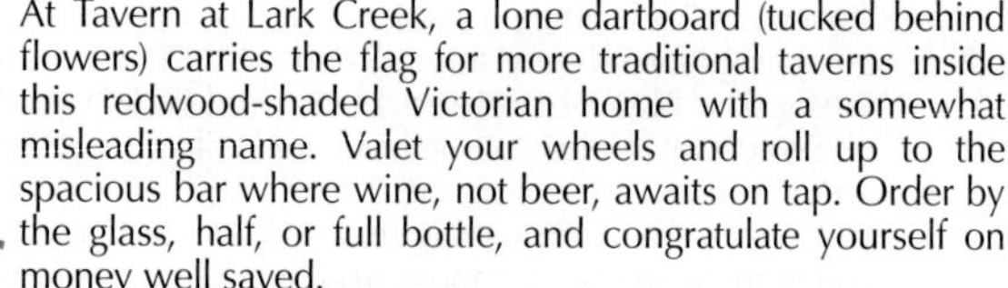

At Tavern at Lark Creek, a lone dartboard (tucked behind flowers) carries the flag for more traditional taverns inside this redwood-shaded Victorian home with a somewhat misleading name. Valet your wheels and roll up to the spacious bar where wine, not beer, awaits on tap. Order by the glass, half, or full bottle, and congratulate yourself on money well saved.

Another bargain may be found in the $29 three-course prix-fixe menu, which changes according to the season. Look for delights such as blue cheese soufflé with arugula, walnuts, and grapes; panko-crusted macaroni and cheese croquettes; and lemon cheesecake brûlée. On weekends, greet the day with brunch at the communal table beneath a massive skylight, or imbibe creative cocktails at dusk.

Tsukiji

Japanese

24 Sunnyside Ave. (at Parkwood St.), Mill Valley

Phone: 415-383-1382 Dinner Tue – Sun
Web: www.tsukijisushimv.com
Prices: $$$

Enclosed by a serene porch in the heart of Mill Valley, Tsukiji is a peaceful sushi spot with outdoor dining in warmer months. Trickling waterfalls recall the Japanese ethos, but a large menu of boldly flavored sushi is more suited to the local American palate. Settle into one of two small dining rooms or pull up a chair at the bar—don't miss the à la carte specials for the day's freshest fish.

Formerly of Sausalito's acclaimed Sushi Ran, the chef turns out such specialty maki as spicy tempura tuna with lemon and red chili aïoli, and a typical Dynamite roll of hamachi, albacore, salmon, and scallions. True sushi lovers will enjoy assorted nigiri: silky toro, *hirame*, and hamachi are served over rice with wasabi and pickled ginger.

Vin Antico

Italian XX

C2

881 4th St. (bet. Cijos St. & Lootens Pl.), San Rafael

Phone: 415-454-4492 Dinner nightly
Web: www.vinantico.com
Prices: **$$**

The scene is comfy and urbane in Vin Antico. Exuding city chic within a small town setting are rich fabrics, handsome hues, Italian marble, *noir* leather, and candle-laden fixtures. Perhaps inspired by Tuscany's venerable reputation for art, framed masterpieces created by local artists grace the brick walls, and Northern Italian culinary treasures are crafted in an exhibition kitchen—solo diners should grab a seat at the counter for maximum viewing pleasure.

The aura is laid-back and the food–most of it hails from Marin County–is gratifying with such gourmet items as handmade sausages; cured meats; and pastas (think parsley fettucine or leek- and lobster-stuffed ravioli).

The bar is a jovial perch for some Italian *vino*.

Park your car without a problem when you see ☞ for valet parking.

Jay Graham

Peninsula

Peninsula

The Peninsula may not be internationally heralded for celebrity chefs and groundbreaking Californian cuisine but, with a diverse population rich in Asian cultures, the area is laden with neighborhood eateries and bountiful markets that appeal to locals craving authentic cuisines. Those seeking a taste of the East can scoop up inexpensive seafood (and links of *longaniza*) alongside the Filipino population at Daly City's **Manila Oriental Market** as well as **Kukje Super Market** (replete with prepared Korean food). Or they can practice the art of chopstick wielding at one of the many Japanese sushi bars, ramen houses, and *izakaya*. Chinese food fans tickle their fancies with traditional sweets such as assorted moon cakes and yolk pastries at San Mateo's cash-only **Sheng Kee Bakery**; while sugar junkies of the western variety chow on authentic Danish pastries at Burlingame's **Copenhagen Bakery**, also known for its special occasion cakes.

In addition to harboring some of the Bay Area's most impressive Cantonese and dim sum houses, Millbrae is a lovely spot to raise one last toast to summer. The Millbrae Art & Wine Festival is a cornucopia of wicked fairground eats—think gooey cheesesteak, Cajun-style corndogs, and fennel-scented sausages. Wash it all down with a glass of wine or a cold microbrew, and kick up your heels to the tune of a local cover band. Speaking of which, **Back A Yard** (in Menlo Park) may be a total dive, but it offers some über flavorful Caribbean food. If, however, it is cooking classes that you seek, head to **Draeger's Market** in San Mateo and sign up for "Indian Cooking Boot Camp" or a lesson in baking "Rustic Italian Breads." While here, also sample artisan and specialty goods (maybe at **Suruki Japanese Market**), or pick up some wine and cheese to-go. Speaking of take-home deliciousness, Half Moon Bay is a must-stop for insanely fresh, seasonal ingredients. Load up on gorgeous fruits and veggies at the many roadside stands on Route 92; and don't miss the town's **Coastside Farmers Market** where you'll find local bounty including Harley Farms goat cheese (from Pescadero), and organic eggs from **Green Oaks Creek Farm** up in the Santa Cruz Mountains.

If seafood is more your speed, **Barbara's Fish Trap**, just north in Princeton by the Sea, serves fish 'n' chips by the harbor. And after all that fish, pork ribs are in order: Join locals et al at **Gorilla Barbeque** for their meaty combos and down-home sides, served out of an orange railroad car on Cabrillo Highway in Pacifica.

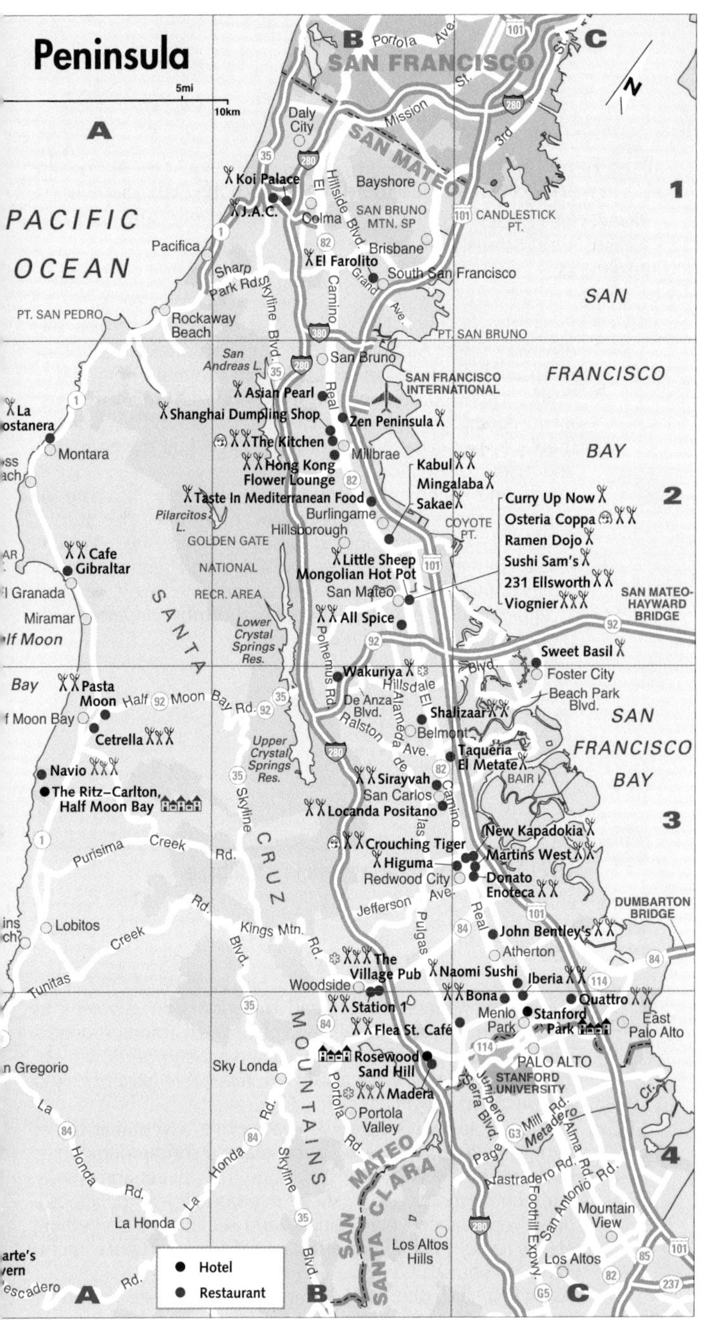
Peninsula
5mi
10km
PACIFIC OCEAN
SAN FRANCISCO BAY
Koi Palace
J.A.C.
El Farolito
Asian Pearl
Shanghai Dumpling Shop
Zen Peninsula
The Kitchen
Hong Kong Flower Lounge
Taste In Mediterranean Food
Kabul
Mingalaba
Sakae
Curry Up Now
Osteria Coppa
Ramen Dojo
Sushi Sam's
231 Ellsworth
Viognier
La Costanera
Cafe Gibraltar
Little Sheep Mongolian Hot Pot
All Spice
Sweet Basil
Wakuriya
Pasta Moon
Cetrella
Shalizaar
Taqueria El Metate
Navio
The Ritz-Carlton, Half Moon Bay
Sirayvah
Locanda Positano
New Kapadokia
Crouching Tiger
Martins West
Higuma
Donato Enoteca
John Bentley's
The Village Pub
Naomi Sushi
Iberia
Bona
Quattro
Station 1
Flea St. Café
Stanford Park
Rosewood Sand Hill
Madera
Hotel
Restaurant
SAN FRANCISCO
SAN MATEO
SANTA CRUZ MOUNTAINS
SAN MATEO
SANTA CLARA
Daly City
Colma
Bayshore
SAN BRUNO MTN. SP
CANDLESTICK PT.
Brisbane
South San Francisco
Pacifica
Rockaway Beach
PT. SAN PEDRO
PT. SAN BRUNO
San Bruno
SAN FRANCISCO INTERNATIONAL
Millbrae
Montara
Burlingame
Hillsborough
COYOTE PT.
GOLDEN GATE NATIONAL RECR. AREA
San Mateo
SAN MATEO-HAYWARD BRIDGE
Foster City
Miramar
Hillsdale
Belmont
Half Moon Bay
San Carlos
Redwood City
DUMBARTON BRIDGE
Atherton
Lobitos
Woodside
Menlo Park
East Palo Alto
PALO ALTO
STANFORD UNIVERSITY
Sky Londa
Portola Valley
La Honda
Los Altos Hills
Los Altos
Mountain View
San Andreas L.
Pilarcitos L.
Lower Crystal Springs Res.
Upper Crystal Springs Res.
BAIR I.
A
B
C
1
2
3
4
N

All Spice

Indian XX

1602 El Camino Real (bet. Barneson & Borel Aves.), San Mateo

Phone: 650-627-4303 — Dinner Tue – Sat
Web: www.allspicerestaurant.com
Prices: **$$**

Drive slowly down El Camino Real or you might miss the driveway up to All Spice, a contemporary Indian restaurant in an unlikely Victorian set back from the main drag. Once inside, a sense of romance wraps you in rich wall coverings, inlaid hardwood floors, intricate moldings, and a crackling fireplace. Get cozy in one of three close-knit dining rooms and ready yourself for a journey.

Chef/owner Sachin Chopra honed his skills in some of country's finest kitchens and now turns out adventurous Indian flavors with muted spice to suit the Western palate. Dishes may include star anise and fennel chicken wings bathed in lemongrass, yuzu, and chili sauce; smoked lavender and cumin scallops; and shortribs *vindaloo* with molten goat cheese and baby bok choy.

Asian Pearl

Chinese X

B2

1671 El Camino Real (at Park Pl.), Millbrae

Phone: 650-616-8288 — Lunch Wed, Sat – Sun; Dinner nightly
Web: N/A
Prices:

Follow the Chinese locals and true dim sum devotees to Asian Pearl, take a number, and line up to sit among strangers in a banquet-style hall where the service can be downright gruff. Nonetheless, what awaits is a moveable feast of baked and steamed delights.

Pushcarts and whirling server trays bring a veritable buffet right to your table. Choose from steamed shrimp dumplings; pork spareribs with nutty sesame oil; sweet-and-smoky barbecue pork buns; and sticky rice noodle rolls deliciously filled with minced beef, ginger, and scallions. If something seems to be missing, just ask a server for a particular menu item and you shall receive it within minutes.

Asian Pearl also offers an à la carte menu for those who prefer to stick out from the crowd.

Bona

Polish

651 Maloney St. (bet. Chestnut Ln. & Oak Grove Ave.), Menlo Park

Phone: 650-328-2778 — Lunch Tue – Fri
Web: www.bonasrestaurant.com — Dinner Tue – Sun
Prices: **$$**

On an easy-to-miss lane in Menlo Park, Bona's authentic fare is just like your Polish grandmother used to make (or good enough to make you wish you had one). Expect delicious sourdough soup, or *zurek*, made from fermented starter for a fabulously tangy broth laden with potatoes, pork sausage, carrots, and herbs; potato and cheese *pierogis* drizzled in melted butter; and stuffed cabbage rolls smothered in mushroom sauce.

This relative newcomer is already packed with Polish and Eastern European families who appreciate the concise menu and taste of home; but its casual vibe, with wood furnishings and burgundy linen-topped tables, is more than welcoming to foreigners.

And if the food sounds heavy, just wear loose pants, skip dessert, and allow time for a nap.

Cafe Gibraltar

Mediterranean

425 Avenue Alhambra (at Palma St.), El Granada

Phone: 650-560-9039 — Dinner Tue – Sun
Web: www.cafegibraltar.com
Prices: **$$$**

The world is small and delicious at Café Gibraltar, the coastal San Mateo county kitchen that melds French, Italian, Persian, and Moroccan flavors all in one big pot—plus a dash of Turkey, Greece, and Spain. Watch the cuisine come to life over the wood-fired oven in the open kitchen, or sink into a floor cushion beneath a tented table tucked away for a sexy North African vibe.

Wherever you sit, prepare to be charmed. Sunny hues and Moorish accents set the scene for Chef/owner Jose Luis Ugalde's aromatic Mediterranean fare. Begin with an ample meze platter laden with flatbread, roasted garlic, olives, and spreads; then meander on to a slow-braised lamb shank in harissa-date-red wine broth. For dessert, indulge in a velvety lavender crème brûlée.

Cetrella

Mediterranean XXX

A3

845 Main St. (at Spruce St.), Half Moon Bay

Phone: 650-726-4090 — Lunch Sun
Web: www.cetrella.com — Dinner nightly
Prices: $$$

If not for the striped banquettes and contemporary accents, Cetrella could be of another place and time—encapsulated in a gold-flecked Mediterranean villa with exposed wood beams peering down on private dining rooms, a glass-encased cheese pantry, wood-burning fireplace, and wine cellar with more than 400 international vintages.

Possibly the most stylish restaurant in Half Moon Bay, Cetrella also serves some of the town's most sophisticated fare. Its market-driven menu might feature red wine-braised lamb ravioli with bitter dandelion greens, or a perfectly seasoned fillet of salmon with bacon-wrapped potato gratin. Desserts fall short of Cetrella's savory accomplishments; opt instead for a nightcap on the terrace.

Crouching Tiger

Chinese XX

C3

2644 Broadway St. (bet. El Camino Real & Perry St.), Redwood City

Phone: 650-298-8881 — Lunch & dinner daily
Web: www.crouchingtigerrestaurant.com
Prices:

A word of warning to the chili-intolerant: this fiery cat will pounce. These Sichuan and Hunan signature dishes ain't for the faint, humming with chilies, chili oil, chili paste, fearlessly kicking up that painful-but-heavenly heat (though tamer options do exist). A popular spot for inexpensive business lunches and family-style dinners, the inviting space sports dark wood furnishings, vibrant touches, and large round tables with lazy Susans.

Get your spice on with a number of delicious goodies, like silky *mapo* tofu with ginger and garlic; flaky white fish filets with sautéed zucchini, carrot, and bamboo shoots braised in red chili sauce; succulent Sichuan prawns; and tender wok-fried Mongolian beef with caramelized onions and oyster sauce.

Curry Up Now

Indian

129 S. B St. (bet. 1st and 2nd Aves.), San Mateo

Phone: 650-477-3000 Lunch & dinner Tue – Sun
Web: www.curryupnow.com
Prices: ⊜

Hurry up now and head to Curry Up Now—one of those rare food carts that has successfully transitioned into a *pukka* diner. This San Mateo curry house prepares mighty flavorful Indian street food in a simple, clean dining room. Yet, local fans don't seem to mind the minimalist mien and pack the den for seasoned faves like the *chicken tikka masala* burrito mingling *chana masala* and spiced rice in a soft flour tortilla. Before the enticing aromas wafting from the kitchen wholly engulf you, notice the chalkboard listing of daily specials; and dive into a deliciously deconstructed *samosa* before moving on to the large *thali* combining *paratha* and delicious *methi pulao* with *keema matar aloo* (ground beef with potatoes and peas) and *desi* hot habanero sauce.

Donato Enoteca

1041 Middlefield Rd. (bet. Jefferson Ave. & Main St.), Redwood City

Phone: 650-701-1000 Lunch & dinner daily
Web: www.donatoenoteca.com
Prices: **$$**

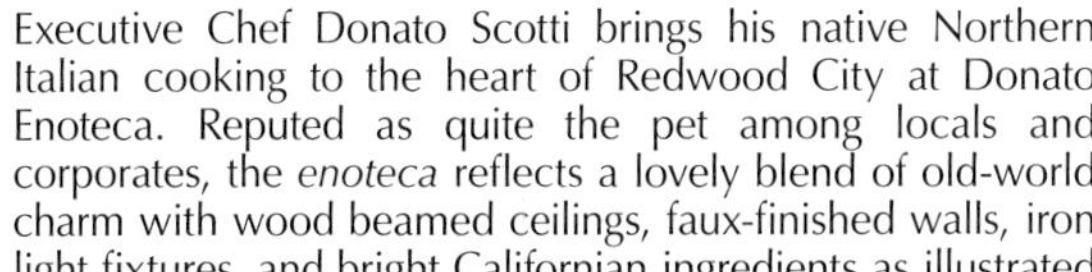

Executive Chef Donato Scotti brings his native Northern Italian cooking to the heart of Redwood City at Donato Enoteca. Reputed as quite the pet among locals and corporates, the *enoteca* reflects a lovely blend of old-world charm with wood beamed ceilings, faux-finished walls, iron light fixtures, and bright Californian ingredients as illustrated in the market-driven menu.

When the sun shines, locals lull in the large outdoor patio shaded by umbrellas and potted plants. The elegant indoors features a well-liked dining counter that overlooks an open kitchen bubbling with preparations like homemade agnolotti stuffed with sausage and veal; wood-fired pizza; or sautéed Mediterranean sea bream.

A lounge-like wine bar offers a solid range of Italian varietals.

Duarte's Tavern

American

202 Stage Rd. (at Pescadero Creek Rd.), Pescadero

Phone: 650-879-0464 Lunch & dinner daily
Web: www.duartestavern.com
Prices: **$$**

Duarte's is a longtime favorite of the food media who are perpetually extolling the virtues of this old-time place with amazing American staples. Naturally, die-hard foodies and tourists pack the 115-year-old family-run tavern, but pulling up to its Pescadero locale, it's easy to wonder if you're in the wrong place: Duarte's surrounds resemble the Wild West, and that's part of the charm.

The legendary duo of artichoke and green chile soups (that locals like to mix) is worth all the hype, but instead of a slice of the overrated olallieberry pie focus on the simply prepared seafood and specials. Coastal proximity means superior swimmers so don't miss outstanding baked oysters, pan-seared abalone, lightly fried calamari, or an aromatic bowl of cioppino.

El Farolito

394 Grand Ave. (at Maple Ave.), South San Francisco

Phone: 650-737-0138 Lunch & dinner daily
Web: www.elfarolitoinc.com
Prices:

San Franciscans are welcome to wait in line at the Mission's location of El Farolito, where super burritos are a tasty cult classic. But, just minutes south of town, this San Francisco locale serves the same satisfying fare to a local working class that is happy to walk right up to the counter and order their hearts' content.

Cleaner than most of El Farolito's outposts, the dining room (if you can call it that) is all about cheap, yummy eats. If the massive grilled chicken burrito packed with black beans, rice, and cheese isn't enough to satiate you, take a gander at shrimp ceviche tostadas; slightly spicy green chile pork tacos; or crispy *taquitos* with smoky carne asada. Cinnamon *horchata* is a sweet addition to a meal—never mind the Styrofoam cup.

Flea St. Café

C4 — Californian XX

3607 Alameda de las Pulgas (at Avy Ave.), Menlo Park

Phone: 650-854-1226 — Dinner Tue – Sun
Web: www.cooleatz.com
Prices: $$$

A cozy neighborhood eatery with small tables and low light, Flea St. Café is a choice spot for date night among Menlo Park locals. Built on a slope, the space houses multiple tiered and intimate dining rooms as well as a quaint front bar where a smoky Napa Valley merlot tastes just right.

A favorite among area restaurants serving Californian cuisine, Flea St. puts the emphasis on locally sourced, organic ingredients. A hint of international inspiration is apparent in such dishes as house-made lamb sausage with spicy peach compote; while down-home flavors shine in fried green tomatoes with avocado and chipotle aïoli. For a fantastic taste of salty-sweet perfection, sink your teeth into the honey-soy glazed duck breast with pomegranate-bacon vinaigrette.

Higuma

C3 — Japanese X

540 El Camino Real (bet. Hopkins & Whipple Aves.), Redwood City

Phone: 650-369-3240 — Lunch Mon – Fri, Dinner nightly
Web: www.higuma-restaurant.com
Prices: ©©

Easygoing and intimate Higuma is housed in a quaint little bungalow on El Camino Real, and is adored by suits and regulars for its honest Japanese preparations. The small cottage is cloaked in wood and wooden accents (Japanese brown bears, *higumas*, dot the space), and feels rustic and cozy. And nothing says cozy better than steaming, comforting bowls of ramen noodles or a miso soup.

The chef's sushi assortment emerges as an ungarnished array of neat packages of fresh fish placed atop rice. Also featured is a large lineup of specialty rolls, sashimi, and donburi. Seats at the tiny sushi bar are at a premium here, but small tables hug each other in the dining room where you will be greeted with friendly service, pretty prices, and top-notch ingredients.

Hong Kong Flower Lounge

Chinese XX

B2

51 Millbrae Ave. (at El Camino Real), Millbrae

Phone: 650-692-6666 Lunch & dinner daily
Web: www.mayflower-seafood.com
Prices: $$

When in Millbrae, do as the local Chinese do and go directly for dim sum at Hong Kong Flower Lounge. No need to look hard—its dramatic, multi-level pagoda-style façade is immediately recognizable. On weekends, bring your morning paper and wait among the crowds craving sticky rice noodle rolls with tender beef and scallions; smoky-salty-sweet sliced barbecue pork; and *Wushi*–style spareribs infused with rice wine, soy, and ginger.

Luckily, 400 seats give Hong Kong Flower Lounge the upper hand; like the namesake city itself, it is a veritable mob scene. Look for the servers in pink jackets if you don't speak Cantonese. Crowds aren't your thing? Forgo the whirling rolling carts at lunch and come for seafood and traditional à la carte fare at dinner.

Iberia

Spanish XX

C4

1026 Alma St. (at Ravenswood St.), Menlo Park

Phone: 650-325-8981 Lunch Mon – Sat
Web: www.iberiarestaurant.com Dinner nightly
Prices: $$

Charmingly housed in a cozy bungalow on a quiet street across from the train station, Iberia celebrates the best and boldest Spanish cuisine. From the avocado relleno stuffed with bay shrimp to crab *buñuelos* in a roasted pepper-hazelnut sauce, offerings showcase a large selection of tapas, ever-changing specials, and more ambitious seafood entrées. Once you're comfortably seated, look forward to an array of delightful delicacies like *paella típica*, espalda *de cerdo* (pork shoulder), or *tarta de Santiago* (orange-almond torte).

The tree-shaded patio makes a perfect spot to sip a glass of the house sangria on a warm day. Next door, The Rock of Gibraltar Comestibles sells quality Spanish ingredients, as well as a sampling of dishes to-go.

J.A.C.

713 Hickey Blvd. (bet. Gateway Dr. & Skyline Blvd.), Pacifica

Phone: 650-359-4522 Lunch & dinner Tue – Sun
Web: N/A
Prices: ⊖⊖

Try the Fairmont shopping center in Pacifica for some honest to goodness, fresh Filipino treats, and nevermind the slow, spacey service. Inside, J.A.C. (Juan de la Cruz Asian Cuisine) is styled in simple, blonde wood furnishings giving off a casual, clean vibe.

Dishes are authentic, flavorful, and homey, ranging from soups and stews to marinated and grilled pork to deep-fried beef short ribs. Begin with *lumpiang* Shanghai with pork and shrimp—crispy spring rolls stuffed with toothsome ground pork and a single, plump prawn served with a sweet-chili dipping sauce. Look for *"ni Juan"* on the menu, indicating house specialties like the hearty *micehado ni Juan*, with tender beef, carrots, and bell peppers stewed in a tasty tomato, soy, and vinegar broth.

John Bentley's

Contemporary 

2915 El Camino Real (bet. Berkshire Ave. & E. Selby Ln.), Redwood City

Phone: 650-365-7777 Lunch Mon – Fri
Web: www.johnbentleys.com Dinner Mon – Sat
Prices: $$$

There's no mistaking a genuine local favorite, and John Bentley's is one such place. Find all the elements necessary to convert patrons into regulars: a trellised entrance entangled with vines; laid-back ambience; comfortable booths; rustic design; and American fare that is consistently good. Expect a working crowd at lunch and a mix of residents for dinner.

To start, John Bentley's serves an ample selection of California-fresh salads and Dungeness crab, in season. Eggplant and portobello mushroom ravioli, cooked al dente with balsamic reduction, is also an exciting first course. Hungrier guests can sink their teeth into a double-cut pork chop, flavorful though perhaps a touch dry, served with a rustic mash of Yukon Gold potatoes and haricots verts.

Kabul

Afghan 

B2

1101 Burlingame Ave. (at California Dr.), Burlingame

Phone: 650-343-2075 Lunch & dinner daily
Web: www.kabulcuisine.com
Prices: **$$**

Sister to the original location in San Carlos, this pleasant Burlingame favorite offers a true taste of Afghanistan amid dark wood furnishings, colorful tapestries, and windowed walls that stream in sunlight. The décor is simple and the service informal, but this local spot is filled with surprises.

The home-style menu may include dishes of *sambosa-e-ghoushti*—fried pastries stuffed with a tender mix of ground lamb and chickpeas infused with garlic and spices. Topped with garlic yogurt, the large, sweet, and silky chunks of pumpkin in *challaw kadu* may actually melt in your mouth. The *kabal-e-gousfand*, skewers of tender marinated lamb, is charbroiled and perfectly completed with fragrant basmati rice and fluffy flatbread sprinkled with poppy seeds.

Bib Gourmand ☺ indicates our inspectors' favorites for good value.

The Kitchen

279 El Camino Real (at La Cruz Ave.), Millbrae

Phone: 650-692-9688 Lunch & dinner daily
Web: www.thekitchenmillbrae.com
Prices: $$

Parked in a largely Asian locale, The Kitchen unfolds top-notch dim sum and delicacy-laden Cantonese specialties to a knowledgeable Asian crowd. Step into their professionally-run dining room freckled with large tables and fish tanks, then merely take a whiff. Rest assured, you will want to return with many friends and family to sample their abounding offerings. Let the Cantonese chronicles at lunch begin with a tasting from the well-versed chef's classics or inventive dim sum such as chive dumplings; a cilantro bean curd salad; and pan-fried bun wrapping pork and veggies. Or turn a leaf to the sizeable dinner menu–think of wasabi-tossed chicken with pork belly or sautéed squab with foie gras and shredded lettuce–and let your palate absorb the rest.

Koi Palace

365 Gellert Blvd. (bet. Hickey & Serramonte Blvds.), Daly City

Phone: 650-992-9000 Lunch & dinner daily
Web: www.koipalace.com
Prices: $$

Koi Palace can seat 400 guests, and the ample parking lot often overflows with cars having to be stationed on the surrounding streets. This phenomenon bespeaks the restaurant's popularity—mostly with a local Chinese clientele who flock here for dim sum at appealing prices.

Walk through the moon gate to spot aquarium tanks swimming with the day's catch; koi ponds in the dining room add aesthetic appeal for adults and provide little ones with entertainment. Try to snag a seat on an aisle for the best service. From here, you can more easily hail the servers who hurry by with a staggering array of items. Offerings include everything from familiar *siu mai* with diced mushrooms or barbecued pork, to exotic fare like poached queen's clam and soya duck slices.

La Costanera ✿

Peruvian ✕✕

A2

8150 Cabrillo Hwy. (bet. 1st & 2nd Sts.), Montara

Phone: 650-728-1600 Dinner Tue – Sun
Web: www.lacostanerarestaurant.com
Prices: **$$$**

Hamid Rafeiri

Discreetly set off Cabrillo Highway, La Costanera's location is simply spectacular. Perched on a beach alcove with views right over the ocean, imagine yourself being swept away from the Peninsula and onto a remote island somewhere. Peek inside this glass-cased Peruvian respite dressed in billowing fabrics, shells, sea-washed wood, and sand, and breathe in the spacious room.

The bar matched with spellbinding outdoor seating, is truly a dream spot to watch the sunset over ample pisco sours. Everyone here is having a great time.

Keeping company with the gorgeous environs is a massive menu of flavorful delights, and warm servers who are happy to indulge your Peruvian-Pacific cravings with the likes of *causa clássica, aji amarillo*-tinged mashed potatoes layered with chicken and drizzled with a green garlic sauce; and *cebiche Chino-Peruano,* ahi tuna excellently mixed with scallion slivers and *aji rocoto.* If the fish special (wahoo with spicy *cau cau*) doesn't wholly bewitch you, the *choclo serrano,* steamed corn on the cob deliciously coated with *huacatay* and *queso fresco*; and *alfajores* with *dulche de leche,* honey-almond cookies creamed with divine *dulce de leche,* will do the trick.

Little Sheep Mongolian Hot Pot

Chinese

215 S. Ellsworth Ave. (bet. 2nd & 3rd Sts.), San Mateo

Phone: 650-343-2566 Lunch & dinner daily
Web: www.littlesheephotpot.com
Prices: $$

You could hop a flight to China, where Little Sheep Mongolian Hot Pot's parent company is based. Or, you could jaunt to San Mateo for lunch and be back in the city for afternoon tea. While quite contemporary, Little Sheep is also reminiscent of its home country with a trickling water fountain, stalks of bamboo, and grassy swaths of paint.

Piquant spices waft from each table where a cauldron of simmering broth sits on a small warming burner: dining here is a do-it-yourself affair. The adventure begins with a high-quality aromatic broth, either original or spicy, but gets exciting when bountiful platters of ingredients arrive. Choose from sliced raw meats, assorted fresh vegetables, and herbs, then toss it all in for a fragrant, group-friendly feast.

Locanda Positano

Italian

617 Laurel St. (bet. Cherry St. & San Carlos Ave.), San Carlos

Phone: 650-591-5700 Lunch & dinner Tue – Sun
Web: www.locanda-positano.com
Prices: $$

San Carlos foodies have good reason to toast this wood-burning pizza oven, imported directly from Italy, at Laurel Street's new Locanda Positano. Fired up and ready to lick thin Neapolitan-style crusts, the oven churns out fragrant, delicious pies such as the Sofia Loren—a signature topped with buffalo mozzarella, prosciutto, fresh arugula, eggplant, artichoke, and zucchini.

The selection of pizzas, simple salads, and a menu for *bambini* make this a go-to favorite for local families. Tasty salads, such as grilled artichokes with spicy arugula in tangy citronette, make way for the star of this show, best viewed from a seat at the counter facing the pizza oven. Larger parties appreciate the friendly Italian servers and chic, contemporary dining room.

Madera ✿

Contemporary

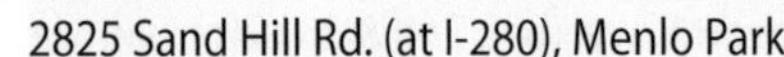

B4

2825 Sand Hill Rd. (at I-280), Menlo Park

Phone: 650-561-1540 Lunch & dinner daily
Web: www.maderasandhill.com
Prices: **$$$$**

Rosewood Hotels & Resorts

Beneath the suitably lofty ceilings of this gorgeously laid-back Rosewood Sand Hill power scene, find Menlo Park's answer to business dining. The vibe here is comfortable and manages not to take itself too seriously, making everything pleasant yet primo (check out the swanky cars in the lot).

Whether heading to the heated terrace or large, attractive dining room, sneak a peek into the open kitchen, where the excellent chefs are preparing a seasonally focused bill of fare that balances modern and creative flair with great ingredients. Expect solid dishes from start to finish, beginning with the likes of braised Snake River Farms pork belly, served meltingly tender and accented with crispy trotters piled atop white asparagus, drizzled with mustard-caviar sauce and *yuzu-kosho* vinaigrette. Everything may sound complex, but in fact the chefs layer flavors to create harmonious and undeniably pleasing combinations that are all too difficult to find. This is equally true of entrées such as Artic char with favas and Oregon Bay shrimp in a pool of English pea purée, and desserts like Earl Grey chocolate tart.

Let the talented sommelier help you chose the right wine to impress those VCs.

Martins West

Gastropub XX

831 Main St. (bet. Broadway & Stambaugh Sts.), Redwood City

Phone: 650-366-4366 — Lunch Wed – Sat
Web: www.martinswestgp.com — Dinner Mon – Sat
Prices: $$

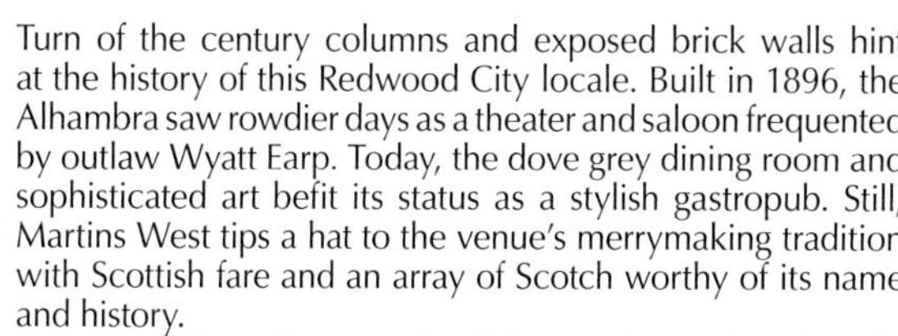

Turn of the century columns and exposed brick walls hint at the history of this Redwood City locale. Built in 1896, the Alhambra saw rowdier days as a theater and saloon frequented by outlaw Wyatt Earp. Today, the dove grey dining room and sophisticated art befit its status as a stylish gastropub. Still, Martins West tips a hat to the venue's merrymaking tradition with Scottish fare and an array of Scotch worthy of its name and history.

Sample traditional tastes in dishes such as tiny Scotch-style quail eggs with a zesty sausage-breadcrumb crust; rich terrines of pheasant; or flaky, ale-battered fish and chips doused in malt vinegar. Then, consider drinking your dessert—the spiked apple cider with Drambuie cream tops the seasonal offerings.

Mingalaba

1213 Burlingame Ave. (bet. Lorton Ave. & Park Rd.), Burlingame

Phone: 650-343-3228 — Lunch & dinner daily
Web: www.mingalabarestaurant.com
Prices: 

Take a break from strolling the shops of Burlingame Ave., and step inside Mingalaba. This quick service hot spot has a loyal and large following, so get here early to avoid a wait. Amidst bamboo wainscoting, modern lighting, and bright walls gilded with Asian artifacts, crowds gather if only to get a whiff of the kitchen's Burmese (and Mandarin) preparations. Most locals know the drill and let cheery servers tempt with bold Burmese fare over more forgettable Mandarin menu options. Begin with a *lap pat dok* (tea leaf salad); move on to a Burmese-style black pepper soup with fish; break at string beans with dried shrimp; and finally, thrill your taste buds with a spicy lamb curry. Cool down at dessert with mango pudding served in a leaf-shaped bowl.

Naomi Sushi

Japanese X

C3

1328 El Camino Real (bet. Glenwood & Oak Grove Aves.), Menlo Park

Phone: 650-321-6902 — Lunch Tue – Fri
Web: www.naomisushi.com — Dinner Tue – Sun
Prices: $$

They say never judge a book by its cover, and the same holds true for this modest Menlo Park sushi spot—for what it lacks on the outside, it more than makes up for on the inside with well-prepared, quality sushi and sashimi. Welcoming patrons as they enter (besides the private parking) is a sushi bar which is the place to park yourself to enjoy a traditional and reasonably-priced omakase.

Two dining rooms recall a rustic seaside tavern dressed up with fishing paraphernalia and murals of the ocean. Here, Japanese dishes exhibit a clear Californian twist as in the 49er roll with spicy yellow tail, white tuna, and avocado; or linguni with grilled chicken and shrimp. Be sure to investigate the daily specials as well as sake samples that spin with the week.

Navio

Californian XXX

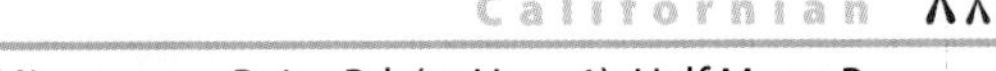

A3

1 Miramontes Point Rd. (at Hwy. 1), Half Moon Bay

Phone: 650-712-7040 — Lunch Sat – Sun
Web: www.ritzcarlton.com — Dinner nightly
Prices: $$$$

Housed in the Ritz-Carlton and boasting spectacular ocean views, Navio begins with a level of refinement that carries through to the barrel-vaulted ceilings, tufted chocolate leather banquettes, and internationally inspired Californian fare from the dramatic exhibition kitchen.

This is the Ritz, so elegance is de rigueur; but it's also the Bay Area, so expect a local bent. The menu highlights area producers in dishes like oxtail ravioli with wilted mustard greens and beef consommé; stuffed quail with butternut squash and cinnamon jus; and Dungeness crab with huckleberries and vanilla gastrique. Not every dish is transcendent here, but a vista of the California sun dripping into dusky Half Moon Bay may be all the epiphany you can handle over dinner.

New Kapadokia

2399 Broadway St. (at Winslow St.), Redwood City

Phone: 650-368-5500 — Lunch Tue – Fri
Web: www.newkapadokia.com — Dinner Tue – Sun
Prices: 

Named for Turkey's region known for ancient underground cities, New Kapadokia is perhaps the most genuine culinary experience this side of the Aegean Sea. Unlike the average Turkish eatery, this family-run restaurant is proud of its heritage and serves only authentic recipes, many of which were handed down from the chef's mother and grandmother. The uninitiated should rely on the knowledgeable staff and the trays of starters or desserts they bring to you to assist with ordering. Kebabs are wrapped in *lavash* and served with garlicky yogurt, sumac, and spicy sauce, while platters teem with lamb and vegetable stews.

Say hello to gracious owner Celal Alpay, and don't miss the spinning Turkish coffee—its service here is quite the performance!

Osteria Coppa

139 N. B St. (bet. 1st & 2nd Aves.), San Mateo

Phone: 650-579-6021 — Lunch Mon –Fri
Web: www.osteriacoppa.com — Dinner nightly
Prices: $$

No wonder Chef Chanan Kamen, a veteran of San Francisco's Quince, was welcomed with open arms when he brought this charming newcomer, Osteria Coppa, to San Mateo. The ingredients are superb, the kitchen is skillful, and the chef's meticulous eye for detail has fashioned a place where–order what you like–everything is good. As expected, Coppa's handmade pastas are a true high point, including *bigoli* tossed with fresh cranberry beans and house-made pancetta. The vibe is casually quaint, with dark wood covering everything from the close-knit wood tables to the floor and bar. Service is friendly, and a few alfresco tables are available on the petite back patio. Consider this a perfect destination for dinner before a movie at the neighboring theater.

Pasta Moon

A3 — Italian XX

315 Main St. (at Mill St.), Half Moon Bay

Phone: 650-726-5125 — Lunch & dinner daily
Web: www.pastamoon.com
Prices: **$$**

It's definitely *amore* when this (Pasta) moon hits your eye. Located on the main drag in charming Half Moon Bay, Pasta Moon is a sure bet for yup, you guessed it, pasta!

Its design can feel like a haphazard and half-finished mix of spaces that afford views of pasta-making during trips to the restrooms; but after a few bites, you won't care that the owner needs to find an architect—stat. Dreamy pastas along with homemade pizzas and breads are divine. You can't go wrong with anything on this Californian-Italian menu. The lasagna strays from grandma's standard with impressive results and is packed with rich, creamy flavor; while crispy *fritto misto* and a Brussels sprout salad tossed with pancetta and cannellini beans are beloved at all times.

Quattro

C4 — Italian XX

2050 University Ave. (at I-101), East Palo Alto

Phone: 650-566-1200 — Lunch & dinner daily
Web: www.fourseasons.com/siliconvalley
Prices: **$$$**

Inside the Four Seasons Silicon Valley, Quattro is inspired by the constant revolution of nature. A garden patio is ideal for warmer months while a roaring fireplace in the lounge wards off a winter chill. In the main dining room, high ceilings embrace glowing natural light while plush chairs invite business travelers and posh couples to get cozy—frosted glass panels lend extra privacy to the banquettes.

A casually refined clientele nibbles focaccia with truffled ricotta while perusing the seasonal menu. Expect such contemporary Italian fare as prosciutto-wrapped quail with saffron-poached kumquats in foie gras sauce; *pizzocheri*, flat buckwheat pasta with Taleggio and earthy mushrooms; and expertly roasted duck breast with apples and parsnip purée.

Ramen Dojo

Japanese

805 S. B St. (bet. 8th & 9th Sts.), San Mateo

Phone: 650-401-6568 Lunch & dinner Wed – Mon
Web: N/A
Prices: ⊜

Busy office types find plenty of time to catch up on the morning paper while in line for lunch at Ramen Dojo, the popular San Mateo Japanese noodle house that often comes with a half hour wait. Add your name to the clipboard at the door and ponder your soup of choice.

The dining room isn't much to look at, and service is quick and minimal, but everyone is here for the hearty, steaming bowls of ramen. Soups are available with three base options (soy sauce, garlic-pork, and soy bean) and three degrees of heat (mild, regular, and extra spicy). All orders come heaped with roasted pork, fried garlic, kikurage mushrooms, scallions, and hard-boiled quail egg, but a list of extra toppings also includes Napa cabbage, shiitake mushrooms, and Kurobuta pork.

Sakae

Japanese

243 California Dr. (at Highland Ave.), Burlingame

Phone: 650-348-4064 Lunch Mon – Sat
Web: www.sakaesushi.com Dinner nightly
Prices: $$

Downtown Burlingame may be the last place one would expect to find authentic sushi, but Sakae hits the spot with fish flown in daily from Japan's Tsukiji Market. While it may be surprising, this stylish eatery is certainly no secret—at lunch, the blonde wood sushi bar and tables are packed with local business types.

For those on the go, affordable combos are an easy treat; but those with time to savor a meal should first check out the boards listing the daily specials. Sample a nigiri plate of albacore and bluefin tuna, kanpachi, and mackerel; or warm up with a bowl of udon noodle soup with seaweed and spicy *togarashi*.

Weekends feature sake flights and live karaoke for all. Also try Yuzu, their sister restaurant in San Mateo.

Shalizaar

Persian XX

B3

300 El Camino Real (bet. Anita & Belmont Aves.), Belmont

Phone: 650-596-9000 Lunch & dinner daily
Web: www.shalizaar.com
Prices: $$

For a taste of Persia on this side of the pond, head to Shalizaar—a large restaurant sleekly attired in wood floors, walls of windows, and French doors that flood the room with light. A central chandelier adorned with leaves sparkles above beautiful wood-wainscoting and a communal table packed with corporate casts and families alike.

An open wood-fired oven in the back is used for baking warm flatbread paired with feta, walnuts, and fresh mint. Served with every meal, this may be chased by ample portions of *tah dig*, crisped rice topped with *gheymeh* (a flavorful stew of ground beef, chickpeas, and Persian spices); *soltani* mingling *barg* and *koobideh* (beef) kabobs with saffron-tinged white rice; and flaky *baghlava* redolent of walnuts and cinnamon.

Shanghai Dumpling Shop

Chinese X

B2

455 Broadway (bet. Hillcrest & Taylor Blvds.), Millbrae

Phone: 650-697-0682 Lunch & dinner daily
Web: N/A
Prices: ⊜

They say that good things come to those who wait. At Shanghai Dumpling Shop, the mmm-mmm goodness comes in the form of delectable soup dumplings, or *xiao long bao* to those in the know. Served with black vinegar and bits of ginger, these tender pork-stuffed morsels may be the gateway to Nirvana. Of course, half the town is lining up at the gates of heaven, so prepare to park it on the sidewalk before claiming a table at lunch.

This particular slice of paradise comes with minimal décor, but the place is packed to the rafters with suits looking to cheer up on authentic and soul-warming Shanghainese treats. Dim sum offerings also include fluffy steamed pork buns; spicy wontons with peanut-chili sauce; and black sesame dumplings bobbing in a rice wine soup.

Sirayvah

Thai XX

366 El Camino Real (bet. Bush & Oak Sts.), San Carlos

Phone: 650-637-1500 — Lunch Mon – Fri
Web: N/A — Dinner nightly
Prices: $$

Sirayvah is a vibrant departure from the ho-hum Thai joints where sauces and spices overwhelm. In this tiny bungalow, homegrown organic herbs and vegetables, free-range and hormone-free meats, and wild-caught fish are allowed to shine in fresh, light, and buoyant preparations. Dishes may be spicy upon request.

The understated, contemporary dining room dressed in dark wood and tan is a relaxed environment for lunch or dinner. If you judge a restaurant by its soup, Sirayvah's inspired interpretation does not disappoint: a *kabocha* pumpkin purée with bits of mixed vegetables and sweet coconut milk is velvety and delicious. Crunchy green beans and bell peppers, as well as delightfully nutty rice, are a surprising highlight in tender *prik khing* chicken.

Station 1

Californian XX

2991 Woodside Rd. (bet. Mountain Home & Whiskey Hill Rds.), Woodside

Phone: 650-851-4988 — Dinner Tue – Sat
Web: www.station1restaurant.com
Prices: $$

Woodside couples and families have a perfect little local haunt in Station 1, a renovated firehouse with an easy, rustic vibe. Jarred candles, vintage wallpaper, and a fireplace add warmth to wood plank tables and matching reclaimed floors in a dining room that packs loads of charm into a teeny space. The covered porch in the back is even more petite and bustles with the noise from the adjacent kitchen.

Earthenware with playful etchings made by a local artist are a quirky backdrop for more refined Californian fare: a $49 three-course dinner may include a delish smoked gnocchi with deep-fried tripe and pickled parsley root; roulade of roast chicken with caramelized cheese grits; and moist hazelnut cake with milk chocolate ganache and apricot jam.

Sushi Sam's

Japanese

218 E. 3rd Ave. (bet. B St. & Ellsworth Ave.), San Mateo

Phone: 650-344-0888 Lunch & dinner Tue – Sat
Web: www.sushisams.com
Prices: $$

Do not be fooled by the no-frills dining space and nondescript exterior—this San Mateo sushi spot is a treasure. Forget the lunchtime bento box and opt for the luscious omakase, which promises that this very good little *sushi-ya* understands excellence.

On this menu, the chef prepares generous slices of their freshest fish, with garnishes that enhance natural flavors. Expect succulent, sweet blue shrimp; silky butterfish topped with tangy pickled daikon and scallions; ponzu-topped wild Japanese yellowtail; or sweet lobster nigiri with creamy *tobiko* mayo and toasted, sliced almonds. Dessert may include mild and velvety *teh kuan yin* panna cotta, delicately embellished with chrysanthemum syrup, poached goji berries, crispy puffed brown rice, and *mochi.*

Sweet Basil

Thai

1473 Beach Park Blvd. (at Marlin Ave.), Foster City

Phone: 650-212-5788 Lunch & dinner daily
Web: www.sweetbasilfoster.com
Prices: ©©

While veggie lovers may head to Basil Cha Cha, the vegetarian sister restaurant in Sweet Basil's former neighboring locale, this new address for the Foster City favorite is now serving the same (often meaty) fare in a refreshed and spruced-up space. Mod red light fixtures, Thai artifacts, and lacquered chairs dress the interior and may be new, but rest assured that the bamboo tabletops will still be heaped with Sweet Basil's beautifully plated, authentic Thai food.

Expect a wait at lunch for tamarind-glazed duck served with fried, crispy shallots, as well as yellow curry with lamb and honey-glazed ginger fish. A plethora of vegetarian options are on hand, of course, including fried basil tofu with bell peppers. Cool your palate with a sweet Thai iced tea.

Taqueria El Metate

Mexican

120 Harbor Blvd. (at Hwy. 101), Belmont

Phone: 650-595-1110 Lunch & dinner daily
Web: N/A
Prices: ꟸꟸ

Cruising along the 101, it's very easy to blast right by this Belmont favorite, which practically sits on the Harbor off-ramp. Don't let the industrial surroundings fool you; inside, find bright, cheery colors, and food that is straight-up *delicioso*. Taqueria El Metate attracts everyone in droves, so expect it to be packed with myriad customers—from businessmen and foodies to sweet *abuelas*.

Stroll up to the counter and place an order for the amazing *tacos al pastor* (wonderfully spiced, slow roasted, moist pork piled onto white corn tortillas and topped with cilantro and onion); or a massive chicken super burrito, so stuffed that it's almost two meals in one. Make sure to specify whether you'd like the burrito "wet" (sauce covered) or "dry."

Taste In Mediterranean Food

Mediterranean

1199 Broadway, Ste. 1 (bet. Chula Vista & Laguna Aves.), Burlingame

Phone: 650-348-3097 Lunch & dinner daily
Web: www.tasteinbroadway.com
Prices: ꟸꟸ

Put simply, this unassuming spot spins out the best *shawarma* and falafel on the Peninsula. It's a pay-at-the-counter kind of place, where refrigerator cases display Mediterranean dips, salads, and spreads, while tempting trays of baklava make the mouth water. On a warm day, grab a table on the dog-friendly sidewalk and enjoy their Medi-Middle Eastern goodness.

A vegetarian plate of crispy falafel hits the spot; made with chickpeas, parsley, garlic, spices, and served with tahini sauce, creamy hummus, and a fresh cucumber, tomato, and red onion salad. If craving meat, go for a lamb *shawarma* pita wrap—shaved slices of spit-roasted lamb heaped into a pita with roasted potato, fresh vegetables, and topped with garlicky yogurt and a drizzle of spicy red aïoli.

231 Ellsworth

Contemporary XX

231 S. Ellsworth Ave. (bet. 2nd & 3rd Aves.), San Mateo

Phone: 650-347-7231 Lunch Tue – Fri
Web: www.231ellsworth.com Dinner Mon – Sat
Prices: $$$

231 Ellsworth remains slightly off the radar, though it may be San Mateo's most seductive fine dining destination. Perhaps it is the dramatic, barrel-vaulted azure ceiling, or the spacious curving booths that lend plenty of privacy for business or pleasure. Or, perhaps credit is due to the elegant place settings and sophisticated contemporary cuisine, which is consistent and skillfully prepared.

At lunch, a well-tailored business set talks shop over forest mushroom tagliatelle with truffle oil; venison with apricot *mostarda*; and delicious Moroccan-spiced peach pavlova paired with a chilled peach soup. The subdued dining room is typically quiet, but the restaurant's bar, with its extensive wine list, does awaken after dark.

Viognier

Contemporary

222 E. 4th Ave. (at B St.), San Mateo

Phone: 650-685-3727 Dinner Mon – Sat
Web: www.viognierrestaurant.com
Prices: $$$

Like fine wine, some restaurants improve with age. Such is the case with Viognier, the Draeger's Market mainstay that now stands on solid terroir thanks to a new toque in the open kitchen. The chef is taking aim at consistency and creative flavor combinations in contemporary American fare made from largely local and sustainable ingredients. Menu highlights may include the creamy bed of bourbon-whipped sweet potatoes, with a crispy-skin duck breast and persimmon *brunoise*.

Despite a fresh face at the stoves, the second floor dining room is filled with the same San Mateo suit-and-tie crowd who blend well into the atmosphere, which is refined but a touch corporate. Opt for a warmer seat in a booth by the central fireplace with views of the pizza oven.

The Village Pub ✿

Gastropub

B3

2967 Woodside Rd. (off Whiskey Hill Rd.), Woodside

Phone: 650-851-9888 — Lunch Sun – Fri
Web: www.thevillagepub.net — Dinner nightly
Prices: $$

Frankie Frankeny

Given its quiet, mountain-rimmed locale in the quaint hamlet of Woodside, The Village Pub would seem an aptly named neighborhood eatery of the kind where everyone knows your name. While one is likely to find a coterie of regulars who come back for house-made charcuterie again and again, those seeking a pub's standard beer and peanuts may be disappointed. The Village Pub is in fact not a typical pub at all.

With linen-topped tables warmed by a roaring hearth and various private dining rooms for high-rolling groups, Chef Mark Sullivan's place combines the comfort of Cheers with all the trappings of fine dining. Dark woods, vibrant florals, and mirrors set a cozy backdrop for artistically executed gastropub fare, while a wood-burning rotisserie provides the smoky character. Perhaps in a nod to the old-school pub, service is friendly but not exactly polished. Yet, all is forgiven with a taste of the chef's pistachio-spiked mortadella.

Additional entrées are similarly meaty, satisfying, and seasonal: a dinner may bring chilled tuna carpaccio with sliced radish, fennel, pea shoots, and Shinko pear; or a pan-roasted Loch Duart salmon with blood orange and poached Maine shrimp ravioli.

Wakuriya ✿

B3 Japanese

115 De Anza Blvd. (at Parrot Dr.), San Mateo

Phone: 650-286-0410 Dinner Tue – Sun
Web: www.wakuriya.com
Prices: $$$$

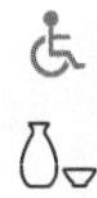

Wakuriya

Modest and informal might be characteristics one easily associates with destination dining; so the fact that this destination is actually a strip mall should not dissuade you from experiencing Chef Katsuhiro Yamasaki's disciplined and delicious Japanese cuisine. Book in advance–far in advance–as its unorthodox locale doesn't seem to be dissuading anyone else, either.

Inside the immaculate space, this husband-wife team runs an organized and professional show with few diversions or embellishments to detract from the main event. That said, you may find that those delicate little sake glasses are vying for your attention. *Drink me.*

Each month, a new crowd-pleasing fixed menu is designed to respect the traditions of Japanese cuisine, with the occasional creative twist for American palates. Appetizers strut the chef's intricate skills and accuracy with the likes of cucumber and *unagi* rolled in omelet, or bean curd and mustard leaf *oshitashi.* From technique to composition, excellence shines through the deep-fried, homemade sesame tofu and Alaskan snow crab served in a thick, clear broth. Desserts are lovingly prepared as delicate berries and sweet red beans suspended in crystal jelly.

Zen Peninsula

Chinese

1180 El Camino Real (at Center St.), Millbrae

Phone: 650-616-9388 — Lunch & dinner daily
Web: www.zenpeninsula.com
Prices: $$

Zen Peninsula is a hugely favored retreat for dim sum and banquet dining in Millbrae. Flooded with Chinese regulars who rub elbows with their neighbors–the dining room, although elegant, is packed with hungry diners–this dim sum den dares to deliver these platters laden with steaming baskets of dumplings and other deliciousness to your table.

Quality ingredients are evident in flavorful *chow fun* mixed with vegetables; marinated chicken feet; pan-fried turnip cakes; shrimp dumplings; and crispy barbecue pork. Beyond dim sum, the vast à la carte menu runs from noodle dishes to clay pot creations, and incorporates delicacies including abalone in oyster sauce and braised bird's nest soup—perhaps the star dish at one of their many wedding receptions?

Red=Pleasant. Look for the red and symbols.

Peter L. Wrenn/MICHELIN

South Bay

South Bay

Tech geeks the world over know the way to San Jose, but foodies typically get lost in San Francisco. It's a shame: tech money plus an international population equals a dynamic culinary scene. Not to mention the rich wine culture descending from the Santa Cruz Mountains, where a burgeoning vintner community takes great pride in its work. In May, sample all 70 area wines at the **Santa Cruz Mountains Wine Express**, at Roaring Camp Railroad in Felton.

Festive Foods

The Valley may have a nerdy rep, but South Bay locals know how to party. In San Jose, festival season kicks off in May with music, dancing, drinks, and eats at the wildly adored **Greek Festival**. Then in June, buckets of corn husks wait to be stuffed and sold at the **Story Road Tamale Festival**, in the fruit orchards of Emma Prusch Farm Park.

In July, Japantown comes alive for the two-day **Obon/Bazaar** and, in August, the Italian American Heritage Foundation celebrates its yearly **Family Festa**. **Santana Row** also keeps the party going year-round: The sleek shopping village is home to numerous upscale restaurants, and its very own farmer's market. Opened in August 2010, San Jose's newest foodie destination is **San Pedro Square Market**, which houses artisan merchants at the historic Peralta Adobe downtown. Farmers and specialty markets are a way of life for South Bay locals: ach city has at least one or more throughout the week.

A Morsel of Vietnam

San Jose is also a melting pot for global culinary influences. Neighborhood *pho* shops and *banh mi* delis sate the growing Vietnamese community, which also heads to **Grand Century Mall** for hard-to-find traditional snacks. Meanwhile, the intersection of King and Tully streets, is home to some of the area's best Vietnamese flavors: Try **Huong Lan** for delicious *bahn mi* sandwiches; cream puffs at **Hong-Van Bakery**; and green waffles flavored with *pandan* paste at **Century Bakery**, just a few blocks away. But that's not all—**Lion Plaza** is another hub for Vietnamese bakeries, markets, and canteens.

Mouth watering for Mexican food? Devotees of South-of-the-Border cuisine pick up still-warm, fresh tortillas at **Tropicana** and surprisingly good tacos from one of the area's 18 **Mi Pueblo Food Centers**. If Cambodian noodle soup is more your cup of tea, look no further than **Nam Vang Restaurant** or **F&D Yummy**. The large and lofty **Dynasty Chinese Seafood Restaurant**, on Story Road, is popular for big parties and is also the local dim sum favorite. In the Asian vein, **Nijiya Market** is a Japanese market (in Mountain View) famed for its specialty goods, fabulous ingredients, and all things Japanese. Long before it was trendy to be organic in America, Nijiya's mission was to bring the taste of Japan in the form of high-quality, seasonal, and local ingredients to the California crowd. Stop by this Far East sanctum for fresh seafood, meat, veggies, and fruit, as well as an array of sushi and bento boxes. Also available on their website are a spectrum of sumptuous recipes ranging from faithful noodle and rice preparations to ethnic specialties.

A Spread for Students

There is more to the South Bay than just San Jose. Los Gatos is home to the sweet patisserie **Fleur de Cocoa** as well as **Testarossa Winery**, the Bay Area's oldest, continually operating winery. Meanwhile, Palo Alto is a casual home base for the students and faculty of reputed Stanford University. Here, locals line up for organic, artisanal yogurts (both fresh and frozen) at **Fraîche**; and delish double-decker sandwiches at **Village Cheese House** (perhaps the vegetarian-friendly Italian Veggie-ball spread with tofu, marinara, and mozzarella?)

If you're craving Korean food, head to Santa Clara where the Korean community enjoys a range of authentic nibbles and delicious spreads at **Lawrence Plaza** food court. And if in urgent need of groceries, shopping along El Camino Real near the Lawrence Expressway intersection is a feast for the eyes. Local foodies favor the caramelized, roasted sweet potatoes at **Sweet Potato Stall**, just outside the Galleria, and **SGD Tofu House** for *bibimbop* or *soondubu jjigae*. Despite the fast pace of technology in Silicon Valley, **Slow Food**–the grassroots movement dedicated to local food traditions–has a thriving South Bay chapter.

Even Google, in Mountain View, feeds its staff three organic square meals a day. For a selection of delicacies, South Bay's eateries and stores dish up gourmet goods and ethnic eats. The rest of us can visit nearby **Milk Pail Market**, known for more than 300 varieties of cheese. Make your pick between such splendid varieties as Camembert, Bleu d'Auvergne, Explorateur, Morbier, Cabriquet, and Perail de Brebis.

Another haunt hugely favored by meat-loving mortals is **Los Gatos Meats & Smokehouse**. This meat mecca has been serving the South Bay community for years via a plethora of poultry, fish, and butcher sandwiches. Revered by all, this salt lick also quenches diners with such "specialties" as prime rib roasts, pork loin, beef jerky, sausages, corned beef, and bacon...regular, pepper, country-style or Canadian?

Pair your charcuterie and cheese with a bottle from Mountain View's famous **Savvy Seller Wine Bar & Wine Shop**—it's a picnic in the making!

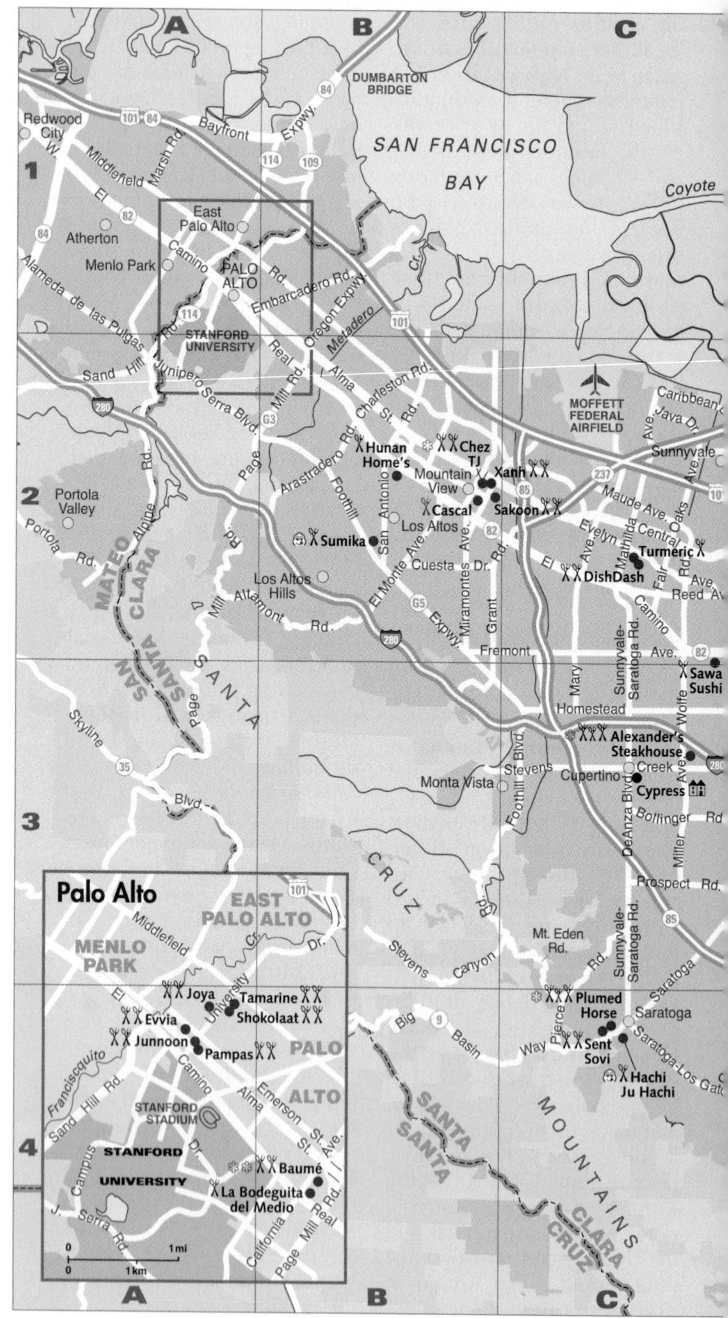

Palo Alto
Hunan Home's
Chez TJ
Xanh
Cascal
Sakoon
Sumika
Turmeric
DishDash
Sawa Sushi
Alexander's Steakhouse
Cypress
Plumed Horse
Sent Sovi
Hachi Ju Hachi
Joya
Tamarine
Shokolaat
Evvia
Junnoon
Pampas
Baumé
La Bodeguita del Medio
SAN FRANCISCO BAY
DUMBARTON BRIDGE
MOFFETT FEDERAL AIRFIELD
STANFORD UNIVERSITY
SANTA CRUZ MOUNTAINS

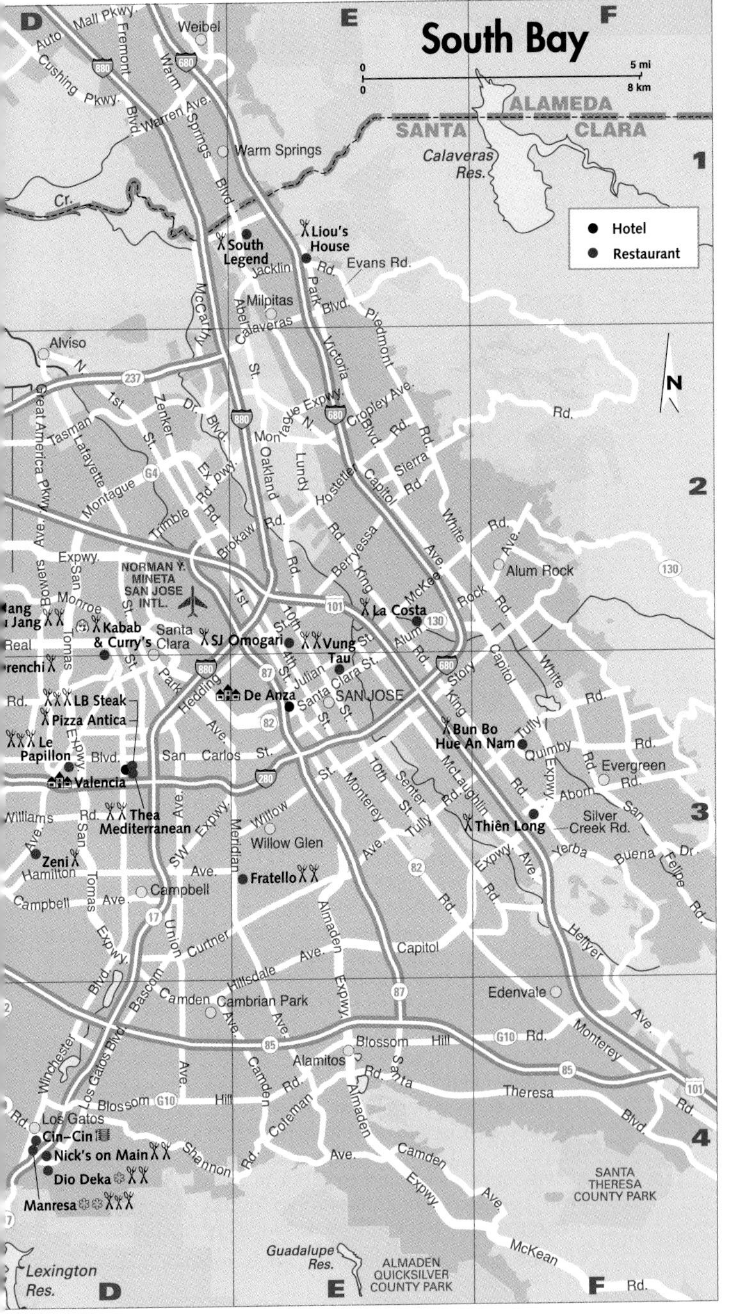
South Bay
Hotel
Restaurant
ALAMEDA
SANTA CLARA
Warm Springs
Milpitas
Alviso
Alum Rock
SAN JOSE
Willow Glen
Campbell
Cambrian Park
Edenvale
Los Gatos
NORMAN Y. MINETA SAN JOSE INTL.
South Legend
Liou's House
La Costa
SJ Omogari
Vung Tau
De Anza
Kabab & Curry's
LB Steak
Pizza Antica
Le Papillon
Valencia
Thea Mediterranean
Zeni
Fratello
Bun Bo Hue An Nam
Thiên Long
Cin-Cin
Nick's on Main
Dio Deka
Manresa
SANTA THERESA COUNTY PARK
ALMADEN QUICKSILVER COUNTY PARK
Calaveras Res.
Guadalupe Res.
Lexington Res.

Alexander's Steakhouse ✿

C3 — Steakhouse XXX

10330 N. Wolfe Rd. (at I-280), Cupertino

Phone: 408-446-2222 Dinner nightly
Web: www.alexanderssteakhouse.com
Prices: $$$$

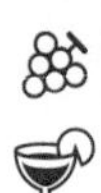

Jeffrey Stout/Alexander's Steakhouse

A quick zoom off Highway 280 in Cupertino makes Alexander's Steakhouse a no-brainer among well-suited Silicon Valley types seeking a pricey house-aged T-bone and full-bodied Napa cabernet. Never mind the shopping center locale and overly scripted staff; this is a venue for a showy business dinner.

A dedicated beef-aging room at the entrance and sweeping staircase lend Alexander's a grand, masculine vibe where spacious candlelit dining areas are done up in charcoal and chocolate hues. Starched white-clothed tables are consistently packed with colleagues and couples; after work, the large back bar buzzes with cocktailing groups.

While the chef's tasting changes nightly, most patrons at Alexander's order from their extensive à la carte menu. A meal here might begin with fusion-style appetizers including a creative tuna tartare accented with mushrooms and *togarashi* aïoli, before beefing up with smoky salt-and-pepper ribeye drizzled with an herbaceous basil oil. Try a side dish or two, such as roasted potatoes in Camembert cream or fresh pea and morel mushroom risotto. Complimentary house-made cotton candy makes for a cheeky finish.

City dwellers can try Alexander's new SoMa sibling.

Baumé ✿✿

B4

201 S. California Ave. (at Park Blvd.), Palo Alto

Phone: 650-328-8899 Lunch Fri
Web: www.baumerestaurant.com Dinner Thu – Sun
Prices: **$$$$**

Peter Giles

Favoring dogma over description, Baumé thrives on its ability to put forth dishes of sublime, seasonal, and very modern fare. In place of menus, expect ingredients listed with neither rhyme nor reason that will surprise you with their magnificence in the hands of Chef Bruno Chemel. This is food in which everyone seems to want to languish; adept servers seamlessly match the pacing to your mood, whether enjoying a relaxed celebration or rushing back to the office for that all-important conference call.

Dishes may offer beguiling simplicity: tiny, sweet beets are perfectly cooked and glazed with their own natural sugars, dotted with carefully placed droplets of liquefied goat cheese, and completed with a bit of "dirt" (dehydrated balsamic vinegar). The stunning care that brings each taste to a new level of complexity is clear in a signature dish like the 62-degree slow-poached egg, served over shaved ham with fresh thyme and tangy vermouth foam. Desserts may unveil a theatrical pear presentation, a DIY dream with smoking vessels and pear pearls that burst in your mouth.

The refined staff and polished, jewel-box interior convey a dedication to excellence from start to finish.

Bun Bo Hue An Nam

F3

Vietnamese

2060 Tully Rd. (at Quimby Rd.), San Jose

Phone: 408-270-7100 Lunch & dinner Tue – Sat
Web: N/A
Prices: ⊜

Take a cue from Vietnamese locals and march into this popular San Jose joint for steaming bowls of fantastic *pho*. Soups and stews are the name of the game here, many of which are jazzed up with ingredients like shrimp cake, soft tendon, fat brisket, and tripe. Slurp down the *bún bò hue*—spicy beef soup with tender chunks of flank steak, pork knuckles, shrimp cake, and rice noodles in a fragrant lemongrass broth, presented with a pile of fresh bean sprouts, mint, cilantro, lemon wedges, and green chilies. Or sample the *pho bò áp chao*—piquant pan-fried beef dressed in a garlic-lemongrass chili sauce, tossed over rice noodles with peppers, onions, basil, cilantro, and mint.

This is the second of two locations–the first is also in San Jose–on Story Road.

Cascal

B2

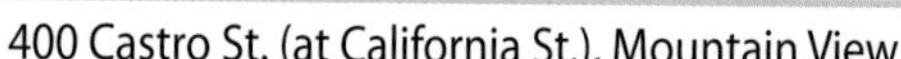

Spanish

400 Castro St. (at California St.), Mountain View

Phone: 650-940-9500 Lunch & dinner daily
Web: www.cascalrestaurant.com
Prices: **$$**

It's no mystery why Mountain View locals adore Cascal: this vibrant eatery shakes infinite and wickedly tempting variations on the mojito, margarita, and caipirinha for a festive after-work crowd enjoying the extensive selection of rum.

Splashy Latin American hues and dressed up Spanish architectural elements, such as wrought-iron fixtures and polished wood tables, hint at the pan-Latin, tapas-style fare. Flavorful dishes include Mexican *sopes* with tender chicken *picadillo* or Cuban roast pork atop crisp masa cakes; lamb *albondigas* with spicy piquillo pepper purée; and wraps stuffed with adobo-marinated pork, cilantro, watercress, and lime. At lunch, Cascal is a popular escape among the cubicle crowd, while dog lovers enjoy family meals on the patio.

Chez TJ ✿

Contemporary XX

B2

938 Villa St. (bet. Bryant & Franklin Sts.), Mountain View

Phone: 650-964-7466 Dinner Tue – Sat
Web: www.cheztj.com
Prices: $$$$

Mark Leet

Even the pickiest of design-savvy gourmands would be hard-pressed to find a more picturesque place to dine than Chez TJ, a Mountain View favorite housed inside the quaintest of Victorian homes with a tree-shaded front lawn and a sweet little back garden.

One need not be an architectural savant to know that this Victorian has been lovingly preserved and restored. Pass the green façade over the threshold of the porch and find yourself in another world, a world where upholstered walls, etched glass, dormer windows, and antiqued mirrors are simply de rigueur. Just a handful of linen-topped tables, frilled with hand-blown glass lamps, fill each in a series of petite, seemingly private dining rooms. In other words, Chez TJ is all about romance.

Same goes for the contemporary cuisine, which waits to woo you with four- and eight-course tasting menus. Begin with a luscious beet panna cotta before courting the velvety heirloom carrot purée. When you get to wild Alaskan halibut in fragrant ham broth or the mouthwatering pork three ways, you'll know things have gotten serious. End this affair with a pure Venezuela Araguani chocolate dessert with olive oil sorbet, pine nuts, and lava salt.

Cin-Cin

D4

International

368 Village Ln. (at Saratoga Los Gatos Rd.), Los Gatos

Phone: 408-354-8006 Dinner Mon – Sat
Web: www.cincinwinebar.com
Prices: $$

Yuppies love Cin-Cin, tucked down a tiny lane in downtown Los Gatos. A neighborhood scene, Cin-Cin hides in a bungalow and bills itself as a wine bar with large, contemporary canvases befittingly depicting images of wine bottles, wine glasses, and wine drinking. Its large dining room (painted a cheery green and accented by light floors, burgundy highlights, and wood furnishings) sets the scene for a spread of shareable small plates.

The bar area can get raucous with the happy hour set as they work up an appetite for an extensive parade of shared plates. Paying homage to global flavors are South Carolina-style pulled pork sliders; Korean *bulgogi* tacos; ricotta gnocchi fragrant with truffled fontina; and light cheesecake beignets with hazelnut honey.

DishDash

C2

Middle Eastern

190 S. Murphy St. (bet. Evelyn & Washington Aves.), Sunnyvale

Phone: 408-774-1889 Lunch & dinner Mon – Sat
Web: www.dishdash.net
Prices: $$

Named after a traditional, cozy piece of Middle Eastern garb, this hoppin' Murphy Street spot captures just that kind of spirit. Notes of sumac and saffron drift through the air, dark wood tables sit against exposed brick walls, and cultural knickknacks dot the dining space. Bold flavors rock a vibrant, pan-Middle Eastern menu, with offerings from tangy chicken *shawarma* salad (spit-roasted chicken atop Romaine, cucumber, tomato, onions, and parsley drizzled with garlicky yogurt) to tasty *beriani dajaj* (potatoes, golden raisins, slivered almonds, and garbanzo beans touched with aged yogurt, alongside saffron rice and garlic-herbed chicken breast).

Sugar craving? Work your sweet way through assorted baklavas: six syrupy choices from cashew to walnut.

Dio Deka ✿

Greek

D4

210 E. Main St. (near Fiesta Way), Los Gatos

Phone: 408-354-7700 — Dinner nightly
Web: www.diodeka.com
Prices: **$$$**

Jack Hutcheson

Situated off a courtyard at Hotel Los Gatos in the quaint but upscale Silicon Valley town of the same name, Dio Deka is just right for its surrounds: posh, unpretentious, and with plenty of substance. This is a go-to for casual, wine-savvy sophisticates.

Legions flock here for an airy, open vibe where light through the soaring windows illuminates rustic plank flooring and the textural surface of a farmhouse communal table. At night, make dinner reservations for a wholly rare and romantic experience. A gleaming fire in the hearth and flickering oil candles cast a gentle glow on potted herbs, high woven chairs, and white linens in the dining room, as well as copper and green tile accents inside the open kitchen.

There you will find a crew of well-choreographed cooks doing magical things with Greek cuisine. Look for an exquisite *pantzaria psita*, ember-roasted strawberry and beet salad with tangy custard; slow-roasted tender pork riblets infused with ouzo and Greek herbs; and *mavros gados*, a couscous-like pasta enriched with fresh peas, lemon, and topped with line-caught black cod. While there are a few mesquite-fired steakhouse options, true-blue foodies leave those for the neophytes.

Evvia

Greek

420 Emerson St. (bet. Lytton & University Aves.), Palo Alto

Phone: 650-326-0983 Lunch Mon – Fri
Web: www.evvia.net Dinner nightly
Prices: $$

Palo Alto denizens are lucky to have Evvia in their town, and they know it. The warmly lit dining room has the rustic coziness of a Greek *estiatorio*, with a roaring stone fireplace, closely-spaced tables, and an open kitchen adorned with hanging copper pots and pans. A lovely backlit wall of shelves illuminates a colorful array of glass bottles of oils, vinegars, and grains.

Frequently packed, the place is popular among the business crowds at lunch and Palo Alto residents at dinner (reservations are recommended). Fresh, flavorful Greek favorites may include roasted artichoke and eggplant souvlaki, served with fresh strained yogurt and house-made pita; or the tender, perfectly seasoned, herb-roasted lamb with dill-flavored *tzatziki*.

Fratello

Italian

1712 Meridian Ave. (bet. Hamilton Ave. & Lenn Dr.), San Jose

Phone: 408-269-3801 Lunch Tue – Fri
Web: www.fratello-ristorante.com Dinner nightly
Prices: $$

Fratello in San Jose might not be fancy-schmancy, but this quaint, casual, and family-friendly spot definitely has its own charm. Its theme is echoed in the terra-cotta-colored walls with paintings of the Italian countryside. The warm-spirited Italian family that runs the show welcomes you and yours with an array of authentic dishes that run the gamut from pastas and panini at lunch to more impressive seafood dishes in the evening.

Twist your fork around the homemade pappardelle topped with veal ragù or savor the charred taste of the tender grilled octopus, drizzled with fresh lemon, olive oil, and a sprinkling of fragrant Sicilian oregano. The crisp-skinned *salmone al brodo*, served in a roasted garlic and lemon broth, is delicious in its simplicity.

Hachi Ju Hachi

Japanese

14480 Big Basin Way (bet. Saratoga Los Gatos Rd. & 3rd St.), Saratoga

Phone: 408-647-2258 — Dinner Tue – Sun
Web: www.hachijuhachi88.com
Prices: $$

Simple chairs and a blonde wood counter may not be much to look at, but the casual Saratoga interior manages to capture the serene essence of Japan. Wise visitors will take the straightforward space as a sign that Hachi Ju Hachi is focused on cuisine.

Delicate à la carte dishes may include cuttlefish with spicy cod roe and pork belly in white miso marinade, but the real adventure begins with a reservation. Folks with a bit of foresight and extra funds may pull up a chair for an elaborate *kaiseki* where the chef himself will comment on every course. Mouthwatering delights include the likes of kombu-burdock roll; hamachi skin and fragrant shiso; yellowtail sashimi with house-made sea salt; and miso-braised beef with blistered shisito peppers.

Hunan Home's

Chinese

4880 El Camino Real (bet. Jordan Ave. & Los Altos Sq.), Los Altos

Phone: 650-965-8888 — Lunch & dinner daily
Web: www.hunanhomes.com
Prices:

If home is where the heart is, then follow yours to Hunan Home's. Chinese may be the cuisine craze in this city, and this restaurant's name may be lost in translation, yet it continues to seduce business and family circles with its wonderfully authentic food. Set in a bungalow beset with shopping stalls, the elevated dining room is cheery with smiling service.

Groups of all sizes gather to ogle the gamut of Chinese delights—from *kung pao* prawns dressed in silky, spicy oyster sauce, to the house specialty of deeply caramelized Peking duck sandwiched in steamed pancakes with scallions and hoisin, to soft tofu cubes sautéed with chili and fermented black bean paste. The same in any language, a dizzying array of complimentary dishes adds incredible value.

Jang Su Jang

D2 — Korean XX

3561 El Camino Real, Ste.10 (bet. Flora Vista Ave. & Lawrence Expwy.), Santa Clara

Phone: 408-246-1212 — Lunch & dinner daily
Web: N/A
Prices: $$

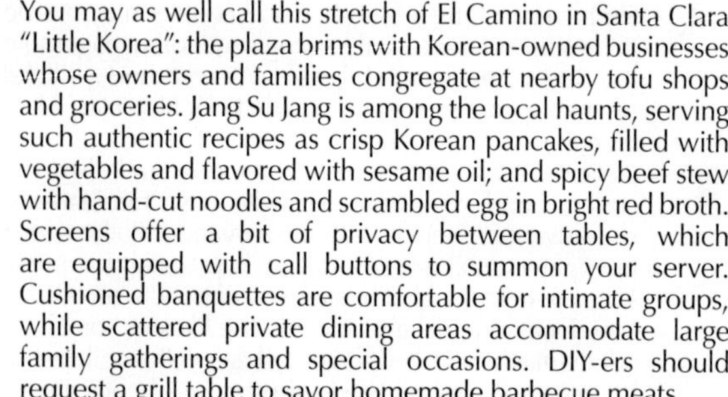

You may as well call this stretch of El Camino in Santa Clara "Little Korea": the plaza brims with Korean-owned businesses whose owners and families congregate at nearby tofu shops and groceries. Jang Su Jang is among the local haunts, serving such authentic recipes as crisp Korean pancakes, filled with vegetables and flavored with sesame oil; and spicy beef stew with hand-cut noodles and scrambled egg in bright red broth. Screens offer a bit of privacy between tables, which are equipped with call buttons to summon your server. Cushioned banquettes are comfortable for intimate groups, while scattered private dining areas accommodate large family gatherings and special occasions. DIY-ers should request a grill table to savor homemade barbecue meats.

Joya

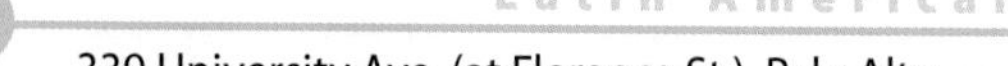

A4 — Latin American XX

339 University Ave. (at Florence St.), Palo Alto

Phone: 650-853-9800 — Lunch & dinner daily
Web: www.joyarestaurant.com
Prices: $$

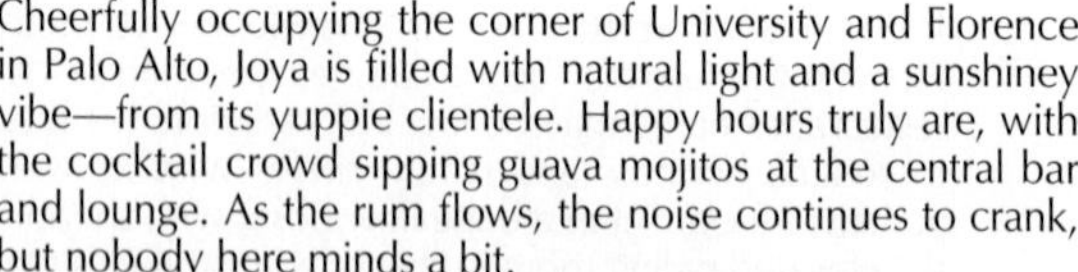

Cheerfully occupying the corner of University and Florence in Palo Alto, Joya is filled with natural light and a sunshiney vibe—from its yuppie clientele. Happy hours truly are, with the cocktail crowd sipping guava mojitos at the central bar and lounge. As the rum flows, the noise continues to crank, but nobody here minds a bit.

Tile floors and leather chairs accent the vivacious space where colorful Latin American small plates and entrées are served in the dining room. Joya is best enjoyed with a group of friends, so grab your pals and share plates of corn *croquetas* deep-fried with English peas and pasilla peppers; roasted chicken *sopes* with chipotle-tomato sauce; and boldly flavored short rib tacos with jicama salsa and horseradish cream.

Junnoon

150 University Ave. (at High St.), Palo Alto

Phone: 650-329-9644
Web: www.junnoon.com
Prices: $$

Lunch Mon – Fri
Dinner nightly

With a sultry dark wood interior, creative cocktails, and patio conducive to warm weather carousal, Junnoon is a perennial favorite among denizens of Palo Alto and Stanford University. Despite rave reviews from national press, this Indian cuisine can be hit-and-miss. While the Darjeeling-steamed dumplings may not wow, they are beautifully brightened by fantastic, über spicy chili-garlic chutney. In fact, some dishes are downright exciting: the chewy roasted garlic naan has rich buttery flavor and arrives piping hot; and tandoori lamb chops, flavored with cardamom and accompanied by vibrant mint sauce, are expertly cooked.

Rather than stay for dessert, arrive early to indulge in exotic libations during happy hour—an undeniable hit.

Kabab & Curry's

1498 Isabella St. (at Clay St.), Santa Clara

Phone: 408-247-0745
Web: www.kababandcurrys.com
Prices:

Lunch & dinner Tue – Sun

If you're hanging around the South Bay at lunchtime and wondering where the area's large Indian and Pakistani population goes to eat, follow the crowd of engineers from Intel and Google to Kabab & Curry's, an authentic eatery that literally serves all you can eat.

Expect a line at the door–this place is a zoo at lunch–but be patient: the $10 buffet is worth the wait at Kabab & Curry's. Here, plates are laden with tender lamb cubes in spicy *vindaloo*; tandoori chicken so moist it's falling off the bone; and velvety chicken *tikka masala*. Every dish is hearty and delicious, the atmosphere is easygoing with plain wood furniture and tiled floors, and the naan is warm, bountiful, and always served with a smile. Come hungry, and leave stuffed!

La Bodeguita del Medio

463 S. California Ave. (bet. Ash St. & El Camino Real), Palo Alto

Phone: 650-326-7762 — Lunch Mon – Fri
Web: www.labodeguita.com — Dinner Mon – Sat
Prices: $$

Palo Alto cigar aficionados head to La Bodeguita del Medio for its adjacent Cigar Divan, a cozy retail space with a walk-in humidor. Connoisseurs should try the house's private label Nicaraguan cigar—pair it with a Hemingway rum cocktail to get the full experience. Non-smokers love La Bodeguita for tasty Cuban cuisine that hails from the restaurant's original Havana locale.

The casual, friendly spot is conducive to sharing fun small plates. Start with a house-cured shrimp ceviche in tangy key lime juice flavored with coconut milk, and don't miss tender *picadillo* pork empanadas with roasted chiles and cabbage slaw. Still hungry? Sink your teeth into moist *masitas*, a roasted pork shoulder with black beans and Rioja-caramelized red onions.

La Costa

1805 Alum Rock Ave. (bet. Jackson Ave. & King Rd.), San Jose

Phone: 408-937-1010 — Lunch & dinner daily
Web: N/A
Prices:

Is it a taqueria, or is it a taco stand? You be the judge at La Costa, a San Jose hot spot where the décor is, well, the great outdoors. Inside, La Costa 's space features a kitchen with red, green, and white tile floors. But never mind that, because you're not going inside.

Belly up to the cashier's window and order your heart's content: Perhaps a tender taco *asado* seasoned with spices and chiles and topped with crunchy salsa? Or maybe a burrito stuffed with strips of grilled chicken, avocado, cheese, and spicy condiments. Whatever you order, expect it to come fast and come outside—the only seating at La Costa is on the covered patio. But the food is cheap, tasty, and enjoys a massive following; regulars include foodies and working class folk alike.

LB Steak

Steakhouse XXX

D3

334 Santana Row, Ste. 1000 (bet. Olin Ave. & Stevens Creek Blvd.), San Jose

Phone: 408-244-1180 Lunch & dinner daily
Web: www.lbsteak.com
Prices: $$$

Shopping and food go hand-in-hand, so after sifting through the racks of this upscale mall, appease your appetite at the casually-chic LB Steak. A good fit for the tony multicenter that it resides in, LB Steak is packed at lunch with businessmen who sink their teeth into gourmet burgers and steak sandwiches; while at dusk, couples stop by for fresh seafood including oysters on the half shell; smoked salmon *pizzette*; fresh fish, lamb, pork, and brawny USDA prime steak, steak, and more steak.

Dishes get a soupçon of French sophistication courtesy of a crowning chef and team—for dessert, look to the pastry cart for more refined treats like a raspberry macaron oozing with vanilla pastry cream and scattered with plump, sweet raspberries.

Le Papillon

French XXX

D3

410 Saratoga Ave. (at Kiely Blvd.), San Jose

Phone: 408-296-3730 Lunch Fri
Web: www.lepapillon.com Dinner nightly
Prices: $$$$

In San Jose, Le Papillon is at once dated but charming in an old-fashioned way: just a glance through its plantation shutters to the luxury cars parked out front indicates a deep-pocketed clientele who finds comfort in massive florals (both in vases and upholstery), white linens, wallpapered wainscoting, and shaded tabletop lamps. Another perk of Le Papillon's old-school manner is its attentive and professional service. Here, the staff is well equipped to please both the corporate crowd at lunch and couples craving a romantic dinner.

French preparations and primo ingredients define the solid cuisine, which might feature ricotta gnocchi with artichokes and morels; pinot noir-braised duck breast with sour cherry sauce; and an airy Grand Marnier soufflé.

Liou's House

Chinese

1245 Jacklin Rd. (at Park Victoria Dr.), Milpitas

Phone: 408-263-9888 Lunch & dinner Tue – Sun
Web: N/A
Prices:

Looking for authentically fiery Hunan cuisine? Drop by Chef Liou's House, near the Summitpointe Golf Club in Milpitas. This cushy family-run restaurant features a large selection of expertly prepared Hunan fare, as well as a zesty sampling of regional Chinese dishes.

The cognoscenti–a sizeable contingent of Chinese residents among them–know to order from the chef's specialties list, which is an insert in the main menu. These dishes are where the talent of noted Taiwanese chef, James Liou really dazzles. "Addictive" best describes the blisteringly hot–as in spicy–nuggets of chicken coated in ground dried red chilies.

Top off such delicious food with warm, friendly service and you've got a go-to restaurant that's worth the trip.

Nick's on Main

American

D4

35 E. Main St. (bet. College Ave. & Pageant Way), Los Gatos

Phone: 408-399-6457 Lunch & dinner Tue – Sat
Web: www.nicksonmainst.com
Prices: **$$$**

Size has zilch to do with sophistication, and Nick's on Main in the hub of Los Gatos is a testimony to the fact. This American bistro is as chic as it is petite (black-and-white painted brick walls match the black-and-white photographs gracing them), even if it is crammed with patrons rubbing elbows at close-knit tables. The ladies who lunch don't seem to mind, and they keep up a steady flow of banter. Luckily, high ceilings help minimize the din at this ten-table pearl.

Bright by day and soft at night, the mood at Nick's is elevated when Chef/owner Nick Difu concocts such comforting dishes as steamed Mediterranean mussels in a spicy Thai broth; pan-roasted duck confit with creamy polenta; and Brussels sprouts sautéed with Applewood smoked bacon.

Manresa ✿✿

Contemporary

D4

320 Village Ln. (bet. Santa Cruz & University Aves.), Los Gatos

Phone: 408-354-4330 Dinner Wed – Sun

Web: www.manresarestaurant.com

Prices: $$$$

Michael David Rose

In the posh little village of Los Gatos, Manresa remains a beacon for savvy, deep-pocketed foodies who will find their favorite restaurant much changed of late. While the chef's exquisite contemporary plates are happily intact, the bungalow's interior is enjoying a sleek second life.

After a brief closure for renovation, Manresa reopened its doors to reveal a stylish space with low sofas decorating a front lounge and an additional dining room where clerestory windows shed soft filtered light. Richly patterned textiles and white tablecloths add warmth to a cream-and-gray palette; chandeliers made of hand-blown crystal spoons add a scoop of whimsy. Try a creative cocktail while you wait for what's to come.

The chef's Californian cuisine is presented in a five-course prix-fixe and served on beautiful sculptural china by a highly polished staff. Made with local, seasonal produce, dishes may include al dente English peas with flavorful geoduck clam, green strawberries, and shiso; seared Monterey Bay abalone garnished with nori and avocado purée; and suckling *porcelet* with creamy whey polenta. Finish with a decadent chocolate-peanut butter dessert crowned with cocoa nib ice cream.

Orenchi

Japanese

3540 Homestead Rd. (near Lawrence Expy.), Santa Clara

Phone: 408-246-2955 — Lunch & dinner Tue – Sun
Web: www.orenchiramen.com
Prices: ₴₴

There are few bowls of soup worth a several-mile drive to a defunct shopping center only to find a line at the door and an inconvenient cash-only policy. But if you are looking for such a soup, Orenchi serves ramen so authentic that Japanese ex-pats come from all over for a piping hot taste of home.

There is no need for décor in this authentic noodle house—you'll be too busy waiting in line and then slurping down soup to notice. Upon arrival, jot your name on the clipboard and consider your options: Orenchi ramen has a *tonkotsu* base with chunks of pork, soft-boiled egg, and enoki mushrooms; Shio ramen comes with seaweed, leeks, and Yuzu zest. Additional menu items include braised pork belly and fish cake tempura. No cash? There's an ATM in the corner.

Pampas

Brazilian

529 Alma St. (bet. Hamilton & University Aves.), Palo Alto

Phone: 650-327-1323 — Lunch Mon – Fri
Web: www.pampaspaloalto.com — Dinner nightly
Prices: $$$

With low slung banquettes, cool earth tones, and chic industrial accents, Pampas' urbane, bi-level interior defies common expectations of an all-you-can-eat affair (as do the sophisticated clientele sipping a full-bodied malbec). The sexy décor befits this Brazilian *churrascaria*, which specializes in authentic *rodízio* meals with limitless roasted meats stealing the scene.

Served on skewers by circulating *passadors*, flavorful highlights include pork loin seasoned with coriander adobo; sirloin filet with garlic and herbs; and spicy linguiça. Try to save room for a trip to the sidebar–not for the faint of appetite–with its heaps of cheese, charcuterie, gazpacho, salads, smoked fish, and hot sides of coconut whipped sweet potatoes or zucchini fritters.

Pizza Antica

Pizza

334 Santana Row, Ste. 1065 (bet. Stevens Creek Blvd. & Tatum Ln.), San Jose

Phone: 408-557-8373 Lunch & dinner daily
Web: www.pizzaantica.com
Prices: $$

Shoppers and others consistently line up at this bistro-style pizza parlor at lunchtime, eager for a taste of the restaurant's thin-crust pies. Dough proofs for three days before being rolled out cracker-thin, topped with a wide range of artisanal ingredients, and baked in the gas oven. "Our Pizza" features set combinations, while "Your Pizza" allows guests to customize their toppings—from pesto to pepperoni. It is equally worthwhile to explore the full menu of fresh salads, pasta, and entrées like herb-roasted breast of chicken and zinfandel-braised boneless short ribs.
High chairs and a kids' menu that doubles as a coloring book make wee diners feel welcome. On sunny days, everyone clamors for the sidewalk seating in this heart of Santana Row.

Sakoon

357 Castro St. (bet. California & Dana Sts.), Mountain View

Phone: 650-965-2000 Lunch & dinner daily
Web: www.sakoonrestaurant.com
Prices: $$

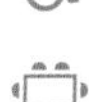

For a sophisticated dose of cheer in Mountain View, make haste for Sakoon, a contemporary Indian restaurant dressed in a virtual riot of color and fun. Bright glass fixtures illuminate large mirrors and vibrant striped and polka-dotted furniture. The bar is backlit with neon hues; a fiber-optic light sculpture changes color every few seconds.
It may sound like a circus, but Sakoon is startlingly stylish and its cuisine is refined. Settle into a booth, order a pomegranate gin Kamasutra, and peruse the menu. Dishes include avocado *jhalmuri*, a fresh and flavorful layered salad; *murgh sakoonwala*, chicken curry stewed with Indian spicies, cardamom, and bell pepper; and Punjabi black lentils simmered in a creamy sauce of tomatoes, ginger, and red chilies.

Plumed Horse ✿

C4 Contemporary XXX

14555 Big Basin Way (bet. 4th & 5th Sts.), Saratoga

Phone: 408-867-4711 Dinner Mon – Sat

Web: www.plumedhorse.com

Prices: $$$$

James Fong

For time immemorial, this wooden house has blended beautifully into its quaint surrounds. Settled along a tree-lined avenue, Plumed Horse preens its feathers in a series of private rooms elegantly appointed with fireplaces, dark wood trim, and white panels. Make your way past an imposing wine cellar to find a luxurious dining lair drenched in a soft glow.

Trolleys of Champagne, Port, Madeira, and cheese tantalize the taste buds, while tables dressed in white linen, crystal, and fresh flowers, set the stage for a lavish feast. Let the brigade of suited staff service your table with accurate plate descriptions; they never miss a beat and make this serene space ideal for special occasions.

The steady chatter between foodies and wine savants will fade into the background once Chef Peter Armellino bestows you with contemporary plates of ahi tuna tartare, prepared tableside in a shiso sorbet; and pan-seared South Texas antelope, cooked to rosy pink perfection and finished with Italian butter beans, stinging nettles, and garlic *saucisson*. The Warren Buffett financier trickled with delicious Armagnac-prune ice cream and quinoa granola is bound to make the "Oracle of Omaha" himself proud.

Sawa Sushi

Japanese

1042 E. El Camino Real (at Henderson Ave.), Sunnyvale

Phone: 408-529-1588 Lunch & dinner Mon – Sat
Web: www.sawasushi.net
Prices: $$$$

At Sawa Sushi, Chef/owner/server Steve Sawa will craft your omakase and then deliver it to you at the sushi bar. Chef Sawa may be deeply dry and his restaurant borders on dingy–the fish cases are empty and plates may be chipped–but you've got to hand it to him: he's made plenty from nothing for over a decade now.

Without a reservation, the chef may question your motives. He may also mention that his super secret recipes come at a premium and are served omakase only. Take a cue from the full house and go with the flow. You'll be treated to the freshest fish even if his sometimes sloppy knife skills leave something to be desired. Expect unique items like slow-poached tuna belly in ponzu, and fresh shrimp topped with creamy uni and sea salt.

Sent Sovi

Californian

14583 Big Basin Way (at 5th St.), Saratoga

Phone: 408-867-3110 Dinner Tue – Sun
Web: www.sentsovi.com
Prices: $$$

In the historic village of Saratoga on a lane shaded by overhanging trees, this petite cottage with sweeping windows and copper wainscoting is the very definition of charming. A honeyed glow fills the space and sets the tone for romantic meals, wherein Chef/owner Josiah Slone showcases sustainable ingredients sourced from local farms and ranches. The ever-changing seasonal offering includes both à la carte items and various tasting menus, which might feature a vegetarian sampling. Highlights may include shaved lamb tongue with fried capers; gnocchi with cardamom and wild mushroom ragù; or a torchon of creamy foie gras with a bruléed crust and pistachioed salad. The concise list of wines and flights is designed for perfect pairing.

Shokolaat

Contemporary

516 University Ave. (bet. Cowper & Webster Sts.), Palo Alto

Phone: 650-289-0719 — Lunch Tue – Fri
Web: www.shokolaat.com — Dinner Tue – Sat
Prices: $$

Such a provocative name calls for provocative desserts, and Shokolaat delivers. Here the headliners are fluffy soufflés and various mousses, gateaux, and tarts. Truly, one would be a fool to pass on the likes of rich opera cake, a little slice of chocolate ganache heaven with silky espresso cream, but that is not where to begin.

Shokolaat is also a lovely little spot for lunch in Palo Alto, which boasts simple savory fare as pleasant as its patio. Nosh on Sicilian focaccia pizzas; lobster salad with crème fraîche and a buttery croissant; or a selection of a sandwiches and panini on house-baked bread. Dinner brings meatier fare, including a bone-in pork chop with rosemary-caramel apples.

Best of all, the breads and sweets are available to-go.

SJ Omogari

Korean 

154 E. Jackson St. (at 4th St.), San Jose

Phone: 408-288-8134 — Lunch & dinner Mon – Sat
Web: www.omogari.biz
Prices:

This homespun, family-owned Korean eatery in San Jose is one to rival any of the cuisine's authentic go-tos in Santa Clara. The traditional *banchan* may be lackluster, but area foodies come anyway for terrific *bi bim bap*, a piping hot stone pot that may be loaded with tender spicy pork, shredded carrot and daikon radish salad, and scallions with an egg on top.

SJ Omogari is a small, simple space with just a few wood tables and little art. And while you won't find the ubiquitous grill-topped tables, you will find most memorable *galbi*–smoky, grilled, and caramelized beef short ribs–from the kitchen. Soft tofu stews arrive with mushrooms or kimchi for vegetable lovers, and all meals are complete with a complimentary scoop of green tea ice cream.

South Legend

E1

1720 N. Milpitas Blvd. (bet. Dixon Landing Rd. & Sunnyhills Ct.), Milpitas

Phone: 408-934-3970 — Lunch & dinner daily
Web: www.southlegend.com
Prices:

South Legend may be located in a shopping center full of markets, Asian-run businesses, and...you guessed it... Chinese restaurants, but ring the alarm as this one stands tall for its bold menu of specialties from China's extra hot Sichuan province. The décor is plain and the service straightforward at this discreet, local haunt; the food is anything but and the likes of Chongqing fish fillets with chili; *mapo* tofu; chili-fried eel; and other sizzling platters are not for the faint of heart.
This is food that will leave you blushing from a flavor-packed smackdown of chili paste, peppercorns, and red chili oil. Not feeling so brave? The Chengdu-style dim sum featuring pork crescent dumplings and yam cakes oozing with red bean paste is sure to sate.

Sumika

Japanese

B2

236 Plaza Central (bet. 2nd & 3rd Sts.), Los Altos

Phone: 650-917-1822 — Lunch Tue – Sat
Web: www.sumikagrill.com — Dinner Tue – Sun
Prices: $$

For a gratifying yakitori experience, venture off the beaten path and behold this authentic *izakaya*. A South Bay haven for the local Japanese folk, Sumika's crowning glory is its glass enclosed *binchotan* charcoal grill. However, *izakaya* faithfuls like dark wood floors and furnishings, soft lighting, and shelves of sake bottles adorn the rest of the space.
A field of families and couples flock to the tables, while the trendier set hovers over a long wood counter for delicious chicken yakitori like *tsukune* (meatballs), *mune* (breasts), and *momo* (thighs). Other grill thrills include juicy Kobe beef skewers freckled with *shichimi togarashi*; fried chicken *karaage* drizzled with lemon; and bacon-wrapped *unagi* glazed with a smoky eel sauce.

Tamarine

Vietnamese XX

546 University Ave. (bet. Cowper & Webster Sts.), Palo Alto

Phone: 650-325-8500 — Lunch Mon – Fri
Web: www.tamarinerestaurant.com — Dinner nightly
Prices: $$

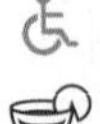

Traditional flavors get a modern makeover at Tamarine, the perennial Palo Alto hot spot serving elegant and contemporary Vietnamese cuisine to cosmopolitan crowds.

By day, the sleek dining room dressed with modern furniture and Vietnamese art, hosts a business clientele. During evenings, the central bar buzzes with locals who come for innovative cocktails and wines by the glass, while chic couples linger over the Tamarine Taste—a delicious sampling of four appetizers that might include shrimp spring rolls, papaya salad, taro root rolls, and tea leaf beef. The menu may go on to include whole fillets of pan-fried snapper lacquered in a sweet and tangy tamarind-, kaffir lime-, and-lemongrass sauce—a perfect match for their crisp *grüner veltliner.*

Thea Mediterranean

Mediterranean 

3090 Olsen Dr. (at Winchester Blvd.), San Jose

Phone: 408-260-1444 — Lunch & dinner daily
Web: www.thearestaurant.com
Prices: $$

The 20-foot-tall olive tree in the center of Thea's soaring dining room sets the stage for a delightful culinary journey through the Mediterranean. Named for the mythical mother of the sun and moon, Thea shines its light on classic Greek and Turkish specialties at honest prices. Begin your trip with an authentic meze sampler of hummus, *tzatziki, htipiti,* and *melitzanosalata* served with homemade pita and fruity olive oil. Then, look to explore the region further in entrées such as spanakopita laden with spinach, leeks, and feta; plump rice- and herb-stuffed dolmades; lemon-roasted half chicken; or Ouzo- and tomato-steamed mussels.

The young, polite staff is swift and efficient—a fact that the Silicon Valley suits who lunch here no doubt appreciate.

Thiên Long

Vietnamese

3005 Silver Creek Rd., Ste.138 (bet. Aborn Rd. & Lexann Ave.), San Jose

Phone: 408-223-6188 Lunch & dinner daily
Web: N/A
Prices: ⊜

Don't have cash? No need to stop at the ATM on your way to this San Jose favorite: Thiên Long's cheap Vietnamese eats are easy on the pockets. It's located in a shopping center that brims with Asian storefronts and is popular among the area's burgeoning Vietnamese community.

With tile floors and wooden chairs, the interior isn't much. But it doesn't need to be: food is fresh and light, and service is friendly. On chilly days, sop up your *bánh mì bò kho,* a chunky beef stew with jalapeño and Thai basil, with a crusty baguette. Or, opt for a noodle bowl laden with barbecue pork and prawns for the perfect flavor combination of smoky, salty, and sweet. Don't miss the tapioca pearl smoothies, including a coffee rendition or exotic durian, jackfruit, and taro.

Turmeric

Indian

C2

141 S. Murphy Ave. (bet. Evelyn & Washington Aves.), Sunnyvale

Phone: 408-617-9100 Dinner nightly
Web: www.turmericrestaurant.com
Prices: ⊜

Located on Sunnyvale's historic and quaint Murphy Avenue, where boutiques and restaurants cram the sidewalks, Turmeric might not be as cute as its neighbors but don't judge this place by its cover. It may not offer much in the way of design and aesthetics, but with delectable Indian food at great prices, who needs fancy digs?

The buffet is well-known and draws droves, but forget traipsing upstairs and take a seat in the dining room for à la carte specialties. Instead of focusing on the typical, the menu gives equal treatment to traditional, regional dishes. Favorites such as chicken *makhani* from Delhi; *murg ka mukul* from Rajasthan; lamb *vindaloo* from Goa; and Malabar fish curry from Kerala take you on a culinary trip around India without the jet lag.

Vung Tau

E3

535 E. Santa Clara St. (at 12th St.), San Jose

Phone: 408-288-9055 — Lunch & dinner daily
Web: www.vungtaurestaurant.com
Prices: ₲₲

Vung Tau's ample space is filled with tables for their hordes of loyal Vietnamese patrons. Despite their rather chaste décor and basic service, the gamut of food offerings keeps them riveted. While the hefty menu can stupefy, rest assured that the home-style food is as authentic as it is tasty.

Imagine a plethora of both unique and classic delights from steaming noodle bowls to seafood and meat dishes. Watch as the faithful order the likes of *bo bia* (soft rolls filled with Chinese sausage and egg); or *tam bi tom cha* (broken rice cloaked with shredded pork and succulent prawns). *Banh khot* are enticingly savory confections, crisp at the edges, depressed at the center to hold a filling of sweet shrimp and minced scallions.

Xanh

B2

110 Castro St. (bet. Evelyn Ave. & Villa St.), Mountain View

Phone: 650-964-1888 — Lunch Mon – Fri
Web: www.xanhrestaurant.com — Dinner nightly
Prices: **$$**

Long a favorite for outstanding Vietnamese fare in Mountain View, Xanh has maintained its mod image over the years. Today, Xanh's über-contemporary design features mesh curtains and bright neon lights, and the 12,500 square-foot space seems deeply devoted to drinks, with a new bar and lounge that starts groovin' to DJ beats on weekends.

For those who like a little nosh with their nightlife, Xanh's Vietnamese food is still good, even if not quite what it once was. Dishes may unveil a roasted duck roll wrapped imperial-style in thin rice paper; bold peppercorn beef sautéed with bell peppers and onion; and tasty fried, shell-on shrimp with sliced hot jalapeños. And finally, don't forget a scoop of the lightly sweet coconut rice.

Zeni

Ethiopian X

1320 Saratoga Ave. (at Payne Ave.), San Jose

Phone: 408-615-8282 Lunch & dinner daily
Web: www.zenirestaurant.com
Prices: **$$**

Ethiopia's cuisine–while roaming the globe–has cultivated a global following. Zeni is a cultural delight luring natives with a deliciously authentic menu and proper set featuring a thatched bar, exotic artwork, and classic furnishings. Amicability reigns as diners dispel with cutlery and chow in communion. With no utensil in sight, visit the wash basin before diving in...fingers first.

Embodying simple food is the *injera*—a fluffy flatbread used to scoop up flavorful meats and sauces. Chatty servers indulge locals with dreamy collard greens; tangy spiced lentils; split peas with turmeric; and veggies gilded with garlic and ginger. *Kitfo* (ground steak with herb butter and chili powder) is perfectly chased down by black tea swirled with honey-spice syrup.

Couverts (X... XXXXX) indicate the level of comfort found at a restaurant. The more X's, the more upscale a restaurant will be.

Peter L. Wrenn/MICHELIN

Wine Country

Wine Country

Napa Valley & Sonoma County

Picnicking on artisan-made cheeses and fresh crusty bread amid acres of gnarled grapevines; sipping wine on a terrace above a hillside of silvery olive trees; touring caves heady with the sweet smell of fermenting grapes: this is northern California's wine country. Lying within an hour's drive north and northeast of San Francisco, the hills and vales of Sonoma County and Napa Valley thrive on the abundant sunshine and fertile soil that produce grapes for some of North America's finest wines.

Fruit of the Vine

Cuttings of Criollas grapevines traveled north with Franciscan *padres* from the Baja Peninsula during the late 17th century. Wines made from these "mission" grapes were used primarily for trade and for sacramental purposes. In the early 1830s, a French immigrant propitiously named Jean-Louis Vignes (*vigne* is French for "vine") established a large vineyard near Los Angeles using cuttings of European grapevines *(Vitis vinifera)*, and by the mid-19th century, winemaking had become one of southern California's principal industries. In 1857 Hungarian immigrant Agoston Haraszthy purchased a 400-acre estate in Sonoma County, named it Buena Vista, and cultivated Tokaji vine cuttings imported from his homeland. In 1861, bolstered by promises of state funding, Haraszthy went to Europe to gather assorted *vinifera* cuttings to plant in California soil. Upon his return, however, the state legislature reneged on their commitment. Undeterred, Haraszthy persisted in distributing (at his own expense) some 100,000 cuttings and testing varieties in different soil types. Successful application of his discoveries created a boom in the local wine industry in the late 19th century.

The Tide Turns

As the 1800s drew to a close, northern California grapevines fell prey to phylloxera, a root louse that attacks susceptible *vinifera* plants. Entire vineyards were decimated. Eventually researchers discovered they could combat phylloxera by replanting vineyards with disease-resistant wild grape rootstocks, onto which *vinifera* cuttings could be grafted. The wine industry had achieved a modicum of recovery by the early 20th century, only to be slapped with the 18th Amendment to the Constitution, prohibiting the manufacture, sale, importation, and transportation of intoxicating liquors in the United States. California's winemaking industry remained at a near-standstill until 1933, when Prohibition was repealed. The Great Depression slowed the reclamation of vineyards and it wasn't until the early 1970s that California's wine industry was fully re-established. In 1976, California wines took top honors in a blind taste testing by French judges in Paris. The results helped open up a whole new world of respectability for Californian vineyards.

Coming of Age

As Napa and Sonoma wines have established their reputations, the importance of individual growing regions has increased. Many sub-regions have sought and acquired Federal regulation of the place names as American Viticultural Areas, or AVAs, in order to set the boundaries of wine-growing areas that are distinctive for their soil, microclimate, and wine styles. Although this system is subject to debate, there is no doubt that an AVA such as Russian River Valley, Carneros, or Spring Mountain can be very meaningful. The precise location of a vineyard relative to the Pacific Ocean or San Pablo Bay; the elevation and slope of a vineyard; the soil type and moisture content; and even the proximity to a mountain gap can make essential differences. Together, Sonoma and Napa have almost 30 registered appellations, which vary in size and sometimes overlap. Specific place names are becoming increasingly important as growers learn what to plant where and how to care for vines in each unique circumstance. The fact that more and more wines go to market with a specific AVA flies in the face of the worldwide trend to ever larger and less specific "branded" wines. Individual wineries and associations are working to promote the individuality of North Coast appellations and to preserve their integrity and viability as sustainable agriculture.

In recent decades, the Napa and Sonoma valleys have experienced tremendous levels of development. Besides significant increases in vineyard acreage, the late 20th century witnessed an explosion of small-scale operations, some housed in old wineries updated with state-of-the-art equipment. Meanwhile, the Russian River Valley remains less developed, retaining its rural feel with country roads winding past picturesque wineries, rolling hills of grapevines, and stands of redwood trees. With easy access to world-class wines, and organic produce and cheeses from local farms, residents of northern California's wine country enjoy an enviable quality of life. Happily for visitors, those same products supply the area's burgeoning number of restaurants, creating a culture of gourmet dining that stretches from the city of Napa all the way north to Healdsburg and beyond.

Note that if you elect to bring your own wine, most restaurants charge a corkage fee (which can vary from $10 to as much as $50 per bottle). Many restaurants waive this fee on one particular day, or if you purchase an additional bottle from their list.

Which Food?	*Which Wine?*	*Some Examples*
Shellfish	Semi-dry White	Early harvest Riesling, Chenin Blanc, early harvest Gewürztraminer, Viognier
	Dry White	Lighter Chardonnay (less oak), Pinot Blanc, Sauvignon Blanc, dry Riesling, dry Chenin Blanc
	Sparkling Wine	Brut, Extra Dry, Brut Rosé
	Dry Rosé	Pinot Noir, Syrah, Cabernet
Fish	Dry White	Chardonnay (oaky or not) Sauvignon Blanc, dry Riesling, dry Chenin Blanc, Pinot Blanc
	Sparkling Wine	Brut, Blanc de Blancs, Brut Rosé
	Light Red	Pinot Noir, Pinot Meunier, light-bodied Zinfandel
	Dry Rosé	Pinot Noir, Syrah, Cabernet
Cured Meats/ Picnic Fare	Semi-dry White	Early harvest Riesling or early harvest Gewürztraminer
	Dry White	Chardonnay (less oak), Sauvignon Blanc, dry Riesling
	Sparkling Wine	Brut, Blanc de Blancs, Brut Rosé
	Light Red	Gamay, Pinot Noir, Zinfandel, Sangiovese
	Young Heavy Red	Syrah, Cabernet Sauvignon, Zinfandel, Cabernet Franc, Merlot
	Rosé	Any light Rosé
Red Meat	Dry Rosé	Pinot Noir, Cabernet, Syrah, Blends
	Light Red	Pinot Noir, Zinfandel, Gamay, Pinot Meunier
	Young Heavy Red	Cabernet Sauvignon, Cabernet Franc, Syrah, Grenache, Petite Sirah, Merlot, Blends, Pinot Noir, Cabernet Sauvignon
	Mature Red	Merlot, Syrah, Zinfandel, Meritage, Blends
Fowl	Semi-dry White	Early harvest Riesling, Chenin Blanc, Viognier
	Dry White	Sauvignon Blanc, Chardonnay, Pinot Blanc, dry Riesling
	Sparkling Wine	Extra Dry, Brut, Brut Rosé
	Rosé	Any light Rosé
	Light Red	Pinot Noir, Zinfandel, Blends, Gamay
	Mature Red	Pinot Noir, Cabernet Sauvignon, Merlot, Syrah, Zinfandel, Meritage, Blends
Cheese	Semi-dry White	Riesling, Gewürztraminer, Chenin Blanc
	Dry White	Sauvignon Blanc, Chardonnay, Pinot Blanc, dry Riesling
	Sparkling Wine	Extra Dry, Brut
	Rosé	Pinot Noir, Cabernet, Grenache
	Light Red	Pinot Noir, Zinfandel, Blends, Gamay
	Young Heavy Red	Cabernet Sauvignon, Cabernet Franc, Syrah, Grenache, Petite Sirah, Merlot, Blends
Dessert	Sweet White	Any late harvest White
	Semi-dry White	Riesling, Gewürztraminer, Chenin Blanc, Muscat
	Sparkling Wine	Extra Dry, Brut, Rosé, Rouge
	Dessert Reds	Late harvest Zinfandel, Port

ıtage	1996	1997	1998	1999	2000	2001	2002	2003	2004	2005	2006	2007	2008	2009
ardonnay **rneros**	Above Average	Outstanding	Average	Above Average	Above Average	Outstanding	Outstanding	Outstanding	Outstanding	Above Average	Above Average	Above Average	Above Average	Above Average
ardonnay **ssian River**	Above Average	Outstanding	Average	Above Average	Above Average	Outstanding	Outstanding	Above Average	Outstanding	Outstanding	Above Average	Outstanding	Above Average	Above Average
ardonnay **pa Valley**	Outstanding	Outstanding	Above Average	Above Average	Average	Above Average	Outstanding	Outstanding	Above Average	Above Average	Above Average	Above Average	Above Average	Outstanding
ıvignon Blanc **pa Valley**	Above Average	Outstanding	Average	Above Average	Average	Outstanding	Outstanding	Above Average	Outstanding	Outstanding	Above Average	Above Average	Above Average	Above Average
ıvignon Blanc **noma County**	Above Average	Outstanding	Average	Above Average	Average	Outstanding	Above Average	Above Average	Outstanding	Above Average	Outstanding	Above Average	Above Average	Above Average
ıot Noir **rneros**	Above Average	Outstanding	Average	Above Average	Average	Outstanding	Above Average	Outstanding	Outstanding	Above Average	Above Average	Above Average	Above Average	Above Average
ıot Noir **ssian River**	Above Average	Outstanding	Above Average	Above Average	Above Average	Above Average	Outstanding	Outstanding	Outstanding	Above Average	Above Average	Outstanding	Outstanding	Above Average
ırlot **pa Valley**	Outstanding	Outstanding	Above Average	Outstanding	Above Average	Outstanding	Above Average	Outstanding	Above Average	Outstanding	Above Average	Above Average	Above Average	Above Average
ırlot **noma County**	Above Average	Outstanding	Above Average	Above Average	Above Average	Above Average	Above Average	Above Average	Outstanding	Outstanding	Above Average	Above Average	Above Average	Above Average
bernet Sauvignon **pa Valley**	Outstanding	Outstanding	Above Average	Outstanding	Above Average	Outstanding	Outstanding	Above Average	Outstanding	Outstanding	Outstanding	Outstanding	Outstanding	Outstanding
bernet Sauvignon **uthern Sonoma**	Outstanding	Outstanding	Above Average	Above Average	Above Average	Outstanding	Above Average	Above Average	Outstanding	Above Average	Above Average	Above Average	Outstanding	Outstanding
bernet Sauvignon **ırthern Sonoma**	Outstanding	Outstanding	Above Average	Above Average	Above Average	Above Average	Outstanding	Above Average	Outstanding	Outstanding	Outstanding	Above Average	Outstanding	Outstanding
ıfandel **pa Valley**	Outstanding	Outstanding	Above Average	Above Average	Above Average	Outstanding	Outstanding	Outstanding	Outstanding	Above Average	Outstanding	Outstanding	Above Average	Above Average
ıfandel **uthern Sonoma**	Outstanding	Outstanding	Above Average	Above Average	Above Average	Outstanding	Outstanding	Outstanding	Outstanding	Above Average	Outstanding	Outstanding	Above Average	Above Average
ıfandel **ırthern Sonoma**	Outstanding	Outstanding	Above Average	Outstanding	Above Average	Outstanding	Outstanding	Outstanding	Outstanding	Above Average	Outstanding	Above Average	Above Average	Above Average

= Outstanding = Above Average = Average

Peter L. Wrenn/MICHELIN

Napa Valley

Wine is the watchword in this 35-mile-long valley, which extends in a northerly direction from the San Pablo Bay to Mount St. Helena. Cradled between the Mayacama and the Vaca mountain ranges, the area boasts some of California's most prestigious wineries, along with a host of restaurants that are destinations in themselves.

A Whirl of Wineries

Reclaimed 19th century stone wineries and Victorian houses punctuate the valley's rolling landscape, reminding the traveler that there were some 140 wineries here prior to 1890. Today, Napa Valley has 325 producing wineries (and more than 400 brands), up from a post-Prohibition low of perhaps a dozen. They are all clustered along Route 29, the valley's main artery, which runs up the western side of the mountains, passing through the commercial hub of Napa and continuing north through the charming little wine burgs of Yountville, Oakville, Rutherford, St. Helena, and Calistoga.

More wineries dot the tranquil Silverado Trail, which hugs the foothills of the eastern range and gives a more pastoral perspective on this rural farm county. Along both routes, picturesque spots for alfresco dining abound. So pick up some picnic supplies at the **Oakville Grocery** (on Route 29), or stop by either the **Model Bakery** in St. Helena or **Bouchon Bakery** in Yountville for freshly-baked bread and delectable pastries. Throughout the valley you'll spot knolls, canyons, dry creek beds, stretches of valley floor, and glorious mountain vistas,

all of which afford varying microclimates and soil types for growing wine. San Pablo Bay has a moderating effect on the valley's temperatures, while the influence of the Pacific Ocean is lessened by the mountains. In the valley, powerfully hot summer days and still cool nights provide the ideal climate for cabernet sauvignon grapes, a varietal for which Napa is justifiably famous.

Among the region's many winemakers are well-known names like Robert Mondavi, Francis Ford Coppola, and the Miljenko "Mike" Grgich. Originally from Croatia, Grgich rose to fame as the winemaker at **Chateau Montelena** when his 1973 chardonnay took the top prize at the Judgment of Paris in 1976, outshining one of France's best white Burgundies. This feat turned the wine world on its ear, and put California

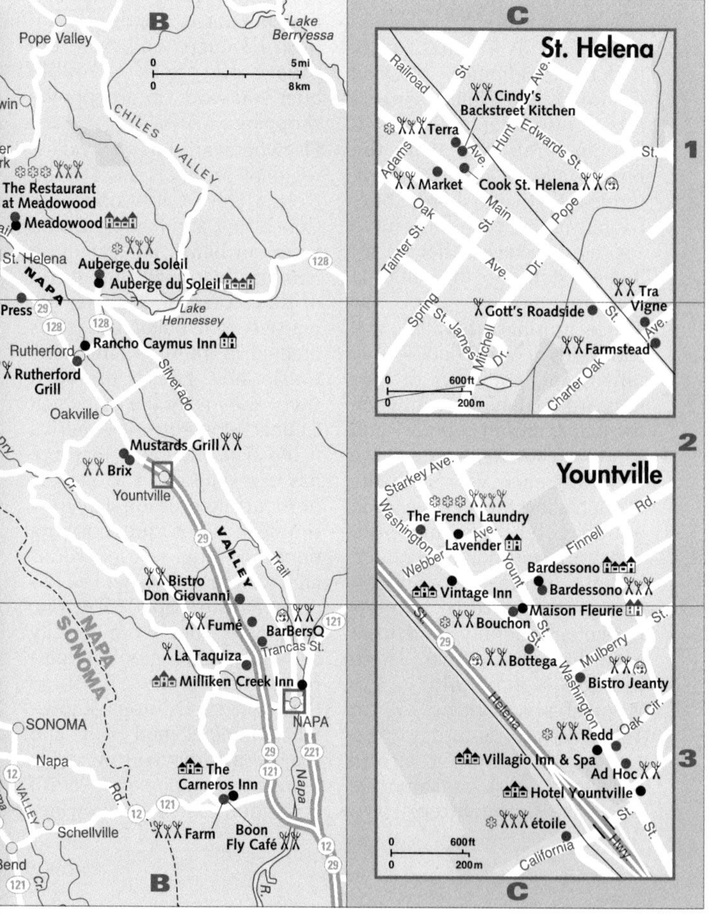

on the map as a bona fide producer of fine wine. Since then, Napa's success with premium wine has fostered a special pride of place. Fourteen American Viticultural Areas (AVAs) currently regulate the boundaries for sub-regions such as Carneros, Stags Leap, Rutherford, and Los Carneros. The boom in wine production has spawned a special kind of food-and-wine tourism: today tasting rooms, tours, and farm-fresh cuisine are de rigueur here. Along Washington Street, acclaimed chefs such as Thomas Keller, Richard Reddington, Michael Chiarello, and Philippe Jeanty rub elbows. Many other well-known chefs hail from the Napa Valley (Cindy Pawlcyn, Jeremy Fox, and Hiro Sone, to name a few) and have successfully raised their local-legend status to the national level.

Those touring the valley will spot fields of wild fennel, silvery olive trees, and rows of wild mustard that bloom between the grapevines in February and March. The mustard season kicks off each year with the Napa Valley Mustard Festival, which celebrates the food, wine, art, and rich agricultural bounty of the area. Several towns host seasonal farmer's markets, generally held from May through October. These include Napa (held in the Wine Train parking lot on Tuesdays and Saturdays); St. Helena (Fridays in Crane Park); and Calistoga (Saturdays on Washington Street). On Thursday nights in the summer, there's a **Chef's Market** in Napa Town Center. Opened in early 2008, **Oxbow Public Market** is a block-long 40,000-square-foot facility that is meant to vie with the Ferry Building Marketplace across the bay. Oxbow brims with local food artisans and wine vendors, all from within a 100-mile radius of the market. Within this barn-like building you'll find cheeses and charcuterie; spices and specialty teas; olive oils and organic ice cream; and, of course, stands of farm-fresh produce. And there are plenty of snacks available after you work up an appetite shopping.

Elsewhere around the valley, regional products such as St. Helena Olive Oil, Woodhouse Chocolates, and Rancho Gordo heirloom beans are gaining a national following. Just north of downtown St. Helena, the massive stone building that was erected in 1889 as Greystone Cellars now houses the West Coast campus of the renowned Culinary Institute of America (CIA). The Culinary Institute has a restaurant, and visitors here are welcome to view the several unique cooking demonstrations—reservations are recommended. With all this going for the Napa Valley, one thing is for sure: From the city of Napa, the region's largest population center, north to the town of Calistoga–known for its mineral mud baths and spa cuisine–this narrow valley represents paradise for lovers of both good food and fine wine.

Ad Hoc

American

6476 Washington St. (bet. California Dr. & Oak Circle), Yountville

Phone: 707-944-2487 — Lunch Sun
Web: www.adhocrestaurant.com — Dinner Thu – Mon
Prices: $$$

A lovely weathered farm table is the centerpiece at bustling Ad Hoc, the third in Chef/owner Thomas Keller's Yountville family. The kind of hangout that Keller himself might frequent at the end of a long night, low-key Ad Hoc epitomizes wine country with a rustic aura, warm hospitality, and plain good food crafted from the most exquisite ingredients.

In keeping with the ease of Napa Valley, Ad Hoc makes the tough decisions for you, serving a nightly four-course prix-fixe. What you see–perhaps smoky Kansas City barbecue or fried chicken–is what you get. Family-style meals begin with a salad such as romaine hearts rich with the flavor of anchovy, and finish with a simple cheese course and a dessert that showcases Keller's heralded knack for pastry.

Angèle

French

540 Main St. (at 5th St.), Napa

Phone: 707-252-8115 — Lunch & dinner daily
Web: www.angelerestaurant.com
Prices: $$$

Located south of the new Napa Riverfront, all traces of the modern age disappear at this winning hideaway inside an historic boathouse overlooking the Napa River. Take advantage of the elements from the breezy covered patio, or relish the friendly interior where a pitched timber ceiling, bistro furnishings, and blue and yellow accents suggest a French Country aspect. Savvy, good-natured service extends from dining room to bar—a recommended stop for those without reservations.

Californian sensibilities enliven this traditional brasserie fare. Watercress and shaved fennel garnish crispy sweetbreads and a caramelized onion tart, while chorizo and peppers spice a pan-seared grouper. Classic renditions include onion soup and *coquilles Saint-Jacques*.

Auberge du Soleil

Californian

180 Rutherford Hill Rd. (off the Silverado Trail), Rutherford

Phone: 707-963-1211 Lunch & dinner daily
Web: www.aubergedusoleil.com
Prices: **$$$$**

Auberge du Soleil

The mood is relaxed and the views are magnificent at the spa-influenced yet very Californian Auberge du Soleil. Whenever possible, dine alfresco here, as the heated terrace offers stunning vistas of the surrounding Mayacama mountains and miles of vineyards from nearly every table.

The Auberge's location in an upscale spa resort may influence some dishes, yet the kitchen's deft hand and finesse have fashioned a sophisticated menu that focuses on the freshest ingredients and remains ambitious without pretense. A variety of prix-fixe menus complement the à la carte options, which may include an elegant starter of silky, fairy-tale pumpkin soup with glazed chestnuts and creamy ricotta cheese. Entrées are composed with harmony of flavors in mind, as in the salmon fillet with a golden crust of crunchy-buttery onion crumbs, served with roasted Brussels sprouts, diced carrots, bacon, and foamy caraway *nage*. Desserts can be intensely decadent as in the exquisite chocolate torte layered with fresh hazelnuts, and rich, dark chocolate ganache accompanied by a shot-glass of pure bliss: icy vanilla milk.

From start to finish, this is a cuisine of very high caliber, bested only by its views.

Azzurro

Pizza

1260 Main St. (at Clinton St.), Napa

Phone: 707-255-5552 Lunch & dinner daily
Web: www.azzurropizzeria.com
Prices: $$

A blue-and-white tiled gas-fired pizza oven gleams in the center of the sleek open kitchen, where a marble bar at the chef's station offers views of the action. The airy dining space features a long wooden banquette, zinc-topped tables, and glossy black chairs.

Ten tasty varieties of thin crust pizza–with combinations for both purists and gourmands–are the specialty at Azzuro. Try the *funghi*, with roasted cremini and wild mushrooms, Taleggio, and thyme; or the *salsiccia*, with fennel sausage, red onion, and mozzarella. Anyone torn between a salad and a slice can go for the *manciata*—baked pizza dough topped with a choice of salads. Rustic pasta and antipasti dishes like Gamberi (grilled shrimp, white beans, sausage and arugula) complete the menu.

Bank Café and Bar

Contemporary 

1314 McKinstry St. (at Soscol Ave.), Napa

Phone: 707-257-5151 Lunch & dinner daily
Web: www.latoque.com/bankbar
Prices: $$

The hotel-like ambience at Bank Café and Bar, off the lobby of the Westin Verasa Napa, does not do this conversation-worthy café any favors. But there is great news: Chef Ken Frank, also of the hotel's La Toque, is notably at the helm here too. Frank's casual fare will transport you from Napa *toute de suite*, off to one of the many French regions that inform his weekly three-course menus.

An Alsace-inspired prix-fixe may bring *pâté de campagne*, pork tenderloin with cabbage, and a tarte Alsacienne. You may also order Californian items à la carte, including bacon-wrapped dates stuffed with spicy chorizo, and a seared duck burger made with artisanal foie gras. Those in the know, and with dollars to spare, may pick from the menu at posh La Toque.

BarBersQ 

B3 — Barbecue XX

3900 D, Bel Aire Plaza (at Trancas St.), Napa

Phone: 707-224-6600 Lunch & dinner daily
Web: www.barbersq.com
Prices: $$

What could be better than good, old-fashioned American classics whipped up outta the fresh bounty of local gardens and farms? Not a whole lot. Here at the ever-popular BarBersQ, Memphis-style barbecue gets a conscientious kick in the pants—sustainable ingredients from grass-fed beef and free-range chicken to organic fruits and veggies (much of which come to the kitchen the same day they're picked), command the hearty menu.
Lip-smackers like wild Atlantic fried shrimp with zingy tartar sauce, or the Q-combo (go for tender brisket and baby back ribs) are sure to satiate. Delish meat sandwiches and sides like warm cornbread with honey butter make it all the more irresistible. The small interior, styled in stainless steel and marble, crowds up quickly.

Bardessono

C2 — Contemporary XXX

6526 Yount St. (at Finnell Rd.), Yountville

Phone: 707-204-6030 Lunch & dinner daily
Web: www.bardessono.com
Prices: $$$

Stone gardens and sculptural fountains at contemporary Bardessono seem to have risen from the soil to blend with the natural landscape. Constructed with 90-percent recycled design, the sleek resort touts itself as the country's greenest. Salvaged Monterey cypress, walnut, and redwood keep the dining room down to earth, while bucolic accents allow the mood to soar.
In keeping with its theme, the menu focuses on local and sustainable ingredients, with à la carte offerings listed as Field & Forest, Ocean, and Pasture & Range. On weekdays, explore the six-course prix-fixe; Sundays bring a four-course supper featuring shrimp scampi with Meyer lemon, or venison with roasted butternut squash. Wines offer many organic and biodynamic options.

barolo

1457 Lincoln Ave. (bet. Fair Way & Washington St.), Calistoga

Phone: 707-942-9900 Dinner Wed – Sun
Web: www.barolocalistoga.com
Prices: **$$**

Wine bar-cum-full-scale restaurant, barolo might have formerly been known as barVino, but there's so much more to this wine country gem than just the local grape juice. After a day of lolling in the mud, or yes, tasting wine at local vineyards, visit this lounge-like spot for a little city chic in the heart of sleepy Calistoga. As might be expected, the wine list has some unique local and small production labels that blend perfectly with their Italian dishes—gourmet mushroom and fontina thin-crust pizza, and deliciously al dente shrimp pappardelle.

This is Italian in that cool, metropolitan way. Not a checkered table cloth red sauce joint, this place is all about red leather booths, metallic fixtures, and a candy apple red Vespa perched on the wall.

Bistro Don Giovanni

4110 Howard Ln. (at Hwy. 29), Napa

Phone: 707-224-3300 Lunch & dinner daily
Web: www.bistrodongiovanni.com
Prices: **$$**

The stars in Galileo's sky aligned in the making of Don Giovanni, the Napa mainstay that owes its success equally to location, ambience, and consistent cuisine. Perched conveniently on Highway 29, the restaurant remains true to rustic Italian form with terra-cotta floors, country-style rattan chairs, and gleaming copper cookware dangling above the *pizzaiolo's* wood-burning oven.

From the kitchen, a bounty of antipasti, seasonal risottos, and house-made pastas refuel locals and wine tasters alike, while savory fried green olives with Marcona almonds or *fettuccine alla Lina*, tossed with porcini and sausage ragù, make for a cocktail-friendly start. High ceilings can't contain the din of the constant crowd but, on sunny days, the real party is on the patio.

Bistro Jeanty

French

C3

6510 Washington St. (at Mulberry St.), Yountville

Phone: 707-944-0103 Lunch & dinner daily
Web: www.bistrojeanty.com
Prices: $$

There is no culinary destination quite like Yountville, where boldface names like Thomas Keller and Michael Chiarello rule a notable restaurant row. Chef Philippe Jeanty may be less recognizable to the Food Network set, but his Bistro Jeanty is still a Washington Street star.

Housed behind a red brick façade with a striped awning and window boxes abloom with roses and geraniums, Bistro Jeanty has all the trappings of a wine country favorite—French antiques inside and woven café chairs and mismatched tables, set with peppermills and cruets of Dijon mustard, on the heated terrace. With a respectful approach to classical fare, the kitchen sends out excellent renditions of pig's foot salad, with al dente haricots verts, and petrale sole meunière.

Boon Fly Café

Californian

B3

4048 Sonoma Hwy. (at Los Carneros Ave.), Napa

Phone: 707-299-4870 Lunch & dinner daily
Web: www.thecarnerosinn.com
Prices: $$

Set in the Carneros Inn (an agri-chic complex amid 27 pastoral acres off the Old Sonoma Highway) is the rustic, red barn-style of the Boon Fly Café. While the café serves breakfast, lunch, and dinner, it is brunch that is a true standout here with plates like green eggs and ham; and poached eggs wrapped in ham served atop golden hashbrowns licked with lemon-leek cream.

With corrugated aluminum walls and porch swings to ease the brunch time waits, this is a decidedly chic roadhouse eatery. The same creative spirit shines at lunch and dinner with entrées like pesto and beer sausage dancing with spaghetti; or crispy chicken and waffles. Heartier appetites will savor homier fare like ribs polished to a fine shine with an orange-habañero barbecue sauce.

Bottega

6525 Washington St. (near Yount St.), Yountville

Phone: 707-945-1050 — Lunch Tue – Sun
Web: www.bottega napavalley.com — Dinner nightly
Prices: $$

In Italian, a *bottega* is a master artisan's atelier. In Yountville, Bottega is both workplace and showplace for TV maestro Michael Chiarello who, despite countless cookbooks and a successful lifestyle brand, isn't kicking back on his laurels. Rather, he leaves the relaxation to his lively, star-struck guests sipping Prosecco on plush couches by the terrace's roaring fires.

Absolutely nothing lacks at Bottega, where the ambience wraps everything in chestnut leather and amber light. When Chiarello isn't charming the dining room with shots of *amaro* and jokes on the house, he's orchestrating the kitchen. Cuisine is simply impeccable, with such dishes as warm polenta "under glass"; fluffy gnocchi with Taleggio and English peas; or Adriatic seafood *brodetto*.

Bounty Hunter

975 First St. (at Main St.), Napa

Phone: 707-226-3976 — Lunch & dinner daily
Web: www.bountyhunterwinebar.com
Prices: $$

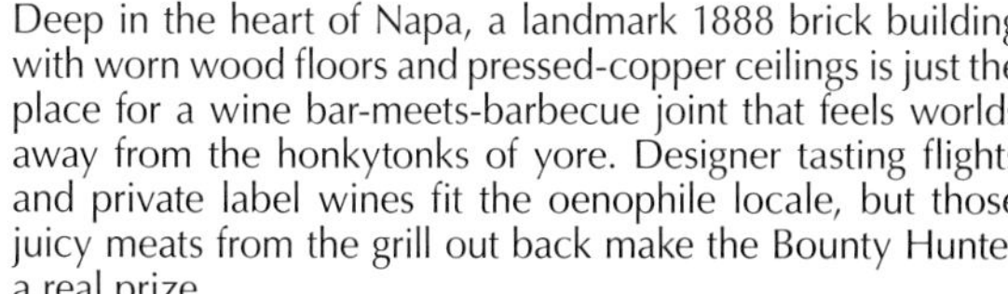

Deep in the heart of Napa, a landmark 1888 brick building with worn wood floors and pressed-copper ceilings is just the place for a wine bar-meets-barbecue joint that feels worlds away from the honkytonks of yore. Designer tasting flights and private label wines fit the oenophile locale, but those juicy meats from the grill out back make the Bounty Hunter a real prize.

Majestic mounted game presides over the saloon-style space where locals pair their wines with shredded crab and red pepper bisque; bone-in rib eyes; and hearty barbecue sandwiches. The beer can chicken is a must, even if it does elicit a sophomoric chuckle—the crispy Cajun-skinned fowl stands upright on a Tecate can. The job of carving the bird is all yours, but so is the reward.

Bouchon ✿

French XX

C3

6534 Washington St. (at Yount St.), Yountville

Phone: 707-944-8037 Lunch & dinner daily
Web: www.bouchonbistro.com
Prices: **$$$**

Bouchon

To eat at Bouchon is to dine in classic French bistro style, with a relaxed and casual Californian energy. Despite an aesthetic that recalls Paris, everything at Chef Thomas Keller's renowned flagship bistro is genuine and without the pretense of lesser imitations. Potted palms, polished brass fixtures, burgundy drapes, decorative tile floors, cushioned rattan seating, blackboards listing daily specials, and that warm, crusty *pain d'epi* placed on each table make locals and tourists glad they are right here in Yountville. In fair weather, terrace dining is equally pleasing. The friendly cocktail and enticing oyster bars are ideal for solo dining.

The words "decadent" and "delicious" can be used to describe much of the menu here, starting with the duck confit—crisp skin and silky meat on a salad of frisée, poached apple, and soft quail egg dressed with creamy foie gras vinaigrette. Hearty entrées may feature a roast leg of lamb served over potato gratin with rich red wine jus. It would be a shame to skip a course of oysters or cheeses, but desserts are de rigueur, so save room for a generous wedge of lemon tart.

Bouchon Bakery is conveniently located next door, should you need more.

Brannan's Grill

A1 American XX

1374 Lincoln Ave. (at Washington St.), Calistoga

Phone: 707-942-2233 Lunch & dinner daily
Web: www.brannansgrill.com
Prices: **$$**

Favorably housed on the main strip in Calistoga, Brannan's Grill dishes up good food for hungry shoppers and spa-fiends. After a soothing mud bath or healing dip in one of the mineral springs, a mountain breeze pouring through large windows and a blazing fire in the stone hearth could be just what the doctor ordered. As if that weren't enough, genuine service; a richly decorated mahogany-paneled dining room dating back to the 19th century; and live jazz on weekends, makes Brannan's the perfect prescription for a cushy night out.

Sealing the deal (and your lips) are classics like smoked salmon carpaccio; Idaho trout *piccata*; filet mignon with bleu cheese scalloped potatoes; and a burger topped with smoked cheddar, crispy onions, and all the fixin's.

Brix

B2 Californian XX

7377 St. Helena Hwy. (at Washington St.), Yountville

Phone: 707-944-2749 Lunch & dinner daily
Web: www.brix.com
Prices: **$$$**

When it comes to ingredients in the Napa Valley, there's local–from one of many nearby farms–and then there's *local*, as in straight from your own backyard. At beloved Brix, expect the red radish and pea shoots that adorn your smoked salmon crêpe to hail from the garden patio out back. There may be no fresher salad in Yountville.

The farm-to-table menu is straightforward with both Italian and Asian inflections: braised pork and chestnut ragù warm the orecchiette pasta; while garden pepper linguini is tossed with Laughing Bird shrimp. If weather permits, enjoy a glass of Carneros pinot noir in the gardens, hugged by rolling vineyards and craggy mountain views. Pick up dessert and a wine country memento at the bake shop and gift boutique.

Bui Bistro

Vietnamese XX

976 Pearl St. (bet. Main St. & Soscol Ave.), Napa

Phone: 707-255-5417 Lunch & dinner Tue – Sun
Web: www.buibistro.com
Prices: $$

Napa Valley denizens craving the flavors of Vietnam are heading to Chef/owner Patrick Bui's namesake bistro in the wine country where Bui serves the same affordable, flavorful fare for which his original Berkeley location is known.

Inside, gilded mirrors dress up sage green walls and rosewood tables; a small granite bar is well suited to singles lingering over glasses of wine and warm bowls of rice noodles, teeming with delicate prawns, scallops and squid, with plates of condiments. French influences can be found in such dishes as Asian duck confit and beef carpaccio, but the tasty Vietnamese mainstays are also here. Look for shaken beef, pepper tuna, and an array of spicy curries. For dessert, moist tiramisu is both an unexpected and chocolaty surprise.

C Casa

Mexican 

610 1st St. (at McKinstry St.), Napa

Phone: 707-226-7700 Lunch & dinner daily
Web: www.myccasa.com
Prices: $$

Bay Area foodies will instantly recognize the Oxbow Public Market, Napa's answer to SF's Ferry Building bursting with kitchen shops and international foodstuffs. Relatively new to the culinary destination, co-owner Catherine Bergen–also former owner of Made in Napa's all-natural pantry products–is translating her taste for healthy gourmet eats to this innovative taqueria.

C Casa is an order-at-the-counter affair, but don't let the casual setting fool you. The market kitchen beats any upscale taqueria with its made-to-order tortillas topped with spiced lamb and grilled mahi mahi. Dig your compostable fork into a lean ground buffalo taco with goat cheese and chipotle aïoli, or try a grilled shrimp cocktail with tomato and cucumber relish.

Celadon

International XX

500 Main St., Ste. G (at 5th St.), Napa

Phone: 707-254-9690 Lunch Mon – Fri
Web: www.celadonnapa.com Dinner nightly
Prices: $$

Chef/owner Greg Cole must be raising a glass to his loyal clientele who, for years, have flocked to this riverfront jewel–Celadon–in order to savor his comfort food influenced by Mediterranean, Asian, and American flavors.

Celadon is as amicable and tranquil as it is accessible. A brick fireplace warms the large covered atrium with an aluminum cathedral ceiling and whitewashed brick walls. Cool gray and green shades coat the interior, where butcher paper and white linens dress the small tables and a quaint bar is ideal for a glass. The menu is as worldly as its wine country patronage, wandering the globe from sweet coconut-fried prawns to a crisp-skinned duck breast perched on roasted spaghetti squash, cranberries, and chestnuts.

Cindy's Backstreet Kitchen

International XX

C1

1327 Railroad Ave. (bet. Adams St. & Hunt Ave.), St. Helena

Phone: 707-963-1200 Lunch & dinner daily
Web: www.cindysbackstreetkitchen.com
Prices: $$

You can almost catch a whiff of fresh-baked pie cooling above the blooming window boxes at Cindy's Backstreet Kitchen, an 1829 country home with swaying arbors and a small stone hearth on the patio. A zinc bar and black-and-white wallpaper depicting fruits and vegetables keep with a modern rural theme, as do the shakes and floats to pair with classic American cuisine.

Chef/owner Cindy Pawlcyn wouldn't be content to remain in Americana alone. Her global palate can be seen in Vietnamese lettuce wraps or *pollo loco* chicken with avocado salsa and stuffed green chile. Pawlcyn brings it back home for dessert with a s'more-sational campfire pie. On Wednesdays and Thursdays, stop by Cindy's Supper Club for a globally-inflected three-course prix-fixe.

Cole's Chop House

Steakhouse XXX

A3

1122 Main St. (bet. 1st & Pearl Sts.), Napa

Phone: 707-224-6328 — Dinner nightly
Web: www.coleschophouse.com
Prices: $$$$

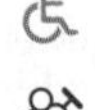

An original open truss ceiling and Douglas fir floors attest to the history of the 1886 hand-hewn stone building now home to Cole's Chop House, a classic meat-and-potatoes destination with a clubby ambience and spendy cuisine: entrées top out at $69 for a 21-day dry-aged Porterhouse. But don't fret, as there are 20 plus pages of wines, including several luscious Napa cabs, or classic and seasonal cocktails to take your mind off the bill.

Boozier pleasures aside, Greg Cole's Chop House serves an American-style menu that is dizzying for omnivores. Look for succulent Iowa pork, New Zealand lamb, and sustainable seafood in addition to such classics as oysters Rockefeller and a chophouse Caesar. Herbivores can wait at Ubuntu, the vegetarian mecca, next door.

Cook St. Helena

Italian XX

C1

1310 Main St. (bet. Adams & Spring Sts.), St. Helena

Phone: 707-963-7088 — Lunch Mon – Sat
Web: www.cooksthelena.com — Dinner nightly
Prices: $$

On Main Street in posh St. Helena, pull over at Cook where a Carrara marble wine bar awaits with local temptations. This spot reflects its wine country locale with taste and whimsy: antique tin-framed mirrors and black-and-white vegetable prints adorn the walls; dark wood covers the floor; and a whimsical bovine lantern is mounted like a trophy on the wall.

While solo diners may prefer a spot at the bar, white cloths topped with butcher paper make the close-knit tables a cozy place to dine. Chef/owner Jude Wilmouth serves reasonably priced Cal-Italian fare, with daily specials on the blackboard. Sample steamed mussels in spicy tomato broth; red trout stuffed with roasted fennel and fingerlings; and flourless chocolate cake dusted with grey sea salt.

Cuvée

American XX

A2

1650 Soscol Ave. (at River Terrace Dr.), Napa

Phone: 707-224-2330 — Dinner nightly
Web: www.cuveenapa.com
Prices: $$

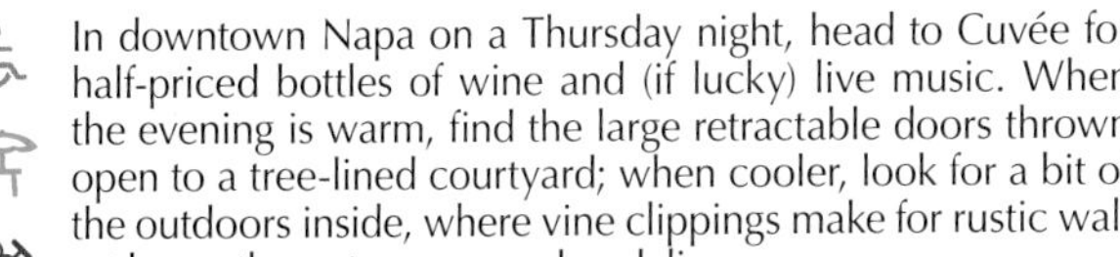

In downtown Napa on a Thursday night, head to Cuvée for half-priced bottles of wine and (if lucky) live music. When the evening is warm, find the large retractable doors thrown open to a tree-lined courtyard; when cooler, look for a bit of the outdoors inside, where vine clippings make for rustic wall art beneath contemporary chandeliers.

Next door to the River Terrace Inn, Cuvée is a favorite among hotel guests and locals hungry for American fare such as pinot noir-braised short ribs and Atlantic salmon wrapped in paper-thin potatoes. For a subtle taste of the Orient, try tuna tartare with crunchy Asian slaw and crisp rice crackers. In true old-world style, the wine selection includes several locally made options on tap, as a barrel tasting.

Farm

Californian XXX

B3

4048 Sonoma Hwy. (at Old Sonoma Rd.), Napa

Phone: 707-299-4882 — Dinner nightly
Web: www.thecarnerosinn.com
Prices: $$$

Don't be fooled by Farm's unassuming gray façade: the stone-paved path lined with potted herbs and flowers leads to another world where the well-dressed clink cocktails by fire pits in an airy, open lounge.

With a certain barn-like *je ne sais quoi*, the spacious dining den is posh yet earthy with oversized murals covering white-trimmed sage walls, and pendant lights casting a sultry glow. Farm's cuisine mimics the ambience with top-notch ingredients in unfussy presentations like Chesapeake Bay soft shell crab with green nettle pesto; succulent Maine lobster risotto drizzled with preserved Meyer lemon oil; and young Petaluma chicken with a delightfully crisp skin. Post dinner, treat yourself to an olive oil financier with crème fraîche sorbet.

étoile 

Contemporary

C3

1 California Dr. (off Hwy. 29), Yountville

Phone: 707-204-7529 Lunch & dinner Thu – Mon
Web: www.chandon.com
Prices: $$$$

Eric Wolfinger

Sullen foodies with a distaste for the picturesque should skip the oak- and vine-lined driveway up to Domaine Chandon's étoile, the Yountville restaurant whose gracious windows provide painfully gorgeous views to the property's gardens, creek and vineyard. Take it from us, this restaurant's address alone promises a quintessentially lovely wine country culinary moment.

Étoile's interior too is nothing if not pretty: oil lamps and bud vases adorn linen-topped tables beneath the vaulted ceiling; while sliding glass doors provide that inside-outside vibe. In warmer months, a bucolic patio takes the party alfresco where you can expect posh tourists celebrating special occasions.

The kitchen's cuisine is equally storybook—just ask the "Fairy Tale" pumpkin "pasta" of pumpkin ribbons and braised duck confit dotted with black trumpet mushrooms and pomegranate seeds. Even Cinderella would certainly have approved. Also look for contemporary takes on Californian classics like a roulade of sole with *cipollinis*, Brussels sprouts, and lemongrass-tarragon cream. For dessert, rendezvous with a French pastry: the quince crêpe with vanilla crème fraîche and pine nuts is a happy ending to any meal.

Farmstead

Californian XX

738 Main St. (at Charter Oak Ave.), St. Helena

Phone: 707-963-9181 — Lunch & dinner daily
Web: www.thefarmsteadnapa.com
Prices: $$

As its name alludes, Farmstead (the restaurant at Long Meadow Ranch) is praised and preferred for its farm-to-table Californian cooking. Likewise, its surrounds are locally-sourced—the wine country-chic barn is clad in wood left over from surrounding redwoods and anchored by a central open kitchen outfitted with a cast-iron grill.

Under airy, vaulted ceilings, dishes are prepared with local and sustainable ingredients and may include *lacinato* kale salad tossed with *chile pequin* and *tuiles* of toasted Grana Padano; wonderfully delicate rock bass fillets spread with a creamy aïoli, and posing atop wood-roasted sausages and potatoes in a cioppino broth; and an expert side of buttery flageolet beans fragrant with garlic and fresh herbs.

Fish Story

790 Main St. (at 3rd St.), Napa

Phone: 707-251-5600 — Lunch & dinner daily
Web: www.fishstorynapa.com
Prices: $$

Ahoy, seafood lovers! This is a yarn about a true fish house on the banks of the Napa River, where a heated patio thaws the bones and a nip from the horseshoe bar warms the belly. Never mind the chill cast from the local maritime temperatures posted on the wall—documented local fishing stories and photos posted in the hall do plenty to authenticate the experience.

Fish Story never veers from its course: silver lures and hooks hang from above, and the day's fresh catch is displayed on ice. Those large kettles are used for brewing the namesake beer, perfect for washing down raw clams and oysters, Maine lobster rolls, or flavorful shrimp and grits. Bargain hunters should reel in the "All at Once Lunch" or "Hook, Line & Sinker" dinner, each under $30.

The French Laundry ✿✿✿

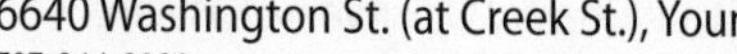

Contemporary XXXX

C2

6640 Washington St. (at Creek St.), Yountville

Phone: 707-944-2380
Web: www.frenchlaundry.com
Prices: **$$$$**

Lunch Fri – Sun
Dinner nightly

Deborah Jones

So much has been said, so little has changed, yet everything continues to evolve at The French Laundry. The stone building's rustic and discreet appearance may seem unassuming, but enter through the lush garden courtyard, with glimpses into the kitchen, to better understand its renowned French-country sensibilities. Inside, flickering candles, stone walls, and carved wood railings add rustic touches to the elegant room that sheds all stuffy formalities.

Meals here are opportunities to dive deeper into the profound culinary knowledge that every server, sommelier, and chef here must inherently possess. In the kitchen, Thomas Keller has anointed Chef Timothy Hollingsworth to honor the path he blazed years ago.

Meticulous skill and delight combine with absolute precision in meals that awaken the palate with the likes of caramelized lemon sorbet over salted, compressed cucumber, blue borage blossoms, and white-sesame *bavarois*. The delicate hands of an artist are clear in a roulade of paper-thin egg crêpe and stinging nettle purée, topped with tomato marmalade. Thankfully, nine-course fixed menus are the only dining option, so there is no foregoing the best cheese course of your life.

Fumé

International XX

B3

4050 Byway East (bet. Avalon Ct. & Wise Dr.), Napa

Phone: 707-257-1999 Lunch & dinner daily
Web: www.fumebistro.com
Prices: $$

Those who seek an unpretentious, friendly atmosphere and comfortable neighborhood vibe head to Fumé, where family-style hospitality and a blaze in the wood-burning pizza oven keep things cozy.

The mood is as jovial as the menu is eclectic in the broad, golden dining room where chatter rises to the exposed rafters and a long bar allows for overflow. The semi-open kitchen dedicates weekday specials to casual themes such as "local" and "little Italy," while Sunday nights bring old-fashioned beef stew. Some of the more wide-ranging dishes might include panko-crusted ahi tuna with tangy Asian slaw or a signature pork chop wrapped in Applewood smoked bacon with whole grain mustard sauce. The respectable list of wines hails from Napa, of course.

Gott's Roadside

American X

C2

933 Main St. (at Charter Oak Ave.), St. Helena

Phone: 707-963-3486 Lunch & dinner daily
Web: www.gottsroadside.com
Prices: ⓢⓢ

For a quick burger in wine country, look no farther than this roadside icon that opened in 1949, long before Napa was renowned for wine. A bit of a naming feud led to the hamburger haven's (formerly known as Taylor's) name change. At Gott's Roadside Tray Gourmet, while the prices seem high, so is the quality—know that juicy Niman Ranch beef lies between buns, beneath toppings like grilled mushrooms or guacamole. The restaurant also churns out hot dogs topped with hearty homemade chile and sides of sweet potato fries. Gott's refreshes with milk shakes, draft beers, and local wines by the glass, half-bottle, or bottle.

All three locations (San Francisco's Ferry Building and Napa's Oxbow Public Market) have picnic tables perfect for alfresco dining.

Grace's Table

A3 International XX

1400 2nd St. (at Franklin St.), Napa

Phone: 707-226-6200 Lunch & dinner daily
Web: www.gracestable.net
Prices: $$

Named for Mother Nature's fabulous bounty, Grace's Table is just as you might expect: a little earthy. Recycled materials in green and brown hues come together for a low-key vibe, while potted plants breathe life onto wooden tables.

Couples and singles can grab a beer and nosh at the 10-seat bar, while tables are preferred for dinners and weekend brunch. The global menu leans toward European comfort fare like tender pork osso bucco with wild mushroom risotto, but it's the seasonal tamale that has become a local legend. If the short rib-stuffed tamale isn't wicked enough, try a slice of the old-fashioned devil's food cake with dark chocolate frosting, Chantilly cream, and a sprinkling of Maldon salt—this dessert is the sweet work of Gaia.

JoLē

A1 Mediterranean XX

1457 Lincoln Ave. (bet. Fair Way & Washington St.), Calistoga

Phone: 707-942-5938 Dinner nightly
Web: www.jolerestaurant.com
Prices: $$

It's ok to be married to your work when you're married to each other, right? It seems to work for husband-and-wife team Matt and Sonjia Spector, the dynamic duo behind JoLē, named for the other fruit of their labor—their two sons.

The sleek, contemporary décor, set with dark wood tables and a marble bar, belies the food. It's wholeheartedly farm-to-table and the food bears a Mediterranean twist. Sample a plate or two of meals ranging from light to heavy, but for a true test of the kitchen's talents, customize a 4, 5, or 6 course prix-fixe menu from the à la carte selections. Pork belly and heavenly coconut cream pie are among many standouts. Didn't leave room for dessert? Ask about The Bakeshop to bring home some sweet goodness.

Kitchen Door

International 

610 1st St. (at McKinstry St.), Napa

Phone: 707-226-1560 Lunch & dinner daily
Web: www.kitchendoornapa.com
Prices: **$$**

A new kid in the Oxbow Public Market block, Kitchen Door preens a roster of internationally-inspired and reasonably priced dishes. Entrée this massive, bright arena via swinging red kitchen doors and place your order at the counter. Then fetch your flatware, find a seat in the dining room or on the patio, and await the affair.

Large communal tables face the open kitchen; while cozy booths allow for reunions. Sealing the family-friendly deal are sky-lit ceilings, hanging pots and pans, and shelves of foodstuffs. As if that weren't enough, there is a dish for every palate—from a porcini salad with *bocconcini*, tomatoes, and arugula, to roast duck *banh mi* spread with duck liver, spicy mayo, and cilantro. A vanilla *affogato* is simple yet exhilarating.

La Taquiza

2007 Redwood Rd. (at Solano Rd.), Napa

Phone: 707-224-2320 Lunch & dinner Mon – Sat
Web: www.lataquizanapa.com
Prices:

Wine country palates on burrito budgets find salvation *con* salsa at La Taquiza, a taqueria with cool local art and Baja-style fresh Mex that defies its Redwood Plaza locale (where taco truck-loving patrons indulge in hefty if average burritos). This chef/owner, a Bouchon Bakery alum, is partial to lighter, more inventive, seafood-driven fare.

Whether fried or grilled, signature fish tacos are a delicious starting point, but the menu's more exotic options whet adventurous appetites. Don't hesitate to sample fresh ceviches, beer-battered oysters, and *pulpo*–grilled, tender octopus ideal for a unique taco–as well as chilled seafood *coctels* and bowls known as *tazones*. Swing by the salsa bar for varying degrees of heat and smokiness to satisfy all tastes.

La Toque ✿

A2 Contemporary XXX

1314 McKinstry St. (at Soscol Ave.), Napa

Phone: 707-257-5157 Dinner nightly
Web: www.latoque.com
Prices: $$$

Melissa Werner, CCS Architecture

Helmed by Chef/owner Ken Frank, La Toque was a wine country favorite well before it relocated to the white-collar Westin Verasa hotel in downtown Napa. Like many resort eateries, La Toque has a bit of a corporate aura, but it doesn't really matter: large windows, rich earth tones, and a blazing fireplace make this admired restaurant perfectly comfortable and warm. Outside is equally pleasing on the sunny covered terrace.

Once settled, cozy up in an intimate banquette in the serene dining room, where a suited waitstaff and soft jazz evoke a fine dining experience without feeling stuffy. Tables are dotted with budding flowers, votives, and only the finest place settings. Come casual but well-heeled, of course.

Chef Frank's contemporary cuisine is presented in prix-fixe meals, so prepare to settle in for a feast. The tasting menu may include ricotta chickpea ravioli in Parmesan and wild mushroom broth; Pacific salmon with morels and English peas; and Moroccan-spiced boneless lamb loin with cumin-scented carrot purée. Enjoy each course with a thoughtfully poured pairing—this is Napa, after all. For the fullest experience, reserve a seat at the chef's table in the partially open kitchen.

Market

American

1347 Main St. (bet. Adams & Spring Sts.), St. Helena

Phone: 707-963-3799 — Lunch & dinner daily
Web: www.marketsthelena.com
Prices: $$

Chef/owner Eduardo Martinez is sharing his American dream at Market, where classics like mac 'n' cheese, dressed up with aged *Fiscalini* cheddar, mingle with little tastes from his Mexico City home—think buttermilk fried chicken and peppery cheddar-jalapeño cornbread, or blackened chicken rolls spiced with chipotle chiles.

There are many reasons to love Market, including pristine oysters on the half shell; a $15 lunch comprised of "soup, sandwich and a treat" (think rice krispies); and a sinfully fabulous butterscotch pudding made with real Scotch, ahem, and served in a waffle cone bowl. Slip into a plush brown leather banquette and get comfy with your latest prize from wine tasting: an anomaly in the Valley, Market generously forgoes corkage fees.

Mini Mango Thai Bistro

1408 W. Clay St. (bet. Franklin and Seminary Sts.), Napa

Phone: 707-226-8884 — Lunch Mon – Sat
Web: www.minimangonapa.com — Dinner nightly
Prices:

This tiny Napa nook has certainly seen more dismal times considering the location has proved a challenge to previous inhabitants. But there is no stopping Mini Mango, a promising Thai bistro that's low on tables but big on flavor. The space does double in pretty weather however, with a roomy front patio ringed in olive trees that bustles when beautiful outside. Thanks to owners Pornchai and Cherry Pengchareon, Mini Mango is a small slice of Thailand in the wine country with a hint of a Californian accent. Pleasant servers overcome the challenges of cramped quarters to deliver such classics as pad Thai along with more audacious options—think Indochine corn fritters with tangy plum sauce; spicy grilled calamari; and tiger prawns preening in tomato curry.

Morimoto Napa

Japanese 

610 Main St. (at 5th St.), Napa

Phone: 707-252-1600 — Lunch Wed – Sun
Web: www.morimotonapa.com — Dinner nightly
Prices: **$$$**

You may not spot celebrity chef, Masaharu Morimoto wielding his knives behind the sushi bar, but your reservation at Morimoto's Napa outpost will be nonetheless worthwhile. In summer, riverfront tables are among the most sought-after in the Valley, and it's a safe bet that you won't find sushi like this elsewhere in the wine country.

A massive staff sees to the curious clientele, answering queries on the seven page seafood menu. Here, local ingredients mingle with delicacies from Tokyo's Tsukiji fish market, flown in daily, and Wagyu beef for land lovers. Diehard sushi fans will enjoy the multi-course omakase, while the pricey à la carte menu features beautiful sashimi, foie gras in a creamy *chawan mushi*, and a whole branzino tempura.

Mustards Grill

B2

American XX

7399 St. Helena Hwy. (at Hwy. 29), Yountville

Phone: 707-944-2424 — Lunch & dinner daily
Web: www.mustardsgrill.com
Prices: **$$**

Well before Thomas Keller staked his flag in Yountville, local favorite Cindy Pawlcyn was serving luxe "truckstop" fare at her already iconic Mustards. Opened in 1983, this wine country roadhouse still draws the crowds for new American fare (think oak-smoked barbecue ribs) and bargain sips from the list of Too Many Wines.

Soak up your favorite California varietal with one the various daily specials scribbled on the blackboard, or try such old favorites as Dungeness crab cakes or grilled quail accented with herbs and vegetables from the restaurant's own gardens. Venture out for a stroll and you just might encounter the chef. If reservations aren't available at Mustards, pick up one of Pawlcyn's many cookbooks and try your hand at home.

Neela's

Indian 

A3

975 Clinton St. (at Main St.), Napa

Phone: 707-226-9988 Lunch Tue – Sat

Web: www.neelasindianrestaurant.com Dinner Tue – Sun

Prices: $$

With a jewel-toned interior and bar streaming Bollywood music videos, this is as close to Mumbai as wine country gets. Raised in old Bombay, Chef/owner Neela Paniz moved from L.A. to Napa to share her native flavors with a town that lacked an Indian eatery. Now, the scent of fresh-ground spices can be traced to Neela's, serving contemporary fare reflective of India's varied culinary styles.

True Indophiles will relish an unexpected artistic edge in *chota haazari* (a variety of unique small plates) that may include a reinterpreted Niçoise salad; while traditional curries and tandoor delicacies are equally pleasing. Wednesdays bring a vegetarian tasting menu; Thursday "bread nights" are carbo-licious; and weekend afternoons are reserved for Indian high tea.

Norman Rose Tavern

Gastropub XX

A3

1401 1st St. (at Franklin St.), Napa

Phone: 707-258-1516 Lunch & dinner daily

Web: www.normanrosenapa.com

Prices: ◎

For everyone who is lagging after the dragging from winery to winery and just wants an ice-cold pint at the end of a hoity-toity day, this place is for you. Those of you who just perked up should cruise over to Norman Rose Tavern, one of the few spots in the Valley with a true-blue penchant for a burger and a PBR (or micro-brew on tap). Plentiful bar seating, walls lined with reclaimed barn wood, and a ceiling of empty "decorative" beer bottles leave no one doubting the theme.

Chef Michael Gyetvan gets it—never mind that his resume includes stints at One Market and Tra Vigne. At his approachable American pub, find plump all-beef hot dogs with tangy relish; milk-braised pork shoulder with gravy and sausage grits; and highbrow junk food at its very best.

Oenotri

Italian XX

1425 1st St. (bet. Franklin & School Sts.), Napa

Phone: 707-252-1022 — Lunch Mon – Fri
Web: www.oenotri.com — Dinner nightly
Prices: $$

The pizza ovens at Oakland's Oliveto have seasoned more than a handful of talented chefs, including Curtis Di Fede and Tyler Rodde who are now blistering their pies in an oven imported from Naples to Napa. Be warned, locals are happy to wait for a taste of that almond- and cherry-wood fire-licked pie.

With sunny textiles, exposed brick, and concrete floors, Oenotri–from an ancient word for "vine cultivator"–is a mix of practicality and pretty. But the design is just a side dish to standout Italian food including the smoky pizza Napoletana; porcini *fidei* pasta with grated tuna heart; and Silverado Trail strawberry *crostata* with Meyer lemon cream. With 30 wines for under $25, Oenotri is ideal for cultivating your palate without breaking the bank.

Pica Pica

Latin American 

610 First St. (at McKinstry St.), Napa

Phone: 707-251-3757 — Lunch & dinner daily
Web: www.picapicakitchen.com
Prices:

Parked at the South end of Oxbow Public Market, Pica Pica's Venezuelan flavors draw in lovers of all things *maize*. Sample white corn arepas oozing with mozzarella cheese, shredded skirt steak, black beans, and fried plantains; corn bread sandwiches (maize'wich) piled with chicken salad and creamy avocado; or griddled sweet yellow corn pancakes (*cachapas*) stuffed with ham and cheddar cheese. Take a budget-friendly break from food shopping for a couple of these tasty takeout style snacks, which could also include empanadas, yucca fries, or colorful salads.

The tiny space sports a few tables and a small bar area where food orders are taken. Choose between a refreshing brew or sangria while waiting for your order and grab yourself a table.

Press

Steakhouse XXX

587 St. Helena Hwy. South, St. Helena

Phone: 707-967-0550 — Dinner Wed – Mon
Web: www.presssthelena.com
Prices: $$$$

Here at Press, there are no sub-par cuts of meat. Those toppings–blue cheese, truffle butter, a fried organic egg–and bounty of tasty sauces may be delicious but are certainly not required on such perfectly prepared beef. Deeper pockets should go for the Kobe Wagyu from Idaho.

The gorgeous St. Helena space fashions a bucolic vibe with its black walnut floors, reclaimed from a Midwestern mill, and bar crafted from a trio of walnut trees. A roaring fireplace warms the contemporary yet rustic interior, while a second hearth and candles add to the patio's ambience and make for an ideal spot to sit and sip a rich, steak-worthy cabernet. The raw bar and many seasonal offerings are just as wonderful and will please those who shy away from the main attraction.

Rotisserie & Wine

American 

720 Main St. (bet 3rd & 5th Sts.), Napa

Phone: 707-254-8500 — Lunch Wed – Sun
Web: www.rotisserieandwine.com — Dinner nightly
Prices: $$

TV chef, Tyler Florence is more than just a pretty face—and he's working hard to prove it. In 2010, T. Flo opened his much-anticipated and straightforward Wayfare Tavern in SF. Now, after delays, he unveils this Napa Valley outpost, Rotisserie & Wine, serving finger-lickin' roasted meats and vintages from "Here" and "There."

Florence is working California's bounty into rich Southern fare. Dig into large *gougères* stuffed with bacon, Vella jack cheese, and Mornay sauce; or the very decadent Sonoma duck and cracklin' on a confit-studded waffle with watercress, a fried egg, and Jack Daniels syrup. The space nods to old-world France, with hand-blown glass *bonbonnes* and hefty wine barrel chandeliers. Belly up to the marble bar for a view to the open kitchen.

Redd ✿

C3 — Contemporary XX

6480 Washington St. (at Oak Circle), Yountville

Phone: 707-944-2222 — Lunch & dinner daily
Web: www.reddnapavalley.com
Prices: $$$$

Andy Katz

Redd is where the cool city kids eat when in Yountville, that food-obsessed wine country town that just couldn't be more idyllic. Here you'll find none of the barrel and vine décor ubiquitous to Redd's neighbors, who might just raise an eyebrow at the lime green resin chairs that arrest the eye from the modern albeit olive tree-lined patio.

Redd, in fact, brings the best of modern design to Napa without going overboard: geometric awnings and a sculptural fountain nod to the outdoors and are anything but rural; inside, gray cushioned Gubi chairs and contemporary whiteware are both minimalistic and serene. Fashionable locals are happy to take their meals at the bar.

Chef/owner Richard Reddington is also a maverick in the kitchen, honing his art on signature Asian-inflected dishes such as stir-fried chicken lettuce cups with eggplant and sesame seeds or yellowfin tuna hamachi with apples, avocado and soy. Main courses flirt with Californian cuisine staples but always pack an edge: a pair of golden scallops canoodles with cauliflower purée, capers, and golden raisins. For dessert, dip into a vanilla bean and quince *granité* parfait with a shot glass of panko-coated farina fritters.

The Restaurant at Meadowood ✿✿✿

Contemporary XXX

900 Meadowood Ln. (off Silverado Trail), St. Helena

Phone: 707-967-1205 Dinner Mon – Sat
Web: www.meadowood.com
Prices: $$$$

Meadowood Napa Valley

A good chef combines the best ingredients and impeccable technique to make something delicious; a great one makes it new and extraordinary. Let there be no doubt that Chef Christopher Kostow has found his footing in this contemporary menu of Californian-French cuisine that shows thought, precision, sophistication, and downright good taste with nary a misstep in sight.

Superlatives fail to describe the cerebral experience of dipping a spoon into the cumin-scented consommé poured over a trio of heirloom beans, with cuttlefish *brunoise* and smoked avocado mousse that gives the illusion of bacon. Entrées may reveal rectangular cubes of goat tenderloin, each topped with fresh dates, carrot spheres, and black lime zest, garnished with Lilliputian vegetables and creamy yogurt. While the à la carte selections are excellent, fixed menus here are vibrant and subtle reflections of savory beginnings and sweet ends, resulting in a level of pleasure that may seem unattainable until you completely experience it.

Inside the circular room overlooking the wine country landscape, white beamed ceilings, wainscoting, and stone fireplaces wrap diners in a sense of rural elegance and romance.

Rutherford Grill

American XX

B2

1180 Rutherford Rd. (at Hwy. 29), Rutherford

Phone: 707-963-1792 Lunch & dinner daily
Web: www.hillstone.com
Prices: **$$**

Temptation starts in the parking lot at Rutherford Grill, where aromas from the wood-fired rotisserie make impatient bellies growl. Just don't arrive too hungry; this popular hangout nearly guarantees a wait. Sidle up to the bar in the meantime for a glass of something local and you might find yourself rubbing elbows with notable Napa Valley oenophiles.

Once summoned from your barstool, step up to a red leather booth and sink into the warm ambience primed for hearty fare. The open kitchen aces menu staples such as artichoke dip; buttery skillet cornbread; and slabs of fall-off-the-bone pork ribs served with shoestring fries and slaw. Rutherford Grill mingles so well with wine country charm that its chain restaurant roots are all but forgotten.

Tra Vigne

Italian XX

C2

1050 Charter Oak Ave. (off Hwy. 29), St. Helena

Phone: 707-963-4444 Lunch & dinner daily
Web: www.travignerestaurant.com
Prices: **$$$**

It's impossible not to love Tra Vigne, the St. Helena retreat evocative of Tuscany with its rugged stone building and vineyard surrounds. On balmy nights, head to the garden patio where tables intertwine with olive trees and white lights twinkle overhead. Cooler weather? No matter. The spacious interior is just as cozy for enjoying rustic Italian fare as it makes its way from the exhibition kitchen.

Tra Vigne is best known for its dishes from the wood-burning oven in hearty portions that highlight seasonal ingredients, as in the cracker-crisp fig pizza topped with spicy arugula and Gorgonzola. The signature and über-creamy mozzarella *al minuto* deserves its buzzing popularity. After dinner, join the locals in savoring a cabernet at the bustling bar.

Solbar ✿

Californian XX

A1

755 Silverado Trail (at Rosedale Rd.), Calistoga

Phone: 707-226-0850 — Lunch & dinner daily
Web: www.solagecalistoga.com
Prices: $$$

Trinette Reed/Solage Calistoga

Envision this as your happy place: olive orchards and palm trees rustle in the breeze that sweeps over a swimming pool and gravel courts where weekenders try their hand at bocce. Water fountains trickle as fire pits blaze, and no one gives you a side-eye for sipping that Napa cabernet in the comfort of your terry cloth robe. Happiness is but a table away at Solbar, inside the Solage Calistoga resort.

With all the trappings of a refined wine country retreat, Solbar brings creature comforts to its outdoor spaces and fresh air into its lofty dining room where concrete floors, a flourishing fireplace, and sleek wood furnishings have a modish bucolic vibe. Groups gather in leather armchairs for innovative cocktails in the lounge, while wine lovers swirl at the bar. All this beauty is garnished with the hand of a talented young chef. Solbar's casually uniformed servers are ready to fill your table with fresh spa fare or heartier dishes, all served with Californian creativity.

Savor the likes of succulent Dungeness crab salad with Meyer lemon, fingerlings, and tarragon; seared Pacific halibut with sweet pea-ramp purée; or a Valrhona chocolate *marquis* with salted almond crème anglaise.

Terra ✿

C1 **Contemporary** XXX

1345 Railroad Ave. (bet. Adams St. & Hunt Ave.), St. Helena

Phone: 707-963-8931 Dinner Wed – Mon
Web: www.terrarestaurant.com
Prices: **$$$**

Hiro Sone

The mood is intimate and the lighting is dim ("watch your step!") at this historic stand-alone stone building in downtown St. Helena. Inside the dining room decked with beamed ceilings and stone walls, a flattering spotlight shines at the center of each high-backed banquette, as if to highlight the decades (or days) of romance that each couple seems to be celebrating. In other words, this is a great date place.

On the menu, Asian and Californian cuisines are combined seamlessly, with just a splash of Italian. Tasty starters like freshly diced tuna tartare with a tangle of *somen*, dark dashi, and a poached egg, become brilliant when finished with shimmering pearls of shad roe that lend a briny pop to each bite, and a tiny scoop of *yuzu-kosho* with its tangy and peppery zip. Entrées like creamy risotto with kuri squash and duck breast make way for wonderfully satisfying desserts that you won't want to split with your date. End with such treats as a flaky phyllo-topped pie, fragrant with cinnamon, tucked over warmly spiced caramelized apples and silky-sweet crème fraîche drizzled with honey.

Check out the new Bar Terra next door which serves lighter fare and doesn't require reservations.

Ubuntu ✿

A3 Vegetarian XX

1140 Main St. (bet. 1st & Pearl Sts.), Napa

Phone: 707-251-5656 Dinner nightly
Web: www.ubuntunapa.com
Prices: $$

Elijah Woolery

When this novel vegetarian restaurant slash yoga studio opened in the town of Napa in 2007, few might have guessed it would last; even fewer, perhaps, would have assumed it would reach cult culinary darlingdom. Named for a Zulu philosophy to do with community and generosity, it seems Ubuntu had its stars aligned from the start.

Those prone to judge a book by its cover will be surprised by Ubuntu's interior: What is masked by a small town storefront façade opens to a lofty contemporary space with no resemblance to more hippie vegetarian establishments. Rich multihued wood flooring and vibrant art provide a splashy contrast to the building's old stone walls, while candlelit bare tabletops and a long communal table keep Ubuntu down to earth. Earth, of course, is the basis of all food here, but rest assured the results are just a little nearer to heaven.

The open kitchen makes miracles of organic local produce: *burrata* cheese and sunchoke purée ooze out of fluffy buns garnished with *fuyu* persimmon and smoked green tomato; while sharp cheddar and goat's whey give life to creamy grits accompanied by fennel frond beignets. Pair with a biodynamic wine from the concise, well-curated list.

Wine Spectator Greystone

Californian

2555 Main St. (at Deer Park Rd.), St. Helena

Phone: 707-967-1010 Lunch & dinner daily
Web: www.ciachef.edu
Prices: **$$$**

Try to conjure the most idyllic wine country setting imaginable, but know your arrival at Greystone will exceed expectations. This historic hilltop château is surrounded by grapevines intertwining like lace through the grounds, as olive trees, rosemary, and lavender pave the way toward a sunny terrace with a trickling fountain.

Inside, the Wine Spectator dining room is massive, with stone walls rising to soaring ceilings and a fireplace in the cozy lounge. Since Greystone houses the Culinary Institute of America's California campus, the three exhibition kitchens provide a veritable dinner theater. On stage: seasonal Californian acts with Mediterranean flair, as in sweetbread vol-au-vent and crispy pork belly with perfectly seared day boat scallops.

Zuzu

Spanish

829 Main St. (bet. 2nd & 3rd Sts.), Napa

Phone: 707-224-8555 Lunch Mon – Fri
Web: www.zuzunapa.com Dinner nightly
Prices: **$$**

Faded tile floors, exposed wood beams, and a weathered tin ceiling salvaged from Mexico set an old-world stage for Spanish and Mediterranean tapas at Zuzu, a self-proclaimed celebration of food, wine, and art. Latin beats are a groovy backdrop for paintings and metalwork by area artisans, while more than 20 off-the-beaten-path wines are poured by the glass at the recycled pine bar.

Feast on crisp fried Manchego cheese with tangy *guajilo* salsa; tender Niman Ranch meatballs with tangy sweet wine and spicy piquillo pepper sauce; or *harissa*-spiked lamb burgers cooled with goat cheese *tzatziki*. Ceviche and paella specials change daily. With few late night spots in Napa, Zuzu is ideal for a bite before or after a Napa Valley Opera House performance.

Sonoma County

Often eclipsed as a wine region by neighboring Napa Valley, the county that borders Marin County claims 76 miles of Pacific coastline, as well as 250 wineries that take advantage of some of the best grape-growing conditions in California. Northern California's first premium winery, **Buena Vista**, was established just outside the town of Sonoma in 1857 by Agoston Haraszthy. Today thirteen distinct wine appellations (AVAs) have been assigned in Sonoma County, where vintners produce a dizzying array of wines in an area slightly larger than the

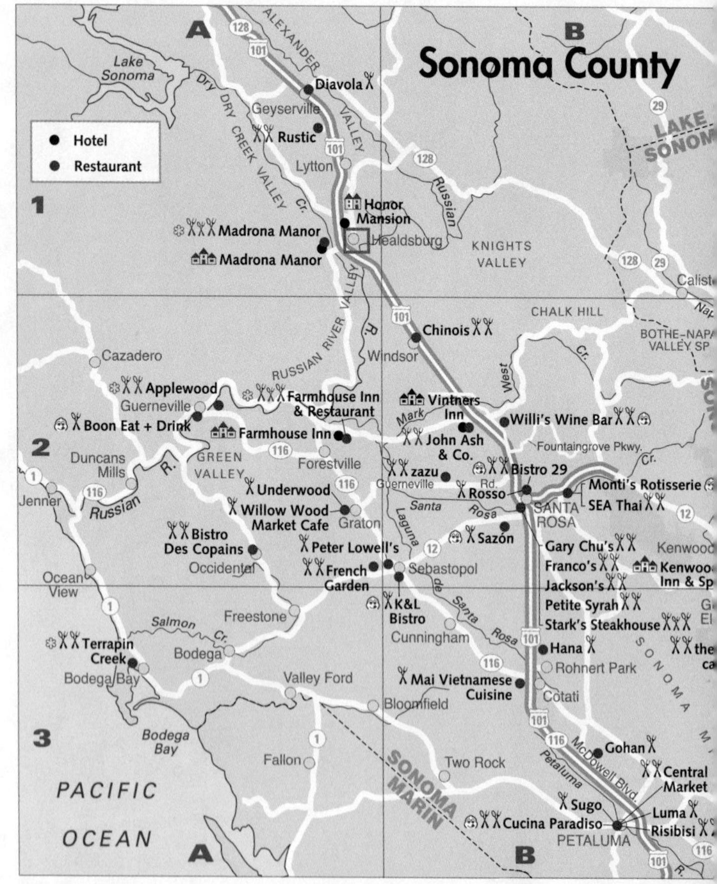

State of Rhode Island. Along Highway 12 heading north, byroads lead to out-of-the-way wineries, each of which puts its own unique stamp on the business of winemaking.

The Russian River Valley edges the river named for the early Russian trading outposts that were set up along the coast. This is one of the coolest growing regions in Sonoma, thanks to the river basin that offers a conduit for cool coastal air. Elegant pinot noir and chardonnay headline here, but syrah is quickly catching up.

At the upper end of the Russian River, the Dry Creek Valley yields excellent sauvignon blanc, chardonnay, and pinot noir. This region is also justly famous for its zinfandel, a grape that does especially well in the valley's rock-strewn soil. Winery visits in Dry Creek are a study in contrasts. Palatial modern wineries rise up along the same rural roads that have

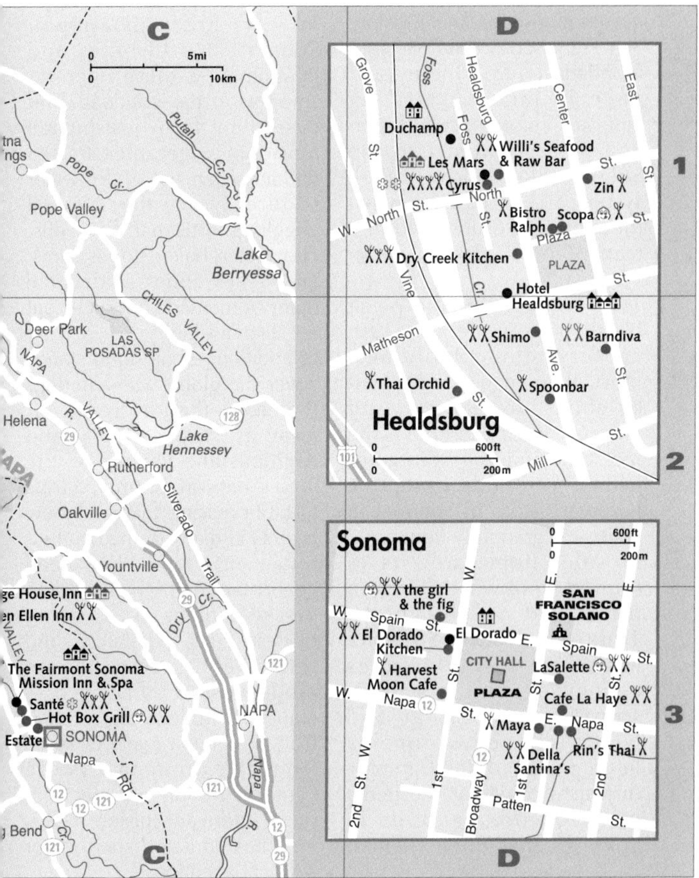

been home to independents for generations; and young grapevines trained into laser-straightened rows are broken up by the dark, gnarled fingers of old vines.

Sonoma County's inlandmost AVAs are Knights Valley and Alexander Valley. These two warm regions both highlight cabernet sauvignon. Nestled between the Mayacamas and Sonoma ranges, the 17-mile-long Sonoma Valley dominates the southern portion of the county. At its center is the town of Sonoma, site of California's northernmost and final mission: San Francisco Solano Mission, founded in 1823. The mission once included a thriving vineyard before secularization and incorporation into the Sonoma State Historic Park system 102 years ago, when the vines were uprooted and transplanted elsewhere in Sonoma.

The town's eight-acre plaza is still surrounded by 19th century adobe buildings, most of them now occupied by shops, restaurants, and inns. Of epicurean note is the fact that building contractor Chuck Williams bought a hardware store in Sonoma in 1956. He gradually converted its stock from hardware to French cookware, kitchen tools, and novelty foods. Today **Williams-Sonoma** has more than 200 stores nationwide, and is a must-stop for foodies far and wide. Just below Sonoma lies a portion of the Carneros district, named for the herds of sheep (*los carneros* in Spanish) that once roamed its hillsides. Carneros is best known for its cool-climate grapes, notably pinot noir and chardonnay.

Pastoral Pleasures

Throughout this bucolic county–called SoCo by savvy locals–vineyards rub shoulders with orchards and farms that take advantage of the area's fertile soil to produce everything from apples and olives, to artisan-crafted cheeses. Sustainable and organic are key words at local farmers' markets, which herald the spring (April or May) in Santa Rosa, Sebastopol, Sonoma, Healdsburg, and Petaluma. At these open-air smorgasbords, you can find everything from just-picked heirloom vegetables to sea urchins taken out of the water so recently that they are still wiggling. Artisanal olive oils, chocolates, baked goods, jams, and jellies count among the many homemade products that are also available.

In addition, ethnic food stands cover the globe with offerings that have their roots as far away as Mexico, India, and Afghanistan. Thanks to the area's natural bounty, farm-to-table cuisine takes on new heights in many of the county's restaurants. Some chefs need go no farther than their own on-site gardens for a variety of fresh fruits, vegetables, and herbs. With easy access to local products such as Dungeness crab from Bodega Bay, poultry from Petaluma, and cheeses from the Sonoma Cheese Factory, it's no wonder that the Californian cuisine in this area has attracted such major national attention.

Applewood 

Californian XX

A2

13555 Hwy. 116, Guerneville

Phone: 707-869-9093 Dinner Wed – Sun

Web: www.applewoodinn.com

Prices: $$$

Christine Gustafson, InnLight

Approaching Applewood, hear the birds chirping and woodpeckers pecking, see the hills rolling and redwoods shading—as if every rustling branch is working to conjure that idyllic wine country postcard. This destination is renowned as a serious spa and charming inn, as well as lovely getaway for Californian cuisine.

That surrounding splendor, visible through floor-to-ceiling windows in the serene and subtly elegant dining room, is exactly what drives this menu that showcases extraordinary, locally sourced ingredients. This is all at once clear when presented with starters like *burrata* from Petaluma. The brilliantly silky-sweet knobs sit atop creamy sorrel sauce strewn with raw green almonds, tiny flower petals, and teardrops of perfect olive oil, for a taste so transporting you may imagine yourself in Puglia. Yet other dishes, like roasted local rock cod with fiddlehead ferns, asparagus, Meyer lemon, and blood orange, have the distinct sensibilities of California's wine country.

Such a relaxed ambience could only be wrought by the hands of a very professional service team at the top of its game. For the full experience, plan ahead to spend the night at the inn or reserve a cottage.

Barndiva

Californian XX

231 Center St. (bet. Matheson & Mills Sts.), Healdsburg

Phone: 707-431-0100 Lunch & dinner Wed – Sun
Web: www.barndiva.com
Prices: $$

If wine country epitomizes fancy farming, then this barn is certainly fitting. Hip and hot, Barndiva (blocks from Healdsburg square) is exalted for its consummate cocktails, magnificent meals, and gorgeous gardens. Mod and charming, the décor is graced with mirrors, lofty ceilings, vivid artwork, and eclectic sculptures.

Just as delicious as the sun-drenched grounds is its dynamic menu. Strutting stuff from local purveyors and food artisans, dishes like asparagus tempura with tarragon aïoli and *fromage blanc* gnocchi sing the praises of the season. Starring Californian flavors are pastas with pristine condiments, and a red velvet cake whirled with creamy goodness. Nurse a local wine or classic cocktail on the thrilling terrace and realize nirvana!

Bistro Des Copains

A2

French XX

3782 Bohemian Hwy. (at Occidental Rd.), Occidental

Phone: 707-874-2436 Dinner nightly
Web: www.bistrodescopains.com
Prices: $$

If you've ever "occidentally" found a great restaurant, it was probably Bistro Des Copains buried in out-of-the-way Occidental. Don your vintage driving gloves and imagine yourself on the Côte d'Azur as you wind your way to this classically-chic bistro. Stunningly set on Bohemian Highway, this green cottage with white trim transports you to Provence via the Cali wine country with French fare like *bœuf en Daube à la Provencal* (braised short ribs with onions, olives, carrots); *lapin à la moutarde* (braised rabbit in mustard sauce with buttery noodles); and roasted chicken.

Reservations are wise, especially on Wednesdays when $1.50 oysters lure locals. The wine bar, warmed by a wood oven in the kitchen, is ideal for sipping on some Sonoma and French labels.

Bistro Ralph

Californian

109 Plaza St. (bet. Center St. & Healdsburg Ave.), Healdsburg

Phone: 707-433-1380 — Lunch daily
Web: www.bistroralph.com — Dinner Mon – Sat
Prices: $$

A pair of sidewalk tables marks the entrance to Chef/owner Ralph Tingle's eponymous bistro overlooking the boutiques of Healdsburg's central plaza. The whitewashed brick interior is studded with metal furnishings and a bar counter lends a view into the open kitchen, where each season's bounty inspires the concise menu.

Order a carefully selected local wine or martini from the respectable vodka and gin offerings, then sit back to enjoy a delightful, no fuss Cal-French meal. Lunch may bring a fully loaded Cobb salad or a tender chicken paillard with capers and shoestring fries. Ravenous appetites can opt for a juicy lamb burger or braised short rib ravioli with freshly grated horseradish. Finish with a cheese board or one of a few homemade sweets.

Bistro 29

French

620 Fifth St. (at Mendocino Ave.), Santa Rosa

Phone: 707-546-2929 — Dinner Tue – Sun
Web: www.bistro29.com
Prices: $$

Named for the county of Finistère in Northwest France, Bistro 29 is a Breton gem in Santa Rosa. Best known for reasonably priced buckwheat crêpes–think homemade sausage with cave-aged Gruyère and apples–the homey spot draws regulars for conversation and comforting Gallic fare. Dinner can bring more sophisticated choices, including pan-roasted duck with mascarpone faro and chanterelles.

The ambience is equally lovely and familiar. Bask in rays of sunshine beaming from the sky light upon interior brick walls and mustard yellow accents. White linen tablecloths and dark wood accents perfect the classic bistro look. After a Gallic meal, indulge your sweet craving with a delicate, buttery crêpe topped with wild huckleberries.

Boon Eat + Drink 

Californian

A2

16248 Main St. (bet. 4th & Mill Sts.), Guerneville

Phone: 707-869-0780 — Lunch Sat – Sun
Web: www.eatatboon.com — Dinner nightly
Prices: $$

The secret is already out. Boon Eat + Drink might be a bit off the beaten path (tucked in the picturesque town of Guerneville) but the seasonal Californian fare attracts foodies from miles around. The modest storefront features a covered patio for outdoor dining and a quaint interior where aluminum chairs and simple wood tables allow the local, sustainable fare to shine.

When in season, Boon's flash-fried Brussels sprouts, with olive oil and red chili flakes, may be the best you've ever had; you may say the same of the house-cured meat and melted provolone sandwich, or desserts like blueberry-thyme compote that lends an herbaceous edge to buttermilk panna cotta. At dinner, try a slow-braised Sonoma lamb shank with preserved lemon and minty pesto.

Cafe La Haye

Californian

D3

140 E. Napa St. (bet. 1st & 2nd Sts.), Sonoma

Phone: 707-935-5994 — Dinner Tue – Sat
Web: www.cafelahaye.com
Prices: $$

Cafe La Haye is the curious yet wonderful collision of a bespectacled former college music teacher with seasonal ingredients and a charming house off Sonoma's town square. A local favorite since 1996, the sunny yellow bi-level dining room with a revolving art collection is constantly packed: make reservations or hold out hope for a seat at the tiny zinc-topped counter.

The open kitchen provides an unobstructed view of the local produce that comprises the Californian cuisine. Expect such dishes as cold smoked salmon with creamy mascarpone on a crisp potato *galette*; Wolfe Ranch quail with artichoke purée, mushroom quinoa, and balsamic jus; and yuzu citrus cheesecake with lemon curd and blackberry-zinfandel sauce. Be sure to ask about the daily risotto.

Central Market

Mediterranean XX

42 Petaluma Blvd. N. (at Western Ave.), Petaluma

Phone: 707-778-9900 Dinner nightly
Web: www.centralmarketpetaluma.com
Prices: **$$**

The lofty 1920s Maclay Building may seem an unlikely spot for an intimate Mediterranean eatery, yet Central Market feels as welcoming as a private invitation to Chef/owner Tony Najiola's own home. Perhaps this is due to his convivial presence around the house.

Foodies take a front-row seat at the zinc counter for the performance in the open kitchen, where the specialty is Slow Food with flourishes from Italy and France. The menu shows passion, as if dishes are made with the hands of an artist. Take time to peruse the offerings over an aperitif and Castelvetrano olives. Then, sample house-made sausages like New Orleans–style seafood boudin; ground lamb cabbage rolls flavored with cumin and coriander; and spicy chorizo that gives zing to stuffed quail.

Chinois

Asian XX

186 Windsor River Rd. (at Bell Rd.), Windsor

Phone: 707-838-4667 Lunch & dinner Mon – Sat
Web: N/A
Prices: **$$**

Chinois' owners have cornered the market on Asian cuisine in this neck of the woods (they also own Ume Japanese Bistro down the road), but in this case, monopolies aren't a bad thing. A delightful gem, delivering fresh flavors that are a welcome change from the sticky sweet sauces of other Asian spots, Chinois is Asian fusion without the confusion.

A little bit of this, a little bit of that, the menu proudly highlights curries from Thailand, dim sum from China, and noodle dishes from all over. It may seem like a tall order to blend so many different styles, but the kitchen executes this task flawlessly. Thanks to its wine country location, the Asian haven touts a respectable list of wines to accompany the beer selections.

Cucina Paradiso

Italian XX

B3

114 Petaluma Blvd. N. (bet. Washington St. & Western Ave.), Petaluma

Phone: 707-782-1130 Lunch & dinner Mon – Sat
Web: www.cucinaparadisopetaluma.com
Prices: ⊜

Nestled in downtown Petaluma, Cucina Paradiso kills with kindness. Chef/owner Dennis Hernandez and his wife, Malena, run their homey mainstay with a strong sense of family: the staff is a tight-knit group, regulars are greeted with kisses and hugs, while the rest of us are simply friends they haven't met yet.

Once a well-kept secret, Cucina Paradiso is flourishing in this spacious dining room bathed in sunny yellow with Gerber daisies smiling from each table, all a far cry from its strip mall origins. The menu of homemade specialties is informed by the chef's Italian training, so as arias fill the air, find harmony in such dishes as rigatoni with spicy pork, red peppers, and creamy tomato sauce; or pillowy Gorgonzola gnocchi with chopped walnuts.

Della Santina's

Italian XX

D3

133 E. Napa St. (bet. 1st & 2nd Sts.), Sonoma

Phone: 707-935-0576 Lunch & dinner daily
Web: www.dellasantinas.com
Prices: **$$**

Benvenuto to Della Santina's, the homespun *ristorante* where family portraits and framed lace napkins adorn the interior walls and a fountain on the trellised brick patio reinforces the rustic Tuscan appeal. Alfresco diners will feel especially comfortable here: the enclosed terrace is heated, spacious, and lovely year-round.

The dining room is a touch more cramped and service, though well-meaning, is somewhat unrefined. Still, Della Santina's can credit over 20 years in Sonoma to its genuine hospitality and solid Northern Italian cuisine. Imagine such treats as lasagna Bolognese; cannelloni Florentine stuffed with grilled chicken and veal, then drizzled with béchamel; spit-roasted meats including duck and rabbit; and daily veal and gnocchi specials.

Cyrus ✿✿

D1

29 North St. (bet. Foss St. & Healdsburg Ave.), Healdsburg

Phone: 707-433-3311 — Lunch Sat
Web: www.cyrusrestaurant.com — Dinner nightly
Prices: $$$$

Andy Katz

It has been said that the gift of great service is anticipation. Perhaps everyone is too distracted by the passing caviar and champagne cart or perusing the five- and eight-course tasting menus, but somehow a crumb never seems to land on the linen tablecloths and little canapés are introduced to the table as if to demonstrate the range of culinary pleasures. And just as magically, empty plates disappear and every diner is leaning a bit farther forward in greater anticipation of the superlative meal to come.

In the kitchen, Chef Douglas Keane shines brightly as he blends Asian influences into his refined menu. Starters such as creamy mussel soup with a fine brunoise of fennel and peppers, aromatic with saffron, lemongrass, and coconut milk, may lead to foie gras torchon with a delicate veneer of pomegranate glass and a warm buttermilk biscuit. Expect tropically inspired fish courses and meats that refuse to be boring. Treat yourself to the well-designed and sophisticated wine pairings.

From its location in the heart of Healdsburg, Cyrus soars high with cloistered ceilings and curving booths, yet remains soft and comfortable with lantern lights and natural landscapes.

Diavola

Pizza

21021 Geyserville Ave. (at Hwy. 128), Geyserville

Phone: 707-814-0111 — Lunch & dinner daily
Web: www.diavolapizzeria.com
Prices: $$

Diavola will forever remain the darling of Geyserville as it there are few serious culinary contenders in the area. At mealtime, cars jam the spaces on the tiny main drag as their occupants anticipate the rustic fare hand-crafted by Chef Dino Bugica.

Artisanal cured meats, sausages, and wood-fired pizzas are the heart of the cuisine here. Bugica has a passion for all things porcine, which figure prominently on the menu—be it in the daily selection of salami; pizza Sonja with prosciutto, mascarpone, and arugula; or roasted asparagus salad tossed with pancetta and truffled pecorino.

A former brothel, the narrow dining space touts its genuine feeling of history with original wood floors, pressed-tin ceilings, exposed brick, and simply dressed tables.

Dry Creek Kitchen

Californian

D1

317 Healdsburg Ave. (bet. Matheson & Plaza Sts.), Healdsburg

Phone: 707-431-0330 — Lunch Fri – Sun
Web: www.charliepalmer.com — Dinner nightly
Prices: $$$

Just look for the lime green façade on Healdsburg's main square and you will have arrived at Dry Creek Kitchen, an airy space where vaulted ceilings hum with the melody of piano and cello. Seafoam walls and a spacious bar and patio supply an aura of relaxation.

A touch stiff, the informed waitstaff can also warm you with the intricacies of new American cuisine. While highlights abound throughout the menu, Charlie Palmer's rotating roster may lend to some inconsistencies. No detail is overlooked in delicacies like sweetbread and confit chicken agnolotti. Flaky halibut poached in olive oil is a dream, and the chocolate-peanut butter *marquis* is layered with flavor and sin.

Naturally, the winning wine selection hails from surrounding Sonoma.

El Dorado Kitchen

Californian

405 1st St. W. (at Spain St.), Sonoma

Phone: 707-996-3030 Lunch & dinner daily
Web: www.eldoradosonoma.com
Prices: $$

A stone's throw from the grassy Sonoma town square, this casual kitchen sates the bellies of guests at the El Dorado Hotel. The chic interior is a rustic reflection of the neighborhood: long hanging lamps bathe a communal table fashioned from a single plank of wood salvaged from a bridge in Vermont; while whitewashed walls and sage green accents give zest to dark rattan furnishings.

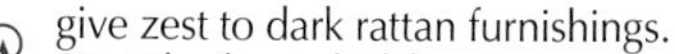

Sit at the far end of the room to view a brigade of chefs in the open kitchen, which turns out such Californian preparations as crispy sweetbreads with green tomato, bacon, and mâche; New York steak with blue cheese–laced potato *dauphinoise*; and apricot tart for dessert. Wednesdays bring half-price wines, while the stone courtyard is prime for a creative Sunday brunch.

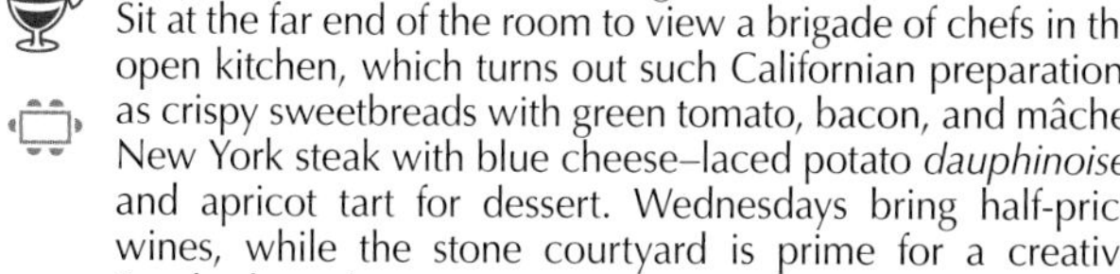

Estate

Italian

400 W. Spain St. (at 4th St.), Sonoma

Phone: 707-933-3663 Lunch Sun
Web: www.estate-sonoma.com Dinner nightly
Prices: $$

With sweeping grounds, gardens, and sumptuous interiors warmed by the hearth, this historic home is worthy of its stately name, minus any doilies or dust. The owners, also of the girl & the fig, infused a touch of avant-garde into a regal space that juxtaposes Victorian architecture with paintings evocative of Italian cinema. The cozy bar is perfect for a pre-dinner Bellini, while the dining room is an opulent setting for Southern Italian fare. Outdoor dining is a must on temperate nights.

Artisanal *salumi* is a wonderful prelude to the likes of lamb meatballs in San Marzano tomato sauce or the decadent *zeppole*, sugar-dusted donut holes with homemade chocolate-hazelnut butter. Groups can go with the *cena di famiglia*, a five-course menu for $26 a head.

Farmhouse Inn & Restaurant 

Californian

7871 River Rd. (at Wohler Rd.), Forestville

Phone: 707-887-3300 Dinner Thu – Mon
Web: www.farmhouseinn.com
Prices: $$$

Tai Power Seeff

As the beautiful Russian River Valley winds its way through vineyards and pine forests, a sense of calm rusticity pervades, making this a very fine setting for the simply named Farmhouse Inn. Inside the turn-of-the-century converted home, find a large fireplace and bucolic murals warming the country-chic room, while a second dining area boasts views of verdant gardens. The Inn's guests and local couples bring a twinkle of romance to the elegant surrounds.

Despite how at ease everyone may feel, the skilled chef brings precision, focus, and attention to detail to each consistently delicious dish. The Californian menu uses local ingredients to meld classic French technique with Mediterranean flair, resulting in the likes of tender ravioli stuffed with a woodsy filling of ricotta cheese and chanterelles in a buttery mushroom ragout, topped with decadent Parmesan foam. Heartier entrées may include a bone-in pork shank, slowly braised and caramelized, alongside mashed potatoes strewn with arugula and chopped green olives.

The three- and four-course fixed menus culminate in thoroughly enjoyable desserts like a pineapple financier with coconut sorbet or the innovative opera cake nouveau.

Franco's

Italian XX

505 Mendocino Ave. (at 7th St.), Santa Rosa

Phone: 707-523-4800 Lunch & dinner daily
Web: www.francosristorante.com
Prices: $$

The flora-lined front patio with its trickling fountain and umbrellas is tough to pass up on a sunny Sonoma day but, for those who skip this inviting garden of Eden, there is still much to be discovered inside. Run by Chef/owner Franco Fabiani, Franco's is a sprawling space that conjures Tuscany, with terra-cotta tiles, glowing fireplaces, timber beams, and rustic frescoes.

Wine is also a way of life here, paired perfectly with creamy Gorgonzola-stuffed fried olives or bubbly lasagna Bolognese. With $10 wood-fired pizzas named for Fabiani's family, Franco's is a kid-friendly eatery that won't break the bank. Elisabetta's pie is topped with mushrooms and garlic, while the namesake Fabiani is heavy with bell pepper and *prosciutto di Parma*.

French Garden

French 

8050 Bodega Ave. (at Pleasant Hill Rd.), Sebastopol

Phone: 707-824-2030 Lunch & dinner Wed – Sun
Web: www.frenchgardenrestaurant.com
Prices: $$

At French Garden, the cuisine blows an air kiss to the classic Gallic bistro, but this actual garden is grounded in California. The Sebastopol favorite sources its leeks, cilantro, and piquillo peppers–to be sautéed with Manila clams for dinner–from its own bio-intensive farm. There you'll also find seasonal ingredients for such expertly adapted plates as traditional frisée salad, with bacon and a poached egg, and fluffy mushroom quiche.

As you would expect, French Garden boasts a pleasing terrace; on cooler nights, find a seat in the airy dining room or near the hearth in the lounge. Desserts are excellent here so don't miss out. With pistachio pastry crust, cranberry coulis, and toasted merinque, the lemon tart may be the most refined you've ever had.

Gary Chu's

Chinese XX

B2

611 5th St. (at Riley St.), Santa Rosa

Phone: 707-526-5840 Lunch & dinner Tue – Sun
Web: www.garychus.com
Prices: ©©

Craving a savory plate of sautéed champagne scallops or bowl of steaming crab and corn soup? You aren't the only one: locals flock to this popular Chinese haunt where the well-priced, creative menu draws everyone in droves. Dark floral banquettes line the apricot walls in this modest space, and a smaller tented area near the entry–intended for larger groups–faces a pristine aquarium of tropical fish.

Start with tasty Sichuan wontons, stuffed with tender ground pork and served with the house secret sauce. For a quick fix at midday, swing by for one of the executive lunch specials, most of which are less than ten bucks and include an entrée, soup, and salad. Sweeten any meal with crispy tempura banana served with caramel sauce and vanilla ice cream.

Glen Ellen Inn

Californian XX

C3

13670 Arnold Dr. (at Warm Springs Rd.), Glen Ellen

Phone: 707-996-6409 Lunch Thu – Tue
Web: www.glenelleninn.com Dinner nightly
Prices: $$

Clandestine lovers would be wise to hide away at the Glen Ellen Inn, a martini bar and grill in the heavily wooded hamlet of Glen Ellen. On a warm afternoon, the patio is ideal for cocktails and oysters, while a fireplace on the porch is snuggle friendly in winter. "Secret" cottages are available for an overnight rendezvous.

Dressed in jewel tones and heavy textiles, the dining room reflects its romantic, rural surroundings. Oddly highfalutin presentation dates the Californian fare, but dishes are pleasant enough. By day, savor a halibut fillet with black bean and corn salsa. At dinner, sink into a panko-crusted Sonoma duck breast with foie gras and cherry Port sauce. If martinis are a touch too 007 for your taste, choose from more than 500 local wines.

Gohan

Japanese 

1367 N. McDowell Blvd. (at Redwood Way), Petaluma

Phone: 707-789-9296 — Lunch Mon – Fri
Web: www.gohanrestaurant.com — Dinner nightly
Prices: $$

Sushi may be an unexpected choice of fuel while shopping at Pier 1 or Michael's, but Gohan is the pride and joy of its strip-mall surrounds at Petaluma's Redwood Gateway Shopping Center. With linen-topped tables, high ceilings, and an LCD fire in the high-tech hearth, this is an undeniably cool spot for lunch.

Serving classics like ribeye teriyaki and fresh hamachi sashimi, Gohan's menu has something for everyone. Fans of creative maki, though, have truly come to the right place. For a view of Chef Takeshige Yahiro in action, slip up to the sushi counter and watch as your fish is neatly sliced and expertly displayed. Don't miss the Cisco roll, stuffed with shrimp, avocado, and green bean tempura topped with crab salad and spicy orange *tobiko*.

Hana

101 Golf Course Dr. (at Roberts Lake Rd.), Rohnert Park

Phone: 707-586-0270 — Lunch Mon – Sat
Web: www.hanajapanese.com — Dinner nightly
Prices: $$

Chef Kenichi Tominaga may have been working in restaurants for decades now, but Hana–in the oddball locale of Double Tree Plaza–has been his favorite child for over 15 years. The chef's heart inspires the experience, where friendly and knowledgeable sushi chefs behind the counter are happy to chat about the food. Feel free to be inquisitive, though the thorough response may evolve into a fish biology lesson.

Imported daily from Tokyo's Tsukiji fish market, seafood here may be simply prepared in fresh nigiri and creative maki, or may arrive in more adventurous forms for those wise enough to indulge in the chef's exquisite omakase. An extensive sake list plus donburi rice bowls and steaming noodles round out the offerings.

Harvest Moon Cafe

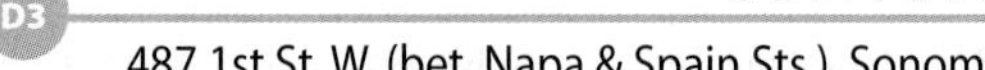

D3 Californian

487 1st St. W. (bet. Napa & Spain Sts.), Sonoma

Phone: 707-933-8160 Lunch Sun
Web: www.harvestmooncafesonoma.com Dinner Wed – Mon
Prices: $$

Harvest Moon is the culinary child of a husband-wife team with true foodie pedigree: Nick and Jen Demarest, the chef and pastry chef respectively, hail from Chez Panisse and La Toque. As expected, the Californian cuisine exhibits a love of local, seasonal produce with just a kiss from the Mediterranean. Begin with Gruyère bruschetta with pork ragù and a fresh fried egg; finish with a bubbly apple-cherry cobbler and tart buttermilk ice cream.

The interior, while relaxed, is narrow despite the large open kitchen. Instead of settling in the dining room, mosey out back where olive, rosemary, and lavender branches festoon a spacious garden patio. Red metal tables provide a charming spot for casual meals; weather permitting, Wednesday is movie night.

Hot Box Grill

C3 American

18350 Hwy. 12 (bet. Calle Del Monte & Hawthorne Ave.), Sonoma

Phone: 707-939-8383 Lunch Thu – Sun
Web: www.hotboxgrill.com Dinner Tue – Sun
Prices: $$

Hot Box Grille is Sonoma's definition of down-home family dining. Chef/owner Norm Owens (formerly of Cafe La Haye) can be spotted daily in the kitchen working side-by-side with his sous chef brother. Owens' wife, meanwhile, holds down the front of the house and his sister-in-law is credited with creating the linoleum prints around the room.

Flower boxes line the front windows with views to the open kitchen, and the back wall doubles as a blackboard boasting the day's dressed-up comfort food specials. Each dish makes the most of local ingredients—think plump duck confit ravioli in spiced broth, or succulent fried Cornish game hen with shells and cheese. With sweet bites like the deliciously campy Valhrona S'mores tart, dessert should be mandatory.

Jackson's

Pizza XX

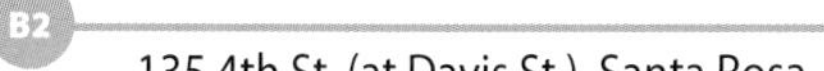

B2

135 4th St. (at Davis St.), Santa Rosa

Phone: 707-545-6900 Lunch & dinner daily
Web: www.jacksonsbarandoven.com
Prices: $$

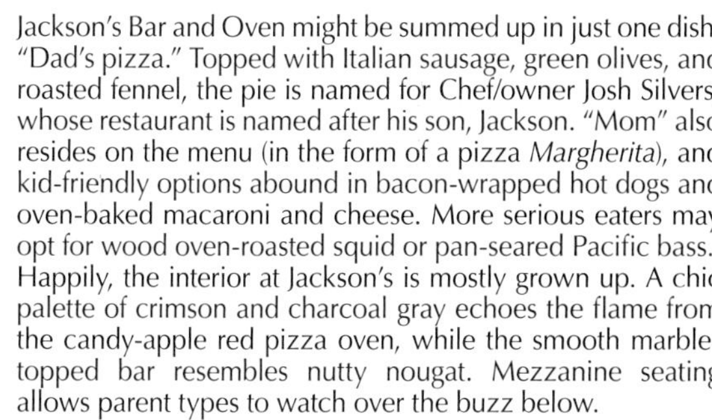

Jackson's Bar and Oven might be summed up in just one dish: "Dad's pizza." Topped with Italian sausage, green olives, and roasted fennel, the pie is named for Chef/owner Josh Silvers, whose restaurant is named after his son, Jackson. "Mom" also resides on the menu (in the form of a pizza *Margherita*), and kid-friendly options abound in bacon-wrapped hot dogs and oven-baked macaroni and cheese. More serious eaters may opt for wood oven-roasted squid or pan-seared Pacific bass. Happily, the interior at Jackson's is mostly grown up. A chic palette of crimson and charcoal gray echoes the flame from the candy-apple red pizza oven, while the smooth marble-topped bar resembles nutty nougat. Mezzanine seating allows parent types to watch over the buzz below.

John Ash & Co.

Californian XX

B2

4330 Barnes Rd. (off River Rd.), Santa Rosa

Phone: 707-527-7687 Dinner nightly
Web: www.vintnersinn.com
Prices: $$$

A trip to John Ash & Co. is the culinary equivalent of getting a massage. Set at the Vintner's Inn in Santa Rosa, the restaurant is surrounded by more than 90 acres of soothing vineyards and gardens and, miraculously, plentiful parking. A sun-soaked patio overlooks the terrain, but the romantic interior is equally plush with a toasty fireplace and terra-cotta hues. White linens set the stage for organic Californian meals with a slight German inflection. Accompaniments of sauerkraut, cabbage, and spätzle hint at the chef's heritage, but the cuisine is generally worldly. A tasting menu might include salmon and cream cheese canapés with dill and briny capers; Canadian lobster tail with celery root purée; and a moist, herbaceous rack of lamb.

K & L Bistro

Californian

B2

119 S. Main St. (bet. Burnett St. and Hwy. 12), Sebastopol

Phone: 707-823-6614 Lunch & dinner Mon – Sat
Web: www.klbistro.com
Prices: $$

Husband-wife duo Karen and Lucas Martin steer the stoves at K & L, a quintessential bistro that takes great pride in its craft. The intimate neighborhood gem typically bursts with Sebastopol locals rubbing elbows at close-knit tables topped with butcher paper. Exposed brick walls and dark wood accents lend a homey polish, while the granite bar is a terrific spot to sit and swirl.

Rusticity reigns in the semi-open kitchen where a crackling mesquite grill turns out French bistro classics and Californian fare. Traditionalists might begin with warm duck confit, while others may prefer grilled Monterey Bay sardines or crispy pork belly with watermelon. A thick-cut pork Porterhouse, simply seasoned with salt and pepper, is a juicy cap to a chilly night.

LaSalette

Portuguese

D3

452-H 1st St. E. (bet. Napa & Spain Sts.), Sonoma

Phone: 707-938-1927 Lunch & dinner daily
Web: www.lasalette-restaurant.com
Prices: $$

LaSalette is a passage to Portugal just off Sonoma's town square. While wooden Port wine crates and pumpkin-hued walls may aim to transport, you'll feel right at home thanks to Chef/owner Manuel Azevedo and his wife, Kimberly, who bring the flavors of his native Azores Islands to wine country. Peek into the open kitchen where a wood-burning oven roasts a variety of small plates for sharing. Try the oven-seared scallops coated with crisp *chouriço* sausage and saffron-rich *molho cru*; pork tenderloin stuffed with olives, almonds and figs; and *cataplana de marisco*, a copper bowl brimming with seafood stew. Named for the chef's mother, LaSalette serves rolls like mom used to make, oven-fresh and kissed by nutmeg and cumin. Dessert is also a must.

Luma

500 First St. (at G St.), Petaluma

Phone: 707-658-1940 Lunch Mon – Fri
Web: www.lumapetaluma.com Dinner Mon – Sat
Prices: $$

The milk chocolate and caramel color palette isn't the only thing sweet about Luma, a Californian eatery that offers after-school specials and crayons for the kiddos on the industrial side of Petaluma. But Luma is also parent-approved with a small wine counter, sunny plant-lined patio, and plenty of savory fare to snack on before the key lime pie arrives.

Pizzas and pears hold court on a menu featuring the Pear & Blue, a thin-crust pie topped with the obvious. Other delights include wood oven-baked pears stuffed with blue cheese, walnuts, and cherries; and a Brie and blue *fonduta* with honey-pear syrup. Dinner may bring ancho-seared skirt steak over cannellini beans and *chimichurri*, or a roasted half-chicken served with mushroom bread pudding.

Mai Vietnamese Cuisine

8492 Gravenstein Hwy. (bet. Cotati Ave. & Hwy. 101), Cotati

Phone: 707-665-9628 Lunch & dinner Tue – Sun
Web: www.maivietnamesecuisine.com
Prices:

The cheery yellow walls, the delightful servers, the abundance of hospitality—this lovely Cotati spot is practically a mood enhancer. Tucked into the corner of a small shopping plaza next to Highway 101, the place is packed with loyal regulars craving fresh, tasty Vietnamese classics.

Dishes like lemongrass chicken and scallop curry share the menu with vermicelli and rice plates, as well as a list of refreshing Vietnamese shakes, including mango and Durian (if you dare). *Pho* lovers can choose from several types, like *pho tai* with thinly sliced steak, vermicelli noodles, white onions, scallions, and cilantro swimming in a ginger-clove broth. Or go with a hearty barbecue plate of prawns, smoky-glazed pork, and egg roll served over rice noodles.

Madrona Manor ✿

Contemporary 

1001 Westside Rd. (at West Dry Creek Rd.), Healdsburg

Phone: 707-433-4231 Dinner Wed – Sun
Web: www.madronamanor.com
Prices: $$$

Madrona Manor

It is a lofty statement to call a place a manor—one imagines an opulent, old-fashioned estate where elegant ladies and gents sip sherry on a wraparound porch or play cards by a hearth in the parlor. Well, such a scene is easily envisioned at Madrona Manor, a majestic Victorian in Healdsburg.

Dating to the 1880s, the historic manse is surrounded by manicured grounds and vegetable gardens that provide a portion of the kitchen's produce. Inside, pastel walls rise to white crown moldings; dark wood antique furnishings are cushioned in floral prints; and tables are set with white linens, vintage silver, and Limoges china. Wicker lawn chairs and potted plants on the patio make for cozy alfresco dining.

Devotees, staff, and chef alike seem to share a reverence for this dignified grand dame: all are polished, sophisticated, and dressed to kill. Romantic and celebratory couples dine on contemporary Californian recipes that may unveil lobster with celery root purée and white chocolate sauce; a tasting of foie gras with watercress and brioche; and grilled lamb loin with sautéed mushrooms, parsley root, and Meyer lemon gelée. Pair with rare and exceptional vintages chosen by the sommelier.

Maya

Mexican 

101 E. Napa St. (at 1st St.), Sonoma

Phone: 707-935-3500 Lunch & dinner daily
Web: www.mayarestaurant.com
Prices: $$

A "temple of tequila" may be an unexpected find at the corner of historic Sonoma Plaza, but that doesn't make it any less intoxicating: the restaurant's central bar, designed to evoke a Mayan ruin, is stocked with the blue agave spirit and topped with the Mesoamerican statue, Chac-Mool. Colorful paintings, stone walls, and swaying hammocks further invoke the vibrant Mexican culture and conjure a festive mood.

Maya infuses the Californian seasonal ethos with culinary influence found south of the border. Dishes might include prawns wrapped in cilantro enchiladas and topped with tarragon cream; pan-seared snapper Veracruz; or a textbook-creamy flan refreshed with berries. All pairs well with a boozy margarita perked up with spicy, toasted pumpkin seeds.

Monti's Rotisserie

American 

714 Village Court (bet. Farmer's Ln. & Hardmand Dr.), Santa Rosa

Phone: 707-568-4404 Lunch & dinner daily
Web: www.starkrestaurants.com
Prices: $$

Wrought-iron accessories, colorful antique doors, and a quirky collection of decorative roosters give Monti's Rotisserie an unusual Mediterranean-cum-Southwest vibe where spit-roasted meats are the common denominator. Since opening in 2004, Monti's long wooden bar has beckoned shoppers to Santa Rosa's Montgomery Village for snacks such as house-made charcuterie, Tunisian Dungeness crab "briks," and to-die-for homemade fries.

Of course, it's the smoky meats turned over smoldering coals that give the place its name. On Wednesdays, belly up for a spit-roasted leg of lamb; and Fridays bring the roast rack of natural-fed veal. On pretty days, take your protein on the trellised patio. Don't miss out on Monti's sister restaurants, including Willi's Wine Bar.

Peter Lowell's

Italian

B2

7385 Healdsburg Ave. (at Florence Ave.), Sebastopol

Phone: 707-829-1077 Lunch & dinner daily
Web: www.peterlowells.com
Prices: $$

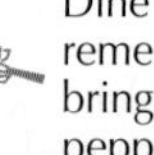

One might call this Sebastopol eatery a "sleeper": once just a little known spot to lunch, Peter Lowell's is enjoying a renaissance thanks to a new chef who is championing the local, sustainable ethos and taking it to new heights with seasonal Cal-Italian cuisine made from organic ingredients sourced in Sonoma County.

Dine inside or out and be patient with the service—remember, good things come to those who wait. Meals might bring a bowl of beans and greens tossed in olive oil, salt, and pepper; cracker-thin pizza topped with squash blossoms and Calabrian chilies; and veal with saffron risotto. To-go orders are popular among busy families, while hardcore locavores line up for weekly Zero Kilometro dinners that celebrate the bounty of Sebastopol.

Petite Syrah

Californian

B2

205 5th St. (at Davis St.), Santa Rosa

Phone: 707-568-4002 Lunch & dinner daily
Web: www.syrahbistro.com
Prices: $$

The Santa Rosa restaurant formerly known as Syrah may have gone petite in name but it hasn't downsized in charm. Petite Syrah is still the same cheery, yellow-painted little haunt Sonoma regulars have come to love, with a flood of natural light filling the vaulted dining room; and a quaint indoor patio that serves Californian fare made with local, seasonal ingredients.

The recently renovated eatery turns out such wine country favorites as roasted beets served with mâche and creamy horseradish panna cotta; olive oil-poached white sea bass crusted with basil breadcrumbs; and local foie gras with pink peppercorns and rhubarb. For dessert, get an *affogato* jolt from fennel-vanilla ice cream spiked with espresso and served with dried cherry-studded biscotti.

Rin's Thai

Thai

139 E. Napa St. (bet. 1st & 2nd Sts.), Sonoma

Phone: 707-938-1462 — Lunch & dinner Tue – Sun
Web: www.rinsthai.com
Prices: 

Set in a charming Victorian cottage that resembles a bed & breakfast, Rin's Thai demonstrates that perfect marriage between Thailand's vivid flavors and its warm hospitality. The inside is clean and open with cheerful yellow walls, soaring ceilings dotted with fans, and the near absence of kitsch. Make yourself at home and wait to be dazzled by their authentic cuisine.

The food and flavors have that lucid Californian sensibility evident in delicacies such as *nuer prig king*, where fresh vegetables and thinly sliced beef tenderloin combine in a pungent garlic-chili sauce. Simple prawns become glorious when bundled whole in egg roll wrappers and lightly fried; while classics like pad Thai and chicken satay are sure to satisfy the less adventurous.

Risibisi

Italian

154 Petaluma Blvd. N. (bet. Washington St. & Western Ave.), Petaluma

Phone: 707-766-7600 — Lunch Mon – Sat
Web: www.risibisirestaurant.com — Dinner nightly
Prices: $$

Named for a favorite risotto in the region of Friuli-Venezia Giulia, Petaluma's Risibisi is a true taste of the Italian city of Trieste. Owner Marco Palmieri hails from the Adriatic seaport and mingles a Californian sensibility with the traditional cuisine of his youth. This Sonoma County charmer also embraces whimsy, with heavy ropes and brightly hued chairs suspended from the ceiling and art works adorning exposed brick walls.

The kitchen makes magic of such familiar fare as *fritto misto*, which here is delicate in texture, bite, and flavor; or spaghetti carbonara bountiful with pancetta and Parmesan. Even that old dessert standby, tiramisu, is more lovingly articulated with the distinct flavors of coffee, liqueur, and fluffy mascarpone cream.

Rosso

Pizza

53 Montgomery Dr. (at 3rd St.), Santa Rosa

Phone: 707-544-3221 Lunch & dinner daily
Web: www.pizzeriarosso.com
Prices: $$

For those who think that vino and *futbol* (read: soccer) don't pair well together, think again. At Rosso, Italian wines live in utter harmony with the flat screen TV. And while the sports channel may feel appropriate to the Creekside Center strip mall locale, the crisp pizza *Napoletana* is a divine departure abroad.

Owner John Franchetti did time at St. Helena's Tra Vigne before opening this pizzeria. Here, amidst an urbane vibe, you'll find crisp salads with smoked chicken and walnuts and, the highlight, chewy 12-inch pies with fresh ingredients that pay homage to the Slow Food Movement. Take a walk on the wild side and order the "goomba" pizza topped with spaghetti, meatballs, and saffron tomato sauce; or stay closer to home with a white pizza *funghi*.

Rustic

300 Via Archimedes (off Independence Ln.), Geyserville

Phone: 707-857-1485 Lunch & dinner daily
Web: www.franciscoppolawinery.com
Prices: $$

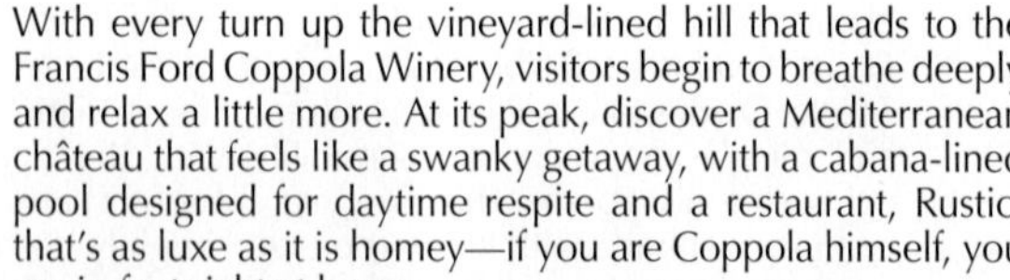

With every turn up the vineyard-lined hill that leads to the Francis Ford Coppola Winery, visitors begin to breathe deeply and relax a little more. At its peak, discover a Mediterranean château that feels like a swanky getaway, with a cabana-lined pool designed for daytime respite and a restaurant, Rustic, that's as luxe as it is homey—if you are Coppola himself, you are in fact right at home.

Themed around "Francis' Favorites," Rustic is a hodgepodge of wine ephemera, movie memorabilia, and foods from the director's past. From the *parilla* (an Argentine grill), look for sweet-and-savory ribs inspired by a Polynesian restaurant from the filmmaker's college days; as well as Mrs. Scorsese's lemon chicken with organic herbs and chocolate mousse "al Francis."

Santé ✿

Californian XXX

C3

100 Boyes Blvd. (at Hwy. 12), Sonoma

Phone: 707-939-2415 Dinner nightly
Web: www.fairmont.com/sonoma
Prices: $$$

Fairmont Sonoma Mission Inn & Spa

Amid the plush grounds of the pink stucco Fairmont Sonoma Mission Inn and Spa, find Santé. A trickling fountain and fire pit lend romance from the outside, while the interior's pale yellow walls, rattan furnishings, French doors, and sisal carpeting reflect elegant comfort through a Mediterranean aesthetic. The menu follows suit in highlighting that same region's fare with distinctly Californian sensibilities.

Each dish here is refined and focused on presenting a high level of sophistication, as haute techniques meet high-end ingredients. Descriptions may seem wordy but are exacting in their ability to convey the many harmonious components of each plate. This is clear in starters such as velvety quail breast, cooked sous-vide and seared, on dollops of onion *soubise* "risotto" with mounds of wilted nettles and green garlic purée, alongside a confit leg of quail coated in herbed breadcrumbs; or entrées like crisp-skinned *bronzini* with marble potatoes, tender rings of calamari, diced chorizo, and a thick, briny Niçoise olive reduction.

The dessert soufflé can be a last-minute decision, in case you decide against (or in addition to) selections from the very enticing cheese cart.

Sazón

Peruvian

B2

1129 Sebastopol Rd. (bet. McMinn & Burbank Aves.), Santa Rosa

Phone: 707-523-4346 Lunch & dinner Tue – Sun
Web: www.sazonsr.com
Prices:

Take a chance on Santa Rosa's divey-looking Sazón, and the only broken heart will be the Peruvian *anticucho de corazon*, or traditional skewered beef heart from the busy open kitchen. It may be a tiny spot in an awkward locale, but know that all this leaves little room for disappointment. Elbow up to the high granite counter or slip into a small corner table; an outdoor counter is open to those in need of fresh air.

On warm days, a cold Inca Cola will help keep things cool. Know that you may need it: spicy *rocoto* and jalapeño peppers enliven the *causas limena*—balls of mashed potato infused with *aji amarillo* and topped with Dungeness crab. Also try creamy prawn chowder (*chupe de camarones*) and *pollo a la brasa*, rotisserie chicken with hand-cut fries.

Scopa

Italian

D1

109A Plaza St. (bet. Center St. & Healdsburg Ave.), Healdsburg

Phone: 707-433-5282 Dinner Tue – Sun
Web: www.scopahealdsburg.com
Prices: $$

Like the lively Italian card game that gives Scopa its name, this Healdsburg hot spot is one big, boisterous family meal brought to the table by Chef Ari Rosen and his wife (and resident oenophile), Dawnelise. The space is pint-sized, but the vibe is bustling, especially on Winemaker Wednesdays, when local vintners work the room and pour their wares at the six-seat marble bar.

Framed Scopa cards set the scene for dinners designed to share. Load up on such *antipasti* as spicy meatballs and crispy, piping hot *arancini*. Try splitting a crusty artisanal pizza topped with thinly sliced prosciutto or the seasonal ravioli, but *nonna's* tomato-braised chicken is a dish that heartier appetites keep to themselves.

Take-home Scopa decks are available for sale.

SEA Thai

Thai XX

B2

2323 Sonoma Ave. (at Farmer's Ln.), Santa Rosa

Phone: 707-528-8333 Lunch & dinner daily
Web: www.seathaibistrosr.com
Prices: $$

Parked on a cozy corner in the bustling Montgomery Village outdoor mall, Tony Ounpamornchai's authentic, upscale Thai-fusion bistro is more than a strip mall stop. Here, crimson walls crawl along a narrow dining space, and upscale Thai gets a Westernized spin in dishes like shrimp bruschetta, made with four squares of fresh, delicious bread topped with avocado, shrimp, cilantro, and spicy homemade Asian pesto. The lunch menu has plenty of goodies to choose from, though curry dishes are only served at dinner. For a fabulous finale, try the banana fritters with coconut ice cream—that should hush the aficionados complaining that prices here are higher than divier joints.

Folks in Petaluma enjoy the older sibling restaurant, SEA Modern Thai Cuisine.

Shimo

Japanese XX

D2

241 Healdsburg Ave. (bet. Matheson & Mill Sts.), Healdsburg

Phone: 707-433-6000 Lunch & dinner Wed – Sun
Web: www.shimomodernsteak.com
Prices: $$

Locals and visitors to the wine country looking for something different are making a haunt of Shimo, the Japanese *izakaya*-meets-steakhouse, named for the marvelous marbling in a prime cut of beef. And since Shimo is housed just off the beaten Healdsburg path, this contemporary find is a special treat for the travelers who happen upon it.

From deliciously textured pepperwood tables–salvaged from Ukiah–to the razor-sharp Damascus steel cutlery, everything at Shimo is executed in style. Same goes for the Japanese-American fusion cuisine which even makes ramen a DIY experience. Build your own noodle bowls or go all out: the latter is easy to do when there's Wagyu tri tip Korean barbecue on the menu. Steak lovers will relish a 21-day, dry-aged bone-in filet.

Spoonbar

Mediterranean

D2

219 Healdsburg Ave. (bet. Matheson & Mill Sts.), Healdsburg

Phone: 707-433-7222 — Lunch Thu – Mon
Web: www.spoonbar.com — Dinner nightly
Prices: $$

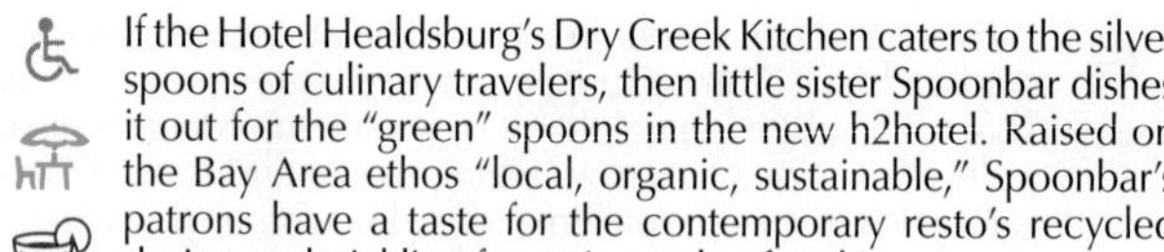

If the Hotel Healdsburg's Dry Creek Kitchen caters to the silver spoons of culinary travelers, then little sister Spoonbar dishes it out for the "green" spoons in the new h2hotel. Raised on the Bay Area ethos "local, organic, sustainable," Spoonbar's patrons have a taste for the contemporary resto's recycled design and trickling fountain made of rocking spoons.

With master mixologist Scott Beattie helming the bar, Spoonbar is a booze hound's paradise with such deftly crafted concoctions as the Corpse Reviver #2. The extensive drinks list is best paired with food—particularly if you're driving home. Sample Mediterranean fare like Sicilian pinenut and raisin meatballs with cucumber salad, or a Moroccan lamb tagine with black chickpeas and mint.

Stark's Steakhouse

Steakhouse

B2

521 Adam St. (at 7th St.), Santa Rosa

Phone: 707-546-5100 — Lunch Mon – Fri
Web: www.starkrestaurants.com — Dinner nightly
Prices: $$$

Fourth in the brood of Mark and Terri Stark (of Willi's Wine Bar and Monti's), Stark's Steakhouse is at last grown up and hitting its stride. On Santa Rosa's historic Railroad Square, Stark's draws suitors with a baby grand piano, a pair of roaring fireplaces, and an ample selection of bourbon and Scotch in the snug bar and lounge, which serves an all day menu.

Unexpected starters like Dungeness crab tater tots or tamarind barbecue prawns show contemporary playfulness, while classics like chilled oysters hint at the experience to come. Stark's tome-lined dining room is best known for its traditional steakhouse dinners of grass-fed and dry-aged beef as well as storied American Kobe. Red meat may rule, but it does share space with omnivorous alternatives.

Sugo

5 Petaluma Blvd. S. (at B St.), Petaluma

Phone: 707-782-9298 Lunch & dinner daily
Web: www.sugopetaluma.com
Prices: $$

Housed behind a well-worn brick façade in Petaluma's Theater District, Sugo Trattoria offers a comely take on dinner and a movie, where classic films silently unfold on a white wall above the open kitchen. If this bit of art house entertainment isn't enough to take your mind off Sugo's strip mall locale, perhaps ambient music and candlelight are enough to transport you at last.

As the name suggests, Sugo's tiered dining room waves its flag for Italy with a hefty selection of bruschetta, including one topped with prosciutto, fig, and Brie; a daily ravioli; and *secondi* starring Californian produce—think pistachio-crusted salmon or artichoke chicken *piccata*. A panzanella salad makes a nice light lunch when paired with five-dollar wines by the glass.

Thai Orchid

1005 Vine St. (at Mill St.), Healdsburg

Phone: 707-433-0515 Lunch Mon – Sat
Web: N/A Dinner nightly
Prices: ⊜

When savvy foodies need respite from foie gras and duck confit, they head to the local strip mall for authentic, affordable Asian eats. Thai Orchid, at Healdsburg's Vineyard Plaza, is one such retreat, with a modest dining room outfitted with only a few wood tables and simple wall carvings.

Despite an unassuming interior, the cuisine explodes with layers of flavor and heat that may sting a sensitive western palate. Heed the knowing stare of the house matriarch whose warning eyes say, "order mild." The broad menu traverses Thailand from familiar to exotic fare. Kick off the expedition with flavorful coconut soup; travel on to *nua nam tok*, beef salad with red onions, basil, and mint; or rekindle your love of the land with a perfect pad Thai.

Terrapin Creek ✿

Californian XX

A3

1580 Eastshore Rd. (off Hwy. 1), Bodega Bay

Phone: 707-875-2700 — Lunch Thu – Sun
Web: www.terrapincreekcafe.com — Dinner nightly
Prices: $$$

Terrapin Creek

Travelers looking for a terrific meal in the coastal hamlet of Bodega Bay can do no better than to dine at Terrapin Creek. It may be off the radar, but rest assured that their flavorful food is not. Happily, the ambience is still country quaint: the owners are likely to seat you; the cooks may smile and wave as you depart; and cutie Ava is often napping by the door.

Inside, the white-trimmed blue house feels casual and convivial with a broad archway connecting two main rooms—one with a few tables and an exhibition kitchen; and the other with a teeny bar and central fireplace that illuminates citrus hues and white linen-covered tables. The atmosphere, while absolutely unassuming, is nothing if not gracious. Servers are polished, polite, and always professional. Good thing too, anything less would do a disservice to the highly skilled cuisine.

Californian fare is presented à la carte with several choices per course. One could easily make a memorable meal of marinated Monterey sardines with a shaved fennel salad; plump rock shrimp and potato gnocchi with earthy mushrooms and English peas; and an excellent crispy-skinned duck breast with Brussels sprouts and caramelized spaetzle.

the fig café

Californian XX

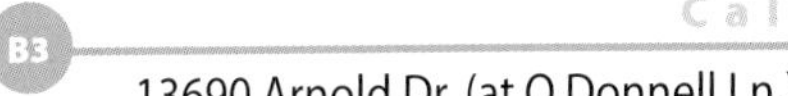

B3

13690 Arnold Dr. (at O Donnell Ln.), Glen Ellen

Phone: 707-938-2130 — Lunch Sat – Sun
Web: www.thefigcafe.com — Dinner nightly
Prices: $$

The fig café is so much a fixture in Glen Ellen that she is practically a landmark. And with a deluge of natural light to illuminate vaulted ceilings and a friendly crowd, it's simple to see why the fig is a favorite among locals. The interior is casual and comfy and the Californian cuisine is consistent, approachable, and beautifully prepared.

Dinners frequently feature local ingredients and might include, you guessed it, a fig and chèvre salad with caramelized pancetta, pecans, and spicy arugula; crispy duck confit with glazed turnips over earthy French green lentils; butcher's steak with blue cheese butter; and fluffy lemon bread pudding with macerated berries and a bit of crème fraîche. In the mood for brunch? See you at the fig on weekends!

the girl & the fig

Californian XX

D3

110 W. Spain St. (at 1st St.), Sonoma

Phone: 707-938-3634 — Lunch & dinner daily
Web: www.thegirlandthefig.com
Prices: $$

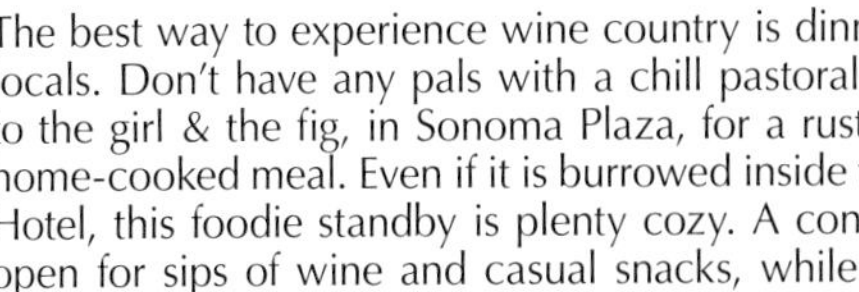

The best way to experience wine country is dinner with the locals. Don't have any pals with a chill pastoral pad? Head to the girl & the fig, in Sonoma Plaza, for a rustic vibe and home-cooked meal. Even if it is burrowed inside the Sonoma Hotel, this foodie standby is plenty cozy. A convivial bar is open for sips of wine and casual snacks, while mint green banquettes in the butter yellow dining room are a comfy spot to linger over Californian dishes with a nod to Provence.

The intricate antique wood bar serves French aperitifs and thoughtful half-glasses to the tasting crowd—paired with a plate of local artisan cheeses. Heartier appetites may indulge in chicken two ways, a crisp-skinned breast and herby leg roulade with roasted root vegetables.

Underwood

A2

9113 Graton Rd. (at Edison St.), Graton

Phone: 707-823-7023 — Lunch Tue – Sat
Web: www.underwoodgraton.com — Dinner Tue – Sun
Prices: $$

The tiny town of Graton is the geographical center of Sonoma's West County, and at its center sits Underwood, a hip little hub known to attract the best local winemakers for a sip and a nosh. Its old-school saloon vibe–red vinyl banquettes, zinc- and copper-topped tables, a nickel-topped bar slinging classic cocktails–make Underwood an ideal spot to pop in any time of day or night.

Befitting this Lilliputian town set smack in the middle of sophisticated foodie heaven, Underwood's menu ranges from American classics, including a darn good ham-and-Gruyère sandwich with crispy hot fries, to such global small plates as Vietnamese lettuce cups, white anchovy crostini, or Thai chili clams. On warmer days, locals slurp oysters on the picturesque mini patio.

Willi's Seafood & Raw Bar

Seafood

D1

403 Healdsburg Ave. (at North St.), Healdsburg

Phone: 707-433-9191 — Lunch & dinner daily
Web: www.starkrestaurants.com
Prices: $$

Healdsburg locals have all new reason to clink glasses of Sonoma County wines: their beloved haunt, Willi's Seafood & Raw Bar, now has room enough for everyone. On the heels of a recent expansion, Willi's rustic-chic interior continues to burst at the seams with regulars and tourists who come for seafood-focused small plates. Not to worry, the fab alfresco dining patio is still perfectly intact.

Ideal for sharing with a jovial bunch of friends, Willi's savory nibbles include fresh hamachi ceviche tossed with *pepitas* and *rocoto* chilies in zesty lime juice; salty, deep-fried Ipswich clams with shisito peppers and citrus aïoli; uni "Mac & cheese" with Sweet Bay scallops; and clam, mussel, or oyster "steamers" with green garlic butter and PBR.

Willi's Wine Bar

International

4404 Old Redwood Hwy. (at Ursuline Rd.), Santa Rosa

Phone: 707-526-3096 — Lunch Tue – Sat
Web: www.starkrestaurants.com — Dinner nightly
Prices: $$

While careening down the dark, tree-shrouded Old Redwood Highway, brake for Willi's Wine Bar, a charming little roadhouse named for the pioneering spot in Paris that pours American wines for the French. Unsurprisingly, the country-chic shack is popular among local vintners who are likely to find their names among the list of 40 wines by the glass that drench the bar in scarlet light.

Opened by Mark and Terri Stark, the husband-wife owners of multiple area restaurants, Willi's Wine Bar is aromatic with eclectic flavors from California, Asia, France, and the Mediterranean. Nosh on interesting small plates like "brick" chicken with harissa and tzakiki; five-spice braised pork belly potstickers; and skillet roasted shrimp with Fresno chilies.

Willow Wood Market Cafe

Californian 

A2

9020 Graton Rd. (at Edison St.), Graton

Phone: 707-823-0233 — Lunch daily
Web: www.willowwoodgraton.com — Dinner Mon – Sat
Prices: $$

Lulu is your hostess at this darling roadside eatery; its genuine country vibe and hospitality marry well with Californian comfort food. While the budget-friendly café remains a rather tinsel market with quirky knickknacks, fans of Americana will be tickled by the Necco wafers and old-time sundries to-go.

Enter this "home" and take a seat. Salads and hot sandwiches are at the ready, but the menu revolves around bowls of "piping hot polenta." The creamy goodness has many guises like garlicky rock shrimp with roasted tomatoes and peppers, but favorites like the black bean soup with a swirl of sour cream or the cheesy skirt steak sandwich will turn back the clock. Nourishing this sense of nostalgia, most items are escorted by crunchy garlic toast.

zazu

Californian XX

B2

3535 Guerneville Rd. (at Willowside Rd.), Santa Rosa

Phone: 707-523-4814 Dinner Wed – Mon
Web: www.zazurestaurant.com
Prices: $$

A little red roadhouse in the middle of nowhere–if you can call Sonoma's sprawl of artisan farms and vineyards "nowhere"–pastoral zazu makes the utmost of its environment, serving pick-it-yourself salads from its onsite garden. Knock the dirt off your shoes and duck inside the narrow dining room where boat lights cast a soft glow and husband-wife chefs, John Stewart and Duskie Estes, provide the extra spark.

The chefs are hog wild for house-made *salumi*, sausage, and bacon, and their rustic interior is suited to Californian cuisine with an Italian accent. Start with rich tomato soup and Carmody grilled cheese, and save room for hand-cut pasta with tender braised boar. For dessert, rose-geranium ice cream is a cool accomplice to strawberry-rhubarb crisp.

Zin

American X

D1

344 Center St. (at North St.), Healdsburg

Phone: 707-473-0946 Lunch Mon – Fri
Web: www.zinrestaurant.com Dinner nightly
Prices: $$

Parked off Healdsburg square, droves of diners unite at diverse Zin for seasonal cuisine. With polished concrete floors, wood beams, high ceilings, and bucolic paintings, this culinary hot spot is *très* cool and casual. Adjacent to the open kitchen at back, zinfandel zealots settle at the bar to ogle a wine list centered on local examples of the zinfandel variety. The affable staff lays upon your table–set with a wooden ladder-back chair–American classics laced with an eclectic spin. Co-owners Jeff Mall and Scott Silva are sons of the soil whose pastoral psyche shines in fried green beans clothed in a mango salsa; succulent shrimp and Andouille sausage atop a crispy grit cake; and a perfectly sweetened latte crème brûlée crowned with oatmeal cookies.

Peter L. Wrenn / MICHELIN

Where to Stay

Stanyan Park

750 Stanyan St. (at Waller St.)

Phone: 415-751-1000
Web: www.stanyanpark.com
Prices: $$

30 Rooms

6 Suites

Stanyan Park

Victorian style, reasonable rates, and a view of Golden Gate Park set this small hotel apart. Built in 1905 as one of a dozen lodgings serving visitors to San Francisco's grand park, the Stanyan alone survives in its original function today. Its handsome three-story Queen Anne-style turret marks the corner of Stanyan and Waller streets.

Exploring the 1,017-acre park from here is a breeze, whether you're walking, biking, or driving. This property is also convenient to the UCSF Medical Center.

While Golden Gate Park may be known for the throngs of tie-dyed-T-shirt-clad hippies who staged throbbing rock concerts in the Speedway Meadows during the 1967 "Summer of Love," the hotel across the street has no claims to hipness. The 36 non-smoking rooms set a tasteful, romantic mood with their floral Victorian wallpaper, quiet colors, and classic furnishings. Reserve one of the larger suites (which range up to 900 square feet) if you need more space; you'll have a comfortable living room, a full kitchen, a separate dining room, and two separate bedrooms at your disposal. Continental breakfast and afternoon tea service are on the house.

Inn at the Opera

333 Fulton St. (at Franklin St.)

Phone: 415-863-8400 or 800-325-2708
Web: www.shellhospitality.com
Prices: $$

30 Rooms

18 Suites

Inn at the Opera

Playing on its proximity to the 1932 Memorial Opera House–home to the San Francisco Opera, the San Francisco Ballet, and the Louise M. Davies Symphony Hall–this 48-room inn is in perfect pitch as a convenient place to stay for performers and theatergoers alike.

At 215 square feet, there may not be space for a *pas de deux* in the Ballet studio, but this unit does offer a kitchenette with a microwave oven, coffeemaker, and small refrigerator. The Concerto junior suite adds separate sleeping and living areas; bigger still, the Symphony suite sleeps four. Divas can book the Opera suite, the largest accommodation. It can hold a small entourage, with two bathrooms and two separate sitting rooms in addition to the bedroom. Comfy bathrobes, turn-down service, a morning newspaper, and complimentary continental breakfast are included with any room.

The newly renovated lobby makes a chic place to meet friends, and fine French fare stars nightly at the hotel's on-site restaurant, Ovation at the Opera. Nearby shopping includes the funky shops of Hayes Street, the Westfield San Francisco Centre mall a short distance down Market Street, and the designer boutiques of Union Square, a mere mile away.

Phoenix

601 Eddy St. (at Larkin St.)

Phone: 415-776-1380 or 800-248-9466
Web: www.thephoenixhotel.com
Prices: **$$**

41 Rooms

3 Suites

Joie de Vivre Hospitality

Bohemian and hip, the Phoenix, admittedly, is not for everyone. It is located at the edge of the Tenderloin neighborhood, an area long known for its mean streets. Today, this diverse district is in transition, and it lures the young and adventurous to its ethnic eateries and nightclubs.

Catering to the rock 'n' roll set, the Phoenix brings in talent that's far from local (think Pearl Jam, the Red Hot Chili Peppers, and The Shins). The hotel is not a quiet place for your grandparents–perhaps not your parents either–since it can get pretty boisterous at times. But for those who want to rub elbows with rock stars by the outdoor heated pool, it's a cool place to hang.

The building retains its 1956 motel configuration, with rooms facing a landscaped central courtyard. Among the courtyard's glorious features, come here to find the amazing pool that incessantly buzzes with even more amazing people. Of the hotel's 44 tropical-toned rooms, the three Deluxe King rooms and the three suites have refrigerators, microwaves, and coffeemakers. After enjoying a complimentary continental breakfast by the pool, feel free to quiz the staff on their favorite city sights.

Adagio

550 Geary St. (bet. Jones & Taylor Sts.)

Phone: 415-775-5000 or 800-228-8830
Web: www.thehoteladagio.com
Prices: $$$

169 Rooms
2 Suites

Jeff Zaruba

A member of the Joie de Vivre Hospitality Group (whose properties include such hotels as the Carlton, Kabuki, and the Vitale among others), the Adagio evokes the quiet grace that its name suggests. This landmark Spanish Colonial Revival structure was built in 1929 as the El Cortez, and knew several different names and owners before it was reopened in 2003.

Clean lines and contemporary furnishings sound a modern note in rooms dressed in tones of walnut brown and terra-cotta. Almost half of the rooms have dramatic views of the San Francisco cityscape. Foremost among these are the two penthouse suites, located on the 16th floor. The larger of the two, the Bolero Suite, adjoins an outdoor terrace. It offers space galore with a king-size bedroom, a separate living room with fireplace, and a dining table for eight.

Come here often? Take advantage of the Adagio's executive luggage storage program. If you're new to the city, sign up for a complimentary tour–your choice of neighborhoods–with a Golden Gate Greeter. Guests also enjoy free town car service within a two-mile radius of the hotel.

Bijou

111 Mason St. (at Eddy St.)

Phone: 415-771-1200 or 800-771-1022
Web: www.hotelbijou.com
Prices: $

65 Rooms

Bijou

Quaint and low-key in the European tradition, the Bijou lies between Union Square and the Tenderloin, and offers good value for its convenient location. In this 1911 hotel, a theater theme and art deco-inspired décor recall the golden years of the silver screen. To illustrate this, each of the 65 rooms is named for a film that was shot in San Francisco.

Rich tones of burgundy, green, and sunny yellow color the well-maintained rooms, which are decorated with still photographs depicting their individual movie motif. Windows are not soundproofed, so if it's absolute quiet you're after, you'll have to sacrifice a street view in a front room for accommodations on the back side of the five-story building (earplugs are provided in all rooms). For security, front doors are locked at 8:00 P.M. each night; guests must show their hotel key card to get in after that time.

Amenities at this well-manicured property include a small desk, large, conventional television, and breakfast pastries, coffee, and tea. Perhaps the best amenity of all here is the nightly double feature. These movies are screened off the lobby in a small theater decked out with vintage, folding velvet-covered seats.

Clift

A2

495 Geary St. (at Taylor St.)

Phone: 415-775-4700 or 800-697-1791
Web: www.clifthotel.com
Prices: $$$

338 Rooms

25 Suites

Clift Hotel

Renowned as "Wonderland for the jet set," the Clift turns the conventional luxury hotel experience upside down. The 1913 Italian Renaissance-style building was reconceived for the 21st century by designer Philippe Starck. True to his style, Starck surprises at every turn in the soaring lobby with a juxtaposition of antique and modern pieces: an Eames chair here; a Salvador Dalí-inspired coffee table there; and a 35-foot-high fireplace as a focal point. This play on scale does indeed tend to make guests feel like they've walked into Wonderland.

Things become less surreal in the guestrooms, designed for tranquility in quiet tones of foggy gray, beige, and lavender. English sycamore sleigh beds on a base of polished chrome add whimsy to the sophistication displayed in gauzy silk curtains and Italian percale linens.

Whether you're in town for business or pleasure, the Clift can oblige. The legendary art deco Redwood Room lounge is a hipster haunt swathed in redwood; while the adjacent Velvet Room is open for business in an equally glamorous setting. Doing business is a breeze with the help of a full-service business center, and rooms to support all facets of video production.

Diva

440 Geary St. (bet. Mason & Taylor Sts.)

Phone: 415-885-0200 or 800-553-1900
Web: www.hoteldiva.com
Prices: **$$**

116
Rooms

2
Suites

Rien van Rijthoven

Steps from Union Square and across from the Curran and the American Conservatory theaters, Diva preserves its edgy Euro-tech vibe. Charcoal gray, taupe, and black lend a hip vibe to the guest rooms, which have been recently enhanced with new bedding and lighting. The ultra-contemporary look uses cobalt blue carpets, streamlined furnishings, contemporary art, and stainless steel accents to make its point. Upgrade your reservation to the Salon floor, and you'll enjoy amenities such as an in-room refrigerator and a complimentary continental breakfast. The Diva has no restaurant, but get your java fix next door at Starbucks.

Kids will go for the Little Diva suites, tailored to the young traveler with pop-art colors, bunk beds, kid-friendly movies, and a karaoke machine for budding American Idols. Parents get the connecting room, so they have their own space, but can easily keep track of the younger members of the family.

Even the meeting room and the Internet lounges are custom designed. The former features a golden onyx and steel underlit buffet, while the lounges credit the likes of skateboarder Pete Colpitts among their designers.

Galleria Park

191 Sutter St. (at Kearny St.)

Phone: 415-781-3060 or 800-792-9639
Web: www.jdvhotels.com
Prices: $$

169 Rooms

8 Suites

Cesar Rubio

Both business and leisure travelers will find a quiet refuge at this 177-room property, which premiered in 1911 as the Sutter Hotel. Taken over by the Joie de Vivre Hospitality Group in 2005, the Galleria Park sits in the heart of the Financial District, a short walk from Union Square and all its fabulous shops.

The lobby is outfitted in a glamorous art deco style, complete with an eclectic collection of furniture and artwork from San Francisco's Lost Art Salon. Likewise, guestrooms have been upgraded with comfy pillowtop mattresses, flat screen TVs, and Frette linens. Shades of chartreuse and plum make a stylish color combination, especially when balanced by clean white trim.

A unique feature, an outdoor jogging track is located on the third floor. Here, you'll also find a landscaped terrace, with benches for relaxing. If jogging's not your thing, you can work out in the little fitness room. The hotel's GPS (Galleria Park Suggests) program offers set packages that provide exclusive access and behind-the-scenes scoops to sights around the city. A free 2-hour guided walking tour of the Financial District is available free of charge to all guests.

The Inn at Union Square

440 Post St. (bet. Mason & Powell Sts.)

Phone: 415-397-3510 or 800-288-4346
Web: www.unionsquare.com
Prices: $$

24 Rooms

6 Suites

The Inn at Union Square

San Francisco's mecca for shoppers, Union Square is the first place many visitors head for when they arrive in the city. From Saks Fifth Avenue and Neiman Marcus to designer boutiques such as Coach, Cartier, and Hermès, ways to exercise those credit cards abound around the plaza that was dedicated as a stage for supporters of the Union Army during the Civil War. And it all lies at the doorstep of The Inn at Union Square.

With upscale shopping at your heels, you would expect a hotel with this address to be equally expensive. In this regard, The Inn at Union Square, a certified California Green Lodging, surprises with its affordable rates, especially given the personalized service that the staff provides. The hotel is small, but the 30 rooms and one suite–recently redecorated in tones of cream, sage, and gold–provide all the comforts of home. Goose down pillows and pillow-top mattresses are nice extras for the price.

Intimate sitting areas on each floor boast wood-burning fireplaces lit with crackling fires in the evening, when wine and hors d'oeuvres are offered free of charge. This is also where guests can mingle over the complimentary continental breakfast set out each morning.

King George

334 Mason St. (bet. Geary & O'Farrell Sts.)

Phone: 415-781-5050 or 800-288-6005
Web: www.kinggeorge.com
Prices: $

151 Rooms

2 Suites

King George Hotel

Potted topiary trees and a prominent awning announce the entrance to this Anglophile's hideaway. Opened in 1914, the King George welcomes guests with European flair, beginning with the lobby, where warm tones of yellow, beige, and gold set off a full-size portrait of the hotel's namesake.

English hunting country may come to mind when you check into one of the 153 rooms, colored in a palette of green, gold, and burgundy. All accommodations include fun and thoughtful touches like jars of candy. If the sweets aren't sustenance enough, the King George also offers 24-hour room service, catered by an off-site restaurant. Given these comforts, and the hotel's location–a block west of Union Square and convenient to the Moscone Center–rates here are a real deal.

King George no longer serves breakfast, but they do set out coffee and tea in the lobby each morning. A proper English tea is available on weekends in the Windsor Tea Room for parties of ten or more; reservations are required. For meals, there are many restaurant options nearby, but for drinks and appetizers, you need not venture farther than Winston's Bar and Lounge. Daily happy hour here features discounted beer and wine.

Mandarin Oriental

222 Sansome St. (bet. California & Pine Sts.)

Phone: 415-276-9888 or 800-622-0404
Web: www.mandarinoriental.com
Prices: $$$$

151 Rooms

7 Suites

Mandarin Oriental Hotel Group

The view's the thing at this sumptuous property, which occupies two towers in one of San Francisco's taller buildings, between the 38th and 48th stories. Glass-enclosed sky bridges connect these towers on each floor, offering spectacular views of the city and beyond.

Exotic touches of the Orient delight at every turn. The lobby's marble floor, for starters, illustrates a stylized Chinese pattern that symbolizes good fortune. On the second floor, Silks restaurant follows suit with Pacific Rim cuisine and silk brocade tablecloths that borrow their design from the robes of the Imperial Chinese Court.

A cinnamon red palette inspires the room décor, enhanced by mahogany furnishings and gold-leaf accents. Every sky-high room claims terrific views from its picture windows. For even better vistas, ask for an Executive Corner room, in which the writing desk cozies up against the window offering a 180-degree cityscape. Or book the Lotus Suite, where you can gaze out the window at the Golden Gate Bridge while you soak in the deep, sumptuous tub.

From the hotel, it's a short walk to Embarcadero Center shopping; all the attractions of Fisherman's Wharf are just a quick cable car ride away.

Monaco

501 Geary St. (at Taylor St.)

Phone: 415-292-0100 or 866-622-5284
Web: www.monaco-sf.com
Prices: $$$

169 Rooms

32 Suites

Fred Licht/Kimpton Hotels

Like every picture, every Kimpton hotel tells a story; the one behind the Monaco is sophisticated world travel. The gold-toned lobby sets the nostalgic tone for 1920s travel with a check-in desk styled like a steamer trunk, and hand-painted ceiling frescoes depicting whimsical skyscapes of hot air balloons and planes. On the landing of the grand staircase, a painting entitled Celestial Lady clearly illustrates that the sky is the limit here.

Vibrant fabrics drape over canopy beds in the guestrooms, and cheery striped paper covers the walls. In-room spa services and a yoga channel add soothing touches to please any jet-setter. Rock 'n' roll fans can rent the Grace Slick Suite, a shrine to the singer's days with the group Jefferson Airplane and later, Jefferson Starship. If hungry, Grand Café provides a great selection of eats and treats that is sure to please and appease.

For tiny tots, the Kimpton Kids program provides complimentary cribs. Older travelers-in-training receive a welcome gift and a pint-size animal print robe to wear in their room; while parents get a list of kid-friendly activities in the city. Even four-legged travelers are welcome here, at no additional cost.

Nikko

222 Mason St. (bet. Ellis & O'Farrell Sts.)

Phone: 415-394-1111 or 800-248-3308
Web: www.hotelnikkosf.com
Prices: $$

510 Rooms

22 Suites

Hotel Nikko San Francisco

Though large, the Nikko offers a comfortable and convenient stay, with a choice of 12 different types of rooms and suites. At 280 square feet, the Petite queens are best for single occupancy, but may also suit two people in search of a good deal. Deluxe rooms, both king and double/doubles, occupy floors 6 through 21. The Imperial Floors (22, 23, and 24) offer added services and amenities, including restricted access and breakfast served in a private lounge. At the top end, the two bedroom, two bath Imperial Suite measures in at 2,635 square feet. City views are divine, especially from the higher floors. The private, aurally perfect, and sophisticated Rrazz Room theater continues to host myriad world-class entertainers such as Ashford & Simpson, Keely Smith, and the American Idols.

A lovely swimming pool, together with a fitness room and sauna, occupy the very large and bright fifth floor atrium. For your business needs, the well-equipped business center can arrange printing, binding, faxing, translation, and secretarial services.

Stop by Nikko's fine dining restaurant, Anzu, for sushi, prime cuts of beef, and a sake martini.

Omni

500 California St. (at Montgomery St.)

Phone: 415-677-9494
Web: www.omnisanfrancisco.com
Prices: $$$$

347 Rooms

15 Suites

Omni Hotels & Resorts

Located in the heart of the Financial District with a cable car stop right outside, this Omni opened in 2002 in an elegantly renovated 1926 bank building. Though only the original stone and brick façade has been preserved, the spacious wood-paneled lobby, floored in rosy marble, takes its cue and its stylishness from a bygone era.

Spread over 17 stories, the 347 rooms and 15 suites follow suit. They are large and classic in style, with details to match, including Egyptian cotton sheets and well-equipped bathrooms decorated in marble and granite. Most guestrooms feature comfortable furnishings and a well-organized space. For upgraded amenities, reserve on the 16th "signature" floor, where rooms come equipped with a Bose Wave radio and CD player, DVD player, and a color copier/printer. Specialty accommodations such as Get Fit rooms (furnished with a treadmill and healthy snacks) and a Kids Fantasy Suite, where bunk beds and kids rule in the second bedroom, are also available. At meal times, Bob's Steak and Chop House will draw the meat-loving guests.

Every Saturday at 10:00 A.M., a guided walking tour departs from the hotel for an overview of the city's history.

Rex

562 Sutter St. (bet. Mason & Powell Sts.)

Phone: 415-433-4434 or 800-433-4434
Web: www.thehotelrex.com
Prices: **$$**

94
Rooms

Patricia Parinejad

Worldly and sophisticated, the Rex styles itself after the art and literary salons rife in San Francisco in the 1920s and 30s. Don't be surprised to see an author signing books in the dark paneled lobby, or folks gathering here for a poetry reading. This is all part of the hotel's literary mystique. Quotes from various regional authors adorn the walls of the different floors as well as at The Library Bar, where a breakfast buffet and compact dinner menu are served.

The artistic theme carries over to the rooms in the custom wall coverings, hand-painted lampshades, and contemporary artwork. Pillow-top mattresses, a mini-refrigerator, and a plasma screen provide many of the comforts of home.

One of the Joie de Vivre Hospitality Group's pet-friendly properties, the Rex has now dropped its pet weight restrictions and additional fees for four-legged guests. Fido or Fifi will be pampered here with their own food bowls, beds, and yummy treats.

Located one block off Union Square, the Rex is convenient to both upscale shopping and the city's Theater District, which further enhances its artsy appeal. Very affordable rates make the Rex a great choice in this otherwise pricey area of town.

Serrano

A2

405 Taylor St. (at O'Farrell St.)

Phone: 415-885-2500 or 866-289-6561
Web: www.serranohotel.com
Prices: $$

217 Rooms

19 Suites

David Phelps/Kimpton Hotels

It's all fun and games at the Serrano, and the games begin with the Check-In Challenge. If you can beat "the house" in a quick game of 21, you could win a free room upgrade or other prizes; if you lose, your voluntary contribution benefits the local SPCA. The fun continues once you settle in; you can call to order a board game from the hotel's library to be delivered to your room.

The centerpiece of this 1924 Spanish Revival building is its dramatic two-story lobby, where the majestic fireplace, beamed ceilings, wood-paneled columns, Moroccan lanterns, and leafy potted plants stitch together an exotic atmosphere.

Bold Mediterranean colors and large windows combine in the rooms in a play of light and warmth, while Spanish and Moroccan accents echo the whimsical feel of the lobby. In a true flight of fancy, the hotel's Wicked Suite transports guests to the Land of Oz with a purple and green color scheme, and a larger-than-life portrait of the Wicked Witch of the West hanging over the bed.

All the great Kimpton Hotel amenities apply, including a nightly wine reception, and coffee and tea service in the lobby each morning.

Sir Francis Drake

450 Powell St. (at Sutter St.)

Phone: 415-392-7755 or 800-795-7129
Web: www.sirfrancisdrake.com
Prices: **$$$**

410 Rooms

6 Suites

Kimpton Hotels & Restaurants

The Sir Francis Drake has enjoyed a long and colorful history as one of San Francisco's landmark hotels. Opened in 1928, this hotel once boasted avant-garde amenities like ice water on tap and radios in every room. History is a large part of the experience here–the doormen still greet guests in the trademark Beefeater uniforms–and the ornate two-story marble lobby perfectly captures the historic grandeur.

Just because it has a past doesn't mean this place forgets all about the present and the future. From its lobby-located Starbucks to its pet-friendly policy, the Sir Francis Drake hotel appeals to modern travelers. Fully renovated, all rooms have been fitted with a sleek and elegant décor complete with patterned chocolate brown carpeting and textured wall coverings in soothing gray. Plum armchairs inject a pop of color in the comfortably sophisticated rooms.

Snag a seat at the bar/lounge Bar Drake, located in the gorgeous lobby, but if you're in the mood for some serious sustenance, beloved Scala's Bistro has all-day dining covered.

Renovations continue at this icon. Next up? The lobby, lobby bar, and fitness center.

Triton

B2

342 Grant Ave. (at Bush St.)

Phone: 415-394-0500 or 800-800-1299
Web: www.hoteltriton.com
Prices: $$

140 Rooms

Markham Johnson/Kimpton Hotels

If you like hip and eco-friendly, head for this member of the Kimpton Hotel group. The Triton's theme–Pop Culture–jumps out at you the moment you step inside the lobby, in the form of fanciful furnishings and whimsical murals in a riot of colors. A rotating selection of work by local artists is on display in the gallery on the mezzanine.

There are no cookie cutter-style rooms here. They come in all sizes, shapes, colors, and comfort levels, so ask for details before you book. Perhaps a standard room meets your needs; the complimentary *New York Times* will update you on world affairs as you sip your morning drink. Other features include iHome docking stations and eco-friendly bath amenities. Or maybe you prefer the panache of a Celebrity Suite, designed by the likes of comedienne Kathy Griffin or rocker Jerry Garcia. Conservation is the name of the game here, where everything is easy on the environment.

Located outside the Chinatown gate–convenient to the Financial District and Union Square–the hotel does not have its own restaurant, but Café de la Presse next door provides room service from its widely appealing French-American bistro menu.

Westin St. Francis

335 Powell St. (at Union Square)

Phone: 415-397-7000 or 866-500-0338
Web: www.westinstfrancis.com
Prices: **$$$$**

1195 Rooms

59 Suites

Mark Silverstein/Westin St. Francis

Doyenne of downtown, the regal St. Francis presides over Union Square as befits a landmark that has graced the square since 1904. In its early days, the hotel was the hub of San Francisco's social scene. "Meet me at the St. Francis" was an oft-heard request, and many a prominent visitor, from presidents to poets, has congregated in the grand 6,000-square foot lobby over the years.

Guest rooms in the Historic Main Building of the Westin St. Francis boast contemporary amenities and Empire style furniture; while Tower suites wear a modern aesthetic. Large bay windows offer a view of the city's skyline. In all the accommodations, ecru, bronze, and brown tones set off the ornate woodwork, high ceilings, and crystal chandeliers. Westin's signature Heavenly Bed and ergonomic desk chairs hail the modern day.

The marble-columned lobby is decorated in shades of cream and chocolate brown, as reproductions of the original beaded globe chandeliers glimmer overhead. The historic 1907 Great Magneta Grandfather Clock has been returned to its rightful place in the lobby, and lures generations of travelers from far and wide. Pop into the adjacent and aptly named Clock Bar for a snack and a cocktail.

Drisco

2901 Pacific Ave. (at Broderick St.)

Phone: 415-346-2880 or 800-634-7277
Web: www.hoteldrisco.com
Prices: $$

29 Rooms

19 Suites

Cesar Rubio

With its sunny setting perched high on the north side of California Street, affluent Pacific Heights contains some of the highest priced real estate in the city. It is here that the Hotel Drisco nestles comfortably amid multimillion-dollar mansions and green parks. In the distance, views of the San Francisco skyline stretch out for all to see.

Built in 1903, this member of the Joie de Vivre Hospitality Group makes a quiet haven removed from the bustle of downtown. Recently redecorated guestrooms have a residential vibe with custom-made furnishings, cast-iron heaters, and white clapboard wainscoting. The daily breakfast buffet (included in the room rates) makes the place feel even more like a B&B. Accommodations vary in size but are consistently graceful in style, and well-appointed with special attention to guests' every comfort. Some rooms offer pleasing city views; others overlook the building's tiny courtyard. A cozy robe and slippers are on hand when you're ready to call it a day.

As for amenities, an on-site workout room and free access to the nearby Presidio YMCA accommodates fitness fiends, while the small business center provides basic services for business travelers.

Kabuki

1625 Post St. (at Laguna St.)

Phone: 415-922-3200 or 800-533-4567
Web: www.hotelkabuki.com
Prices: **$$**

218 Rooms

Matthew Millman

An Asian spirit imbues this hotel with Zen-like tranquility, from the sleek lobby to the Japanese garden and koi pond just adjacent.

A renovation in 2007, the year the Joie de Vivre Hospitality Group purchased the hotel, revealed spacious rooms attractively appointed with modern furniture, including working desks and new Serta mattresses. East and West dovetail in lodgings where Japanese artwork and Asian tea kettles mix with amenities like flat screen televisions, iPod docking stations, and radios.

For added luxury, reserve a deluxe corner king room, equipped with extras such as a chaise lounge, a dining table, and a traditional Japanese soaking tub. Also in these rooms, sliding glass doors lead to a wraparound balcony. A stay on the club level will grant you a complimentary continental breakfast.

Located in the heart of Japantown, the reasonably priced Kabuki hotel is also close to Western Addition jazz clubs and Fillmore Street restaurants and boutiques. More traditional experiences await in sake and small plates at on-site O Izakaya Lounge, and in the communal baths at nearby Kabuki Springs and Spa, to which hotel guests have complimentary access.

Laurel Inn

444 Presidio Ave. (at California St.)

Phone: 415-567-8467 or 800-552-8735
Web: www.thelaurelinn.com
Prices: $$

49 Rooms

Joie de Vivre Hospitality

Steps away from Presidio National Park and Sacramento Street shopping, the Laurel Inn borders the quiet residential neighborhood of Laurel Heights. Ignore the bland exterior; inside, the inn tastefully plays on its 1963 pedigree courtesy of its current owners, the Joie de Vivre Hospitality Group.

Designed like urban studio apartments, the 49 sleekly furnished guestrooms include 18 larger units with kitchenettes. The latter are perfect extended stays, for which the hotel offers discounted rates. Be sure to bring the whole family; pets are welcome here, and special treats are provided for them.

Even at the regular rate, this place is a great value. Bold strokes of color enliven the rooms, where large windows open to let in fresh air (the hotel is not air-conditioned). Rooms on the back side feature pleasant city panoramas and are quieter than those facing the street, though all are efficiently soundproofed. Amenities–a complimentary continental breakfast and wine hour, concierge services, and access to the fitness center across the street among them–measure up to much pricier hotels.

Next door, Swank Cocktail Club lives up to its name with a cool style and killer drink menu.

Majestic

D4

1500 Sutter St. (at Gough St.)

Phone: 415-441-1100 or 800-869-8966
Web: www.thehotelmajestic.com
Prices: $

49 Rooms

9 Suites

MICHELIN

Isolated from the downtown bustle, the Majestic embraces its early 20th century heritage with grace and style. Built in 1902 as a private residence, this structure survived the 1906 earthquake to become San Francisco's oldest continuously operated hotel. (The fires that resulted from the quake were stopped a mere two blocks away.)

English and French antiques fill the rooms, while elements such as claw-foot tubs and sumptuously swagged four-poster beds bespeak the charm of the Victorian era. Standard rooms are on the small side, so reserve a junior or a one bedroom suite if you need more space.

When it's time to turn in, don the monogrammed robe provided and nestle in amid the feather pillows. Cookies placed on your bed at turndown assure sweet dreams…just keep an ear out for the mischievous resident ghost, who is said to roam the fourth floor.

Edwardian elegance decks out the lobby with antiques, marble columns, comfy sofas, and etched glass. If you're here on business, make sure you take advantage of the hotel's complimentary sedan service to either the Financial District or Union Square on weekday mornings.

Carlton

A3

1075 Sutter St. (bet. Hyde & Larkin Sts.)

Phone: 415-673-0242 or 800-922-7586
Web: www.hotelcarltonsf.com
Prices: $

161 Rooms

Carlton Hotel

A certified Green Business, the Carlton proudly claims to be the first hotel in San Francisco to be solar powered. In conjunction with the property's other energy-saving measures, 105 solar panels were installed on the hotel's roof in early 2008.

This forward-thinking attitude continues in the ample amenities, which make this place a great value for the price. In the same vein, afternoon beverages and an evening wine reception are offered gratis, as are shuttle services to and from the San Francisco International airport.

The guest rooms are understated and tasteful, their soft colors splashed with accents of persimmon and saffron. Like the hotel's public spaces, they are decorated with photographs of exotic destinations. The higher of the building's seven stories afford unobstructed city views.

Though accommodations are not air-conditioned, rooms keep their cool with ceiling fans on those rare hot days. "Peace through travel" is the philosophy espoused by the Carlton's staff, an international team that speaks more than a dozen languages. Another exotic touch is the restaurant, Saha, that serves contemporary Middle Eastern cuisine at breakfast and dinner for all guests.

The Ritz-Carlton, San Francisco

C2

600 Stockton St. (bet. California & Pine Sts.)

Phone: 415-296-7465 or 800-241-3333
Web: www.ritzcarlton.com
Prices: $$$$

276 Rooms

60 Suites

Spa

The Ritz-Carlton, San Francisco

When it opened in 1909 as the western headquarters of the Metropolitan Life Insurance Company, this neoclassical landmark flanked by a row of stately Ionic columns was lauded as a "Temple of Commerce." A century later, as The Ritz-Carlton, the edifice crowning the eastern slope of Nob Hill can justly be called a temple of luxury.

A museum-quality collection of 18th- and 19th-century antiques and artwork adorns the public areas. Treasures such as Waterford crystal candelabras, 18th-century portraits, and Regency silver abound throughout the hotel.

Restored with European charm, your home-away-from-home here comes with a featherbed and down comforter, a cozy robe and slippers, and a marble bath with a rain showerhead. On the Club Level, a dedicated concierge, continuous culinary offerings, and a private business lounge provide unparalleled pampering.

All the expected amenities apply. Take the time to work out in their fitness facility, then relax those tired muscles in the steam room before your soothing massage. Later in the day, the lobby lounge makes a gracious venue in which to linger over afternoon tea or a cocktail before retiring for the night.

The Fairmont

B2

950 Mason St. (at California St.)

Phone: 415-772-5000 or 866-540-4491
Web: www.fairmont.com
Prices: **$$$**

528 Rooms

63 Suites

The Fairmont San Francisco

This Gilded Age palace atop Nob Hill survives as a monument to James "Bonanza Jim" Fair, who profited mightily off Nevada's Comstock silver Lode, and on whose land the hotel's foundations were laid in 1902. Ironically, The Fairmont was scheduled to open on April 18, 1906, the day the devastating earthquake rocked the city. The structure survived, but the ornate interior was ravaged by fire.

Today, the hotel's public spaces sparkle again with turn-of-the-20th century splendor. The lobby shows off the restoration of architect Julia Morgan's original Corinthian columns, alabaster walls, marble floors, and vaulted gold-trimmed ceilings. Soak up the atmosphere over a meal in the domed Laurel Court. Or, for a different kind of nostalgia, drop by the newly restored Tonga Room, a tiki hideaway, complete with staged rainstorms and live music.

Renovated rooms–divided between the original building and a 23-story tower added in 1961–shine with refined fabrics. Eco-minded folks can choose the Eco Chic Suite. In this tower suite, guests enjoy views from wraparound windows, amid furnishings made from organic and recycled materials. Local biodynamic wines stock the mini-bar.

Nob Hill

835 Hyde St. (bet. Sutter & Bush Sts.)

Phone: 415-885-2987 or 877-662-4455
Web: www.nobhillhotel.com
Prices: **$$**

52
Rooms

Nob Hill Hotel

Unlike many of its ritzier neighbors, this 1906 hotel named for its lofty location offers prices that are better paired with consumers' current financial belt-tightening. It may not have all the upscale amenities of its brethren, but the Nob Hill Hotel hands out plenty of value for the price.

Rates include an evening wine tasting, access to a 24-hour fitness center, and a continental breakfast. In-room spa services are available, and the hospitable staff can accommodate speakers of Spanish, French, Italian, Greek, and Chinese.

Though small, rooms are clean and individually decorated in a plush crush of romantic Victoriana and period antiques. Some rooms, including two penthouse suites, have private terraces; several suites feature whirlpool tubs. Mini refrigerators and microwaves are provided, along with CD players, hairdryers, and coffeemakers. The atmosphere is hushed and the rooms are quiet, whether they face the courtyard or the street. Smokers beware: a hefty cleaning fee applies if you're caught lighting up in this smoke-free haven.

As an incentive to eat in, guests who choose to dine on Italian food at the on-site Columbini Bistro will receive a complimentary glass of wine.

Orchard Garden

466 Bush St. (at Grant Ave.)

Phone: 415-399-9807 or 888-717-2881
Web: www.theorchardgardenhotel.com
Prices: **$$$**

86 Rooms

Orchard Garden

Green is more than just a color used in decorating this Nob Hill hotel; it's a way of life. California's first hotel built to U.S. Green Building Council standards, the Orchard Garden prides itself on its commitment to Mother Earth—and its LEED certification.

Opened in 2006 at the top of steep Powell Street, the hotel is constructed of eco-friendly materials including concrete made using the ash that results from recycling coal. Sustainably-grown maple provides the wood for the custom-crafted furniture in the guestrooms, and fabrics all contain recycled content. You won't sacrifice any comfort, though. Stylish rooms are luxuriously outfitted with soft sheets of washable Egyptian cotton, down pillows, plush cotton robes, and natural bath products, while a spacious desk leaves lots of room for getting down to business. Your key card also activates the lights and temperature control, adjusting both automatically to save energy when you leave your room.

Downstairs, Roots restaurant makes it easy to be green by choosing local produce, naturally raised meats, and sustainable seafood to craft its American fare. So no matter how you look at it, you can feel good about staying here.

Argonaut

495 Jefferson St. (at Hyde St.)

Phone: 415-563-0800 or 866-415-0704
Web: www.argonauthotel.com
Prices: $$

239 Rooms

13 Suites

David Phelps/Kimpton Hotels

Over the decades, the area known as Fisherman's Wharf has slowly morphed from a rough-and-tumble port into San Francisco's most visited tourist attraction. The Argonaut hotel, lodged in a 1907 waterfront warehouse at The Cannery, recalls the neighborhood's hardworking heritage in its original brick walls and massive wood beams.

Likewise, the interior design takes its cue from the area's rich nautical history. Bold stripes and stars in bright marine blue and yellow spiff up the room décor, and all the modern amenities apply. Many rooms look out over the bay and the historic ships of the San Francisco Maritime National Historical Park, whose visitor center shares space with the hotel.

Kids will love the hotel's proximity to the ships berthed at Hyde Street Pier, the rides at the wildly popular Pier 39, and the tasty chocolate treats at Ghirardelli Square. Exhausted adults will no doubt appreciate the hotel's complimentary wine hour at the end of each day.

Named for Jason's mythical ship, the Argonaut is all about adventure. After you've explored all there is to see at Fisherman's Wharf, the Powell-Hyde cable car line (just steps from the hotel's door) will take you on new adventures.

Bohème

C3

444 Columbus Ave. (bet. Green & Vallejo Sts.)

Phone: 415-433-9111
Web: www.hotelboheme.com
Prices: $$

15 Rooms

Hotel Bohème

This quaint boutique hotel at the foot of Telegraph Hill in the heart of North Beach takes its inspiration from the bohemian Beat Generation of the 1950s. And well it might, as poet Allen Ginsberg once slept here. Steps away you'll find Vesuvio Café and City Lights Bookstore (founded by poet Lawrence Ferlinghetti), two hangouts still haunted by Beat spirits.

Built in the 1880s and rebuilt after the earthquake, the Victorian structure has been nicely adapted to its current role. Its 15 rooms reflect a certain 1950s countercultural style in their bright colors and eclectic furniture; they are small, romantic, and meticulously clean. Whether you pick a "cozy," "comfortable," or "inviting" room, rest assured that they are all dressed with queen beds, antique armoires, and private baths. About half of them face Columbus Avenue, which makes for good people-watching, but not much peace and quiet. The surrounding neighborhood is great for strolling and sipping coffee; from here you can walk up Telegraph Hill to Coit Tower and explore up and down the Filbert Steps.

The courteous staff at the Hotel Bohème is glad to help make reservations for restaurants, theater performances, and tours.

Four Seasons

757 Market St. (bet. Third & Fourth Sts.)

Phone: 415-633-3000 or 800-819-5053
Web: www.fourseasons.com
Prices: $$$$

231 Rooms

46 Suites

Mary Nichols/Four Seasons San Francisco

Sightseeing may be the only reason to leave the Four Seasons San Francisco, which occupies the first 12 stories of a residential high-rise in the Yerba Buena Arts District. Almost everything else you could wish for lies within the hotel's walls.

Start with the Sports Club/L.A., accessible from the fourth floor. Open to hotel guests, this huge facility has it all: a state-of-the-art gym, exercise studios, a full basketball court, and a junior Olympic-size pool. This is also where you'll find the cocoon-like spa, where signature treatments promise to detoxify and de-stress.

On the fifth floor lobby, Seasons restaurant serves Californian-inspired cuisine for breakfast, lunch, and dinner; while the clubby bar and lounge specializes in small plates and cocktails.

Art is everywhere, as the hotel showcases throughout its public spaces a considerable collection of paintings, sculpture, and ceramics by Bay Area artists. Rooms, as they ascend from the 6th to the 17th floor, offer more and more stunning views of the city. Generously sized, accommodations are done in restful tones with floor-to-ceiling windows. Young guests are welcomed with milk and cookies and child-size bathrobes.

InterContinental

B3

888 Howard St. (at 5th St.)

Phone: 415-616-6500 or 888-811-4273
Web: www.intercontinentalsanfrancisco.com
Prices: $$$

536 Rooms

14 Suites

Rien van Rijthoven/InterContinental Hotels

Contemporary in style and voluminous in size, the InterContinental ranks as one of the city's most sumptuous hotels. The eye-catching landmark pierces the SoMa skyline with its 32-story blue glass tower, and is equally sought out by those traveling on business and pleasure.

The former make good use of the two formal ballrooms and 21 meeting rooms, for a total of 43,000 square feet of flexible meeting space. They also appreciate the hotel's 24-hour business services and close proximity to the Moscone Convention Center.

Leisure travelers get fired up about glorious rooms appointed in rich wood and marble. Large picture windows frame the San Francisco skyline in all its glory. And who wouldn't like the full-service I-Spa and indoor lap pool on the sixth floor?

Down on the lobby level, grappa is the signature cocktail at Bar 888, while local products star in the contemporary American cuisine served at the stellar restaurant Luce (pronounced LOO-chay; Italian for "light").

In these days when recorded phone messages are the norm, the InterContinental offers guests the luxury of pushing a button on their room phone and connecting directly to a customer service manager.

The Mosser

B2

54 4th St. (bet. Market & Mission Sts.)

Phone: 415-986-4400 or 800-227-3804
Web: www.themosser.com
Prices: $

166 Rooms

The Mosser

In the hip SoMa district, this family-owned boutique hotel hits a high note with its own recording studio. The only hotel in San Francisco to offer this amenity, The Mosser caters to musicians and media pros with first-rate digital and analog technology in the Studio Paradiso.

There's plenty here to lure non-musicians as well. Within a two-block radius, you can walk to Yerba Buena Gardens and the SF Museum of Modern Art, the Moscone Convention Center, Westfield Centre mall, and the cable car line to Fisherman's Wharf.

With all that action nearby, you might fear that rooms here would be noisy. Happily, this charming 1913 Victorian structure has been retrofitted with double-pane windows to screen out the din. To ensure complete peace, reserve a less expensive room facing the courtyard. The clean, crisp décor includes platform beds, whitewashed walls, and geometrically-patterned carpet for a comfortable Danish-modern effect. Some rooms feature lovely bay windows with window seats that overlook the street; all are equipped with ceiling fans.

Though all guests at The Mosser enjoy very affordable rates, if you're on a strict budget book one of the 54 economical rooms that share a bath.

Palace

2 New Montgomery St. (at Market St.)

Phone: 415-512-1111 or 888-625-5144
Web: www.sfpalace.com
Prices: $$$$

519 Rooms

34 Suites

Palace Hotel

Having celebrated its 100th anniversary in 2009, the Palace reigns as the grand dame of downtown hotels. During its long history, the hotel has entertained such notables as Queen Victoria, Italian inventor Guglielmo Marconi, and President Woodrow Wilson (who gave his League of Nations speech in the Garden Court). Originally built in 1875, the property was destroyed in the 1906 earthquake. The year 1909 marked the unveiling of the new Palace; its centerpiece was the Garden Court, crowned by a stunning leaded-glass dome and flanked by a double row of Italian marble columns. Today you can take breakfast, lunch, brunch, or afternoon tea in this resplendent space, which drips with Austrian crystal chandeliers.

For its anniversary, the hotel upgraded its 553 guestrooms with 37-inch LCD flat screen TVs. Mahogany furniture–including a large work desk–and creamy tones with federal blue accents set a traditional scene in rooms that all boast 14-foot-high ceilings and windows that open.

Classic cocktails are in good company downstairs in Maxfield's Pied Piper Bar, which showcases a mural of the Pied Piper of Hamelin painted for the 1909 reopening by American illustrator Maxfield Parrish.

Palomar

12 4th St. (at Market St.)

Phone: 415-348-1111 or 866-373-4941
Web: www.hotelpalomar-sf.com
Prices: **$$$**

179 Rooms

16 Suites

David Phelps/Kimpton Hotels

Touting a theme of "art in motion," the Palomar flashes its bohemian spirit on the 5th through the 8th floors of a landmark 1908 building. Art is everywhere you look here, on the wall, in niches and nooks, even on the lobby floor—where the parquet displays a trompe l'oeil pattern suggesting the work of M.C. Escher.

In the rooms, taupe alligator-print carpeting lies underfoot, and unexpected bursts of color enliven the contemporary ambience. Other modern day comforts may include in-room spa services, complimentary newspapers, and even a companion goldfish can be delivered to the guest rooms. Downstairs, a recent update has rendered the famed Fifth Floor restaurant a stylish spot to dine on contemporary cuisine.

Located where 4th Street meets Market, the hotel couldn't be better situated. Art museums, shopping, and the Moscone Convention Center are all an easy stroll away. The concierge can direct you to the best of the nearby arts, while the new "What's in Store?" program highlights promotions from stores such as Bloomingdale's, Nordstrom, and Adidas. Packets filled with special savings coupons are available in all the guestrooms to carry with you while you shop.

St. Regis

125 3rd St. (at Mission St.)

Phone: 415-284-4000 or 877-787-3447
Web: www.stregis.com
Prices: $$$$

214 Rooms

46 Suites

Joe Fletcher

The fact that the lobby of the St. Regis was conceived by acclaimed Toronto interior design studio Yabu Pushelberg should clue you in to the level of luxury you'll experience here. A neutral palette of beige and gray forms the backdrop for the striated Zebrano wood and Italian travertine marble of the lobby. As you enter the soaring lobby, a 16-foot open fireplace catches your eye. From there it's all sleek lines and contemporary art installations.

A landmark 40-story high rise designed by Skidmore, Owings, and Merrill, this building houses the hotel on its first 20 floors, and condominiums above. Next door is the San Francisco Museum of Modern Art; across the street sit all the attractions of Yerba Buena Gardens.

Spacious rooms and suites overlook Yerba Buena Park, or have expansive city views. Exquisite finishes and unique design features pair with Pratesi linens and a touchscreen on the nightstand that controls the room's temperature, curtains, and lighting.

Remède Spa recently introduced customized treatments—does the Stillness Ritual or a Four Hand Massage sound tempting? For dining, Chef Hiro Sone's modern fusion cuisine delights palates downstairs at the scrumptious Ame.

Vitale

8 Mission St. (bet. Steuart St. & The Embarcadero)

Phone: 415-278-3700 or 888-890-8688
Web: www.hotelvitale.com
Prices: **$$$**

180 Rooms

20 Suites

Cesar Rubio

Flagship of the Joie de Vivre Hospitality Group, the Vitale occupies a prime piece of real estate across the street from the Ferry Building–its marketplace teeming with gourmet delights–and the elegant Embarcadero promenade. All the attractions and eateries of Market Street, Rincon Hill, and the Financial District are easily accessible from the hotel.

An understated luxury permeates the public spaces. Rich wood paneling, rough-hewn stone columns, large softly curtained windows, and sleek furnishings create a Scandinavian modern aspect in the lobby. Luminous and well-soundproofed rooms wear soothing tones that play off the natural light that streams in from large windows. Ask for a water view room, and you'll look out on San Francisco Bay by day, and an awesome silhouette of the Bay Bridge all lit up by night.

Since the hotel's name translates to "vitality" in Italian, you'll want to save time for a trip to the YMCA next door (guests get free passes), then to the penthouse spa to unwind. Your pets will be equally pampered here with special toys and treats. When it's time to eat, you need go no farther than the hotel lobby for stylish Italian fare at Americano restaurant.

W - San Francisco

181 3rd St. (at Howard St.)

Phone: 415-777-5300
Web: www.whotels.com
Prices: **$$$**

404 Rooms

W San Francisco

Part of a hotel chain that is known for its innovative, eclectic, and contemporary ambience, the W San Francisco finds a fitting and well-situated home in the hip and artsy enclave that is the SoMa district.

Each of the recently redesigned rooms boasts a panorama of the city, along with such Asian-inspired details as platform beds, Chinese checkers, and origami butterflies. Signature pillow-top mattresses and a Sweet Dreams pillow menu assure comfort when you turn in for the night, and window nooks make great places to take in the cityscape or curl up with a good book. Lemon and sage bath amenities come courtesy of the hotel's 5,000-square foot Bliss Spa.

The octagonal, three-story Living Room, as W calls their lobby, has been refreshed with eye-catching artwork and textured walls. Comfy seating around a redesigned modern fireplace offers a hip spot to meet and greet, while live DJ music entertains from Wednesday through Saturday evenings. Lighting colors change throughout the evening, adding another dimension to this airy public space.

Those wanting to explore more than the hotel are walking distance from the Moscone Convention Center, several museums, and shopping on Market St.

Claremont Resort & Spa

C2

41 Tunnel Rd., Berkeley

Phone: 510-843-3000 or 800-551-7266
Web: www.claremontresort.com
Prices: $$$

263 Rooms

16 Suites

Bob Bryant Photography

Surrounded by 22 lovely landscaped acres in the hills overlooking San Francisco Bay, this gleaming, white, castle-like edifice has been pampering guests since 1915. The grand tradition of 19th century resort spas continues here today, as the Claremont fulfills its promise to wrap guests in elegance.

If you like lodgings with plenty of activity, the Claremont is for you. Start with the fitness facility, where weight equipment, aerobics classes, and personal training are available. Then there are the ten tennis courts (six of which are lit for evening play), and two heated pools—one dedicated to lap swimming, the other to recreation. For families, the hotel features a Kids Club, with babysitting services, games, movie nights, and other activities tailored to the young set.

Dining options include the Paragon Bar and Café, where live jazz entertains guests on Friday and Saturday nights. For a more refined experience, Meritage overlooks much of the Easy Bay. Chef Josh Thomsen's seasonal Californian cuisine keeps up with the posh surroundings.

Accommodations offer three degrees of comfort, all luxurious. One caveat: request a quiet room since some of them face a loud refuse area.

Lafayette Park

B1

3287 Mt. Diablo Blvd. (bet. Carol Ln. & Pleasant Hill Rd.), Lafayette

Phone: 925-283-3700 or 877-283-8787
Web: www.lafayetteparkhotel.com
Prices: $$

138 Rooms

Lafayette Park

Sister property to the Stanford Park hotel, the Lafayette Park displays all the splendor of a French château, just off the I-24 freeway. Indeed, that's what this stately structure, with its mansard roofs and turrets, brings to mind.

Beginning with the three-story domed lobby, common areas exude elegance. Wings of the hotel surround a lovely central courtyard, ideal for relaxing to the sound of a trickling fountain. Stucco walls frame the tranquil outdoor heated pool, which is flanked on one end by a small full-service spa, and on the other by a well-equipped fitness room.

Traditional American style defines the oversized guestrooms, decked out with cherrywood furnishings, granite vanity countertops, and ample work desks; many rooms have fireplaces and vaulted ceilings. Beware bargain room rates; you get what you pay for here (for a few more dollars a night you can ensure that you overlook the courtyard). Friendly service takes on a laid-back California attitude, and occasionally misses the mark, but for high style and comfort, the Lafayette Park stands out as a welcome upscale alternative to the corporate chain hotels that predominate in this area.

Casa Madrona

A3

801 Bridgeway, Sausalito

Phone: 415-332-0502 or 800-288-0502
Web: www.casamadrona.com
Prices: $$$

63 Rooms

Casa Madrona Hotel & Spa

Climbing up Sausalito's hillside from the waterfront, Casa Madrona envelops the best of old and new within a charming complex well-situated for exploring both San Francisco and the northern wine country. Of course, Sausalito affords ample opportunities of its own for waterfront dining and shopping in chic boutiques.

Accommodations, from historic suites to contemporary rooms, satisfy a range of tastes. Highest in terms of vantage point, the 1885 Casa Madrona mansion crowns the complex, offering bewitching bay views. Victorian style pervades the rooms; most romantic are the bay view chambers furnished with wood-burning stoves and private, flower-bedecked balconies.

A covey of quaint cottages have been built into the hillside since 1976. Connected by brick pathways lined with flowers and waterfalls, these rooms may be either contemporary or historic in décor. Last but not least, ultramodern rooms populate the newest wing of the hotel. Four-poster king-sized beds and large, luxurious bathrooms with oversized soaking tubs fill these rooms.

When you're not in your room, you can treat yourself to a rejuvenating session at the hotel's spa, and fine Northern Italian dishes at Poggio.

Cavallo Point

601 Murray Circle (at Fort Baker), Sausalito

Phone: 415-339-4700 or 888-651-2003
Web: www.cavallopoint.com
Prices: $$$$

142 Rooms

Kodiak Greenwood

Some hotels pin their appeal on history, others on their setting, while some tout their eco-friendly efforts. Cavallo Point boasts all of these enticements and more. On the grounds of Fort Baker, this lodge-like property offers incredible views of the Golden Gate Bridge, the bay, and the city skyline.

Rooms seesaw between classic and contemporary. The former are housed in the original fort buildings, while the latter occupy new structures. None of the facilities are air-conditioned, but who needs it when constant bay breezes cool the site? Meals at Murray Circle restaurant feature outstanding Californian cuisine, while more casual fare can be had at Farley Bar. Aside from eating, guests can visit the healing arts center and spa or enroll in the on-site cooking school. There's a complimentary shuttle to the center of Sausalito, but for those craving more exercise, the surrounding Marin Headlands contain a web of hiking trails.

In addition to the normal hotel taxes, Cavallo Point levies an extra fee on its guests. This money goes toward the operation of Golden Gate National Recreation Area, in which the property is located. To save a few bucks, insist on self versus valet parking.

The Inn Above Tide

30 El Portal (at Bridgeway), Sausalito

Phone: 415-332-9535 or 800-893-8433
Web: www.innabovetide.com
Prices: **$$$**

29 Rooms

The Inn Above Tide

Every room in this bayfront beauty boasts spectacular water views that extend across to San Francisco, Alcatraz, and Angel Island. As you go up the price scale, king rooms add gas fireplaces, while accommodations in the deluxe category feature private decks that extend out over the bay and provide comfy teak chairs for waterside reflection.

Standard amenities encompass plush robes and slippers, Bvlgari toiletries, and DVD players with access to the hotel's film library. Another thoughtful touch, each sandy-toned room comes with a pair of binoculars for honing in on the scenery. And if that's not enough, a complimentary continental breakfast is served in the guest lounge adjacent to the small lobby—or the staff will deliver it to your room, if you prefer.

At happy hour, wine and cheese are on tap, gratis of course! A short menu of in-room spa services can be arranged for a fee.

The city is just a short ferry ride away, but there's plenty to keep you occupied in Sausalito. Stroll the waterfront and check out the shops, then have a leisurely lunch in one of the bayside restaurants. The inn's concierge can arrange a host of other activities, including biking, boating, and wine tours.

Nick's Cove

A1

23240 Hwy. 1 (near Miller Park), Marshall

Phone: 415-663-1033
Web: www.nickscove.com
Prices: $$$$

9
Rooms

3
Suites

Val Atkinson

You just got elbowed (again) on the sidewalk. Someone haggled you for your spare change. And the last thing that lit up for you was the elevator button. Sounds like you need to get out of the city—but where? Nick's Cove. Close enough to San Francisco and the Bay Area for a quickie getaway, Nick's Cove feels a million miles away from the hustle and bustle. The best part? The only tweet you'll hear is the sound of seabirds.

Perched on Highway One, half an hour south of Bodega Bay, Nick's has 12 charming cottages with a romantic fishing village feel. Hear the lapping of the bay from your cottage or enjoy the scene from your Adirondack chair on your deck. When it's high tide, bayside decks stretch out over the water. Relaxing with a cup of coffee or glass of wine and listening to the sea birds and the gentle waves will surely wash away any thoughts of inboxes or deadlines.

Wake up to freshly baked goodies (or whatever else your heart desires) with breakfast delivered straight to your cottage. Lunch and dinner are available in the waterside restaurant.

Sure, there's plenty to do in this gorgeous part of Cali, but with this gentle pace, you might never want to leave.

The Ritz-Carlton, Half Moon Bay

1 Miramontes Point Rd. (at Hwy. 1), Half Moon Bay

Phone: 650-712-7000 or 800-241-3333
Web: www.ritzcarlton.com/hmb
Prices: **$$$$**

239 Rooms

22 Suites

Mark Norberg

Overlooking miles of rugged Pacific coastline from its bluff-top perch 30 miles south of San Francisco, The Ritz-Carlton, Half Moon Bay presents a convincing argument for leaving the city.

Start with the public spaces, where plush furnishings, large stone fireplaces, and a collection of fine art recall the grand seaside lodges of the 19th century. All of this, however, pales before the magnificent ocean views, seen through floor-to-ceiling windows.

Then there are the accommodations, done in subdued tones so as not to distract from the scenery. Of the total number, two-thirds of the rooms have coastal views, and from every one you can see the green fairways of the hotel's golf links. Marble bathrooms and feather beds with down duvets are standard amenities.

Follow the path to the secluded beach, where relaxing is de rigueur. Beyond the beach, six lighted tennis courts, jogging trails, a basketball half court, and two oceanside golf courses ensure you'll never be bored. That's not to mention the fitness facility and the lavish spa.

With all this activity, you're bound to work up an appetite. Take care of that with tasty Californian cuisine at Navio—along with an ocean view, naturally.

Rosewood Sand Hill

2825 Sand Hill Rd. (at I-280), Menlo Park

Phone: 650-561-1500 or 888-767-3966
Web: www.rosewoodsandhill.com
Prices: $$$$

91 Rooms

32 Suites

Rosewood Hotels & Resorts

It might be possible to have the best of both worlds after all, or at least while staying at Rosewood Sand Hill. This luxury resort is just minutes off I-280 in Silicon Valley, but its serene setting on 16 sprawling acres with views of the nearby Santa Cruz Mountains feels a million miles away from it all.

The resort blends a laid-back Californian ranch style with a contemporary elegance. The accommodations are decorated with soothing earth tones, and amenities (king beds, spacious desks, walk-in closets) are especially thoughtful. Bigger is always better when it comes to bathrooms, and these modern chrome-fitted spaces with large marble tubs and oversized showers don't disappoint.

The grounds are immaculate, and courtyard gardens and landscaped patios are a pleasant buffer between resort buildings. Downtime is cherished, especially at the state-of-the-art Sense Spa and beautiful outdoor heated pool. The garden view fitness center is especially well appointed, and after those feel-good endorphins kick in, treat yourself to a trinket at high-end Stephen Silver jewelry.

Madera is a hugely beloved destination unto itself for its locally-inspired, wood-fired cuisine.

Stanford Park

100 El Camino Real (at Sand Hill Rd.), Menlo Park

Phone: 650-322-1234 or 866-241-2431
Web: www.stanfordparkhotel.com
Prices: **$$$**

134 Rooms

29 Suites

Stanford Park Hotel

In contrast to the Spanish-inspired archways and red tile roofs of Stanford University, the Stanford Park hotel, located just adjacent, stands out with its dark cedar shingles and crisp white trim. English Colonial is the style displayed by this four-story lodging, which makes a convenient retreat for university visitors.

Spacious and residential in feel, sparkling clean guest rooms flaunt a traditional ambience—cultivated by vaulted ceilings, granite fireplaces, and canopied beds in many of them. Courtyard rooms also have vaulted ceilings and views of the manicured gardens or the heated lap pool. Spa robes, CD players, and coffeemakers number among the many room amenities, and the on-site gym sees to your fitness needs.

When happy hour rolls around, drop by the Lounge at the Park for a classic cocktail or a glass of wine—from California, of course. A menu of small plates will tide you over until dinner. Then it's off to the hotel's Menlo Grill for casual American cuisine served in a cozy contemporary setting.

Antiques and museum-quality objets d'art grace the lobby, which contains a library of literary masterpieces for guests' use—a nod to the hotel's erudite neighbor.

Cypress

10050 S. De Anza Blvd. (at Stevens Creek Blvd), Cupertino

Phone: 408-253-8900 or 800-499-1408
Web: www.thecypresshotel.com
Prices: **$$**

224 Rooms

David Phelps/Kimpton Hotels

You can count on the Kimpton Hotel group to deliver luxury, and the Cypress is no exception. You get the idea when you stroll through the entrance colonnade, where urns hold sculpted topiaries, and clusters of comfortable seating invite you to relax.

In the rooms, bold contemporary style echoes the creative spirit of Silicon Valley in polka dot wallpaper, striped drapery fabric, and bright sculptural headboards. Yet warm colors soothe the psyche, and new beds fitted with Frette linens cushion the body. A morning newspaper arrives at your door with the hotel's compliments—as does a nightly wine reception and a 24-hour fitness facility.

Being in the heart of Silicon Valley, the Cypress provides ample space for meetings—5,000 square feet to be exact. The Parkview Ballroom boasts an adjoining patio perfect for cocktail receptions. When it's time to get down to business, the Boardroom accommodates 25 for private meetings, and a second ballroom can be subdivided to provide more space. Catering and room service are provided by the adjacent Park Place restaurant, whose recently renovated dining room is a stylish oasis of neutral tones and fresh American cuisine.

De Anza

E3

233 W. Santa Clara St. (bet. Almaden Blvd. & Notre Dame Ave.), San Jose

Phone: 408-286-1000 or 800-843-3700
Web: www.hoteldeanza.com
Prices: $$

80 Rooms

20 Suites

Alex Johnson

Recognizable by its pink façade, the Hotel De Anza provides pleasant downtown San Jose digs for both business and leisure travelers. A neutral palette and blonde wood furniture warm the bedrooms without overdoing it. With such exquisite attention to detail including two TVs, three phones, and a DVD/VCR (videos are complimentary), finding a comfortable yet stylish room here shouldn't be a problem. On the lower level, the business center offers a range of services, and the hotel can accommodate meetings of up to 70 people. In the rooms, a large glass-topped desk ensures adequate work space.

La Pastaia restaurant, off the lobby, serves Italian cuisine in a colorful osteria setting. Even more attractive is the Hedley Club Lounge with its sophisticated art deco design—an ideal spot for a cocktail. And lest you go hungry, cookies and fresh fruit are available throughout the day in the comfortable pastel-hued lobby; purified ice and water are on tap on each floor above. In fact, the De Anza even features a "Raid Our Pantry" service offering sandwiches and snacks to satisfy those late-night munchies.

Last but not least, your petite pet–15 pounds or less–can accompany you here.

Valencia

D3

355 Santana Row (bet. Olin Ave. & Tatum Ln.), San Jose

Phone: 408-551-0010 or 866-842-0100
Web: www.hotelvalencia-santanarow.com
Prices: $$$

196 Rooms

16 Suites

Hotel Valencia

A plethora of shopping, dining, and entertainment options lie just outside your door when you check into this gracious hacienda, set smack in the middle of Santana Row. Shopping is the draw for many of the guests here, but young Silicon Valley business types also find the Valencia a fitting and well-located haven.

Contemporary Cal-Med describes the hotel's shiny style, including the spacious third floor lobby, which feels like a lounge with its low lighting, comfy couches, and hidden nooks. Service is friendly and informal, in keeping with a young Californian sensibility.

Whether your stay is for business or pleasure, you'll find ample room in the well-kept accommodations that sport plenty of counter space for the paper chase, as well as a leather club chair and ottoman for chilling out. Soundproofing is a minus; light sleepers may be bothered by hallway noise or clamor from the street outside.

Best perks? The complimentary breakfast served at the glorious open air restaurant, and the sunny rooftop pool. On the seventh floor, Cielo lounge serves up impressive Silicon Valley views with its cocktails, a buzzing happy hour spot in warm weather.

Auberge du Soleil

B1

180 Rutherford Hill Rd. (off the Silverado Trail), Rutherford

Phone: 707-963-1211 or 800-348-5406
Web: www.aubergedusoleil.com
Prices: **$$$$**

31 Rooms

21 Suites

Auberge du Soleil

Olives aren't the only things that thrive on the sunlit slopes of Rutherford Hill. Tucked in among the silvery trees are the cottages of the "Inn of the Sun," a favorite Napa Valley hideaway that has been flourishing for 25 years.

Over the years, the property has catered increasingly to well-to-do sybaritic visitors. Auberge du Soleil opened with its much-acclaimed restaurant in 1981; the hotel was added a few years later. Then came the spa in 2000. Here, the valley's signature product is pressed into service for signature treatments such as a grape seed crush body exfoliation. Unlike many hotel spas, this one is open exclusively to resort guests.

Scrambling down the hillsides, sophisticated rooms and suites all occupy cottages with private terraces and surroundings that could just as well be Mediterranean. King, or Maison, rooms measure 520 square feet and feature fireplaces and large bathrooms with luxurious soaking tubs. Suites at least double that space, adding a separate living room, a dining table, butler's pantry, and full-size refrigerator.

Toasting the setting sun with a glass of Napa Valley wine on the restaurant's breezy terrace is a wine country must before you leave.

AVIA Napa

1450 1st St. (at School St.), Napa

Phone: 707-224-3900
Web: www.aviahotels.com
Prices: $$

83 Rooms

58 Suites

Alex Hayden

If you're craving a taste of the wine country but not feeling the farmhouse vibe, AVIA Napa is the hotel for you. This urbane hideaway is perfect for city slickers who wish to enjoy the wine, food, and vistas of Napa without leaving their chic city lifestyles behind. Set in downtown Napa, AVIA offers a different slant on the wine country lifestyle. You won't look out over vineyards, but you can hit up the famous Oxbow Public Market for tasty provisions or take a short stroll to visit the shops, galleries, and award-winning restaurants of this culinary capital.

There's no need to go far for good food though, since AVIA's Kitchen and Wine Bar serves a yummy breakfast buffet and offers sophisticated, locally sourced cuisine at dinner. The Terrace, outfitted with porch swings and a fire pit, is plain heavenly for sipping a glass of wine.

AVIA is distinctly Californian, offering a countrified chic design in its public spaces. Where else would you find a farmhouse-type table reception area juxtaposed with bordello-style antique mirrors and red velvet seating? The rooms and suites flaunt a more modern approach and are accented with soothing earth tones and sleek, contemporary styling.

Bardessono

6526 Yount St. (at Finnell Rd.), Yountville

Phone: 707-204-6000 or 877-932-5333
Web: www.bardessono.com
Prices: $$$$

62 Suites

Sammy Todd Dyess

What's greener than grape vines in Napa? Bardessono, a 62-room hotel that stands out as a feat of eco-engineering. Constructed with 100,000 square feet of salvaged wood, the hotel uses photovoltaic solar collectors to create electricity, and geothermal wells to heat the rooms and water. Motion sensors turn off lights when guests are not in residence; settings are automatically restored when they return. Stone paths lined with flowering plants meander between the low-rise buildings that compose the complex.

Guest suites are tranquil sanctuaries, well-appointed with organic cotton bed linens, deep soaking tubs, and private patios or balconies. The carefully thought-out design places a comfy sitting area in front of the gas fireplace and the flat screen TV. Bathrooms conceal a massage table for in-room spa treatments, but there's also a full-service spa for those who desire a more in-depth experience.

For exercise, you can swim in the rooftop pool, or use one of the complimentary bicycles to explore the valley. And while the hotel lies within an easy walk of some stellar restaurants, you won't go wrong if you stay on-site to dine on contemporary Cali fare in the main restaurant.

The Carneros Inn

4048 Sonoma Hwy., Napa

Phone: 707-299-4900 or 888-400-9000
Web: www.thecarnerosinn.com
Prices: $$$$

76 Rooms

10 Suites

Mark Hundley

Located at the southern gateway to the Napa Valley, the Carneros wine region wins raves for sparking wine, chardonnay, and pinot noir. The appellation takes its moniker from the Spanish word for "sheep," animals that once grazed on the hillsides where straight rows of grapevines now grow. The inn named for this region fits well into this pastoral setting, its 86 cottages punctuating 27 acres of vineyards. Use of water recycling and geothermal heating and cooling systems for all of the guest accommodations respect the local environment.

The property is set up like a small village, with many gardens and paths crisscrossing the site. Walking is the preferred manner of transportation to get to the spa, the meeting halls, or any of the three restaurants. The latter include the Hilltop dining room, the casual Boon Fly Café, and Farm, which gathers its ingredients from the surrounding farms and ranches.

Natural light bathes tastefully decorated cottages, where Italian bedding and wood-burning fireplaces set the scene for a tranquil stay. In the bathrooms you'll find heated slate floors and deep soaking tubs. Two infinity pools and two hot tubs provide additional places to relax.

Hotel Yountville

6462 Washington St. (at California Dr.), Yountville

Phone: 707-967-7900 or 888-944-2885
Web: www.hotelyountville.com
Prices: **$$$$**

71 Rooms

9 Suites

Hotel Yountville

Considering Yountville's status as a world-class destination for jet-set foodies with first-class taste, the new Hotel Yountville is a good value for well-heeled travelers seeking R&R. City dwellers might especially appreciate the genuinely tranquil vibe: with oak and olive trees shading jasmine-scented grounds, Hotel Yountville seems to respect its wine country surrounds.

Housed in a collection of small river stone-clad buildings, 80 rooms are dressed in Napa Valley chic—read casual but elegant with just a touch of a rustic accent. Your plush four-poster bed rests beneath a vaulted ceiling, and rooms are warmed by gas fireplaces and candles lit at turndown. Contemporary sofas, semi-private patios, and jetted soaking tubs all have an eye toward in-room serenity. Toss in a sprinkling of lavender bath salt and let the vacation begin.

When you tire of your room and feel the need to get out, don the plush robe and make for the spa. The 4,000 square foot relaxation hub has a beautiful outdoor pool and is open exclusively to guests. Enjoy breakfast at the hotel's Hopper Creek Kitchen but plan to go out for dinner: after all, that's probably why you're in Yountville in the first place.

Lavender

2020 Webber Ave. (bet. Yount & Jefferson Sts.), Yountville

Phone: 707-944-1388 or 800-522-4140
Web: www.lavendernapa.com
Prices: $$

8 Rooms

Lavender

Napa Valley finds the south of France at this enticing gray clapboard house, trimmed in bright blue and nestled amid a profusion of lavender and roses. Inside, Provençal prints and vibrant colors create a sunny palette worthy of Avignon.

You'll find joie de vivre in each of the inn's eight spacious rooms, all cheerfully decorated with country charm *à la française*. Two rooms are located in the main house. The remaining six cottage rooms surround the house and garden; each has its own private entrance and patio. After a day of wine tasting or biking around the valley, slip on the comfy robe provided and kick up your feet in front of the gas fireplace in your room. For a true romantic getaway, ask for room No.7; its private patio comes with an outdoor jetted spa tub.

The little things that can add up elsewhere are included here: a buffet breakfast; afternoon wine, tea, and hors d'oeuvres; freshly baked cookies; and chocolates with turndown service. The wraparound porch and the fragrant terrace garden make perfect spots to enjoy your morning coffee or an afternoon glass of wine.

Guests have pool privileges at neighboring Maison Fleurie, also a member of the Four Sisters Inns group.

Maison Fleurie

C3

6529 Yount St. (at Washington St.), Yountville

Phone: 707-944-2056 or 800-788-0369
Web: www.maisonfleurienapa.com
Prices: **$$$**

13 Rooms

Maison Fleurie

Oozing French country charm inside and out, the "Flowering House" makes the perfect romantic wine country getaway. This member of the Four Sisters Inns welcomes guests amid Provençal-inspired fabrics and furnishings, and a huge stone fireplace in the lobby. Constructed in 1849, back when the valley was known for growing walnuts and olives, the rustic main house contains seven of the property's 13 rooms. Elsewhere on the grounds, two Carriage House rooms have private entrances, while those in the Bakery Building boast fireplaces and whirlpool tubs.

Before setting out to explore the valley, whether by car or complimentary mountain bike, you'll need a hearty breakfast. The inn complies with a spread of hot and cold dishes—perhaps a quiche, potato casserole, and soft-boiled eggs, along with fruit, cakes, toast, and English muffins. Drop by the lobby lounge for wine and hors d'oeuvres each evening. A small refrigerator in the common area offers complimentary soft drinks all day.

True to its name, Maison Fleurie abounds in lovely landscaped flora, from the roses that surround the hot tub area, to the grape vines that climb the walls and trellises scattered around the pastoral grounds.

Meadowood

900 Meadowood Ln. (off the Silverado Trail), St. Helena

Phone: 707-963-3646 or 800-458-8080
Web: www.meadowood.com
Prices: **$$$$**

41 Rooms

44 Suites

Meadowood Napa Valley

Serenity prevails in the 85 cottages and lodges nestled on 250 acres of wooded hills off the Silverado Trail. What is now a world-class resort began in the 1960s as a small club for local winemakers. It still doubles as a chic country club for Napa notables, and its décor and ambience say as much.

When there's a chill in the air, guests bunk in secluded cottages, warmed by wood-burning stone fireplaces. White wainscoting and exposed beams lend a bucolic feel, while glorious French doors lead to private decks perfect for soaking in nature's bounty.

The valley's most famed product is celebrated in Meadowood's wine-education program. Lessons begin at the afternoon wine reception, where all guests are invited to a complimentary tasting of two local wines. More in-depth tastings, conducted by the resort's master sommelier, are offered for a fee. But, don't miss an evening at The Restaurant at Meadowood, where the superb cuisine pays homage to the area's farm-to-table tradition.

If you find yourself with time to spare, the grounds also encompass a nine-hole golf course, seven tennis courts, two croquet lawns, two lap pools, and a fitness center and relaxing spa...with its own spa menu!

Milliken Creek Inn & Spa

1815 Silverado Trail, Napa

Phone: 707-255-1197 or 800-835-6112
Web: www.millikencreekinn.com
Prices: $$$

11 Rooms

1 Suite

Milliken Creek Inn & Spa

There are just some times in life when you need to reboot (and no, not your Blackberry or MacBook). Milliken Creek Inn & Spa is the antidote to the hustle and bustle. This quietly charming hotel is right off the Silverado Trail, but tucked away on three lush acres on the banks of the Napa River. Take a seat on the porch, sit by the roaring fireplace, or settle into a feather bed in one of 12 rooms and you'll soon be tssking your multi-tasking ways.

Canopy beds, fireplaces, and tree-shaded private porches with lovely views are just some of the "standard" features of this hotel. It's not just the country charm of the rooms that takes your breath away—the grounds are breathtaking. Have breakfast by the river to the sound of rushing water and singing birds, but be sure to join civilization at the evening wine and cheese Magic Hour. This is no run-of-the-mill social (it is wine country, after all). If the verdant setting hasn't quelled your anxiety, the holistic therapies at the private spa will.

Of course, a whole world exists right outside the grounds, with everything from winery tours and tastings, biking, hot air ballooning, and fine dining. That is, if you ever want to leave.

Napa River Inn

500 Main St. (at 5th St.), Napa

Phone: 877-251-8500
Web: www.napariverinn.com
Prices: $$$

68 Rooms

Napa River Inn

Surrender your car keys at check in at the Napa River Inn, since you won't need to drive anywhere once you're ensconced within this historic property. All of Napa's charms–art galleries, top-notch restaurants, Summer Chef's Markets, and area wineries–are within reasonable distance from this hotel located on the River Walk. The charming Napa Valley Wine Train, which skirts through the countryside vineyards, is also just steps away.

The Napa River Inn is an exquisite, independently owned hotel hidden inside the Napa Mill, a National Registered Landmark built in 1884. This former warehouse shares its special history but it's far from stuck in the past. Guests are treated to luxurious accommodations featuring the finest in everything from high-quality linens to the latest technology.

This intimate property impresses with its bountiful amenities, including four restaurants. Sweetie Pies provides fresh baked goods for complimentary breakfast, Angèle and Napa General Store have the country-chic style down pat, and Celadon shares a worldly cuisine. Feelin' groovy? Silo's Jazz Club is a cool cat's heaven. Imbibed too much chardonnay? Opt for one of 25 treatments at the refreshing spa.

Rancho Caymus Inn

B2

1140 Rutherford Rd. (off Hwy. 29), Rutherford

Phone: 707-963-1777 or 800-845-1777
Web: www.ranchocaymus.com
Prices: $$

25 Rooms

1 Suite

Rancho Caymus Inn

Owned for some 20 years by the Komes family, who runs Flora Springs winery, Rancho Caymus captures the spirit of the early days of Alta California in both its name and its hacienda-style buildings. The name comes from a sprawling *rancho* built on this site in the 1830s, after Spanish general Mariano Vallejo awarded this land to pioneer George Yount (for whom the town of Yountville is christened).

The inn's buildings, each of which bears the name of a historic Napa Valley personality from Robert Louis Stevenson to Black Bart, house one- and two-bedroom suites. Hand-carved black walnut headboards, 100-year-old reclaimed oak ceiling beams, and white stucco walls imbue the accommodations with a sound sense of the past. Standard amenities, such as televisions, air conditioning, a wet bar, and a refrigerator cater to modern comfort. Many of the rooms have beehive fireplaces, and private outdoor balconies or sitting areas. Designed as "split levels," the sleeping areas are set up a step in each room.

Complimentary continental breakfast is served each morning in the main dining room. Like The Rutherford Grill, there are several great restaurants in the immediate area.

Solage

755 Silverado Trail (at Rosedale Rd.), Calistoga

Phone: 707-226-0800 or 866-942-7442
Web: www.solagecalistoga.com
Prices: $$$$

83 Rooms

6 Suites

Spa

Solage Calistoga

There's no place like wine country to indulge in the good life, and Solage capitalizes on what is best about this area. The first property from Auberge Resorts' new Solage Hotels & Resorts brand, this eco-friendly cottage-style resort and spa spreads out over 20 acres off the Silverado Trail.

The resort's 89 rooms are tucked inside bungalows that fashion urban lofts in a pastoral environment. Modern day amenities (flat screen TV, iPod docking station, mini refrigerator) mix with vaulted ceilings, contemporary furniture, polished concrete floors, and semi-private patios. Colors run to leafy greens, and sizes range from one bedroom studios to spacious suites. Each cottage is equipped with a pair of bikes for exploring.

Guests want for little here. There's a large outdoor heated pool flanked by cabanas, and a state-of-the-art fitness center where classes are complimentary. Solbar restaurant serves up healthy Californian cuisine for breakfast, lunch, and dinner. But the pièce de résistance is the resort's 20,000-square-foot spa. And this being Calistoga–a small town with a big reputation for its mineral-rich mud–a visit to the spa's signature Mud Bar is an absolute must.

Villagio Inn & Spa

6481 Washington St., Yountville

Phone: 707-944-8877 or 800-351-1133
Web: www.villagio.com
Prices: $$$

86 Rooms

26 Suites

The Vintage Estate

Tuscan style defines the two-story buildings and the grounds of elegant Villagio, where sybarites want for little. Fluffy duvets, fine linens, and cozy robes make for cushy quarters, swathed in Tuscan gold tones and warmed by fireplaces when it's cold outside. Room rates include a Champagne breakfast, afternoon tea, and Friday evening wine tastings.

Some of the valley's best restaurants are literally steps from the complex, but if intent on an evening indoors, room service can oblige with a Tuscan Carpet Picnic for two. This in-room treat fosters romance with wine country cuisine, candlelight, Italian music, and throw pillows to sit on.

If work is the reason you're here, Villagio accommodates business functions with 26,000 square feet of meeting space—but it's not unusual for break out meetings to take place in the adjacent vineyard or Michael Chiarello's Bottega restaurant.

Indulge yourself at Spa Villagio. This plush 3,000-square foot retreat has separate wings for men and women, and offers Swiss showers, steam and dry saunas, and outdoor thermal soaking tubs. Treatments pamper with everything from a hot stone massage to the signature facial that features a mask of crushed pearls.

Vintage Inn

6541 Washington St., Yountville

Phone: 707-944-1112 or 800-724-8354
Web: www.vintageinn.com
Prices: $$$

72 Rooms

8 Suites

The Vintage Estate

Sharing a 23-acre estate with Villagio, the Vintage Inn is the older of the two, but is no less charming in its Gallic demeanor. A Provençal feel pervades the grounds, abloom in season with lavender and roses. Paths and footbridges connect the two-story French country-style buildings within this intimate complex.

A complimentary bottle of wine welcomes guests to airy rooms with vaulted ceilings, where French antiques, toile de Jouy fabrics, plush robes, and down duvets set the tone for luxurious comfort. Every room boasts a wood-burning fireplace and a bathroom equipped with an oversized whirlpool tub.

A signature of both properties, a lavish Champagne breakfast comes compliments of the house. You won't need lunch after tackling a buffet laden with egg dishes, quiche, salmon mousse, fresh fruit, homemade breads, and pastries. At dinnertime you need only meander Washington Street to sample Yountville's justly famous restaurant lineup, which encompasses Bouchon, The French Laundry, Redd, and Ad Hoc. Michael Chiarello's regional Italian restaurant, Bottega, is right next door at V Marketplace.

For those "aah" moments, guests at Vintage Inn have access to Villagio's Spa.

Duchamp

421 Foss St. (at North St.), Healdsburg

Phone: 707-431-1300 or 800-431-9341
Web: www.duchamphotel.com
Prices: **$$$**

6 Rooms

David Duncan Douglas

French Dada artist Marcel Duchamp was known for his unconventionality, and so this small hotel echoes the artist's spirit by its departure from conventional wine country accommodations. A not-so-well-kept secret within minutes of Healdsburg's downtown plaza, the Duchamp displays a sleek, modern aspect that trumps country charm.

Owner Pat Lenz–an artist herself–and her husband, Peter, named the hotel's six freestanding bungalows after modern artists (the seventh bungalow serves as a reception area). The design of each reflects the style of namesakes such as Picasso and Warhol. The grouping surrounds a heated swimming pool with a sundeck and Jacuzzi.

Each room is large and minimalist in style, with whitewashed walls and decorative murals to add a spark of color. French doors let in natural light, and lead out to a private patio. King beds and down comforters promise a good night's rest; white tiles dress the large bathrooms, which highlight two washbasins and a spacious shower.

Convenient to the wineries of the Russian River, Dry Creek, and Alexander valleys, the hotel offers a unique amenity: the innkeepers will arrange private tastings at nearby Duchamp Winery, which they also own.

El Dorado

D3

405 1st St. W. (at W. Spain St.), Sonoma

Phone: 707-996-3220 or 800-289-3031
Web: www.eldoradosonoma.com
Prices: $$

27 Rooms

Erin Kunkel

Laid out by Mariano Vallejo in 1835, Sonoma Plaza holds a lot of history in its eight acres. Among the historic structures that flank this square, the El Dorado hotel nods to the area's past while furnishing guests with a reasonably priced place to stay in the wine country.

Light and color set the hotel's 27 rooms aglow; the 23 accommodations in the main building, and the four independent bungalows were recently refurbished in a clean simple style. French doors open onto private balconies or terraces and admit a wash of sunlight into the rooms. Some look over the historic plaza; others face the restaurant's terrace, which is shaded by a fig tree. Every Friday evening, the hotel holds a complimentary wine tasting in the lobby, spotlighting wineries from El Dorado Kitchen's extensive wine list.

The property recently applied a range of green initiatives, from using non-toxic cleaning products and environmentally-friendly bath amenities to employing solar panels to collect heat for the small pool. Following suit, the hotel's popular restaurant–El Dorado Kitchen–has formed a partnership with local Benziger Winery Biodynamic Farms to grow organic produce for the seasonal menu.

The Fairmont Sonoma Mission Inn & Spa

C3

100 Boyes Blvd. (bet. Arnold Dr. & Hwy. 12), Sonoma

Phone: 707-938-9000 or 800-441-1414
Web: www.fairmont.com
Prices: $$$

166 Rooms

60 Suites

Spa

The Fairmont Sonoma Mission Inn

Some spas claim to bottle their own oils. Others claim to grow the herbs and flowers used in the treatments, but how many can say that they have their own geo-thermal mineral water source? The Fairmont Mission Inn & Spa has been attracting visitors for years with its healing waters (and the area's pinot noir and pinot grigio aren't bad therapy either). Originally built in 1927, the Inn blends historic flavor with modern niceties. The lobby is a bastion of typical Mission-style architecture with wrought-iron chandeliers, beamed ceilings, and stonework; while the rooms and suites gently echo the historic look.

The *piece de resistance* at this resort is the 40,000-square-foot spa. Those geo-thermal waters are highlighted with a unique bathing ritual, while the treatment menu looks to the region for its inspiration. If you're so inclined, the fitness center is well-equipped to keep you in shape, but with an exceedingly comfortable pool deck and delicious restaurant, you might wish to be a bit more indulgent.

There is enough to (not) do within the resort's lush grounds, but with Sonoma's award-winning vineyards just outside your door, take advantage of the gracious staff's advice.

Farmhouse Inn

A2

7871 River Rd. (at Wohler Rd.), Forestville

Phone: 707-887-3300 or 800-464-6642
Web: www.farmhouseinn.com
Prices: $$$$

6 Rooms

12 Suites

Tai Power Seeff

Make "country" the operative word when visiting the wine country and head for the charming Farmhouse Inn. This gracious getaway has definitely cornered the market on peace and quiet.

Set in an idyllic area of Forestville in the Russian River Valley, the Farmhouse Inn is surrounded by groves of trees and miles of vineyards. Away from it all and offering just eight cottages, two guestrooms in the main house, and eight rooms in the barn, this hideaway is the ultimate retreat. The cottages, with pale yellow and white trim, and impeccable flower beds, exude an Anne of Green Gables charm, while inside they are graciously appointed with a mod rustic style. This isn't your grandfather's farmhouse, so you won't be forsaking any of your city slicker comforts.

The Farmhouse Inn blends down home appeal with sophisticated touches. Farm-fresh breakfasts, locally made and organic bath and beauty products, and cookies and milk delivered to guests each afternoon are among the country charms, while the full-service spa and wine tasting classes with a master sommelier are seriously sophisticated. Also topping the list of luxurious amenities is the Michelin-starred namesake restaurant.

Gaige House Inn

13540 Arnold Dr. (at Railroad St.), Glen Ellen

Phone: 707-935-0237 or 800-935-0237
Web: www.gaige.com
Prices: $$$

12 Rooms

11 Suites

Paul Dyer

Built in the 1890s by Glen Ellen's butcher at the time–a man with the surname of Gaige–this Sonoma County landmark now cossets visitors to the area in luxurious accommodations designed with an Asian flair.

With a full menu of spa services, an expanded continental breakfast (included in the rates), and a lovely heated swimming pool, this new member of the Joie de Vivre Hospitality Group merits a detour off the beaten track. It is located just north of Sonoma, couched amid three acres of lush gardens along Calabazas Creek. The cottage suite that overlooks this creek through its floor-to-ceiling windows features a private deck for reveling in the natural setting. Offering true tranquility, stand-alone Zen suites are the inn's largest, showing off Japanese-inspired elements such as an interior atrium garden and a large granite soaking tub. Standard rooms, all ten of which are located in the main house, bespeak a luxury all their own. In some, tatami mats cover hardwood floors, and rice paper screens decorate the walls; others feature fireplaces.

Unwind and treat yourself to indulgent body treatments such as the Thai herbal poultice massage, enjoyed in your room, or in the Spa Loft.

Honor Mansion

14891 Grove St. (bet. Dry Creek Rd. & Grant St.), Healdsburg

Phone: 707-433-4277 or 800-554-4667
Web: www.honormansion.com
Prices: $$$

13 Rooms

The Honor Mansion

Romance waits behind the façade of this restored 1883 house, located less than a mile away from the tony boutiques, tasting rooms, and fine restaurants lining Healdsburg's downtown plaza. Owners Cathi and Steve Fowler have anticipated guests' every need in the 13 individually decorated rooms and suites. Rooms in the main house vary in size and style, while four separate Vineyard Suites (the priciest accommodations) foster *amore* with king-size beds, gas fireplaces, and private patios complete with your own whirlpool (robes and rubber ducky included). On the four-acre grounds, landscaped with rose gardens and zinfandel vines, you'll find a lap pool, a PGA putting green, bocce and tennis courts, a croquet lawn, and a half basketball court.

Following the Fowlers' hospitable lead, the staff will provide you with a picnic basket and a list of places to pick up picnic fare. They'll also make arrangements for everything from private winery visits to poolside massages. A hearty multicourse breakfast, and an afternoon wine and hors d'ouevres reception are included in the room rate.

On weekends, count on a minimum stay of two nights in low season, and four nights in high season.

Hotel Healdsburg

25 Matheson St. (at Healdsburg Ave.), Healdsburg

Phone: 707-431-2800 or 800-889-7188
Web: www.hotelhealdsburg.com
Prices: $$$$

51 Rooms

4 Suites

Hotel Healdsburg

Natural elements of wine country combine in this three-story garden hotel to create a serene retreat on Healdsburg's town square. Spacious rooms are decorated with soothing wine country tones, Tibetan wool carpets, and pecan wood floors; most have French doors leading to private balconies. Teak platform beds dress in down duvets and Frette linens. In the oversize bathrooms, you'll find Italian glass tile, walk-in showers, separate soaking tubs, and organic bath amenities courtesy of the hotel's full-service spa.

A hearty breakfast comes with your stay. Whether you plan on wine tasting, getting acquainted with the shops and wine bars around the square, or working out in the hotel's fitness room, and relaxing by the olive- and cypress tree-shrouded pool afterwards, the selection of baked goods, smoked salmon, eggs, cereals, and fruit will fortify you for the day's activities.

Dining options are plenty in downtown Healdsburg, but you can eat just as well on-site. Check out the grappa bar in the lobby before retiring to the Dry Creek Kitchen for seasonal Californian fare; or walk down the street to their new sibling and sustainable inn, h2hotel, and grab a bite at Spoonbar.

Kenwood Inn & Spa

10400 Sonoma Hwy. (bet. Kunde Dr. & Kunde Winery Rd.), Kenwood

Phone: 707-833-1293 or 800-353-6966
Web: www.kenwoodinn.com
Prices: $$$$

27 Rooms

2 Suites

J. Nichole Smith

Dreaming of the Mediterranean but can't get away? Book a room at Kenwood Inn & Spa: with a gorgeous garden courtyard and archways trellised with blooms, this vine-hugged, villa-style retreat might be the next best thing.

The 25-room gem feels European through and through with thick draperies, wrought-iron accents, and shutters punctuating heavy doors that open onto, well, *aaaaahhhh*. In fact, it is surprisingly easy to feel cut off from the world at the serene Kenwood Inn. While the rooms are equipped with WiFi for vacation-challenged business types, the hotel isn't about to supply you a desk—or even a TV. Just forget work and concentrate on chilling out. With cozy fireplaces and deep soaking tubs in every spacious room, it's really not that hard.

For those who need an extra nudge in the relaxation department, put on your slippers and plod down to the pump house, with a working water wheel and koi fish swimming about. There you'll find a lovely spa and oak tree-shaded pool. In the mornings, take your coffee and pastries in the charming courtyard; later, join guests only for lunch and supper in the dining room. With such romantic surrounds, you might find it difficult to leave.

Les Mars

D1

27 North St. (bet. Foss St. & Healdsburg Ave.), Healdsburg

Phone: 707-433-4211 or 877-431-1700
Web: www.lesmarshotel.com
Prices: $$$$

16 Rooms

Les Mars

Good things come in small packages, as Les Mars–just off Healdsburg's central square–proves beyond the shadow of a doubt. The hotel only has 16 rooms, but each is a study in old-world elegance. Perhaps your room will wear a classic Parisian décor, draped in warm earth tones and a four-poster canopy bed. Or maybe you prefer a regal red and burgundy palette, with a jetted hydrotherapy soaking tub. There are also chambers in the grand château style, impeccably dressed in French toile underneath 20-foot-tall beamed ceilings. Whatever your preference, in all the rooms you'll revel in period antiques, a gas fireplace, marble bath, and sumptuous Italian linens.

Attention to detail reveals itself in vases of fresh flowers on each floor, Bvlgari bath amenities, and locally produced artisan cheeses offered at the nightly wine reception. The place oozes luxury, from the 17th-century Flemish tapestry that hangs in the lobby to the hand-carved walnut panels and leather-bound books that line the library.

Attention all foodies: Les Mars is ideally situated and is only a few steps from some of the best and most delicious restaurants in Sonoma County.

Madrona Manor

1001 Westside Rd. (at West Dry Creek Rd.), Healdsburg

Phone: 707-433-4231 or 800-258-4003
Web: www.madronamanor.com
Prices: $$$

17 Rooms

5 Suites

Madrona Manor

Built for San Francisco businessman John Paxton, the stately, three-story Victorian mansion has graced this wooded knoll above the vineyards of the Dry Creek Valley since 1881. Whether your pleasure is simply strolling along sun-dappled paths lined with flowers, having an elegant dining experience, or visiting some of California's finest wineries, you will be well-situated to do all of those things here.

Of the 22 handsome rooms on-site, nine are located in the historic landmark mansion itself; all of these have king-size beds and fireplaces. Four large rooms on the second floor boast original antique furniture; two of them have balconies. The remainder of the rooms and suites are scattered around the eight-acre wooded grounds in buildings such as the original carriage house and school house. All accommodations are individually decorated with an eye to Victorian style, and are fitted with pillow-top mattresses and terrycloth robes. To foster tranquility, there are no TVs in any of the rooms.

Guests need not leave the property to find creative contemporary cuisine. Nightly menus are based on market-fresh ingredients, including vegetables, herbs, and fruit from the on-site gardens.

Vintners Inn

B2

4350 Barnes Rd. (at River Rd.), Santa Rosa

Phone: 707-575-7350 or 800-421-2584
Web: www.vintnersinn.com
Prices: $$$

44 Rooms

Vintners Inn

An idyllic wine country retreat just north of Santa Rosa, this small lodging focuses on romance—with weddings frequently held here. There are many charming settings a couple can choose from to tie the knot, given that the four picturesque Tuscan-style structures that compose the Vintners Inn cuddle in the midst of a 90-acre vineyard. And with catering by the acclaimed John Ash & Co. restaurant on-site, it's a sure bet that the food and wine will include some of the best products of the Sonoma Valley.

Cozy nests feathered with down bedding, bathrobes, and a complimentary bottle of wine roost on the two floors of the tile-roofed buildings. All have either private patios or balconies, and second-floor chambers boast vaulted ceilings and exposed wood beams. Windows look out on either the surrounding vineyards or the brick-paved courtyard and central fountain around which the structures are arranged. Rates include a buffet breakfast.

In 2009, Vintner's Inn was awarded the highest honor in the State of California's Green Lodging Program, thanks to the efforts of owners Don and Rhonda Carano (of Ferrari-Carano Winery) in minimizing waste, recycling, and conserving energy.

Peter L. Wrenn/MICHELIN

Indexes

Where to **Eat**

Where to **Stay**

Alphabetical List of Restaurants

A

B

K

L

M

S

Restaurants by Cuisine

Contemporary

Cuban

Eastern European

Ethiopian

Filipino

French

Fusion

Gastropub

Greek

Indian

Indonesian

International

Italian

Japanese

Korean

Latin American

Polish

Portuguese

Seafood

Southern

Spanish

Steakhouse

Thai

Turkish

Vegan

Vegetarian

Vietnamese

Cuisines by Neighborhood

San Francisco

Castro

Civic Center

Financial District

Marina

Marin

Peninsula

WINE COUNTRY

Napa Valley

Starred Restaurants

Within the selection we offer you, some restaurants deserve to be highlighted for their particularly good cuisine. When giving one, two, or three Michelin stars, there are a number of elements that we consider including the quality of the ingredients, the technical skill and flair that goes into their preparation, the blend and clarity of flavours, and the balance of the menu. Just as important is the ability to produce excellent cooking time and again. We make as many visits as we need, so that our readers may be assured of quality and consistency.

A two or three-star restaurant has to offer something very special in its cuisine; a real element of creativity, originality, or "personality" that sets it apart from the rest. Three stars – our highest award – are given to the choicest restaurants, where the whole dining experience is superb.

Cuisine in any style, modern or traditional, may be eligible for a star. Due to the fact we apply the same independent standards everywhere, the awards have become benchmarks of reliability and excellence in over 20 countries in Europe and Asia, particularly in France, where we have awarded stars for 100 years, and where the phrase "Now that's real three-star quality!" has entered into the language.

The awarding of a star is based solely on the quality of the cuisine.

Exceptional cuisine, worth a special journey

One always eats here extremely well, sometimes superbly. Distinctive dishes are precisely executed, using superlative ingredients.

Excellent cuisine, worth a detour

Skillfully and carefully crafted dishes of outstanding quality.

A very good restaurant in its category

A place offering cuisine prepared to a consistently high standard.

Bib Gourmand

This symbol indicates our inspector's favorites for good value. For $40 or less, you can enjoy two courses and a glass of wine or a dessert (not including tax or gratuity).

Under $25

Brunch

Indexes ▶ Brunch

Late Dining

Alphabetical List of Hotels

Peter L. Wrenn / MICHELIN

The Michelin Adventure

It all started with rubber balls! This was the product made by a small company based in Clermont-Ferrand that André and Edouard Michelin inherited, back in 1880. The brothers quickly saw the potential for a new means of transport and their first success was the invention of detachable pneumatic tires for bicycles. However, the automobile was to provide the greatest scope for their creative talents. Throughout the 20th century, Michelin never ceased developing and creating ever more reliable and high-performance tires, not only for vehicles ranging from trucks to F1 but also for underground transit systems and airplanes.

From early on, Michelin provided its customers with tools and services to facilitate mobility and make travelling a more pleasurable and more frequent experience. As early as 1900, the Michelin Guide supplied motorists with a host of useful information related to vehicle maintenance, accommodation and restaurants, and was to become a benchmark for good food. At the same time, the Travel Information Bureau offered travellers personalised tips and itineraries.

The publication of the first collection of roadmaps, in 1910, was an instant hit! In 1926, the first regional guide to France was published, devoted to the principal sites of Brittany, and before long each region of France had its own Green Guide. The collection was later extended to more far-flung destinations, including New York in 1968 and Taiwan in 2011.

In the 21st century, with the growth of digital technology, the challenge for Michelin maps and guides is to continue to develop alongside the company's tire activities. Now, as before,Michelin is committed to improving the mobility of travellers.

MICHELIN TODAY

WORLD NUMBER ONE TIRE MANUFACTURER

- 70 production sites in 18 countries
- 111,000 employees from all cultures and on every continent
- 6,000 people employed in research and development

Moving
for a world

Moving forward means developing tires with better road grip and shorter braking distances, whatever the state of the road.

CORRECT TIRE PRESSURE

RIGHT PRESSURE

- Safety
- Longevity
- Optimum fuel consumption

-0,5 bar

- Durability reduced by 20% (- 8,000 km)

-1 bar

- Risk of blowouts
- Increased fuel consumption
- Longer braking distances on wet surfaces

forward together
where mobility is safer

It also involves helping motorists take care of their safety and their tires. To do so, Michelin organises "Fill Up With Air" campaigns all over the world to remind us that correct tire pressure is vital.

WEAR

DETECTING TIRE WEAR

The legal minimum depth of tire tread is 1.6mm.

Tire manufacturers equip their tire with tread wear indicators, which are small blocks of rubber moulded into the base of the main grooves at a depth of 1.6mm.

Tires are the only point of contact between vehicle and road.

The photo below shows the actual contact zone.

NEW TIRE

WORN TIRE
(1,6 mm tread)

If the tread depth is less than 1.6mm, tires are considered to be worn and dangerous on wet surfaces.

Moving forward
means sustainable mobility

INNOVATION AND THE ENVIRONMENT

By 2050, Michelin aims to cut the quantity of raw materials used in its tire manufacturing process by half and to have developed renewable energy in its facilities. The design of MICHELIN tires has already saved billions of liters of fuel and, by extension, billions of tons of CO2.

Similarly, Michelin prints its maps and guides on paper produced from sustainably managed forests and is diversifying its publishing media by offering digital solutions to make travelling easier, more fuel efficient and more enjoyable!

The group's whole-hearted commitment to eco-design on a daily basis is demonstrated by ISO 14001 certification.

Like you, Michelin is committed to preserving our planet.

Chat with Bibendum

Go to
www.michelin.com/corporate/fr
Find out more about Michelin's
history and the latest news.

QUIZ

Michelin develops tires for all types of vehicles. See if you can match the right tire with the right vehicle…

A 1

B 2

3

C

4

D

5

E

F

6

G 7

Solution : A-6 / B-4 / C-2 / D-1 / E-3 / F-7 / G-5

Notes

Michelin

Notes

Michelin

Notes

Michelin

Notes

Michelin

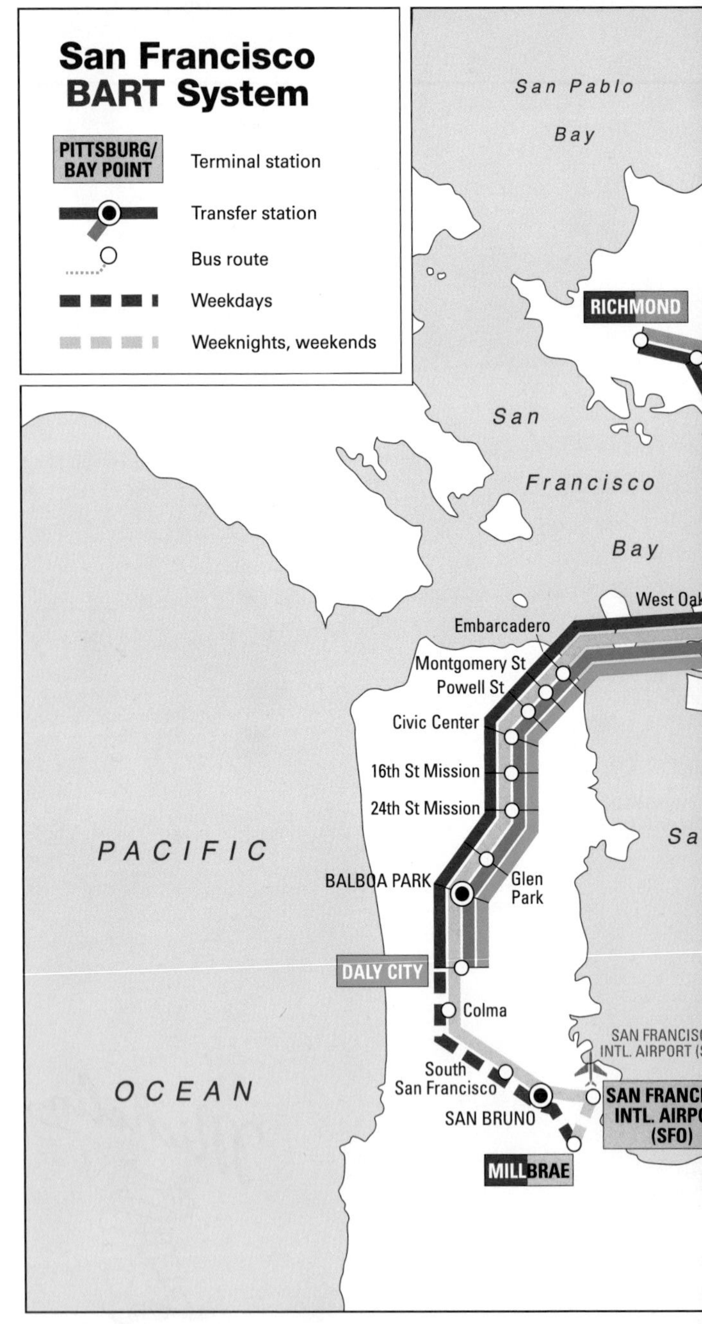
San Francisco
BART System
PITTSBURG/
BAY POINT
Terminal station
Transfer station
Bus route
Weekdays
Weeknights, weekends
San Pablo
Bay
RICHMOND
San
Francisco
Bay
West Oak
Embarcadero
Montgomery St
Powell St
Civic Center
16th St Mission
24th St Mission
PACIFIC
BALBOA PARK
Glen
Park
DALY CITY
Colma
SAN FRANCISC
INTL. AIRPORT (S
South
San Francisco
OCEAN
SAN BRUNO
SAN FRANC
INTL. AIRPO
(SFO)
MILLBRAE

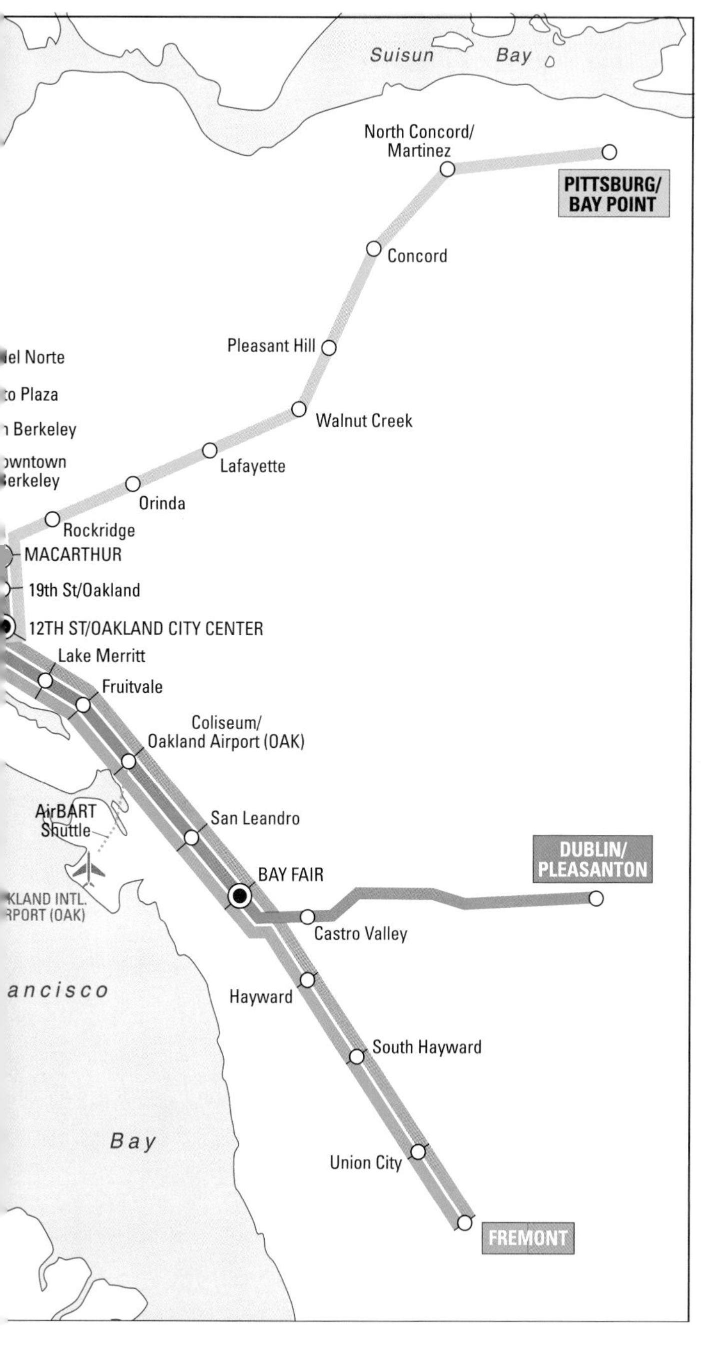

Suisun Bay
North Concord/ Martinez
PITTSBURG/ BAY POINT
Concord
Pleasant Hill
Walnut Creek
Lafayette
Orinda
Rockridge
MACARTHUR
19th St/Oakland
12TH ST/OAKLAND CITY CENTER
Lake Merritt
Fruitvale
Coliseum/ Oakland Airport (OAK)
AirBART Shuttle
San Leandro
BAY FAIR
DUBLIN/ PLEASANTON
Castro Valley
Hayward
South Hayward
Bay
Union City
FREMONT

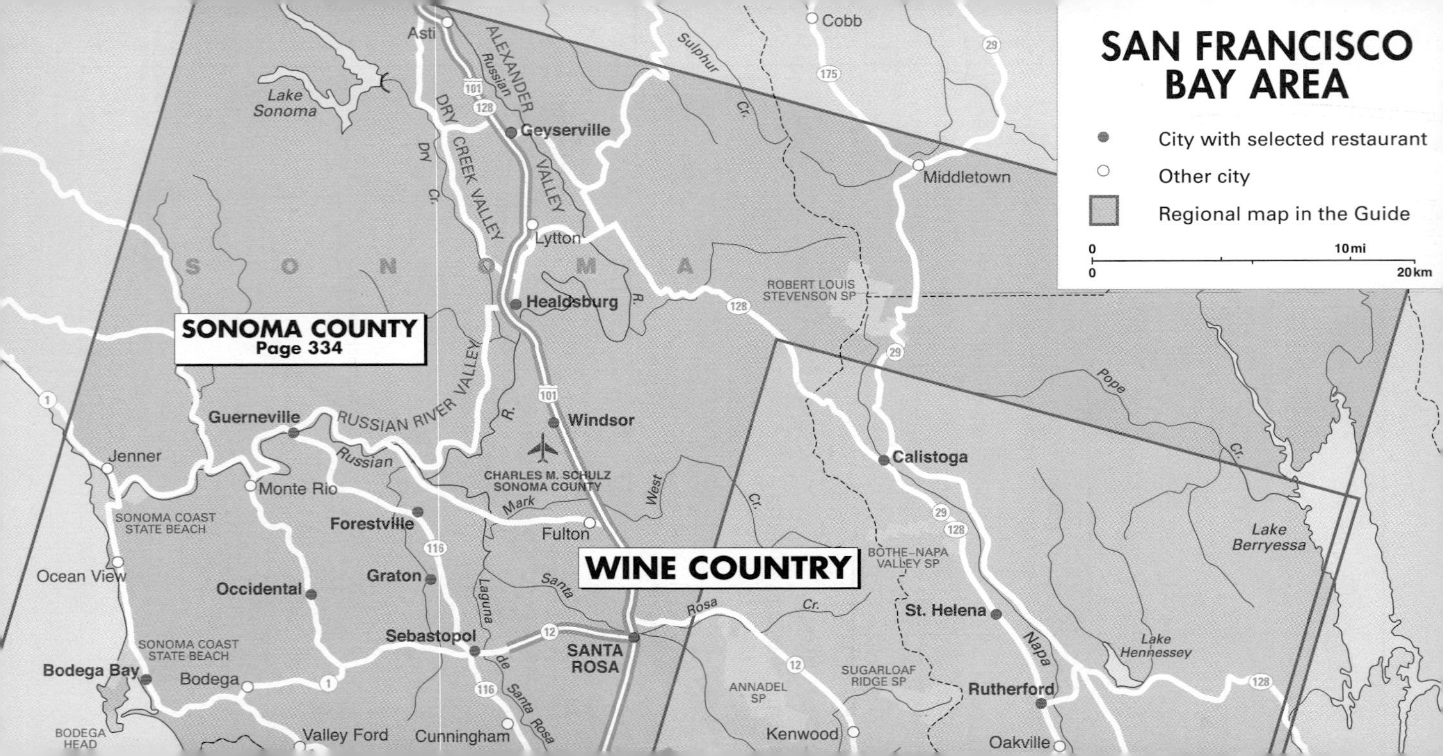

SAN FRANCISCO BAY AREA
City with selected restaurant
Other city
Regional map in the Guide
0
10 mi
0
20 km
SONOMA COUNTY
Page 334
WINE COUNTRY
S O N O M A
Asti
Cobb
Sulphur
Cr.
Lake Sonoma
Russian
ALEXANDER
VALLEY
DRY
CREEK VALLEY
Dry
Cr.
Geyserville
Middletown
Lytton
Healdsburg
R.
ROBERT LOUIS STEVENSON SP
Pope
RUSSIAN RIVER VALLEY
Guerneville
Windsor
Russian
CHARLES M. SCHULZ SONOMA COUNTY
Jenner
Monte Rio
Mark
West
Calistoga
Cr.
SONOMA COAST STATE BEACH
Forestville
Fulton
BOTHE-NAPA VALLEY SP
Lake Berryessa
Ocean View
Graton
Occidental
Laguna
Santa
Rosa
St. Helena
Sebastopol
SANTA ROSA
Napa
Lake Hennessey
SONOMA COAST STATE BEACH
Bodega Bay
Bodega
de
Santa Rosa
ANNADEL SP
SUGARLOAF RIDGE SP
Rutherford
BODEGA HEAD
Valley Ford
Cunningham
Kenwood
Oakville